PO...
LEA...

D0175454

WITHDRAWN

ALSO BY EVAN THOMAS

The Wise Men
(coauthor with Walter Isaacson)

The Man to See

The
VERY
BEST
MEN

FOUR WHO DARED:
THE EARLY YEARS
OF THE CIA

EVAN THOMAS

SIMON & SCHUSTER
New York London Toronto Sydney Tokyo Singapore

SIMON & SCHUSTER
Rockefeller Center
1230 Avenue of the Americas
New York, NY 10020

Copyright © 1995 by Evan Thomas
All rights reserved,
including the right of reproduction
in whole or in part in any form.
SIMON & SCHUSTER and colophon are
registered trademarks of Simon & Schuster Inc.
Designed by Irving Perkins Associates
Manufactured in the United States of America

10 9 8 7 6 5 4 3

Library of Congress Cataloging-in-Publication Data

Thomas, Evan.
The very best men : the early years of the CIA / Evan Thomas.
     p.   cm.
   Includes bibliographical references (p.   ) and index.
   1. United States. Central Intelligence Agency—History.
2. Intelligence service—United States—History.   I. Title.
JK468.I6T455   1995
327.1273′092′2—dc20   95-21316   CIP

ISBN 0-684-81025-5

To Louisa and Mary

CONTENTS

INTRODUCTION   9

Chapter One
Crusader: *"Fair play? That's out."*   15

Chapter Two
Rollback: *"We've got a job to do! Don't hold us up!"*   32

Chapter Three
The Cavalier: *"The culture was wild."*   44

Chapter Four
Empire Building: *"I don't know if I can keep this up."*   60

Chapter Five
**The War Lover: *"I think he did the right thing,
don't you?"***   75

Chapter Six
A Mind of His Own: *"You do it to fight Providence."*   87

Chapter Seven
**Running the World: *"Dools, Dools, do you take
us for fools?"***   98

Chapter Eight
Coup: *"How are you going to keep this a secret?"*   107

Chapter Nine
The Spy War: *"Jesus Christ, it's been blown!"*   127

Chapter Ten
**Collapse: *"SOS SOS SOS . . . THE FIGHTING IS VERY
CLOSE NOW . . ."***   142

Chapter Eleven
Brother's Keeper: *"If you knew what you'd done to me . . ."*   153

Chapter Twelve
High Flier: *"Was it really wise to do that the first time?"*   164

Chapter Thirteen
A Clandestine World: *"I took to covert action like a duck to water."*   179

Chapter Fourteen
Plots: *"We thought of Daddy as James Bond."*   203

Chapter Fifteen
Shoot-Down: *"Beware the lesson of Icarus . . ."*   216

Chapter Sixteen
Plausible Deniability: *"They were mad dogs."*   230

Chapter Seventeen
Invasion: *"He was building a tar baby."*   237

Chapter Eighteen
Fiasco: *"What did we buy with all that hocus-pocus?"*   261

Chapter Nineteen
Secret Armies: *"We gave them this! We gave them that! How can they not win?"*   273

Chapter Twenty
Hard Target: *"Bobby wanted boom and bang . . ."*   285

Chapter Twenty-One
Blowback: *"Now we'll never know."*   305

Chapter Twenty-Two
Casualties of War: *"He was full of rue."*   318

Acknowledgments   342

Author's Note   344

NOTES   349

INDEX   411

INTRODUCTION

GENERAL WILLIAM "WILD BILL" DONOVAN, the founder of the Office of Strategic Services, America's World War II spy agency, liked to hire Wall Street lawyers and Ivy Leaguers to commit espionage. "You can hire a second-story man and make him a better second-story man," Donovan explained, referring to the cat burglars sometimes employed by investigative agencies. "But if you hire a lawyer or an investment banker or a professor, you'll have something else besides." Donovan wanted a higher class of men; although the OSSers were teased for being socialites, they tended to be confident and intelligent. On the other hand, they didn't have much of a knack for, or experience with, the planning and execution of second-story jobs.[1]

Donovan's hiring philosophy was embraced by the OSS's Cold War successor, the Central Intelligence Agency. Its top ranks were filled with Wall Streeters, many of whom were OSS veterans, and academics from leading eastern colleges. They were especially noted—at once admired and resented—at the upper levels of the Directorate of Plans, the CIA's operations arm, also called the clandestine service and, by reporters of a later era, "the Department of Dirty Tricks." Operating in secret, they were not public figures, though in their heyday, the 1950s and early 1960s, they were very powerful. Within the CIA, the men who ran the clandestine service were known for their courage and élan, as well as for their occasional recklessness.

This is the story of four of these men: Frank Wisner, Desmond Fitz-Gerald, Tracy Barnes, and Richard Bissell. It begins with Wisner at the outbreak of the Cold War. An OSS veteran who had seen firsthand the Russian takeover of Eastern Europe as an American spymaster in Romania at the end of World War II, he felt an urgent, almost personal need to stand up to the Soviets. The OSS had been abolished after the war, replaced by a very weak intelligence organization lacking in manpower or leadership. Wisner started a small, highly secret agency, blandly named the Office of Policy Coordination (OPC) to take a more activist role battling Soviet subversion. His outfit was later merged into the CIA, and in 1951 Wisner became the agency's chief of covert action.[2]

Wisner believed it was necessary to fight back with the same tools that the Russians used: espionage, blackmail, bribery, sabotage, and propaganda. Following Donovan's dictum, Wisner in turn recruited FitzGerald and Barnes, both Harvard-trained Wall Street lawyers who had fought bravely in World War II, and Bissell, a brilliant Yale economics professor who helped organize the Marshall Plan to rebuild Europe after the war. Together, these men built the clandestine service, which extended American power around the world; in many developing countries by the late 1950s, CIA station chiefs functioned as modern proconsuls, influencing, if not dictating, affairs of state.

These men were not a secret cabal. Their views on the need for covert action against the Soviet Union and communist insurgencies around the world were widely shared at the upper levels of government and generally accepted by the politicians and press of the era. If their masters in Congress and the executive branch did not know precisely what the CIA's spymasters were up to in this era, it is in part because they did not wish to know. Nonetheless, it is also true that the men described in this book took their freedom and ran with it.

This group biography is intended to be in some ways a companion to *The Wise Men*, a book I wrote with Walter Isaacson in 1986 about six men who helped rebuild Europe and shaped U.S. foreign policy after World War II. The Wise Men were statesmen—diplomats and policymakers—who created a doctrine of containment which, over the long run, helped vanquish Soviet communism without a global conflagration. The four CIA officials portrayed in this book came from similar backgrounds, shared the same worldview, and were devoted to the same cause. But they had the difficult, messy job of waging a real if secret war against communism, not just in Europe but all over the world, with results that were often frustrating and sometimes tragic.

There are many good histories of the CIA in this period, and there will be more as still-secret agency records are eventually disclosed. My purpose here is different. This is in many ways a social history. It is my belief that the actions of the men who ran the CIA during the early Cold War cannot be understood without examining the web of friendships, the class and culture that made them. Too much can be made of the old school tie, but it is difficult to imagine an environment in which shared values and associations counted for more than in the clandestine service of the CIA in the 1950s.

Public service was supposed to be the ethos in schools like Groton in the era before World War II, when Richard Bissell and Tracy Barnes were students there together. On Sundays, the Rector preached about the duties of privilege. Most boys only half listened and headed off to make money or to spend it. But some served memorably.

For Barnes and Bissell, as well as for Wisner and FitzGerald, the catalyst was World War II. They found in their wartime experiences a sense of drama and meaning that could not be matched back at their law firms or lecture halls in peacetime. They saw the opportunity of American predominance and reached out to seize it.

The experience produced a type that is quite at odds with that stereotype of Cold War fiction, the deeply cynical spymaster. George Smiley and his ilk are jaded and spent, no longer able to tell right from wrong, or much interested in trying. The title of John le Carré's novel *The Honourable Schoolboy* is meant to be read with appropriate irony. But in the beginning, at least, Wisner, Bissell, Barnes, and FitzGerald were full of conviction. "We didn't talk about it, but we felt like we were at the center of the world, just as we feel like we aren't now," said Susan Mary Alsop, a close friend. "The feeling then was, it's our responsibility. What should we do about the Italian elections?"[3]

They believed they were moral. The title used by former CIA Director William Colby, a Princeton graduate and OSS veteran, for his memoir of the CIA's early days, *Honorable Men*, is not meant to be ironic in the least.[4] The top CIA men were, for the most part, quite liberal in their politics. The CIA has been widely regarded as a reactionary force, propping up dictators against popular movements. But in the early 1960s, when the CIA was at the limits of its global power, the senior men in the agency saw themselves as interventionists in the cause of freedom.[5]

Wisner, Bissell, Barnes, and FitzGerald could not exist in modern Washington, with its layers of bureaucracy and inquisitive press. "They were their own power centers," recalled Ed Applewhite, a former deputy inspector general of the CIA who worked with all four men. "They arrogated to themselves total power, with no inhibiting precedent. They could do what they wanted, just as long as 'higher authority,' as we called the president, did not expressly forbid it. They were extremely aristocratic in their assumptions, extremely parochial about life between men and women, very romantic and arrogant. They had a heaven-sent obligation and, God knows, what opportunity! They ate it up." Asked how they seemed so cheerful under such stress and adversity, their White House counterpart, National Security Adviser McGeorge Bundy, answered, "They were having a marvelous time."[6]

Patriotic, decent, well-meaning, and brave, they were also uniquely unsuited to the grubby, necessarily devious world of intelligence. "They were innocents," said John Bruce Lockhart, a senior official in the British Secret Intelligence Service who knew the four men from his service as the SIS liaison to the CIA in the 1950s and as chief of operations in Europe, the Middle East, and Africa. By "innocent," Lockhart meant incapable of wickedness and naive about the difficulties and risks of what he called "a life in secrets."[7]

Confidence and naiveté can be a lethal mix. At first, their mistakes did

PORTLAND COMMUNITY COLLEGE
LEARNING RESOURCE CENTERS

not seem to matter. In Stalin, the United States was up against practiced evil; Hitler, too, had seemed formidable, but in time America's citizen soldiers had triumphed. Failures, in the early days of the Cold War, were kept largely hidden from the public. Only much later did Americans learn about the CIA's excesses—the LSD experiments, the illegal break-ins and buggings, the plot to hire the Mafia as assassins. Then the damage was severe. Many people went to the other extreme and came to suspect that the CIA was capable of doing almost anything wrong. After the movie *JFK*, a work of fiction, polls showed that many Americans believed that the CIA had a role in the assassination of President John F. Kennedy.[8]

For Wisner, Bissell, Barnes, and FitzGerald, the personal cost was high as well. The careers of two were ruined; one killed himself; only one lived past the age of sixty-two. They could not see that the mortal enemy was within, that they were being slowly consumed by the moral ambiguities of a "life in secrets."

Among their friends and family, there is a kind of puzzled sadness that such gallant men could have been brought down by their lives in the clandestine world. After recalling, with great affection, the bravery and dash of Tracy Barnes and his friends, his widow, Janet, pondered for a moment the fiasco of the Bay of Pigs, of which her husband was a principal architect. She asked, somewhat plaintively, "How could they have been so dumb?"[9]

Barnes's old colleagues from the CIA sometimes shake their heads over the blunders of the early days—"flaps," as they were called at the CIA. But these colleagues point out that they were up against a tough and more experienced adversary. It is hard, after the Cold War, to remember how frightening the world looked in the early 1950s. Pentagon planners had actually picked a day—July 1, 1952—for the Soviet invasion of Western Europe. Some policymakers thought that the Kremlin would not need tanks to take over Europe; the continent was so riddled with communist subversion that it would just fall into Stalin's hand, like overripe fruit. All-out war against the Soviet Union was unthinkable, yet something had to be done. "We were given jobs that were impossible," said Carleton Swift, who ran espionage operations in China in the early 1950s. "If the Army and Navy couldn't do it, we got the job. My job was to get the agenda of the Chinese Communist Central Committee in real time. I never did. But I tried."[10]

Former officials of the CIA are now quite frank about their experiences. Because the Cold War is over, or perhaps just because they are getting old, most were willing to speak freely about their successes and failures, and they readily acknowledge that there were more of the latter. I interviewed sixty-six former officials of the CIA for this book; almost all spoke on the record.

The Central Intelligence Agency is also beginning the slow and somewhat painful process of opening up its classified records. Under an arrangement worked out after a long negotiation (described in the acknowledgments and an author's note on page 344), I became the first "outsider"—journalist or historian—ever permitted to see the CIA's own secret histories of its operations in the first two decades of its existence. Written by intelligence officers, these histories can be turgid, and they are not always complete. But they allowed me to see the CIA as it saw itself. They reveal no great secret victories or hidden defeats. The early operations of the CIA are by now fairly public. This book attempts to explain the less well understood story of the men who made it.

Chapter One

CRUSADER

"Fair play? That's out."

IN THE FALL of 1948, Frank Wisner, the newly appointed director of the Office of Policy Coordination, was looking for the very best men. He needed to find them quickly, to staff his new outfit, a top-secret organization created to run covert actions in the Cold War.

Wisner wanted amateurs, not ex-FBI agents, former cops, bureaucrats, or, as he called them, "whiskey colonels" who couldn't wait to get to the Officers Club in the evening. Wisner spoke of the "added dimension" that he couldn't find among the paper pushers and timeservers working in the federal buildings along the Mall. He wanted men who would show initiative, who would be innovative, a little quirky if necessary, but bold. They needed to be fluent in foreign languages, and they needed grace and confidence under pressure. The place to find these men, he believed, was on Wall Street, among the bankers and lawyers who had joined the OSS, the wartime intelligence agency, and then drifted back to their peacetime jobs; and from among the graduating classes at their old schools, which generally meant Harvard, Yale, and Princeton.[1]

The code name for the CIA's connection to the Ivy League was "the P Source" (not hard to crack; "P" stood for professor). For some years in the 1950s, the CIA recruiter at Princeton was the dean of students, William Lippincott. "How would you like to serve your country in a different way?" he would ask promising young men. Another recruiter in the early years was the Yale crew coach, Skip Walz. He would work the boathouse and the field house, Mory's and fraternity row, looking for strong young shoulders and quick minds. When the Korean War called for some beef, he broadened his recruiting ground to the National Football League, producing twenty-five former players who would be trained, he was told, for parachuting behind enemy lines. Once every three weeks Walz would meet with his agency contact at the Reflecting Pool in Washington. Walz would pass on his names; he "did not know, or wish to know," Robin Winks writes in *Cloak and Gown*, which ones actually signed on—or what became of them. (He had heard that his first two recruits died in the field.)[2]

In 1950, Walz took a job with a company that manufactured precision gunsights, and he shifted his recruiting territory to the club car between Greenwich and New York. One can imagine what it was like, in this era of the Man in the Gray Flannel suit, for that restless young lawyer riding the 6:43. Perhaps he is bored by probating wills or flyspecking debenture statements. Perhaps, if he is a veteran, he feels a nostalgic longing for the danger and camaraderie of the war. Along comes Skip Walz to chat about the Harvard-Yale boat race—and, by the way, something else. . . .

Many Yale (and Harvard and Princeton) men felt a longing to escape. Their lives were so prescribed, beginning with their college "careers." This romantic urge to get off the safe treadmill is captured by the "Whiffenpoof" song, the sweet, sad ballad (lifted from a drinking song by Rudyard Kipling) that Yalemen link arms to sing:

> *We're poor little lambs who've lost our way,*
> *Baa! Baa! Baa!*
> *Little black sheep who have gone astray*
> *Baa! Baa! Baa!*
> *Gentlemen songsters off on a spree*
> *Damned from here to Eternity*
> *Lord have mercy on such as we*
> *Baa! Baa! Baa!*[3]

Frank Wisner's OPC offered young men a chance to serve their country, in Dean Lippincott's carefully chosen phrase, "in a different way." Bill Colby, a Princetonian and OSSer who signed on (and later became the director of Central Intelligence), credited Wisner with creating "the atmosphere of an order of Knights Templars, to save Western freedom from Communist darkness. . . ." Joining the OPC was "a rather glamorous and fashionable and certainly a

most patriotic thing to do," writes Colby in his memoirs, *Honorable Men.*[4]

World War II had ended American squeamishness about spying. In 1929, Henry Stimson had abolished the Black Chamber, a code-breaking outfit, under the quaint notion that "gentlemen do not open other gentlemen's mail." Hitler, and now Stalin, clearly did not qualify. In 1947, American moviegoers watched the hero of *Cloak and Dagger*, played by Gary Cooper, listening to his OSS instructor, played by Jimmy Cagney, lecture on the reality of secret war: "The average American is a good sport, plays by the rules. But this war is no game, and no secret agent is a good sport—no living agent. . . Fair play? That's out."[5]

Spying, covert action, and psychological warfare were in. To work for Frank Wisner was romantic and dashing. Over time the amateurs would become cynics, and intelligence would become a cult. But in 1948 it was still a crusade.

FRANK GARDINER WISNER had grown up in a world that was, like the one the CIA would help create, secretive, insular, elitist, and secure in the rectitude of its purpose.[6]

Wisner's family built nearly all of the town of Laurel, Mississippi—the schools, the churches, the museum, the bank, the parks, the golf course, the cemetery. All the land and many of the buildings were donated by the Gardiner and Wisner clans, paid for with the money made cutting and sawing logs at the local mill, which they also built. The company headquarters, erected in 1910, the year Wisner was born, looks incongruous today, backing on a shopping mall. The building is an exact copy of the sixteenth-century casino of Cardinal Alessandro Farnese in Caprarola, Italy.

In later years, Wisner was regarded, even by intimates, as a remote figure; capable of charm and warmth, yet somehow not quite all there. Certainly his upbringing set him apart, in ways that at once elevated and burdened him. The Wisners and Gardiners believed in moral uplift. The Eastman/Gardiner Company did not exploit its workers like some other southern lumber companies; it went to a ten-hour day before the law required and built sanitary housing in the lumber camps out of old railway cars.[7] "My family believed it was from Mississippi, but not Mississippian," said a Gardiner descendant, Charles Reeder. By that he meant that his family had no plantation roots and was decent to blacks,

which took some courage in a state where night riders planted burning crosses on the lawns of "nigger lovers." "We believed every person was a child of God," said Jean Lindsey, whose mother, Frank Wisner's sister Elizabeth, discovered and promoted the black opera singer Leontyne Price. ("Leontyne used to call herself our chocolate sister," said Lindsey.) Wisner and Gardiner children were expected to "go forth and do good," said Jean Lindsey. "We were told that to whom much is given, much is expected. It was all very Victorian: never complain, never explain."

It was also privileged and self-contained. As a little boy, Wisner did not dress himself; he merely lay on his bed and raised his arms and legs for his maid. His playmates were almost invariably his cousins. "The only people he saw were his own family," said Lindsey. "We had a kind of enclave," said Admiral Fred Reeder, who married a Gardiner after the First World War. "You didn't need any outside contact. You had all you needed right here."

Wisner was an intense child. His cousin Gardiner Green recalled that he never walked anywhere; he always ran. Somewhat small and sickly, he built himself up by lifting weights (like his hero, Teddy Roosevelt). His father tried to build his spirit by enrolling him in the St. Andrew's Society, under the mentoring of a World War I pilot–turned–Episcopal priest who taught the boys to be "young Galahads," said Charles Reeder. "You pledge to spend time in service to your fellow man, to be a straight shooter, and to pray a lot." The praying part did not take; when he got older, Wisner infuriated his father by refusing to go to church.

Wisner's moral training was matched by a love of games. Beneath a fey manner, his mother was highly competitive, and Wisner learned to compete fiercely at everything from football to parlor games like mah-jongg. Wisner's aristocratic sensibility, as well as his insularity, was further refined at Woodberry Forest School, in Orange, Virginia. Founded by a Confederate captain after the Civil War, Woodberry preached chivalry. "Give me clean hands, clean words, and clean thoughts," begins the school prayer. "Help me stand for the hard right against the easy wrong." The school was run under an honor code. There were no locks or keys; boys left a white handkerchief on the door if they did not wish to be disturbed.[8]

The University of Virginia, where Wisner went to both college and law school, was more like a private school than "State U." in the 1930s. The young gentlemen at Mr. Jefferson's university wore

coats and ties and stood up when a teacher entered the room. They also wildly drank grain alcohol punches at their fraternities on the weekend. The great honor was to be tapped by the Sevens, a society so ostentatiously secret that the names of its members were not revealed until death.

Compact and restless, with a gap-tooth grin and bright eyes, Wisner was a great sprinter and hurdler at U.Va., good enough to be asked to the Olympic trials in 1936. His father said no; it would be more character-building to work the summer in a Coca-Cola bottling plant. He had a somewhat ornate sense of humor, which he showed by telling elaborate tall tales and drawing cartoons. In bankruptcy class one day Wisner handed his seatmate, Arthur Jacobs, a drawing of "the courts squeezing debtors, with the creditors lined up with their tongues sticking out to get the droppings." Still, Wisner was regarded as more serious and mature than the hell-raisers in the DKE house. He could drink beer on fraternity row, but he was more apt to be found at a professor's for dinner. He was, inevitably, tapped for the Seven Society.[9]

This combination of high moral purpose and gamesmanship, acted out on a self-consciously higher plane, stayed with Wisner all his life. Years later his nephew Charles Reeder lived for a time with the Wisners in London, where Frank was the CIA chief of station. "Somewhere deep in him," said Reeder, "you knew it was the evil empire versus the good guys. You knew it was part of him. And that it was a great game, to be played with great ferocity." The problem, Wisner discovered after he got to Washington, was that the moral issues were not always so black and white, and the victories against more ruthless opponents, like the Soviet Union, were rare.

WISNER WITNESSED the greatest moral outrage of his life, the Soviet takeover of Romania, as a spy during World War II. Bored as a Wall Street lawyer, he had enlisted in the Navy six months before Pearl Harbor. But he was relegated to shuffling paper in the Navy censor's office and yearned to see action. (He had been mortified, shortly after America entered the war, when passengers on a subway stood and applauded him as he entered, wearing a naval uniform, hobbling on crutches. His "war wound" was an ankle twisted in a weekend touch football game.) In July 1943, Wisner arranged a transfer to the OSS through Robert Gooch, an old professor from

U.Va., a former Rhodes scholar who had an interest in espionage.

Wisner's early experiences at spying ranged from marginally useful to comical. After an uneventful tour in Cairo, he landed in June 1944 in Istanbul, where he worked for a man named Lanning "Packy" MacFarland. Ordered to meet MacFarland at a nightclub there, Wisner tried to be inconspicuous, to preserve his cover as a consular clerk. But when MacFarland made his entrance the music stopped, a spotlight picked him out on the steps leading to the dance floor, and the orchestra struck up a song called "Boop, Boop, Baby, I'm a Spy!" MacFarland, who had two girlfriends, one working for the Soviets, the other for the Germans, later went AWOL.[10]

Wisner's war didn't really begin until he arrived in Bucharest, Romania, just as the Germans were pulling out in August 1944. His first assignment was to organize the return of 1,800 American fliers shot down over the Ploeşti oil fields (a success: Wisner commandeered every bus in the city), but his real job soon became keeping an eye on the Russians.

Within a month Wisner was reporting "from a dependable industrial source" that "the Soviet Union is attempting to subvert the position of the government and the King." Not only that, but "Russian sources" were telling Wisner of the Kremlin's goal of "political and economic domination of Southeast Europe, including Turkey." Headquarters in Washington wasn't quite ready to hear that its wartime ally was turning into the Red Menace. General William Donovan, the head of OSS, cautioned Wisner in October "against speech or action" that might show "antagonism to Russia." Wisner responded defensively that he was "at all time exercising the utmost care" not to appear to be siding with the Romanian government against the communists.[11]

In fact, he was deeply involved in palace intrigue in Bucharest, a city that fancied itself as the Paris of the Balkans. Wisner had requisitioned the thirty-room mansion of Romania's largest brewer, Mita Bragadiru, along with his Cadillac Eldorado. He befriended the brewer's wife, Tanda Caradja, a twenty-four-year-old Romanian princess (descendant of Vlad the Impaler) with a wide sensuous mouth and close ties to the royal family. "I became his hostess," she said. "He wanted to meet everyone right away in court society," which she was able to arrange because, she explained with a smile, "when you're rich and above all a good-looking girl, you know a lot of people." She threw elaborate parties for

King Michael's advisers (so young they were known as "the Nursery") and invited the Russians as well, advising Wisner to coat his stomach with olive oil for the vodka toasts.

Wisner naturally gravitated to the local elite. He soon became close to King Michael and the Queen Mother, who invited him to her castle and found him well-mannered and self-assured. "Il est tellement calme et tranquille dans ces propos," she told Caradja in her court French. Wisner became an informal adviser to the royal family and, according to Caradja, the life of the party. "He loved dancing and entertainment. He did magic tricks and charades and played backgammon." A photo in a Wisner family album shows Wisner, in the uniform of an American naval commander, squinting at a makeup mirror as he tries to fire a shotgun backwards over his shoulder.[12]

Some of Wisner's staff were put off. A member of Wisner's group recorded, "After about two months, the American Military Unit decided to move away from the Bragadiru residence on the Alea Modrogan. Eating, working, sleeping, drinking, and loving other men's wives all under one roof while husbands and enlisted men were around was just a bit too much for some of us." Beverly Bowie, a staffer assigned to Bucharest, later lampooned Wisner in the novel *Operation Bughouse* as Commander Downe, a manic OSS operative who sets up headquarters in the large house of Madama Nitti and immediately implores Washington to declare war on the Soviet Union.[13]

Wisner actually did use the names of germs for his codes (his own was Typhoid), but he was not being paranoid about the Russians. On January 6, 1945, Stalin ordered the Red Army to round up all men aged seventeen to forty-five and all women eighteen to thirty who could be determined to be "of German ethnic origin, regardless of citizenship." They were to be deported to the Soviet Union and "mobilized for work." In Bucharest, this caused an appalling scene: Russian troops hauled Transylvanians whose families had been long settled in Romania out of their homes and put them on boxcars for Stalin's work camps. Wisner knew many of these Volksdeutsche from Princess Caradja's soirees. The desperate wife of her architect called him in the middle of the night. They were taking away her husband. Wasn't there anything the Americans could do? Wisner tried. He drove around the city in his jeep, personally trying to stop Russian soldiers from pulling Romanians from their beds. He had some success; the Russian soldiers did not want to make a scene with their wartime ally. But Wisner was unable to save the architect; by the time Wisner arrived at the train station, the man had already vanished, like thousands of others. Wisner could only watch as the Romanians, weeping and begging for help, were herded onto boxcars.[14]

Wisner's wife and children later said that this experience of watching the Russians round up innocents and take them off to misery or death had the most profound influence on his life. Wisner himself talked about his Romanian episode so much and so vividly that Frank Wisner Jr. was startled to learn, when he got older, that his father had spent less than six months in the country.[15]

Throughout the fall and early winter, Wisner had been reading cables from Moscow as they circulated through the Romanian Communist Party, which his agents had penetrated. It was clear to him that the Kremlin meant to take over all of Eastern Europe or, as Stalin's orders to Red Army commanders put it, impose a "broad democratic basis" on the region. Wisner could see as well that the Russians understood who their future foe would be. In late December he warned Washington that the Russians had permitted two trapped Nazi divisions to escape in order to attack American units fighting in the Ardennes in the Battle of the Bulge.[16]

Wisner's cables stirred great interest in Washington, as they were among the first clear warnings of what was to come. But in Wisner's view Washington wasn't doing enough to stop communism from coming to Romania. "He was disgusted," said Caradja. On March 1 the Russians took over the newspapers, the police headquarters, and the palace. A new government under a fellow traveler was set up, and King Michael was driven into exile. Many of the Romanian friends whom Wisner had made in Bucharest were rounded up and simply disappeared.[17]

By then, Wisner was gone, pulled back to Washington at his own request, for reassignment. He was sent to Germany, to work out of the OSS station in Wiesbaden. Postwar Germany held no allure for Wisner. "It is not the same as Bucharest," he wrote Caradja on August 17. "There are no nice people—no opportunities for any pleasure or relaxation from the long hours I put in at my desk. I think often of Romania. It was one of the most interesting and pleasant experiences, and it was you who were responsible for so much of that. . . ."[18] In Germany, Wisner could already see the sparks of the next war in the embers of the last. His cables back to headquarters reported on Russian mischief. One told of a socialist leader in the Russian zone who "expressed in rather strong terms his opposition to the Communist Party"—and promptly disappeared "in the company of several Russian officers." Another described an anti-American "whispering campaign" fomented by Russian propaganda specialists to spread rumors around Berlin that American soldiers were robbing elderly, well-dressed German women.[19]

Policymakers did not want to hear what Wisner was telling them. Having fought and won a war, almost no one in Washington wanted to think about another. The Russians were communists and not trustworthy, but they had been allies, and official Washington still wanted to find a way to make common cause in the postwar world. Arthur Schlesinger Jr., an OSS sergeant in Wiesbaden, found Wisner obsessed with Russia. "He was already mobilizing for the cold war," Schlesinger told Burton Hersh for his book *The Old Boys.* "I myself was no great admirer of the Soviet Union, and I certainly had no expectation of harmonious relations after the war. But Frank was a little excessive, even for me."[20]

As Wisner was gearing up for a spy war, Washington was gearing down. Ever eager to protect his own turf, the FBI's J. Edgar Hoover had, through a campaign of leaks and innuendo, convinced Harry Truman that the OSS in peacetime would be an "American Gestapo." In September 1945, Truman folded up the OSS, leaving a vestigial intelligence organization, the Strategic Services Unit (SSU), languishing in the War Department. Wisner rushed back to Washington to argue for more resources. When Colonel William Quinn, the head of the SSU, turned down Wisner's request for two hundred bicycles, to be given Germans so they could ride through the Russian zone of Berlin and record Soviet troop movements, Wisner quit. As he turned in his commission, he told Colonel Quinn, "You're cutting our throat."[21]

GRUDGINGLY, WISNER went back to his Wall Street law firm, Carter Ledyard, in the winter of 1946. In Germany, he had worked under Allen Dulles, the OSS's top spymaster in Europe. Dulles, like Wisner, had returned to Wall Street to his own law firm after the war. The two men began having lunch together to talk about old times and to discuss the need to build a strong peacetime intelligence service. Peter Sichel, who worked with both men in Germany, went to one of those lunches, at the Down Town Association:

"They were pining to get back. They were boy scouts who were bored in their law jobs. They were like fighter pilots in England after the Battle of Britain. They couldn't adjust. They were both great romantics who saw themselves as the saviors of the world."[22]

As it became clear that the country was beginning a Cold War against the Soviet Union, Wisner increasingly began to ponder ways to join in. He toyed with the idea of going to Washington and joining up with the remnant of the wartime OSS, the SSU, but he considered the organization to be weak and badly run. (There is some evidence as well that the SSU was not eager to have him; the Army colonels who dominated the intelligence agency at the time were wary of Wisner as "another ['Wild Bill'] Donovan who'll run away with the ball," according to author William Corson.)[23]

By the spring of 1947, Wisner was unable to stay away any longer. In Europe, the winter had been the worst in memory, and England, France, Italy, and especially Germany were threatened by famine and unrest. Washington was rising out of its postwar torpor: at the State Department, Dean Acheson could see that the time had come for the United States to take over Britain's imperial role. The Truman Doctrine, declared in March, promised that America would aid "free peoples" everywhere in the fight against communism.[24]

In 1947, in the opening days of the Cold War, the State Department was the place to be for an ambitious Cold Warrior like Wisner; the best men with the best minds were there—Undersecretary Dean Acheson, Soviet experts George Kennan and Chip Bohlen. That summer Wisner took a job, at Acheson's urging, as the number-two man in the State Department's Office of Occupied Territories. His boss, Charles Saltzman, was a former head of the New York Stock Exchange and a Carter Ledyard client.[25]

Wisner was also State's representative on the State–Army–Navy–Air Force Coordinating Committee, an interagency group that was supposed to study "psychological warfare" to counter Soviet ambitions. The threat had been vividly described in Kennan's famous "Long Telegram," the Russian expert's warning of Soviet global ambitions that had been received from Moscow and passed around by anxious officials in Washington. Stalin was implementing Trotsky's strategy of "neither war nor peace" by a campaign of subversion, propaganda, and intimidation. Washington did not at the time fear a Soviet invasion of the West, but rather a slow rotting from within, fomented by communist agents bribing politicians, taking over labor unions, infiltrating the army and the police. The feeling was that the Kremlin had plenty of experience in this area; the West almost none.[26]

How to fight back? In the summer of 1947, Wisner traveled to his new State Department domain, the occupied territory of Germany. While he was there he visited the "displaced persons" (DP) camps set up to handle the flood of East Europeans who had fled before the Red Army as it drove west in 1944–45. There were 700,000 people in these camps, almost all of whom hated communism. There were Ukrainians, and Czechs, and Poles, and Hungarians who had fought against the Russians; perhaps they could be persuaded to fight again. Here, Wisner realized, was an entire army—a potential secret army that could be recruited and trained to infiltrate the lands they had lost. True, many of its would-be recruits had worn Nazi uniforms during the war. Some of them presumably had committed acts that would be regarded as war crimes. But that had been a matter of expediency in wartime. In any case, the common enemy was clear.[27]

Back in Washington, Wisner set up a study group looking into "Utilization of Refugees from U.S.S.R. in U.S. National Interests." By May 1948, it had cranked out a proposal for a major effort to use "native anti-communist elements . . . which have shown extreme fortitude in the face of Communist menace." Wisner was fascinated by the communists' ability to use innocuous-seeming civic organizations—student groups, farmers' collectives, labor unions, study groups—as tools of propaganda and subversion. If the communists could use these techniques, he reasoned, the West could, too. And who better to fight back than the victims of Soviet oppression, the thousands of refugees who had fled Stalin's boot? While other government officials saw the displaced persons camps as a burden, squalid bogs of hunger and want, Wisner saw them as recruiting grounds for a force that could fight fire with fire. In language that would prove overly optimistic, the interagency committee document praised the émigrés' " 'know how' to counter communist propaganda," their knowledge of "techniques to obtain control of mass movements." The émigrés, Wisner believed, could ape the communists' ability to manipulate "Socialist, trade union, intellectual, moderate right wing groups and others." The program, code-named Bloodstone, called for $5 million, appropriately laundered for "secret disbursement."

It was an ambitious plan, but as Wisner was well aware, there

was no one to carry it out. The State–Army–Navy–Air Force Coordinating Committee was a talk shop. It had no capacity to conduct operations. What was needed, Wisner urged his fellow
planners at State and the Pentagon, was "an entirely new propaganda agency within this Government."[28]

WHEN WISNER moved to Washington, he bought a farm on the
Eastern Shore of Maryland and rented a house in Georgetown. He
immediately fell in with a crowd that was unusually lively and
self-confident. At the center were two rising Soviet experts from
the State Department, Charles "Chip" Bohlen and George Kennan. Bohlen was especially charming and gregarious. He loved to
argue with his college clubmates Joseph Alsop, a well-connected
newspaper columnist, and Paul Nitze, another young comer at the
State Department. Kennan, while admired for his intellect, was
less socially at ease; he was prone to periods of brooding.
    The young couples, lawyers down from New York, diplomats
returned from abroad, bought or rented small eighteenth- and
nineteenth-century row houses in Georgetown. The New Deal and
wartime had transformed the neighborhood from a backwater, in-
habited largely by lower-middle-class blacks. The new crowd felt a
sense of arrival and belonging. They were not stuffy, like the
old-time "cave dwellers" of Washington society, yet they were
confident of their place in a new order that placed the United
States on top. Susan Mary Patten, the daughter and wife of diplomats (and later Joe Alsop's wife), felt the euphoria on a trip home
from Paris as she walked down the streets of Georgetown, past
"the black maids sweeping the steps of the little brick houses and
saying their beaming 'Good morning, how are you?' . . . Washington is the coziest capital in the world and it's nice to feel the
optimism and the sense of controlled power," she wrote her friend
Marietta Tree. "Life is much less luxurious than when we were
girls, but people give delightful little dinner parties with next to no
help in the kitchen. . . ."[29]
    Along with America's rise in the world came the rise of the
"Washington political dinner party," said Townsend Hoopes, a
young Yale graduate who had taken a job in the Pentagon after
serving in the Marines. Tables of twelve would gather and argue
over how best to fight communism. "There was a great intensity,"
said Hoopes. "It had to affect policy. Dinner parties were an ex-

tension of the working day." For all its global reach, Washington was still small. There was in 1948 none of the vast modern apparatus of foreign policy making, no national security staff or think tanks, but rather a fairly informal circle of friends who had known one another through their schools, banks, and law firms before coming to Washington. "You'd go to the F Street Club for lunch and there'd be [Undersecretary of State] Bob Lovett in one corner and [Secretary of Defense] James Forrestal in the other," said Hoopes.[30]

The Wisners and their friends were determined, in a relaxed way, to have fun while doing good. The style showed itself in an institution known as the Sunday Night Supper. "We'd get bored with our children on Sundays and abandon them and have dinner with each other," said Tish Alsop, wife of Stewart Alsop, Joe's brother and fellow columnist. What began as maid's night out, just a few couples having potluck, became, without anyone quite realizing it, a much-sought-after invitation in the insular world of post-war Washington. There was the night that Averell Harriman turned off his hearing aid and stared straight ahead rather than talk to Richard Nixon (who had been invited as a last-minute guest); and there was the night that Chip Bohlen, forgetting where he was in the heat of debate, tried to throw Joe Alsop out of his own house. The idea was to leave by 11 P.M. "But I remember Stew pushing Chip [Bohlen] out the door at 4:30 A.M.—'Goddamn Chip! I've got to get some sleep,' " recalled Tish Alsop. The survivors of these dinners marvel at the stamina it took to keep pace. "Chip, of course, trained in Russia," said Mrs. Alsop. "You either dropped dead or learned how to deal with it."[31]

The Wisners were often the last to leave the party after midnight. There was always time for one more drink, one more point to make. "Frank loved to tie one on and dance all night in those days," said Ella Burling, a Georgetown hostess. "He used to do a dance called the crab walk. He loved parties; he was exotic and interesting." He could also seem, at times, a little self-satisfied. At one party he grabbed Elizabeth Graham. "Have you ever seen such a collection of beautiful women?" he asked. "It made me a little mad," said Graham. "It was: 'We have the best, the best wives, the best everything.' " At other times he was funny and light, spinning ornate southern tales.

At the Sunday Night Suppers, Wisner, Kennan, Bohlen, the Alsop brothers, and the various movers and shakers who were invited to join them engaged in ferocious debates. The argument most often focused on what to do about the Soviet Union. The debate had moved beyond ends—whether or not to stand up to the Kremlin—to the question of means. Another war was out of the question. The economic aid generated by the Marshall Plan was the best bet, perhaps, but there was no assurance in the winter and summer of 1948 that Congress would foot the entire bill, or that the aid would not be somehow blocked or subverted by the active communist insurgencies in Western Europe, especially France and Italy. It seemed possible that the governments of these countries would go communist, or at least be paralyzed by social chaos. There needed to be some way, Frank Wisner argued, of beating the Soviets at their own game.

ALL THROUGH history national leaders have felt the need to take actions for which they do not wish to be held accountable—spying; sabotage; blackmail; bribery; subversion; disinformation; *in extremis*, assassination. At least since King Henry II cast about for someone to "rid" him of a troublesome priest, Thomas à Beckett, some eight centuries ago, national leaders have from time to time confronted a quandary: how to make others do their dirty work without blame attaching to the sovereign? In modern times the answer has been called the doctrine of "plausible deniability."[32]

Wisner believed, as did many of his friends and colleagues, that the United States needed the capacity—an "entirely new agency"—that could carry out acts that could be plausibly denied.

Actually, in 1948 there already existed an organization that could be used for this purpose. Though weak, the postwar vestige of the OSS had survived through bureaucratic shuffles and a succession of new acronyms. In 1946 the Strategic Services Unit (SSU) had been partly reincarnated as the Office of Special Operations (OSO) and placed under an umbrella organization, the Central Intelligence Group, rechristened, in 1947, as the Central Intelligence Agency (CIA). The CIA was essentially a shell in its early days, and its operations arm, the OSO, was supposed to engage in espionage, not political action; it was set up to gather and analyze information, not to take "active measures" like propaganda.

Still, the OSO had been used successfully that spring of 1948 in the Italian elections. The situation had been deemed an emergency. The communists appeared very strong in Italy, and Washington feared that if the Kremlin's campaign of subversion was allowed to proceed unchecked, Moscow would be able to make Italy go communist one day just by "picking up the phone." To fight back, the OSO adopted Russian tactics: bribes had been paid, newspaper editors suborned, labor unions co-opted. Paying for the operation had been touch-and-go; at one point, old intelligence hands like Allen Dulles had literally passed the hat in their New York clubs, the Brook and the Links, to raise cash to buy right-thinking politicians. But Italy had not gone communist.[33]

Having created an organization capable of effective covert action, the top officials in Washington decided not to use it. The secretary of state, General George C. Marshall, wanted the United States to have a covert action capacity, but he did not want it in the State Department. Diplomacy, he believed, would be undermined. Secretary of Defense James Forrestal was a strong advocate of covert action, but not in the Pentagon, at least in peacetime. Neither Marshall nor Forrestal—nor, for that matter, any other major policymaker—wanted to have his fingerprints on anything that might smack of a "dirty trick." Even the CIA, they believed, was too accountable. Under the 1947 National Security Act, it reported to the newly created National Security Council of the president's top advisers. None of the members of that august group wanted to be held responsible for a program of covert action.

Frank Wisner had the solution, the "entirely new agency" he began lobbying for in the spring of 1948. Wisner was a formidable pleader. He had an urgency of manner, he was well-spoken, if orotund when he got wound up, and he knew everyone. He found an ally and sponsor in Defense Secretary Forrestal, who shared his anticommunist passion and interest in propaganda and "psychological warfare." Wisner's friend George Kennan, the State Department seer who had most articulately warned of the Soviet threat in his cables home from Moscow in 1946, also strongly believed in the need for a covert action capacity. The White House, under political pressure to do something to counter Russian adventurism, signed on. Under national security memorandum NSC 10/2, drafted by Kennan and dated June 18, 1948, a new organization was created, named with intentional vagueness the Office of Special Projects, then quickly renamed, even more innocuously, the Office of Policy Coordination (OPC).

The language of its secret charter was more vivid: the organization's purpose would be to counter "the vicious covert activities of the USSR, its satellite countries and Communist groups to discredit the aims and activities of the U.S. and other Western powers." OPC's covert operations were to include all the tools the Russians had perfected: "propaganda, economic warfare; preventive direct action, including sabotage, antisabotage, demolition and evacuation measures; subversion against hostile states, including assistance to underground resistance groups, and support of indigenous anti-Communist elements in threatened countries of the free world." These efforts were supposed to be "so planned and conducted" that if they ever surfaced publicly, the U.S. government could "plausibly disclaim any responsibility."[34]

Having helped to create the secret new organization, Wisner was now asked to run it. The new chief of the Office of Policy Coordination kept a copy of NSC 10/2 in a safe in his office. Anyone who wanted to see the directive had to sign a special request. One of Wisner's assistants later told author Thomas Powers that he couldn't quite understand the aura of mystery Wisner attached to the document: "All it said was, they do it, and therefore we have to do it, too."[35]

To Wisner, it was a broad license. OPC was attached to the CIA, but only for "quarters and provisions"—essentially for housing and salaries. The CIA director, Admiral Roscoe Hillenkoetter, exercised almost no control over Wisner. Nor did anyone else in government. Nominally, Wisner reported to Kennan, the head of the State Department Policy Planning Staff, as well as to a pair of generals in the Pentagon who had their own unrealistic demands for behind-the-lines guerrilla warfare. Kennan, once enthusiastic in his support for covert action, was experiencing second thoughts by the winter of 1949. He felt the reaction to his warnings about Soviet aggression had been overwrought, its message distorted by minds less supple than his own.[36]

At the time Kennan did not resist Wisner's ambitions. Moody and insecure, Kennan simply withdrew to his private study at the Library of Congress. Wisner was left to deal with Bob Joyce on the Policy Planning Staff. Since Joyce was an old OSS friend who knew Wisner from Romania days, he did not exercise much restraint.[37]

Wisner had, at last, the job he really wanted. But when William Harding Jackson, one of Wisner's partners at Carter Ledyard, heard about Wisner's new job, he was troubled. Jackson was a perceptive man, known by his law partners for his uncanny intuition. During the war he had served in the OSS and become an expert on the British intelligence services, which had long experience in the spy trade. Jackson knew both Wisner and the job he was getting into. Wisner would be crazy to take it, he told one of his partners, Edward Clark. "It will kill him," Jackson said.[38]

Chapter Two

ROLLBACK

"We've got a job to do! Don't hold us up!"

WISNER REALIZED THAT he would need a year to plan and organize his new intelligence agency before he could put any operations into the field. But in the fall of 1948 there didn't seem to be much time. A communist takeover in Czechoslovakia that winter had created a war scare in Washington, and in the summer only a massive airlift had averted an armed confrontation over Berlin. Wisner was under tremendous pressure from the Pentagon to gear up for war with the Soviet Union. OPC veterans would later shrug at the demands: scores of coordinated, well-armed "stay-behind" groups to harass the Red Army as it rolled through Western Europe. The Pentagon also wanted OPC men trained to sabotage two thousand Russian air bases to prevent Soviet planes from taking off in the event of an invasion.[1]

These were absurd requests for an organization that began with an office in an old Navy Department building and a staff of ten. Wisner wisely resisted the more ridiculous "requirements" from the military, but he was fascinated by "psychological warfare," a term, much in vogue at the time, used to describe propaganda and political subterfuge. Dwight Eisenhower described psychological warfare as "the struggle for the minds and wills of men." The ability of Madison Avenue to manipulate consumers with clever advertising, the great success of deception plots against the Germans in World War II, and the popularity of "grifter" novels like *The Big Con* had all combined to make policymakers believe in the power of artful persuasion. Henry Luce's "American Century" had given them the duty to bring these tools to the great cause of spreading freedom around the world, by devious means if necessary.[2]

To sharpen these techniques, Wisner hired Joe Bryan, a well-born Virginian known as "the Duke of Richmond," to run a Psychological Warfare Workshop. Bryan put together a bright group, but he seems to have recruited from the Princeton *Tiger*, his college humor magazine. He brought on the writer Finis Farr and a famous practical joker, Hugh Troy ("the most eminent practitioner of the art," according to Groucho Marx). The early work of Bryan's staff was "college boy stuff," said Thomas Braden, a Dartmouth/OSS vet who organized anticommunist front groups for OPC. "They had a lot of screwy ideas," said Braden. As a propaganda stunt, one of the cutups on Bryan's staff suggested dropping extra-large condoms—labeled "medium" in English—on the Soviet Union, in order to make Russian women think all American men were exceptionally virile. These were not serious proposals, just a way of "letting off steam," said Thomas Parrott, a Princeton/OSS man recruited by Wisner. The psywar staff did carry out some propaganda missions, including funding the Hollywood production of George Orwell's *Animal Farm*, an animated allegory of communist domination. (As a measure of thanks, Bryan arranged for Mrs. Orwell to meet Clark Gable.)

The Soviet Union, we know now, was not about to invade Western Europe. But its intelligence service, the NKVD and MGB (renamed, in 1954, the Komitet Gosudarstvennoy Bezopasnosti, the Committee for State Security, or KGB), was formidable indeed. It had been operating in Russia and around the globe for thirty years. Its resources were plentiful and its officers among the smartest the Soviet system could produce. CIA men mocked their foes as rubes: "How will I know which one is the Russian?" asked David Phillips when he was a neophyte spy working for the CIA in Chile in the early 1950s. "Look for the guy with pant cuffs so wide they flap," answered his handler. "He'll be the KGB agent." But the CIA felt outmanned and outgunned by their Soviet counterparts. When Harry Rositzke, an old CIA hand, wrote a book about the KGB in 1981, the subtitle was "the secret operations of the world's best intelligence service."

To fight back, Wisner hired some colorful operators. One was Michael Burke, a Penn football star and former OSS agent who had been the model for Gary Cooper in *Cloak and Dagger* and served as "technical adviser" to the movie. Burke, who in later life would run a circus and then the New York Yankees, was put to work parachuting agents into the East Bloc and Soviet Union. Another more exotic recruit, far more effective than the lampooners in Bryan's shop, was Carmel Offie; who was distinguished by his physical ugliness. He had bulging eyes, fleshy lips, and a swollen face; an open homosexual at a time when most stayed in the closet, Offie liked to disconcert other men by pinching his nipples in the midst of a conversation. He had been discovered before the war by a group of talented Russian experts—Chip Bohlen, Charles Thayer, and George Kennan—at the American embassy in Moscow, where he worked as an all-purpose troubleshooter for the ambassador, William Bullitt. After the war Offie had been tossed out of the foreign service for using the diplomatic pouch for illegal currency transfers (he also dealt in diamonds, rubles, and in one smuggled shipment, three hundred Finnish lobsters). Though corrupt, Offie was useful and, according to his friends, quite considerate. In Washington, he would stay ahead of the diplomatic cables by rising at 4 A.M. and calling his sources in the European embassies six or seven hours ahead of the State Department.

Bohlen persuaded Wisner to take on Offie at OPC. He immediately proved his worth on several fronts. For Mrs. Wisner he hired a very good cook, and for the Wisner children there were movie showings on rainy Saturday mornings. For Wisner he located former German officers and diplomats who could be used against the Soviet Union. One of them was Gustav Hilger, a career German diplomat who had specialized in recruiting collaborators to fight against the Red Army. Offie knew that Hilger would be very valuable in carrying out Wisner's plan for a secret émigré force, first described in the State–Army–Navy–Air Force Coordinating Committee documents as Operation Bloodstone.[3]

Wisner put Offie in charge of refugee matters—in essence, recruiting an émigré army from the displaced persons (DP) camps scattered throughout Western Europe, with the mission to spy on and "destabilize" the Soviet Union and its satellites. Wisner's friends at the State Department—Sovietologists Bohlen, Thayer, and Kennan—regarded Hilger and other former German diplomats, like Hans "Johnny" Herwarth von Bittenfield, as "good Germans." They were by and large aristocratic and anti-Nazi, close to the upper-class plotters who tried and failed to kill Hitler in 1944. When Offie suggested bringing Hilger to the United States in the spring of 1948, George Kennan enthusiastically seconded the idea (in the same memorandum, Kennan scrawled a note of thanks to Offie for intervening to pay the transatlantic passage of a couple of servants for Kennan's own household).

Kennan, still a covert action enthusiast at this point, believed that former German officers like Hilger could help organize an underground army of anticommunists in Eastern Europe and the Ukraine. If Hitler had listened to political warfare experts like Hilger, argued Charles Thayer, he might have succeeded in defeating Russia. Hilger was smart and presentable, but he was also guilty of war crimes. He had been the German Foreign Office's liaison to the SS during the invasion of Russia; he had participated in the creation of the SS Einsatzgruppen, the mobile killing squads that went around shooting thousands of Jews and Gypsies as the Germans advanced eastward. Hilger had also helped to round up and imprison Italy's Jews for transportation back to the German death camps.[4]

In 1982, John Loftus, a prosecutor with the Office of Special Investigations at the U.S. Justice Department, wrote a book, publicized on the CBS News show *60 Minutes*, that accused Wisner of methodically recruiting Nazi war criminals. The book paints a lurid and somewhat unfair portrait of Wisner, who was vehemently anti-Nazi.[5] Wisner was certainly aware that some of the émigrés imported by the CIA had unsavory backgrounds. He arranged to have them exempted from the immigration laws, which barred war criminals. Chip Bohlen was sent up to Capitol Hill to soothe congressmen anxious on this score. When Congress passed the CIA Act of 1949, opening the door to a hundred émigrés a year whom the CIA found useful but who might not otherwise pass muster with Immigration, Wisner complained that the quota was too small.[6]

Generally speaking, "We knew what we were doing," said Harry Rositzke, a Soviet expert in the CIA. "It was a visceral business of using any bastard as long as he was anti-communist." Wisner did not inquire too closely into the bastard's past. But on the other hand, Wisner did not concern himself with the particulars of recruitment. He was probably unaware of the sordid pasts of some of the émigrés rounded up by Carmel Offie. "Some of the people Frank brought in were terrible guys, but he didn't focus on it," said James Critchfield, a CIA officer who served as a liaison to the Gehlen organization, a German Army intelligence unit that was preserved intact by the U.S. Army to spy on Russia. "At 6:30 in the evening, Wisner would put his signature on things that Carmel Offie put in front of him. He wasn't paying attention."[7]

Wisner was focused on the difficult task of penetrating the East Bloc. Out of the displaced persons camps, the Army had recruited 40,000 refugees into Labor Service units to help clean up rubble from the war. The labor units provided convenient cover for Wisner's secret army. Some 5,000 volunteers were trained as a "post-nuclear guerrilla force" to invade the Soviet Union after an atomic attack. Others were organized into "stay-behind" units to blow up bridges in case the Red Army overran Europe. A number of brave volunteers were picked for secret missions behind the Iron Curtain. Beginning in September 1949, the CIA began dropping scores of parachutists into the so-called denied areas to spy or link up with resistance groups. In the Ukraine, there was a sputtering revolt against the communists that Wisner hoped to exploit. Ukrainian refugees, many of whom had fought with the Nazis, were recruited to jump in and join their countrymen waging a furtive shooting war in the Carpathian Mountains. These were hopeless missions; the Kremlin's highly efficient security services rounded up the infiltrators as they crushed the resistance movements. "It was a horrible mistake," said Thomas Parrott, who supervised some of the drops. "None of them survived."[8]

The recruits were a brave but sad lot. "You'd go to a refugee camp and say, 'Here, Joe, you want to join a special project?' Most of these people were like the homeless," said Peter Jessup, an OPC operative who worked on an operation, code name ZRELOPE, to recruit émigrés.* Not surprisingly, some saw a chance for profit. The thirst for intelligence inside the Iron Curtain gave rise to a whole new industry, paper mills churning ever-more fantastic tales of revolt and intrigue in the "denied areas." One U.S.-financed émigré group, known as TsOpe by its Russian initials, even blew up its own headquarters and blamed the KGB. The idea was to show that the Russians really feared TsOpe, and thus Washington should increase its funding.[9]

It was not beyond the Russians to try to blow up or murder their adversaries. The KGB had a branch, the 13th Directorate, devoted to "wet affairs"—kidnapping, sabotage, and assassination. Their

---

* The cryptonyms of CIA operations are preceded by a two-letter "diagraph" for signals security.

targets were usually defectors who were preaching anticommunism in Europe. To silence émigré editors and broadcasters, the KGB used exotic weapons—poisons and dart guns that left no trace to fix the cause of death.[10] Inevitably, Wisner and his men had to decide whether to do likewise. OPC officials later testified that no assassinations were ever carried out. CIA agents were apparently prohibited from shooting anyone except in self-defense. "This license-to-kill stuff is bullshit. We never did kill anyone. We were stumblebums," said Arthur Jacobs, a law school classmate of Wisner's who acted as a kind of informal inspector general. "I am Mr. Wisner's conscience," Jacobs once announced to a case officer; his colleagues nicknamed Jacobs, who was a tiny man, the "Ozzard of Wiz."[11]

With his moralistic background, Wisner may have been bothered at some level by the dirty work of spying, but he never showed it. The ability to swallow one's qualms, to do the harder thing for the greater good, was regarded as a sign of moral strength by men like Wisner. At meetings with his staff, he seemed moved less by squishy scruples than by practical necessity. "We talked about assassinations," said Jim McCargar, one of Wisner's top aides. "Wisner's attitude was that the KGB was better at it." He was not anxious to get into a spy war in which spies were human targets. The "talk" about assassinating Stalin did get at least to the planning stages. In his 1994 biography of Allen Dulles, Peter Grose writes that in 1952 Wisner considered a plan to assassinate Stalin if the Kremlin leader came to Paris to attend a four-power summit suggested by the French. The idea was to plant a bomb in his car. The summit never took place; in any case, CIA Director Walter Bedell Smith "rejected out of hand" the proposal.[12] As a practical matter, there was an informal truce between the Americans and the KGB; neither side killed the case officers of the other. Low-level informants were another matter. The punishment for a double agent in the émigré community was sometimes death. Washington, in those hectic years of trying to catch up to a stronger and more ruthless opponent, looked the other way.

WISNER'S GREAT ambition was to penetrate the East Bloc and, ultimately, to break it into pieces. In 1953 alone, according to one of the CIA's in-house histories, the agency spent almost $100 million on operations in Eastern Europe, about half of it on paramilitary training and operations. Wisner believed that, given proper underground aid—arms caches, radios, propaganda—the local populations of Eastern Europe could be persuaded to throw off their communist oppressors. This was a very ambitious goal, and Wisner was not completely unrealistic about the chances of success. But he felt obliged to try, to probe and test, to see if OPC could find a fissure and drive a wedge.[13]

The first target of opportunity was Albania. The tiny country was poor and isolated, cut off from the rest of the East Bloc by Greece and Yugoslavia. Yet it was a strategic threat—the Soviets were building a submarine base at the Albanian port of Sasseno, from whence they could control the Adriatic. Trying to overthrow the repressive regime of Enver Hoxha in Albania would be a "clinical test" of the West's ability to "roll back" communism in Eastern Europe, Wisner told his staff. A successful revolt in Albania might stir insurrection elsewhere. In any case, a victory in Albania would prove the worth and effectiveness of OPC.

The Albanian operation, code name BGFIEND, began as a British idea. There was among the British sentimental support for the deposed King Zog, living in exile in Cairo, and a desire by Whitehall to hang on to some influence in the Mediterranean. The British Secret Intelligence Service (SIS) began to draw up plans to infiltrate agents into Albania in order to make contact with resistance groups. There was one problem: the British were broke. "Church mice don't make wars," a foreign office official told Neil "Billy" McLean, the SIS man handling Albania.

Wisner was happy to help. He had enormous respect, as well as some envy, for the British, who had vastly more experience with spying than the Americans. The British would provide the knowhow, and in the beginning at least, the manpower; the Americans would provide the cash. Wisner was taken with the idea of using the British to inherit their role as global power. "Whenever we want to subvert any place, we find the British own an island nearby," Wisner told the SIS liaison in Washington, Kim Philby. On April 14, 1949, Wisner and McLean signed the deal, with a handshake, over lunch at Buck's Club in London.

The base for the operation was Malta, one of Britain's handy islands. The trainers, British special operations vets from World War II, referred to their charges, Albanians recruited out of the DP camps, as "untidy little men" and "pixies." The first twenty "pixies" were sprinkled ashore on the Albanian coast by the yacht *Stormie Seas* in October 1949. Most of them stumbled back out a few months later through Greece. They reported that Hoxha's men had been waiting for them in ambushes, and that the locals did not seem eager for an uprising. Four of the infiltrators had died. The British were somewhat discouraged and signaled their lack of enthusiasm for further forays. But Wisner was not too disappointed. A 20 percent loss rate was deemed normal for these types of operations, and the survivors had picked up some useful information. Wisner wanted to try again. He sent Mike Burke, the OSS vet with Hollywood experience, to open a new base of operations in Athens. Wisner discussed details of the operation over lunch with the British SIS's Philby. Well spoken (despite an upper-class stutter), well educated (if slovenly dressed), and shrewd in the ways of secret operations, Philby impressed Wisner greatly. The American spymaster did not know that his British counterpart was also a Soviet mole, betraying him to Moscow.[14]

WISNER'S COLLEAGUES were struck by his physical presence. He seemed coiled, said one, still the low hurdler, constrained by a vest. "He tried to give the impression of a very strong man, in command, which he achieved," said Jim McCargar, who helped run the Albanian operation. "But I think it was a deliberate display." Wisner, who rolled up his sleeves in the office, had a habit of working his fists and making the tendons and muscles ripple up the length of his arm. McCargar would watch and wonder whether he was consciously flexing or the habit was just a physical tic.

In Georgetown, at their house on P Street, Wisner and his wife, Polly, "ran a boardinghouse for ambassadors," said Tom Braden. The constant entertaining was work and, over time, wearying. But in the early days, when there seemed to be so much to do and such vivacious people to do it with, Wisner was as much enlivened as he was fatigued by the blur of duty and social life. Bourbon in hand, he would revive as he chatted with generals and undersecretaries and their wives.[15]

Wisner's staff was at once slightly jealous and grateful for their boss's tireless presence in the salons of Georgetown. It gave OPC a leg up on the other agencies of government. In theory, OPC just executed policy decisions handed down by the White House, State, and Defense, but Wisner sought a wider stage for himself. "Wisner would tell us to keep our mouths shut because we weren't supposed to make policy," said Charles Whitehurst, who worked on the Far East desk. "I thought this was odd—because he clearly cared so much about policy." Whitehurst figured that Wisner was making policy "at night" with social friends like Bohlen and Nitze from State and Clark Clifford from the White House. "I would be at a meeting where it was obvious that the decision had been made the night before at a dinner party."

Wisner's approach to management was to foster competition. The winners in Wisner's office were the managers who could produce the most projects. His model was a law firm: the more clients, the more cases, the more reward. Competition raised productivity, but the results were sometimes chaotic. He would sometimes assign the same project to more than one person. McCargar was astonished, at a meeting on the Albania situation, to discover a man he had never met setting up charts and graphs to show how he would accomplish a mission that had been assigned to McCargar. Wisner's men admired his energy, deferred to his power, and laughed at his long and often ribald Mississippi stories, told with animation through a gap-tooth smile. But they were worn out by him.[16]

He did not get much guidance from the State Department. Bob Joyce, State's liaison officer to OPC, "was more CIA than the CIA," said Gilbert Greenway, one of Wisner's aides. Kennan's notions about the organization he had helped to create with his Policy Planning Staff papers were hopelessly naive. "It did not work out at all the way I conceived it," Kennan later confessed. "We had thought that this would be a facility which could be used when and if any occasion arose when it might be needed." Instead, covert action projects were pouring out of OPC by the hundreds. All over Europe, OPC operatives were handing envelopes full of cash to politicians, newspaper editors, and union leaders to enlist them in the crusade against communism. Money was no object. Wisner had arranged to siphon off funds from the Marshall Plan. Under the plan Western European countries matched every dollar sent by the United States; up to 5 percent of that money—about $200 million a year—was to be set aside in local currency for the use of the United States. This money became a slush fund for OPC, available to agents who called it "candy." The funds were unvouchered, to make them harder to trace. "We couldn't spend it all," said Greenway. "I remember once meeting with Wisner and the comptroller. My God, I said, how can we spend that? There were no limits and nobody had to account for it. It was amazing."

Over at Central Intelligence, Lawrence Houston, the agency's general counsel, watched with growing unease as Wisner's men had their way. Typical of the breed, in Houston's eyes, was Merritt Ruddock, one of Wisner's recruits who had been sent to London as OPC representative. Ruddock, who wore riding boots in the office, wanted the CIA to pay to stable his horses. Under OPC's charter the CIA was supposed to handle OPC's "quarters and rations," but this was going too far. "You want to go to jail?" demanded Houston. "Ruddock's attitude was, We've got a job to do! Don't hold us up!" said Houston. The CIA lawyer had little power to stop them. "Wisner would think these things up and get them cleared by Bob Joyce at State," said Houston. "He didn't want to clear anything with my office. He tried to keep me out of it. But his recruits would come to me and say, 'What are we doing?' There was a lot of consternation. What was going on with all those funds?"[17]

The concern was most strongly felt in the Office of Special Operations (OSO), the espionage and counterintelligence branch of the CIA that had been pushed aside when Wisner created OPC. The OSOers, most of whom were career government servants, regarded themselves as professionals. The OPCers, with their Yale manners and Wall Street swagger, were amateurs. "We thought they were a bunch of cowboys," said George Holmes, who was with OSO in Belgium. Yet OSO was a static organization, and OPC was growing by leaps and bounds. The OSOers were especially galled that OPCers of the same or lesser rank and experience were better paid—Wisner had arranged to have his troops come in at higher GS levels than the OSO. In the field OSO and OPC tripped over each other. With more money to hand out, OPC brazenly stole some of OSO's foreign agents.

The OSO versus OPC feud sounds like a petty bureaucratic struggle. But the difference between the two organizations represents a divide that ran through the CIA for decades, a fundamental conflict in the role and mission of an intelligence agency. Clandestine operations embrace two separate activities. One is covert action—seeking to influence or change the way a country is governed. The other is espionage—secretly gathering information about a friend or foe. The two missions attract different sorts of personalities. Covert action operatives, like the ones who worked for

OPC, tend to be activists. Results are more important than process. Espionage operators, like the ones who worked for OSO, tend to be more passive. They are cautious, prudent, careful. The goals of covert action and espionage are often in direct conflict. Covert action is almost by definition noisy, since operatives plunge themselves into the struggle for power. Espionage must be quiet to be effective. It "never announces itself," writes Thomas Powers. The foreign government official who is on the payroll, feeding the CIA secrets, must never be identified as an agent. Yet covert action is also risky—it tends to "go wrong" and expose spying networks carefully laid by the espionage operators.

The differences between OPC and OSO were personally felt. "The OPCers had that missionary zeal in their eyes. We distrusted missionary zeal," said Peter Sichel, who went into OSO after the war. The OSOers had a "card file mentality," said Ed Welles, an OPCer in Europe. "People with card files always want to know if number 23 is out of place, not whether the information on it is accurate." Frank Wisner was contemptuous of OSO, which he described as "a bunch of old washerwomen gossiping over their laundry." Wisner did not have much to do with Admiral Hillenkoetter, the director of Central Intelligence, whom he regarded as "an amiable lightweight," said Houston. The CIA, the umbrella organization for OPC and OSO, was just a place to hang one's cloak, and not a very nice place at that. The quarters provided OPC by the CIA were some seedy "temporary" buildings on the Reflecting Pool that had never been torn down after World War II.[18]

Wisner's indifference to the CIA came to an abrupt halt with the outbreak of the Korean War in June 1950. The reason, ironically, was the failure of the CIA to predict anything right. The fledgling intelligence agency had not anticipated the Czech coup in 1948 or anti-American riots in Bogotá that threatened the visiting U.S. secretary of state, George Marshall, that year.[19] When the CIA failed to see the Korean War coming, that was the last straw for President Truman. He eased out Hillenkoetter and brought in a no-nonsense commander, General Walter Bedell Smith.

Winston Churchill had called "Beetle" Smith "America's bulldog." Smith had been Eisenhower's chief of staff at D-Day. It was said that he was even-tempered, that his mood never changed: he was always angry. He was angrier after half his stomach, along with some ulcers, was removed in the summer of 1950. A product of the Indiana National Guard, not West Point, Smith was suspicious of privilege. He inspected the parking lot of the CIA and observed the OSOers going home in their Chevrolets and Fords and the OPCers going home in their MGs and Jaguars. His sympathies, if he had been capable of sympathy, were with the grunts in OSO. In any case, he was not about to tolerate Frank Wisner's independence.[20]

Wisner was tipped off by his friends at State that the new DCI was going to make a move to take control of OPC. Wisner's aides asked for a new table of organization and a legal directive. General Smith said he didn't need any piece of paper. "Wisner," he growled, "you work for me."

Wisner was not happy with the new arrangement, especially when he learned that he was going to be layered by more than Beetle Smith. The CIA would now have a number two under Smith, as well as another new position innocuously named deputy director/plans. The "DD/P" would serve as an adviser to the director on covert action and, after the eventual merger of OSO and OPC, as chief of the clandestine service. But Wisner's mood improved when he learned the identities of his new bosses. Smith's second-in-command would be William Harding Jackson, a Wall Street lawyer who had first hired Wisner at Carter Ledyard in New York in the 1930s and was his partner for a couple of years after the war. The new DD/P was to be Allen Dulles, the former OSS masterspy who had shared long lunches with Wisner in New York, plotting how to create a peacetime intelligence establishment.[21]

The Korean War also meant new business for Wisner. He knew that OPC would grow even faster to meet the military's demand for behind-the-lines spying and sabotage. He began to cast around his old recruiting grounds on Wall Street for brilliant amateurs who also knew something about fighting a war in Asia. He found one in Desmond FitzGerald.

Chapter Three

THE CAVALIER

"The culture was wild."

THERE WAS A predictable course for a man like Desmond FitzGerald, who was thirty-four years old in 1945, returning home from the war to resume his life in New York. He would become a partner in his Wall Street law firm (Hotchkiss Spence had saved a place for him). He would move from his large apartment on Park Avenue to a larger apartment on Park Avenue. He would summer on Long Island, and belong to the Piping Rock Club, the Racquet, the River, and the Brook (he already did). He would serve on boards and give to causes.[1]

But FitzGerald was interested in a wider world, and war exposed him to it. As a U.S. Army captain serving as liaison officer to a Chinese battalion in Burma, he had eaten monkey brains (enjoyed them, he insisted) and engaged in a technical debate with his troops over the proper way to banish a Chinese ghost.[2] He had shed some of his prejudices and become both harder and more thoughtful. He was full of ideas about the civilizing mission of America and, even more so, about the role of the individual in a world of dangerous mass movements.

FitzGerald could be autocratic and cutting, and his elitism, by modern standards, was offensive. A colleague in the CIA, Russell Jack Smith, once described him as a man with "the silken grace and easy manners of a courtier and the imagination and dash of a Renaissance soldier of fortune. I often thought that Des would have been in his element in the Elizabethan or Stuart era of sixteenth- or seventeenth-century England." He was, in fact, born out of his time; he would perhaps have been happier as a nineteenth-century British gentleman. Still, he had the ability to stand back from his situation and see that what was "normal" was in fact quite odd and that what was different was, in a different context, normal. When contemplating a CIA operation, he would sometimes quote Lewis Carroll's *Through the Looking Glass:* "It's a poor sort of memory that works only backwards."[3] While proper and somewhat stiff, he had a sense of fun and adventure, and though he was to all appearances an old-school traditionalist, he was immensely curious and had a highly developed sense of public service. His esprit was contagious; his subordinates felt they were, by association with him, the brightest men doing the best work.

AFTER PEARL Harbor a well-connected thirty-year-old lawyer with a wife and child might have arranged for a commission and a safe rear-echelon job. FitzGerald instead enlisted as a private. His attitude was, "If there's a war, jump in! Don't worry about rank," said an old schoolmate, Charles Francis Adams.

He had some misgivings about his democratic approach by the time his troop train from New York to Camp Blanding, Florida, had passed Washington. "My seat mates are without any doubt the dumbest pair I have ever met in the Army, and how could I ever say more?" he wrote his wife, Marietta, on March 10, 1942, from a railroad car "somewhere in Virginia." The seatmates irritated FitzGerald by not bothering to look up at the Capitol. "I think what angers me about the local dopes is the fact that they are so utterly uncurious. For instance, the larger cretin with whom I am sitting has never traveled outside New York City."[4] At Camp Blanding he was temporarily relieved to be assigned to an intelligence unit and then plunged into "despair" by another transfer, to work for a colonel in the Judge Advocate General Corps. The colonel is "an unctuous stinker," he wrote his wife. FitzGerald saw himself fated to spend the rest of the war practicing "the subspecies of criminal law practised in court martial," all because the colonel couldn't find another man "who ever quibbled or mumbled pig-latin."[5]

FitzGerald wanted to be a combat officer. He finally wrangled a transfer to Officer Candidate School and was relieved to be crawling about in the mud and learning how to read a compass. "I think, in a lovely fashion, that I am potentially hot stuff as a combat officer," he wrote, in an uncharacteristic burst of boastfulness,

though he admitted "my voice in command is acclaimed the drea-
riest on the reservation." (The troops apparently had difficulty
understanding orders delivered in Locust Valley lockjaw.)[6]

His first command was an entire platoon of blacks, to whom he
referred, with prejudice typical of his time and class, as "boogies,"
"jigaboos," "dinges," and "dusky dopes." At times he would despair over their lack of discipline and initiative. In one letter he
described the punishments he had meted out to various miscre-
ants, including an attempted suicide who drank a bottle of iodine
"with entirely too much flourish." The man "thinks he has a fool-
proof way of getting out of the army by acting nuts," FitzGerald
wrote home. "I delayed administering the antidote (starch) and
the guy was in lots of pain and scared bleach. When he gets out of
the hospital I will give him more work than he ever got in the
reformatory he came from. (I am a hard and bitter man, boogie-
woogie.)"[7] But just when FitzGerald would begin to sound more
bitter than amused in his letters, he stepped back and made an
effort to understand his charges. He observed that while the southern blacks tipped their forelocks while endeavoring to do as little
as possible to help their white masters, the midwestern blacks
were different—eager to become officers and pilots, wanting to
better themselves. It was an early lesson for FitzGerald that culture, not race, is what matters.

"These chronicles begin to look like Booker T. Washington's
memoirs, but the subject of the negro is a brand new one to me and
fascinating," he wrote home. He lectured his troops on the virtue
of democracy and found that "democracy doesn't need much plug-
ging." He even warmed a little to the men: "With all their short-
comings, which are educational and cultural and not inherent, I
believe most of them are awfully likeable—I wish I understood
them better," he wrote his sister, Eleanor.[8]

FitzGerald was desperate to get in the fight. When his family
tried to convey their pride in his service, he responded, a bit
piously, "The only measure of success for a combat soldier is combat." A year of drilling enlistees in the Alabama heat was hard to
bear. "This place with its sea of blank black faces puts me in frenzy
of thwartedness," he confided to his sister in November 1942.
When the orders finally came in August 1943, he "turned pirou-
ettes and got horribly drunk."[9]

He was sent to a remote corner of the war, the China-Burma-
India theater, where he joined General "Vinegar Joe" Stilwell's

campaign to recapture Burma from the Japanese. He tried to be a
good sport about the tedium and physical discomfort: "I am not in
the least disillusioned—I never did expect a joust and a hot bath.
I knew and I now realize that war always paints things brown."
When FitzGerald was awarded a medal, he wrote home, "The joke
of the week is that they went and presented me with the Bronze
Star. This is a very important decoration, ranking just below the
mothball cluster and the Mexican border ribbon. It is, shall we say,
not uncommon even in a theater where it is sometimes difficult to
find a sufficient pretext for paying us."[10]

His self-deprecation notwithstanding, FitzGerald had what the
British call "a good war." It was much more harsh than his letters
allowed. Barbara Tuchman, General Stilwell's biographer, describes the mountainous jungle where FitzGerald marched "as forbidding fighting country as any in the world." The official Army
history shows that in one operation in which FitzGerald fought,
Operation Galahad, there were—in addition to the 93 combat
deaths and 293 wounded—503 cases of amoebic dysentery, 149
cases of scrub typhus, 296 cases of malaria, and 72 cases of "psy-
choneurosis." Some soldiers cut out the seat of their pants, so
severe was their dysentery as they marched.[11] FitzGerald never
complained of being sick, indeed insisted his health was "perfect."
Yet in the jungle he contracted a skin condition so persistent that
whenever he went out into the sun for the rest of his life, he was
compelled to cover his exposed skin in a thick layer of ointment.

FitzGerald was a liaison officer to a regiment of Chinese troops.
Years later he told his daughter, Frances, that he had wondered
whether his Chinese troops would cut and run. They had fled once
before with Stilwell across Burma to India. Retrained and resup-
plied, they were expected to take on a Japanese division that had
captured Singapore. The Chinese never became the most aggressive attacking force; still, FitzGerald became an admirer of their
capacity to carry on. He enjoyed the exotic life of the bush, smok-
ing opium with Burmese chieftains and complaining about the
sheer awfulness of listening to a Chinese opera ("Imagine 'Lucia'
played by a male falsetto with an orchestra composed of two spit-
toons, a rattle, and a couple of one-string fiddles"). He had hope for
the "New Chinese": "Amid the mass new values are being born
and for the coolie, new hopes." He did not sound at all like the
scornful young fop on the train to boot camp. In one letter to his
wife he called for "sympathy and understanding" for the Chinese

and felt ashamed of ugly Americanism. "You would be appalled by the percentage of soldiers who, by their 'God-damned Wop (Frog, Limey, Chink)' attitude utterly ruin the effect of our giving [help to the natives]."

As FitzGerald marched toward China he was entranced by the "Alice-in-Wonderland" atmosphere that "pervades everything for the average American. If I were a spectator at the croquet game or a guest at the mad tea-party, I would be amused but never astonished."[12] He was proud of his troops' success against the Japanese. Properly equipped, an Asian force can fight under American leadership, he wrote. The key, he believed, was understanding the Asians and keeping them well equipped with an efficient system of airdrops.[13] These were important military lessons that FitzGerald would apply, with mixed success, when running secret wars in Southeast Asia.

FITZGERALD WAS "indulging in some small-scale infantry maneuvers against the Japs in Hunan Province" when he received news of the atom bomb. For most soldiers far from home, the end of the war meant relief, the comforting prospect of a return to some kind of normalcy. FitzGerald's turn of mind was more inquiring and unsettled. "My first reaction to the atom's behavior was one of personal futility. My battalion of people were capable of causing approximately $\frac{1}{300}$ as much damage as the crew of the B-29 and I felt like a tired stone axe. . . ." He imagined an interstellar spectator saying, " 'Oops! There goes another world whose wisdom couldn't keep up with its knowledge.' I may be unduly pessimistic about the atomic future but the Bomb seems to me analogous to passing out loaded tommy guns at a Christmas Tree," he wrote his in-laws. "The Peace seemed almost an anticlimax to the Bomb but as I am fundamentally for peace and in favor of getting home, I didn't let it spoil my pleasure." Still, the new superweapon haunted FitzGerald. He sensed the broader implications for weapons of mass destruction and the threat it posed to the well-ordered, individualistic society he prized.[14]

FitzGerald returned home in the fall of 1945 to learn that his marriage was failing. Before the war he had married Marietta Peabody, a long-necked New England beauty who had been, for most of her life, in full revolt against her family. Her grandfather was Endicott Peabody, the formidable Rector of Groton, and her mother was a starchy Bostonian who "was basically against people having a good time," according to her granddaughter Frances FitzGerald. During the war Marietta had finally been allowed to live her own life, getting a job as a researcher at *Life* magazine, modeling for *Vogue* and *Harper's Bazaar*, and playing in cafe society. She had also fallen in love with John Huston, the movie director.

FitzGerald learned of this, literally, as he got off the boat. Marietta told him she wanted a divorce. FitzGerald managed to persuade her to see a therapist, but the marriage was doomed. In the summer of 1947, Marietta went to Reno, Nevada, to get a divorce, over the bitter objections of her mother and father. She had found a new man, wealthy British diplomat Ronald Tree. FitzGerald appeared fatalistic. On a boat trip to England in the spring of 1947, he had pointed to Tree and told a friend, "There is the man my wife is going to marry."

FitzGerald remarried a year later, to an effervescent Englishwoman, Barbara Green Lawrence, who had been briefly married to an American Air Force pilot with a drinking problem and had a small daughter of her own. FitzGerald badly missed his own daughter, Frances, who had moved with her mother to England. But he was generally not one to reveal his feelings. "Des was very handsome," said one of his oldest friends, Susan Mary Patten (later Alsop), "with sparkling eyes, color in his cheeks. He could be very smooth, discussing the best restaurant in Paris, or very serious. He had the clearest mind, and he was very concise, with command of the language. I thought he was open-minded and wise, but he could be arrogant. I loved Des, I adored him. But he was cold."[15]

FitzGerald was restless in New York. Bored with his law firm, he began dabbling in politics. New York City was run by Tammany Hall, and FitzGerald had a low opinion of the Irish pols in Mayor William O'Dwyer's administration. Together with some other Republican "reformers," FitzGerald formed the grandly named Committee of Five Million to investigate official corruption. FitzGerald was being idealistic. Most men in his circumstances regarded politics, particularly the kind of machine politics practiced in New York City, as something to be avoided. FitzGerald was not so squeamish. He had a more British view of public service, which included not only a sense of noblesse oblige, but also a willingness to do whatever was necessary.

FitzGerald's reform movement was embarrassed when a private

investigator hired to spy on Tammany was caught illegally wire-tapping. FitzGerald himself was not named in the indictment, and he was probably unaware of the illegal act. But the headlines in the *New York Times* soured his enthusiasm for public politics.[16]

Off and on during the late 1940s, FitzGerald had been urged by Paul Nitze, a friend and classmate from Harvard, to come work for the government. A good group had come down to Washington—or simply stayed on there after the war, said Nitze—men like Frank Wisner, who was setting up a new secret intelligence agency.

FitzGerald knew Wisner from Wall Street and meetings at the Council on Foreign Relations, an establishment bastion that worked to encourage America's larger role in the world. When the Korean War broke out in the summer of 1950, Wisner called Fitz-Gerald and asked him to join his agency. Though he and Barbara had just bought a new brownstone on East 62nd Street, FitzGer-ald accepted. That November he received a letter from Colonel Richard Stilwell, one of Wisner's deputies: Wisner "has the high-est possible estimate of your abilities . . . Frank and I would like to have you join our team, for an extremely important assignment here just as soon as practicable." FitzGerald wrote back that he would be there as soon as he could get away, "to devote 100 per-cent of my time (up to 24 hours a day), and all of my thoughts, to the job in hand."[17]

WISNER MADE FitzGerald the executive officer in OPC's Far East Division, handling the Korean War and communist insurgencies from the Philippines to Thailand.

Veterans of CIA operations in the Far East talk about the Ko-rean War period with a sense of wonder and chagrin. At indoctri-nation, trainees were shown a film called *I Was a Communist for the FBI* and given a red-hot speech about fighting the evils of Stalinism. At the end they invariably jumped up cheering and shouting. "The culture was wild," said Donald Gregg, who signed on out of Williams College as a "PMer" (paramilitary specialist, also known as a knuckledragger) to parachute into northern Viet-nam on a secret mission that was, fortunately for him, scrubbed. Gregg was trained to recruit agents by "instructors who had never recruited anyone before. Mostly, they taught us how not to do things."

The CIA instructors were veterans of the last war, a more

straightforward affair than the struggle looming in Asia. For all the courage it required, jumping into France to hasten the departure of the Nazis or fighting the Japanese in the Burma jungles was not really adequate preparation for the more subtle and ultimately frustrating task of trying to penetrate communist insurgencies. "We thought it was going to be like World War II," said James Lilley, who was based on Taiwan. "Instead we got led into lies, deceit, deception, and traps. We were children in a big boy's game."[18]

Frank Wisner had established an OPC presence in the Far East before the Korean War. In 1949, General Claire Chennault, the U.S. Army Air Forces commander who was close to Generalissimo Chiang Kai-shek, had approached Washington with a plan to destabilize the Chinese communists. The State Department had turned him away: Dean Acheson, the secretary of state, wanted nothing to do with Chennault or his Chinese patron, the "G'mo." But Wisner thought that Chennault was a man of action. Lobbied by Thomas "Tommy the Cork" Corcoran, the New Deal fixer, at a series of social events in the winter of 1949, Wisner bought Chennault's airline, Civil Air Transport, for $950,000. Based in Taiwan, CAT turned out to be the CIA's air arm for clandestine activities in the Far East for the next twenty years. OPC's early attempts to roll back communism were as unsuccessful in the Far East as in Eastern Europe. In 1949, hoping to save the island of Hainan off the coast of southern China from the Chinese communists, Wisner sent "a pot of gold" to the ruling warlord, a Chinese Nationalist general, according to one of Wisner's deputies, Frank Lindsay. Unfortunately, said Lindsay, the communists paid him more, and Hainan was folded into the People's Republic.[19]

With the outbreak of the Korean War, Wisner staffed up OPC's base on Taiwan, sending more than three hundred operators to provide guerrilla training, radio broadcasts, propaganda, aerial reconnaissance, and balloon drops. OPC poured so much money into "Western Enterprises," the agency's front company on Taiwan, that Washington worried about the impact on the Nationalist Chinese currency. The 8,500 guerrillas trained on Taiwan did not have much impact on the mainland. The CAT dropped 75 million leaflets, and the guerrillas made eighteen raids and committed eleven "marginal" acts of sabotage, according to an in-house CIA history.

Wisner knew that Chiang Kai-shek's Nationalist Chinese (the

KMT) were corrupt and weak, and hardly likely to "take back the mainland." As another alternative, he hoped to create a "Third Force" movement in China that would offer a democratic alternative to communism and the discredited KMT. Based on false reports (Hong Kong, like the German DP camps, had its share of Cold War entrepreneurs who would make up convincing-sounding intelligence for a fee), Wisner and his Far East chief, Richard Stilwell, believed that there were 500,000 guerrillas on the mainland waiting for American support to rise up against Mao. Even if the revolution failed, Wisner figured, the Third Force movement would divert the Red Chinese, who had jumped into the Korean War in November 1950.[20]

Colonel Stilwell had a "hell of a lot of brass," said Carleton Swift, who was an operative for OSO in the Far East. A combat infantry veteran with the 90th Division in Europe, Stilwell would wear a Confederate forage cap to CIA Christmas parties and emit rebel yells. A West Pointer, he was a yes-sir, can-do officer. At OPC he summoned Swift and demanded to know why OSO had been unable to identify the 500,000 waiting guerrillas. "I've got an order to roll back communism, I've got an airline, I've got a training base. Let's go!" he barked. Swift tried to explain that there weren't any guerrillas on the mainland.[21]

Stilwell decided to go ahead anyway. Chinese agents were trained at a $28 million CIA compound on Saipan and parachuted into the Manchurian provinces of Liaoning and Kirin. The first group (Team Wen) was to be extracted in November 1952 to report on its progress stirring insurrection. The pickup method was harrowing: the agents were to be yanked off the ground by planes flying slightly faster than stall speed, 60 miles per hour. One of the CIA case officers along for the ride on the first pickup out of Manchuria was John Downey, a member of the Yale class of '51. He had abandoned his plans for a law career after listening to the CIA's campus recruiter spin tales of parachuting behind enemy lines and setting up resistance networks. "Hey," he recalled. "That was as glamorous as anything we could ever hope for."

Downey ended up spending twenty-five years in a Chinese prison. His operation had been penetrated. The CIA plane was shot down as it approached the pickup zone; the pilots were killed and Downey was captured. The box score on the Third Force movement was pitiful: of the 212 Chinese agents who parachuted into the mainland between 1951 and 1953, 101 had been killed, usually on the spot by "outraged peasants," and 111 captured. By the end of the Korean War, the CIA had purchased $152 million worth of foreign weapons and ammunition for guerrilla groups that never existed. ("I think we did have some mounted horsemen in Mongolia," Swift recalled.)

The CIA had only slightly better luck infiltrating guerrillas into North Korea. Wisner had sent Hans Tofte, an OSS veteran with a genius for self-promotion, out to the Far East to run guerrilla operations. Tofte's early efforts were not auspicious. He sent back a film to Washington which, he claimed, showed his guerrillas clambering ashore behind enemy lines. Wisner wanted to use the film to try to impress some Pentagon brass, who were dubious about OPC. (The American commander in Korea, General Douglas MacArthur, was especially hostile.) Wisner's aide, Arthur Jacobs, observed during the showing that the infiltration was taking place in broad daylight. Could this be possible? Was Tofte that reckless? Tofte had to admit that the film was of a training exercise, not a real operation. A secret CIA history of operations in Korea notes that Tofte's guerrillas were dressed in "captured army uniforms and Korean civilian clothing, but unfortunately wore self-incriminating U.S. Army issue underwear."

Tofte finally did send forty-four guerrilla teams into Korea between April and December 1951, some by air, most by sea. He later claimed that the operations were a "tremendous success." There is some evidence that the enemy felt some very small stings. Although only 3,000 guerrillas were involved, the CIA intercepted some messages from Beijing warning field commanders that there were 30,000 guerrillas operating behind their lines. And Tofte's agents did appear to pick up valuable information about Chinese troop movements. But it later turned out that most of them had been "doubled" by the communists and fed disinformation, which they duly relayed to their unsuspecting masters at the CIA. "The CIA's contribution to the Korean War was minimal," dryly stated Richard Helms, longtime CIA hand and the agency's director in the late 1960s and early 1970s.[22]

FITZGERALD'S PROJECT during the Korean War was a well-intentioned flop. In 1949 several thousand Chinese Nationalist troops fleeing the communists had crossed into Burma under their general, Li Mi. OPC's Hong Kong station chief, Alfred Cox, suggested that these "ChiNats" be used as a diversionary force on China's southern flank, invading Yunnan Province and forcing Beijing to divert troops away from Korea. CIA Director Beetle Smith was highly skeptical of this plan. He noted that the Chinese communists had several million men under arms, and a harassing movement by a few thousand poorly trained, poorly equipped marauders two thousand miles from the front was not likely to make much difference. But the White House was eager to try something to distract the Chinese, who were chewing up MacArthur's army on the Korean peninsula.

FitzGerald was enthusiastic about the operation. From his experience fighting with Chinese troops, he believed that, properly equipped and led, they could be effective. The key was air support, which the CIA's secret air force stood ready to deliver. "Des told me he knew this territory, he knew these bastards," said Charles Whitehurst. "This was up his alley. He was a natural for it."

More experienced hands regarded FitzGerald as eager and charming but green. The more cautious bureaucrats in OSO, which was being slowly merged with OPC by Bedell Smith, were wary of FitzGerald, worried that his amateurish activism would burn their espionage networks. Whitehurst, who was running OSO's China desk, was summoned one morning by an angry FitzGerald. Why, FitzGerald demanded, was Whitehurst trying to fire a certain OPC man in Hong Kong? FitzGerald had a very high opinion of the man, who had parachuted behind German lines in World War II. Whitehurst was less enthusiatic. FitzGerald's war hero was a scam artist; he had turned in six months of expenses on the back of an envelope. What's more, the man knew nothing about tradecraft—the rules of espionage, carefully designed to protect secrecy. He was as "overt as a big red sign," said Whitehurst. "But FitzGerald didn't give a damn about trade craft. Trade craft was an excuse for doing nothing. He went across the hall, yelling and screaming to my division chief to have the guy put back on the payroll."

FitzGerald's eagerness went deeper than a desire to be involved and a familiarity with the local territory. Well read in English literature and politics, FitzGerald had a romantic notion of the individual. Like the young British officers who had come home from the trenches of World War I disgusted by the impersonal wholesale slaughter, FitzGerald was especially wary of the modern age of mass movements and mass destruction. The CIA appealed to him in part because it was a small elite force—a knighthood—that could apply force more discreetly and, he believed, more efficiently than a blundering army, no matter how modern its weapons. "He would have preferred," said his daughter Frances, "to fight the Cold War by single combat. By jousts. Brave individuals fighting each other." FitzGerald was appalled by what he had heard or knew of Chinese communism, with its brutal subjugation of the individual, its herding of whole populations and collective brainwashing. Dubious about the U.S. Army's efforts to take on the Red Chinese—the largest army in the world—through conventional warfare, FitzGerald harbored a hope of fomenting insurrection against Beijing through guerrilla movements.

His inspiration was the British Empire. FitzGerald's jauntiness about the spy world was very British. Commander Mansfield Cummings, known as "C," the head of the British Secret Service during World War I, referred to espionage as "capital sport." In the nineteenth century, the British had used guile, pluck, and a certain ruthlessness to tame the natives and outfox the Russians in the "Great Game" of Central Asia. Just as the British had used mountain tribes, like the Gurkhas of Nepal, as their allies, FitzGerald wanted to make common cause with a local warlord, Li Mi, to attack the Red Chinese.[23]

Beginning in March 1951, air operations, run by the CIA front, the Overseas Southeast Asia Supply Company—Sea Supply, as it was familiarly known—dropped supplies and American advisers down to Li Mi. When Li Mi's men were driven back into Burma after a brief incursion in April, FitzGerald argued against shutting down the operation, ignoring protests from the State Department that Li Mi's roving bands were ruining relations with Burma. "The psychological effect of the operation had been remarkable," Fitz-Gerald wrote in a memo on August 10. "Anti-communist Chinese spirit throughout the Far East had been given a shot of Adrenalin." FitzGerald recommended encouraging Li Mi to create "small, mobile hard-hitting groups" to work behind enemy lines. Bedell Smith, an old Army man, remained a skeptic about Li Mi's brigands, who had been named the Yunnan Province Anti-Communist National Salvation Army. "All those guys do is skate up and down the wrong side of the border," he scoffed. In any case, their cover was soon blown; the *New York Times* reported on February 11, 1952, that witnesses in Burma had seen Li Mi's men sporting brand-new American weapons. Soviet diplomats at the United Nations fulminated; Secretary of State Dean Acheson denied any U.S. involvement.

By summer, General Li Mi's force had grown to 12,000 men, and once more it invaded Yunnan. The CIA-backed ChiNats made it sixty miles before being driven out by the People's Liberation Army. As was typical of CIA operations in this era, this one had been thoroughly penetrated: General Li Mi's radio operator at Sea Supply in Bangkok was a Chinese communist agent who would periodically fill in Beijing on Li Mi's location and troop strength.

Li Mi refused the CIA's entreaties to relocate to Taiwan, and instead became a drug lord in Burma and north Thailand. His troops farmed poppies for opium in a region that would later become known as the Golden Triangle. The Burmese, in keeping with their isolationist history, closed up their borders and froze out the United States.[24]

FitzGerald's standing at the CIA rose in the wake of the Li Mi affair. "Li Mi helped Des. To get promoted in those days you needed a real disaster," laughed Carleton Swift, but he noted, more seriously, that while the Korean War may be half forgotten forty years later, at the time it looked as if it could lead to Armageddon. General MacArthur wanted to bomb the Chinese mainland and "get it over with." Under tremendous pressure from the Republican Right, who kept demanding "Who lost China?" (implying that it was the Democrats and "pinkos" at State), President Truman needed to do something about the Red Chinese, but not something so draconian that it might drag the United States into a world war. Covert operations seemed like a measured response. After all, Swift noted, the Li Mi operation "didn't use up any American lives. And it got publicity." Lacking many of the essential details, the newspaper articles did not paint the operation as a defeat, but rather as a clandestine attempt to stir trouble on China's flank. It was proof that the Truman administration was not just sitting idle. Knowledgeable officials within the agency knew that the operation had been "ill-conceived and ill-run," said Swift, but their attitude was, "Well, these are hard operations to run. It's tough to roll back communism in the Far East."

FITZGERALD'S ATTEMPT at harassing the Chinese communists had not succeeded, but on a different front he was able to contribute to a significant success at containing communism in the Far East. In later years Edward G. Lansdale would be remembered as the model for Graham Greene's *The Quiet American* and for Lederer and Burdick's *The Ugly American*—the earnest, feckless agency man who does wrong while trying to do right. But in the Philippines in the early 1950s, Lansdale gave the CIA its greatest victory against communist aggression in Asia.[25]

It would be an exaggeration to say that FitzGerald "ran" Lansdale, an Air Force colonel on loan to the CIA. An iconoclast and a loner, Colonel Lansdale preferred to operate on his own, with as little interference as possible from headquarters. But as the acting Far East chief for OPC, whose overall responsibilities included the Philippines, FitzGerald was smart enough to see that Lansdale was an original, highly effective on his own, and best left alone.

Lansdale's cover was as military adviser to the Philippine Army, but his real job was to stop the communist Hukbalahap insurgency from taking power. Lansdale was an avid practitioner of the art of psychological warfare. He would forge orders for a massacre by the Huks and then mail the "captured document" to the *Manila Times*, which would splash it on page one. (The Huks helped give credibility to such "black" propaganda by slaughtering the patients in a hospital with bolo knives.) In the villages of Luzon, Lansdale's operatives spread the rumor that men with evil in their hearts would be attacked by the local vampire, the *asuang*. To bring home the point, they took the body of a dead Huk, poked two holes in its neck, drained out the blood, and left it lying in the road. The villagers began to regard the Huks as vampire bait. More concretely (and probably with more effect), Lansdale engaged in "nation building" by giving land and money to Huk rebels who surrendered.

As an alternative to communism, Lansdale offered up Ramón Magsaysay, the defense minister with whom he had a Svengali-like relationship. Magsaysay and Lansdale were inseparable; they slept in twin beds in the same room. Lansdale's basic method with Magsaysay was to listen carefully and then restate what the Philippine politician had said in a way that clarified and subtly reshaped the meaning, until Magsaysay adopted the message and reasoning as his own. Lansdale could, at times, take stronger measures. FitzGerald liked to tell the story of Lansdale and Magsaysay arguing over whether to give a certain speech. Lansdale got so worked up that he hauled off and punched Magsaysay, knocking him out.

Lansdale was mortified but Magsaysay reassured him. "I understand," he told his American adviser, "it is because you care so much about the Philippine people."[26]

FitzGerald was fascinated by Lansdale. Here was an individual who really could make a difference in the struggle against communism. "Des loved Lansdale's ability to manipulate politics," said John Horton, who worked with both men in the Far East. Lansdale was a bit of a con man with his own superiors. "He snookered Des," said Horton. "He would send back these hysterical cables—things are falling apart! He would make up the whole situation to prove that only he could solve it. Des never figured out that he was dishonest." Even so, FitzGerald had enough sense to stay out of the way, and he was able to supply Lansdale with some valuable know-how from an unlikely source. One of FitzGerald's cohorts on the ill-fated Committee of Five Million in New York had been the lawyer Gabriel Kaplan. FitzGerald recruited him to work with Lansdale on the Philippine elections. He put together the National Movement for Free Elections (NAMFREL), supposedly organized by various civic groups but actually run by Kaplan and funded by the CIA. NAMFREL pushed for clean elections while making sure that Magsaysay would be the one elected. In 1953, Magsaysay was overwhelmingly elected president (earning for his CIA handler the nickname "Colonel Landslide"). The Philippine politician, who actually was an effective leader and whose death in 1957 would be a tragedy for Filipinos, spent election day cruising Manila Bay on the yacht of the American naval commander. A photo shows him asleep on a deck chair, Lansdale awake by his side.[27]

Lansdale's work in the Philippines was a model of counterinsurgency. The agency would try to repeat it all over the developing world, with less success, in coming decades. The *New York Times* called the Philippines a "showcase of Democracy," and President Eisenhower declared, "Now, this is the way I like to see an election run."

By 1953, FITZGERALD was effectively running the Far East Division of OPC. Frustrated by OPC's lack of success, Colonel Stilwell had gone back on active service in the Army in 1951, leaving FitzGerald in charge. On Bedell Smith's insistence, OSO and OPC were merged in 1952, despite the immense animosity, and the newly created Far East Division of the CIA was headed by

OSOers—first Lloyd George, then George Aurell. Both were upstaged by their deputy, FitzGerald. Most operatives accepted setbacks against a difficult foe; what they admired was FitzGerald's enthusiasm and stamina. Everyone in "FE" understood that FitzGerald was the true boss. He saw the Far East as a great and fascinating battlefield of the Cold War, and he set out, with flair and assurance, to make it his domain.[28]

Chapter Four

EMPIRE BUILDING

"I don't know if I can keep this up."

THE CIA'S SUCCESS in the Philippines in the early 1950s stands against a backdrop of failure: of agents betrayed; dropped into the waiting arms of the communist security apparat; dragged before people's tribunals; interrogated, tortured, and shot. In Germany, CIA case officers painfully listened on Moscow radio to the show trials of agents they had unwittingly delivered into communist hands. "It was all tragic, all lost," said the Reverend William Sloane Coffin, who was recruited out of Yale in 1949 and handled OPC parachute drops into the "denied areas." "But it was war. You buried your buddies and kept fighting."[1]

Because agency operations were secret and "compartmented" on a need-to-know basis, many of the defeats were not generally known, even within the agency. The only man who really knew the extent of failure was Frank Wisner, and it was the nature of his character that he never let on. Wisner's expression for his world-wide propaganda operation, the "Mighty Wurlitzer," can be seen as a cheeky put-on or as an early symptom of Wisner's mania. In his biography of Richard Helms, author Thomas Powers writes: "Wisner's boast was that he could sit down at his mighty Wurlitzer and play just about any tune he liked, from eerie horror music (Moscow is planning a purge of the Western parties!!!) to light fantasias." Wisner's men were irreverent about the Mighty Wurlitzer; it didn't occur to most of them that Wisner was perfectly serious.[2]

The Wurlitzer's loudspeakers were known as "the Radios"—giant transmitters located in Munich, blasting propaganda across the Iron Curtain. During their long lunches at the Down Town Association right after the war, Wisner and Allen Dulles had talked about using radio broadcasts as a propaganda tool. With Wisner's backing, Dulles and other prominent New Yorkers, like C. D. Jackson of Time-Life, set up the front organization, the National Committee for a Free Europe, in 1949. Radio Free Europe began broadcasting, over a mobile transmitter borrowed from the Army by Carmel Offic, into Czechoslovakia in 1951. Radio Liberation followed in 1953, reaching into the Soviet Union. Both radios quickly expanded operations and were soon penetrating communist airwaves in seven languages. Another front also launched balloons to drop leaflets, over 400 tons—300 million leaflets—into the "denied areas" over the next two decades. The CIA footed the bill, $30 to $35 million a year.

The radios would, over time, play an important role in keeping alive the idea of freedom in the East Bloc. When the Iron Curtain finally disintegrated in 1989, there were numerous testimonials to the power of its message. In the early days, the radios were blunt instruments. RFE repeatedly broadcast the "Document on Terror," supposedly captured from a dead NKVD official, that described how the Russians used terror against civilian populations. There were sections on "general terror" (murders, hangings, etc.), "enlightened terror" (use of agents provocateurs), and "creating the psychosis of white fear." The "captured document" was widely distributed (to the *Congressional Record* and *Reader's Digest*, among other places) as proof of what the West was up against. The charges rang true, but the document itself later turned out to be a forgery, whose origins traced back to the Nazi intelligence service, the SD.[3]

Wisner believed that East and West were engaged in a moral and psychological struggle. He had a "vast program" targeted at intellectuals, who tended to be left-leaning—"the battle for Picasso's mind, if you will," said Tom Braden, a Dartmouth/OSS man enlisted by Wisner to run the International Organizations Division. Western culture was a weapon in the struggle. In 1952 the CIA paid to send the Boston Symphony Orchestra to Europe. The agency infiltrated the Congress for Cultural Freedom and placed an agent on its magazine, *Encounter*.

Hiring intellectuals and subsidizing symphonies to battle communism seem excessive in retrospect, but in 1952 Wisner was hardly exceptional in seeing the world through an ideological prism, and he was a good deal less crude than the fanatics of the Far Right, who searched for Reds under every bed. His views, while more passionately expressed, were quite conventional among members of the national security establishment. "Psychological warfare" sounds like a "five-dollar, five-syllable word," presidential candidate Dwight Eisenhower told an audience in October 1952, but it was really just a commonsense approach to fighting communism. "The state of mind was such that people accepted the notion that a totalitarian system, where kids were taught in the art of agitprop, was very dangerous, very real," said Arthur Cox, who worked on the CIA's psychological warfare staff in the early 1950s. "The feeling was we had to fight fire with fire, to use communist methods to fight communists. We had to be better organized and tougher."

The communists had long made effective use of front organizations—of women, youth, farmers, workers, students, academics. "They had stolen the great words," said Braden. In the minds of many young Europeans, "peace, freedom, and justice" were associated with "communism." In the early 1950s, Braden and others proposed to Wisner that the CIA push back. He agreed, and a new division, International Organizations (IO), was created in the agency to set up a broad network of fronts.

The competition for students and labor was especially avid. The CIA used a variety of student fronts: in 1957, for instance, the agency recruited members of the Yale Russian Chorus who were attending a youth festival in Moscow. One of the Yalemen bravely stood on the steps of Lenin's Mausoleum in Red Square and read from a report on Soviet aggression. The largest unions in France and Italy were controlled by a communist front, the World Federation of Trade Unions. To counter them, the CIA began funneling money through an AFL-CIO official, Jay Lovestone, a former secretary of the American Communist Party who had seen the light. The funds—some $2 million a year—went to pay off dockworkers and union leaders in places like Marseilles, where the communists were trying to stop ships from unloading Marshall Plan aid. It was the source of some concern that the CIA never received a full or accurate accounting of the way its money was spent. But the CIA's European bagman, Irving Brown, was effective: the ships were unloaded.[4]

Wisner's OPC was growing fast: In 1949, OPC had a staff of 302 and a budget of $4.7 million (not counting the "candy" or counterpart funds that OPC could use in Europe). By the beginning of 1952, OPC had 2,812 operatives working in 47 stations around the world and a budget of $82 million, heading for $200 million by the end of the year.[5] There was no way Wisner could keep track of it all, but he tried. Desmond FitzGerald later described Wisner as a "watchmaker in Detroit." No matter how massive his factory grew, Wisner insisted on trying to control even the smallest and most intricate parts.

For brief moments, Wisner would tire of the task. At 8:30 one evening he told Thomas Parrott, who worked in the Soviet Division in the early 1950s, "I don't know if I can keep this up. My wife has me on the social circuit and I work all night and I work all day." Wisner told Arthur Jacobs ("the Ozzard of Wiz") that "he had outgrown Wall Street and the law, but that he wasn't going to stay in Washington, which had a rat race of its own." But the fact was that Wisner had become a prisoner; he was trapped in a Manichaean struggle that, while deadly enough in the world outside, was fiercest in his own mind.

Some subordinates chafed under his unrelenting need to control. "He was an obsessive second guesser," said Parrott. "He had to get in on everything. You'd send him a memo and it would come back with writing all up and down the sides and on the back." Wisner was especially obsessive about trying to control the news. "Orchestrate" was one of his favorite words. When Magsaysay won in the Philippines, Wisner took credit for amassing the large number of Western journalists who publicized the event. He considered his friends Joe and Stewart Alsop to be reliable purveyors of the company line in their columns, and he would not hesitate to call Cyrus Sulzberger, the brother of the publisher of the *New York Times*. "You'd be sitting there, and he'd be on the phone to [*Times* Washington bureau chief] Scotty Reston explaining why some sentence in the paper was entirely wrong. 'I want that to go to Sulzberger!' he'd say. He'd pick up newspapers and edit them from the CIA point of view," said Braden. Wisner kept wire service tickers across the hall from his office. "A story would come over and he'd get on the phone. Get something out! The Mighty Wurlitzer! He was compulsive about answering everything," observed William Colby, one of his chief operatives in Rome. "You could go crazy this way.

A few subordinates did think that Wisner was getting a little too passionate. Cord Meyer, who succeeded Braden as head of International Organizations, received phone calls from Wisner at odd hours suggesting ever grander propaganda campaigns. "You began to wonder," said Meyer. When Wisner handed Sam Halpern, an official in the Far East Division, a long, personally drafted editorial that Wisner wanted placed in an Asian newspaper, Halpern questioned whether Wisner's rhetorical efforts were really going to make a difference to far-off peasants struggling to eat. "How is that going to look in Urdu?" Halpern asked.[6]

FROM THE moment he became director of the CIA in the summer of 1950, Bedell Smith was bound to clash with Wisner. Smith was a ground soldier, skeptical about psychological warfare. In his deadpan way he praised his number two at the CIA, William Harding Jackson, as the most effective psychological warrior of World War II. Jackson, who had coordinated massive leaflet drops over Germany for the OSS, warning the citizenry to surrender, preened at Smith's rare praise. Smith went on to say that one of the heavy sacks of leaflets had failed to open and sunk a German barge in the Rhine. That, Smith dryly noted, had been the most successful "psy op" of World War II.[7]

Smith dispatched Jackson to inspect Joe Bryan's Psychological Warfare Workshop. Jackson reported back that he had found the merry pranksters shooting at balloons in their office with BB guns. This was about what Smith expected. When one OPCer was shipped off to St. Elizabeth's mental hospital for demonstrating a passion for farm animals, Smith demanded, "Can't I get people who don't hire people who bugger cows?" To one of Bryan's psy-warriors, he growled, "If you send me one more project with goddamned balloons I'll throw you out of here."[8]

Smith was especially tough on Wisner. Allen Dulles, who shared Wisner's enthusiasm for covert action, was also lashed by the director, but he was able to joke about it. "The general was in fine form this morning, wasn't he?" Dulles would say to his aides, and guffaw in a way that was meant to lighten the moment. Wisner was more likely to take it personally. Going to a meeting with "Bedell" Smith was like getting whacked around in a squash court, he told Lawrence Houston, the CIA general counsel. Smith believed that Wisner had surrounded himself with dilettantes, and he ordered fifty of them fired. "I don't care whether they were blabbing secrets or not," he declared. "Just give me the names of the people at Georgetown cocktail parties."[9]

To inspect the front lines of the Cold War, Smith picked his wartime comrade General Lucian Truscott as his "special representative" to Germany. Truscott, who had invaded Anzio and driven an armored division into Germany, shared Smith's suspicion of covert operators. "I'm going to go out there and find out what those weirdos are up to," he told Smith as he headed out to Frankfurt in April 1951.[10]

With 1,400 operatives, the CIA's German station was booming. Psywar operators set off stink bombs at communist youth festivals and mailed out glossy invitations to attend nonexistent diplomatic receptions at East Bloc embassies. A delegation from the Yale Class of '50 was being given parachute training outside Munich for paramilitary raids inside the Iron Curtain. ("The whole thing was silly," said Jim Critchfield, a CIA case officer in Germany. "Their wives would come out in their convertibles to watch.") Unmarked planes were being flown over the "denied areas" on dark nights to drop in émigré spies. To forge Russian passports for them, the CIA had gone to an extraordinary effort, building its own paper mill to reproduce the Soviets' distinctively shoddy paper. Nazi spies had been betrayed by their phony passports in World War II because German staples, made out of stainless steel, did not rust like Russian staples.[11]

Some of the operations got out of control. "Our impression was that headquarters would approve anything," said Peter Jessup, a CIA man assigned to General Truscott. Eager to learn about the latest Soviet weaponry, Wisner authorized the payment of $400,000 to a former Polish Air Force officer who said he could buy a Russian MiG on the black market. The Polish pilot holed up instead in an expensive hotel in Munich and spent as much money as possible on champagne and girls. In 1950 a CIA case officer recruited about a hundred members of the far-right League of Young Germans as a "stay-behind" unit in case the Red Army overran Germany. The organization was paid $50,000 a year and given weapons and explosives. It turned out, however, that in the event of a Soviet attack, the plan of the Young Germans—many of whom were not young scouts but old SS officers—was to kill about forty top Social Democratic officials. It is unlikely that the CIA case officer knew about the hit list, but he had an embarrassing time explaining this to the German government when the story leaked to the papers in October 1952.[12]

Truscott was determined to "put a lid" on this kind of activity. After the Young German scandal broke, Allen Dulles came through Germany, and Truscott presided over a kind of star chamber prosecuting the more hopeless operations that Dulles and Wisner had authorized. Dulles tried to deflect Truscott with his hearty laugh, but when he got up to leave Truscott ordered "Sit down!" and started in again. Wisner came through about a year later and got the same treatment from Truscott, who demanded, after a few drinks, "Why can't you write in plain English?"[13]

Wisner was not a pushover for either Truscott or Smith, by any means. He admired Truscott, even if he sometimes felt scorned by him. Wisner managed to keep the old generals from undoing most of his covert operations, and he could laugh at his tormentors from time to time. He understood that Smith needed to vent, whether or not the occasion warranted an outburst. John Bruce Lockhart, the British SIS liaison to the CIA from 1952 to 1954, was summoned from a Washington golf course one day in 1952 and given a vicious tongue-lashing by Smith, for reasons that were not entirely clear to Lockhart. As the British official left Smith's office, Wisner handed him a tumbler of neat whiskey. Wisner was smiling broadly.

WISNER'S REAL problem, Lockhart believed, was that he failed to appreciate the toughness of his adversary. Like many British SIS men, whose tradition of spying and deception ran back at least to Elizabethan times, Lockhart felt that his American cousins were naifs at intelligence work. The OSS had not been properly trained; by the time the OSS really jumped into the war, Hitler was in retreat. Despite his Romanian experience, Wisner himself had not seen the "hard end" of the war, said Lockhart, when the Gestapo was still a formidable foe. Lockhart had served two years as MI-6's chief of operations in Germany after the war. "I realized we were getting nowhere. Unlike World War II, we had no SIGINT [signals intelligence, like the Enigma code breakers], no POWs to debrief, and no aerial reconnaisance," added Lockhart. He gave up trying to infiltrate agents into the Soviet Union. It was pointless. They were quickly killed or turned into double agents.[14]

Some in the CIA at the time recognized the futility of airdrops of émigré agents behind the Iron Curtain. "The only thing they're proving is the law of gravity," said Tom Polgar, one of Truscott's aides. Others realized that the agents could not possibly foment an uprising, but they hoped to plant some long-term agents. They failed; "on the other hand, we learned how not to do it," recalled David Murphy, who supervised the airdrops for the CIA.[15]

By the end of 1952, the last radio signals were dying out from agents parachuted into the Ukraine. The Soviets were hunting down resistance fighters in their caves, where they were hiding so their feet would not leave tracks in the snow. Still, the agency had high hopes for another group of freedom fighters, Wolnosć i Niepodlenosć (Freedom and Independence)—known as WIN after their Polish initials. Emissaries from WIN had approached the CIA in London, claiming an active underground movement of 500 men in Poland, with 20,000 sympathizers, waiting to take up arms against their Soviet oppressors. They needed guns, radio equipment, and financial aid. The CIA provided over $1 million in gold sovereigns. The OPC man assigned to be WIN's control agent told General Truscott that the operation was "too secret to be committed to paper." WIN had supplied him with some photos of their sabotage, blown-up barracks and burnt-out Red Army vehicles.

The whole thing was an elaborate communist ruse. WIN did not exist; the pictures were fakes, and the gold was gone. In the 1920s, in a sting operation called the Trust, the communist secret police had created phony resistance networks to entrap the enemies of the state. WIN was the same trick aimed at the West. On December 27, 1952, the communists jeeringly revealed their scam over Radio Warsaw. They added to the injury with the kind of psywar that Wisner envied. Radio Warsaw reported that the Americans had been fooled into divulging to the double agents of WIN something called the Volcano Plan, a kind of scorched-earth strategy for World War III. In the event of war, the Americans planned to hold Europe for three months—just long enough to destroy the farms and industry of England, France, Germany, and Italy. The Volcano Plan was pure fiction, but it was also clever disinformation.[16]

The collapse of WIN was devastating. Unlike other failures, it was highly public. Wisner had to listen to his work being mocked all over Europe. The embarrassment particularly rankled, coming on the heels of one of the great betrayals of the Cold War, the perfidy of Kim Philby.

THE OUTBREAK of the Korean War had only enhanced Wisner's desire to score a coup in Eastern Europe. Small and isolated, Albania remained the most promising target. Although the early infiltrations into Albania in 1949 and 1950 had not gone well, Wisner pressed on. Out of the DP camps in Germany the CIA created Company 4000, 250 Albanians willing to take the risk of jumping into their homeland. In 1951 and 1952 some sixty of these "pixies" infiltrated by sea or air. They were almost all captured or killed; one team was burned alive in the house where they were hiding. The Albanian security service always seemed to be waiting for them.

The British gradually realized the futility of the operation and withdrew. Until they did, the "joint commander" was Harold "Kim" Philby, the British SIS liaison officer in Washington from 1949 to 1951.

Philby was a Soviet mole, the most effective "deep penetration agent," in the formal jargon of spying, in modern history. He was a member of a ring of Cambridge University students recruited by the Kremlin during the 1930s who had burrowed into the upper ranks of the British civil service. A rising star in the SIS, he was on track to become "C," the chief of British intelligence. He had been a brilliant contributor to Anglo-American deceptions in World War II, feeding disinformation to Hitler. With his mannered charm, Philby got on with Americans who were eager to learn from their more experienced "cousins." He was a natural choice to serve as liaison to the American intelligence community. In that role he had exceptional access: to American war plans against the Soviet Union (code name Trojan, a massive A-bombing campaign against fifty Russian cities), to American troop movements in the Korean War, to every single CIA operation against the Kremlin in the Baltics, Ukraine, and Albania. In the basement of his house on Nebraska Avenue in Northwest Washington was encoding equipment that Philby used to transmit America's secrets back to the Kremlin.

Philby worked closely with Wisner. Like Des FitzGerald and many other CIA men, Wisner was a strong Anglophile with a romantic sense of the British Empire. (Wisner's favorite book as a child was Rudyard Kipling's *Kim,* all about the "Great Game" of spying in the subcontinent.) He wanted to get on with Philby, the son of a famous British agent in the Middle East (who had nicknamed his son after Kipling's hero). At the end of their working sessions Wisner would "produce Bourbon from his office bar, after which we would debate the wisdom of again abandoning our wives for a regular-guy evening on the town," writes Philby in a biting memoir. Wisner was not really a friend, Philby later wrote: "I thought him too pompous? self-opinionated? aggressive? too stout and too bald for his age? a shade too cordial towards the British liaison officer? Perhaps all of those things."

Wisner was not totally lulled by Philby. After working and socializing with the British liaison for more than a year, he had become suspicious. When a series of CIA/SIS operations were compromised in the fall of 1950, Wisner told Bob Joyce, the OPC liaison at State, that there was perhaps a traitor in their midst. In Washington, only a small circle, including a couple of CIA men, Joyce, and Philby, knew the details of the operations. By a process of elimination, Joyce later recorded in an unpublished memoir, Wisner had arrived at Philby as the most likely culprit. It is not clear what Wisner did next, save for continuing to meet with Philby as if nothing was amiss, perhaps to avoid arousing Philby's own suspicions. But it is likely that he told the CIA's counterintelligence chief, William Harvey, to keep an eye on the British liaison.

A small-town midwesterner and former FBI agent, Harvey would become a legendary spook, "America's James Bond," as he was once supposedly billed to John F. Kennedy. In 1951 he was an unregimented gumshoe who had been unable to conform to J. Edgar Hoover's petty rules. Unlike the CIA's Ivy Leaguers, Harvey felt no affinity for wellborn Englishmen, especially after one of them, a diplomat from the British embassy, Guy Burgess, got drunk and humiliated Harvey's wife by drawing an obscene caricature of her, legs spread, at a dinner party at Kim Philby's in January 1951. Harvey began to poke about in Philby's past, to review certain coincidences—the fact that Philby's first wife had been a communist, his association with a Soviet spy in World War II. Slowly, he began to make connections that others had overlooked.

In the winter and spring of 1951, Philby was feeling the pressure. From his exceptional access, he knew that FBI code breakers were closing in on a spy code-named Homer. Homer was Donald Maclean, Philby's Cambridge classmate and fellow traitor who had helped steal the secret of the atomic bomb. Maclean was now a senior official in the British Foreign Office. Philby's house-guest at the time was another Cambridge chum, Guy Burgess—drunk, charming, foul, and dangerous to the plotters. Burgess was dispatched by Philby back to London to tip off Maclean that his arrest was imminent. Maclean fled to Moscow, but to Philby's horror, Burgess ran (or was ordered to run) with him. The escape of the wellborn Soviet moles caused an international sensation. For Harvey, the flight of Burgess was the final clue to the identity of "the Third Man." In early June, Harvey slapped a damning file on Philby down on the desk of Bedell Smith. The U.S. government threw the SIS liaison out of the country, declaring him persona non grata. To a friend in London, Smith wrote, "I hope the bastard gets his. I know a couple of Albanian tribesmen who would like to have half an hour with him."

Wisner was hurt and betrayed by the scandal. Philby's perfidy would stay with him, a lingering wound he was never able to salve. It meant that every single operation he had run against the Soviet Union since the creation of the OPC three years before had to be considered in some way compromised. No network of agents was safe anymore. The Kremlin had to be presumed to know all.

Incredibly, Wisner continued to order agents dropped into Albania. Some thought he was being resolute, if pigheaded. Others observed a certain fatalism in his character. In fact, in late 1952 the secret radio messages coming out of Albania seemed promising. The agents reported progress organizing a resistance movement and asked for more help. Wisner sent more, although his counterintelligence people worried that the "fist"—the individual style and pattern that distinguishes telegraph operators—didn't seem quite right. It wasn't: the agents had been rolled up or turned. A series of highly publicized show trials in Tirana, the capital of Albania, in early 1954 made a mockery of the CIA's operation.[17]

BY THEN, one of Wisner's first and most enthusiastic lieutenants had lost heart. Frank Lindsay represents a beginning and an end—or at least what should have been an end—to the covert attempt to roll back communism. During World War II, Lindsay had been OSS; he had fought bravely and well with the partisans against the Nazis in the mountains of Yugoslavia. He was a believer in the power of guerrilla warfare. In 1947 he and Charles Thayer had written one of the first memos recommending that the United States create a covert guerrilla force to fight the Cold War. The paper had attracted the attention of Frank Wisner, who was Thayer's friend and had met Lindsay in Cairo in 1943. When Wisner formed OPC, he asked Lindsay to come on board to run his European operations.

Lindsay was, in the beginning, very gung ho. "George Kennan was saying that there was a fifty-fifty chance of war within a year," he recalled. "That was the mood. The atmosphere was, my God, we're right back into the trenches." Summoned out to Omaha to brief the Strategic Air Command, Lindsay was confronted by General Curtis LeMay, banging his fist on the table, demanding to know how Lindsay planned to rescue downed fliers inside the Soviet Union. Lindsay helped set up "stay-behind" groups in Western Europe and to launch the Albania operation.

But as time went on Lindsay began to realize that covert action was not working against the communists. Yes, there were occasional successes: Lindsay was particularly proud that he had been able to secretly ship five boatloads of weapons to Marshal Tito in Yugoslavia to help him stand up to Stalin. But there were more failures. Although he did not advertise his discouragement, Lindsay was troubled to send all those émigrés parachuting to death and imprisonment inside the East Bloc. ("I do not know what happened" to these agents, Kim Philby later wrote with a ghoulish wink, "but I can make an informed guess.") "I began to have real doubts about rolling back the Iron Curtain," said Lindsay. "It was peacetime, not wartime. The stuff that had worked against the Germans did not work against the Russians, who seemed impervious. It was time to back off and think this business through."[18]

For half a year in 1951, Lindsay toured the CIA stations of Europe. He realized that the people of Eastern Europe were just too worn out by the last war to rise up and start another one. "Only every two or three generations are people willing to go through a terrible internal war. They had just had a war, and they'd had a bellyful," said Lindsay. He also realized that the communist security services were hardly the crude peasants some of his colleagues made them out to be. In practice, they were more efficient than the German Gestapo.

Lindsay believed it was too easy to blame the Albanian fiasco on Kim Philby. "I don't think the Kremlin wasted Philby on Albania," said Lindsay. "I think the operation went down the drain because we couldn't maintain security in the DP camps and because the communist security apparatus was so damn strong."

On his tour of the field offices, Lindsay began asking some questions that probably should have been asked earlier of the men running the airdrops into the "denied areas." Talking to the leader of a Russian émigré group working with the agency, Lindsay said, "Imagine if you have the best person you can conceive of in Russia, fully documented, in place, the ideal for leadership. Now how long would it take before he could raise the subject with another recruit? The answer was, if they had been working together, about six months. I said, assume he's built the first cell of ten to fifteen people. What is the probability that he will have picked up a secret police penetrator? The answer was 50 percent. So the odds are almost 100 percent that the nascent resistance would be fully penetrated before it expanded to a size that would make any difference."

Lindsay did not expect to turn around Wisner with his qualms. Still, Wisner was willing to listen. He agreed to Lindsay's proposal to set up a "murder board" to shut down the least successful operations.

Lindsay's change of heart and the creation of the murder board might have marked a turn at the CIA away from high-risk covert action to more carefully conceived and executed operations. And in fact, about a third of all OPC-inspired operations were weeded out by the murder board in 1952.[19] But then, after a brief lull, more— and more ambitious—operations against a greater variety of targets were started. Instead of pulling back and consolidating, the CIA became more bold—and reckless. The agency entered a new era in 1953, one that took it in a direction that would, in time, make the early days of OPC seem innocent and tame by comparison.

THERE ARE a number of reasons for this escalation, but one of the most important is the character of Allen Dulles. After the Republicans won the White House in 1952, the CIA went through a changing of the guard. Bedell Smith was sent over to State by his wartime boss, Dwight D. Eisenhower, to be deputy to the new secretary of state, John Foster Dulles. Dulles's brother, Allen, became head of the CIA.

On a Saturday morning in the late autumn of 1952, a weary and somewhat disillusioned Lindsay went to see Dulles in his office. Lindsay explained his findings that rollback had been a flop and offered cautious recommendations for containing the communist threat. This was not what Allen Dulles wanted to hear. He was counting on becoming the next Director of Central Intelligence in a Republican administration pledged to rolling back communism. "Frank," said Dulles, "you can't say that." Lindsay recalled, "I thought he would have a heart attack."[20]

Still, Allen Dulles was cagey. Republican rhetoric notwithstanding, he would as a practical matter steer away from operations aimed directly at liberating the "slave states" of Eastern Europe. Instead, he would look to a new battleground, the developing world, where communism was on the march, yet not quite so formidable as it was closer to home.

Dulles was a deceptive figure.[21] With his white brush mustache, pipe and tweeds, and hearty ho-ho-ho laugh, he seemed professorial, especially when he was wearing carpet slippers for his gout. His brother, Foster Dulles, was regarded as a grim and pompous moralist. Allen Dulles, by contrast, had a twinkle in his eye (a roving eye, to be sure) and a jolly, avuncular manner. But he was actually a hard man. Briefed about the agents sent to their doom in the East Bloc, Dulles commented, "Well, at least we're getting good experience for the next war."[22] "He was a hale fellow, but his laugh was humorless," said Louis Auchincloss, the novelist of manners who as a young lawyer worked for Dulles at Sullivan and Cromwell, his Wall Street firm. "I thought Foster was maladroit, but, beneath it all, warm. Allen was shrewd—but cold as ice."

Dulles does not seem to have been in the least troubled by the moral ambiguities of intelligence work. He was "a man capable of an amiable encounter with the enemy and the Devil; he learned to deal comfortably in perfectly bad faith, without ever violating a personal sense of moral rectitude and decency," writes his biographer Peter Grose. Dulles took offense at the suggestion that spying was somehow disreputable. John Bross, a senior CIA official, recalled a rare show of Dulles's anger when a German visitor suggested it was difficult to attract good men to go into the intelligence service "for intelligence is so *schmutzig*—filthy."[23]

Allen Dulles cited the Bible for its use of spies (by Joshua into Jericho). When he built a new building for the CIA in 1961, he chose to have engraved on the wall of the lobby the quotation from the New Testament "And ye shall know the truth, and the truth shall make you free." According to the official CIA history of the Dulles years, a few agency officials suggested that some might find this inscription offensive, because "they might feel it was in bad taste to cloak the covert operations of the agency behind the words of Jesus. Dulles earnestly protested that intelligence was the search for the truth. If it fought the Devil with his own weapons, it did so for a good cause."[24]

In spite of, or because of, his dour Presbyterian upbringing in upstate New York, Dulles was a bon vivant. After a weekend aboard the 190-foot yacht of Greek shipping magnate Stavros Niarchos, Dulles confided to Clare Boothe Luce, the diplomat and wife of Time/Life's Henry Luce, "You know, all my life, I've wanted a yacht like this. And I know I'll never have one." He was a well-known ladies' man whose long-suffering wife, Clover, was said to console herself by visiting Cartier every time Dulles began a new affair.

Dulles was a romantic about spying. Within the agency he became known as the "Great White Case Officer" because he liked to run "vest pocket" operations of his own. He was drawn to flamboyant agents who traveled about the Middle East bribing local officials and fomenting plots.[25]

Dulles was also a snob. It was well known in the CIA that he cared, perhaps too much, about social pedigree. He would ask prospective case officers not only where they went to college, but also what clubs they belonged to as undergraduates. (He was less particular about foreign agents, who were often necessarily low-lifes. Of General Reinhard Gehlen, a German Army officer recruited by the CIA for his anticommunist intelligence network, Dulles said, "One needn't ask him to one's club.")[26]

As his top advisers, Dulles wanted men who were bold and adventurous and came from the right background. Tracy Barnes fit that description, and Dulles reached out to him as soon as he became director in February 1953.

Chapter Five

THE WAR LOVER

"I think he did the right thing, don't you?"

CHARLES TRACY BARNES HAD proved his bravery, with panache, in World War II. Many young men in 1941 wanted to go to war, to defend their country or test themselves in some way, but Barnes wanted to go to war more than most. "Tracy invited danger. He couldn't wait for it," said his widow, Janet Barnes Lawrence. Before the war Barnes had worked on Wall Street for Carter Ledyard, the same blue-stocking law firm as Frank Wisner. "It gave him hives. It drove him crazy. He was bored by trusts and estates," she said. "He would tie a leash to his Labrador retriever and roller-skate down the East River Drive." The Monday morning after Pearl Harbor Barnes enlisted "without waiting for breakfast," said Janet. Commissions were easily arranged for well-connected thirty-year-old lawyers, but Barnes refused to take one. "He didn't want help, he wanted to be a man in the ranks," said his cousin and college roommate, Marshall Dodge. He ended up as a private at an air intelligence school in Harrisburg, Pennsylvania.[1] Barnes did not take well to military discipline. He later told a friend that he "hated saluting and spit and polish." Shivering on the parade ground in Harrisburg one morning in the winter of 1942, he was accosted by a second lieutenant who ordered him to stand up straight. Tracy, who was about six one, looked down. "I won't," he said.[2]

Barnes was rescued from Harrisburg by Tommy Hitchcock, a polo-playing World War I hero who was serving as air attaché in the London Embassy. "Hitchcock recognized Tracy's name in the society pages and got him a commission," said Marshall Dodge. By the winter of 1942, Barnes was overseas, serving as Hitchcock's aide in London.[3]

His scruples against accepting a commission worn down by the second lieutenants of Harrisburg, Barnes fell back a step: he would not accept a promotion until he was given active duty. Barnes began writing Janet long and melodramatic letters, telling her how much he loved her and the children, but that he needed to get into the fight and might not ever return.

"He'd get morose and have a few drinks and write that goddamn stuff," said Benno Schmidt, Barnes's roommate in London. "It wasn't really like him." Tempting fate was more in character. Their apartment, at 1 Gore Street, "seemed to be on the main bombing run for the Germans," said Schmidt. "German bombers always dropped flares to illuminate their targets. So when a flare dropped close to you, you were supposed to take cover." Predictably, Barnes went to look out the window. "I said, 'Tracy, get away!' The first bomb blew him across the room. We got dressed and went and pulled people out of the wreckage. The buildings on either side were destroyed. It was pure luck that ours was still standing," said Schmidt. The two men watched in horror as an adjoining wall collapsed, crushing the rescue workers.

Barnes continued to complain bitterly about his desk-bound assignment. "Goddamn it, I didn't join the Army to sit in the U.S. embassy. I want in on the action," he told Schmidt. "If I can't do it through channels I'm going to join the British merchant marine and go on the Murmansk run." At the time the Luftwaffe and German U-boats were sinking half the convoys to Russia. Schmidt told Barnes, "If your purpose is to get killed so you'll be a hero, we'll find a better hero role for you."[4]

He found the role in the OSS. He was hired by John Bross, the senior prefect in Barnes's class at Groton. "Tracy came to me . . . looking for something active," Bross later wrote in a private memoir. "If we couldn't give him some kind of combat service, he was going to get a job as a waist gunner in the air force." Bomber crews over Germany at the time had about the same life expectancy as sailors on the Murmansk run. "I rather got the impression that he wanted specifically to look death in the eye," wrote Bross. Barnes's classmate got him assigned to the Jedburgh program, training commandos to drop behind German lines and link up with the French resistance.[5]

At Jedburgh training at Milton Hall in Peterborough, Barnes

was instructed by British commandos in the black arts: how to blow up a bridge, code a message, operate a radio, forge documents, silently strangle someone from behind.[6] The regimen did not remove him or the other Jedburghs from an active social life. The men from that era are slightly sheepish when they talk about how much fun they had during the London blitz. The women are more forthright: "We had an absolutely wonderful time," said Evangeline Bruce, whose husband, David, was the head of OSS operations in London. "The parties were nonstop."[7]

Tracy parachuted into France on August 5, 1944. His Silver Star citation reads, through the bureaucratese, like the treatment for a movie:

> Captain Barnes (then First Lieutenant) was parachuted into the Brittany Peninsula, as an intelligence officer, to assist in establishing a communications system between the Third United States Army and resistance forces and to direct resistance activities. The liquidation of a detachment of several hundred of the enemy was largely attributable to his courage and initiative, when, after unsuccessful attempts to effect a surrender, he and a French officer, armed only with carbines, opened fire, constantly changing firing position to convey the impression of a large force. They bluffed the enemy into evacuating the city, and upon the arrival of armored forces, Captain Barnes rode the first tank to direct the pursuit.[8]

Barnes himself told the story in later years as a "comic turn," said his former son-in-law, novelist John Casey. Barnes would laugh about how he and the French officer ran around like Indians circling the wagon train, "shooting guns, the Germans throwing up their hands. Tracy would say, 'We didn't know what we were doing.' " Barnes had joined up with a group of maquis, fighters in the French underground. He would imitate being greeted by these tough French peasants, who kissed Barnes on both cheeks, threw their arms around him, and offered him wine. Later, when he had reached down for his knife and wallet, they were gone.[9]

Barnes delighted in playing the liberator. His cousin Marshall Dodge saw him riding into Paris in September 1944 on the back of a tank, holding a big bottle of champagne and catching bouquets from the girls. The "nonstop" party in London had moved south. Barnes hooked up with an old friend, Paul Nitze, at the Ritz, which had been requisitioned as a barracks by Barnes's cousin John Hay Whitney. "Tracy's pockets were full of cash," said Nitze. "He invited us to a party at Le Nite Club, which had prospered under German occupation. They were joyous days. That's a horrible way of putting it, but they were."[10]

Barnes was in a sober mood when he returned to London. He stopped a Groton schoolmate, Douglas Auchincloss, on the street near Grosvenor Square and suggested a drink. There was something on his mind that was "really bothering" him, he said. As Barnes recounted the story, he had captured three or four German officers while he was operating with the resistance. The prisoners were badly wounded. Barnes had had to move on, but he knew that the vengeful maquis would torture the Germans, whom they blamed for atrocities in the local village. Barnes had considered what to do. He had taken out his sidearm and finished off the Germans. "It bothered the hell out of him," Auchincloss recalled. This was not the sort of moral dilemma that Groton had prepared him for, but what was he to do? "I think he did the right thing, don't you?" Auchincloss said, recalling the incident forty years later. "But it weighed on him."

Barnes apparently told no one else at the time. There is no official record of this incident in the OSS archives. But he did, after the war, tell his wife. "Tracy told me he wasn't allowed to take prisoners," she recalled. "One of them begged him, 'I'm married. I have a wife and three children. I've never done you any harm.' Tracy was really eaten up by this. But no one was as cruel as the maquis."[11]

Barnes was dropped a second time into France in September 1944. The jump was a botch. He landed inside American lines by mistake and was nearly shot by his own troops. He couldn't wait to jump again. On leave in London, he told an OSS colleague, Tom Braden, that he had gotten clearance to practice parachuting "out of four different airplanes." Braden was "startled. I told him that I didn't like jumping out of airplanes. I wouldn't do it for fun. But Tracy loved the thrill. I'm not sure danger ever occurred to him." Braden was struck by Barnes's physical presence. "He was tall and blond, with his hair combed straight back into a pompadour. He was beautiful. Not just handsome, but beautiful."[12]

Barnes's dashing figure and great magnetism caught the attention of another, more senior OSS official that autumn. Operating out of Bern, Switzerland, Allen Dulles was the OSS's best-placed spymaster. He had forged a back channel to German military intelligence, the Abwehr, which was hedging its bets, just in case the United States decided to join Germany in the fight against Russia. Dulles needed a man for a job that would require not only daring, but also looks and charm and the willingness to use them. On December 3, 1944, Dulles wrote David Bruce, his OSS superior in London: "I have met Tracy Barnes here today and am anxious to get him to Switzerland as soon as possible. . . . We can find useful work for him."[13]

Barnes arrived in Bern within a few days. The medieval city was a hothouse of spies who all seemed to know one another. "We all ate at the Bellevue Hotel," recalled one of Dulles's staffers. "At one table would be all the Polish agents, at another would be the Nazi agents, another would have all the British, another all the Americans. There was an informal agreement to respect each other's privacy." The "useful work" Dulles had in mind for Barnes was securing the diaries of Galeazzo Ciano, Mussolini's son-in-law and foreign minister until he was hanged for treason in 1944. His wife, Edda, had escaped to Switzerland with his diaries, which were said to be full of valuable information about the Axis powers (as well as titillating gossip about Hitler and Eva Braun).[14]

Barnes was daunted by his task. On December 15 he cabled London headquarters, "Edda is a psychopathic case under influence Swiss psychoanalyst whose motives and connections dubious. She promises diaries as good-will gesture one day and the next asks large monetary payment to protect interest children and also some letter of acknowledgment. Naturally matter requires most discreet handling from every view point."[15]

Barnes's charm eventually worked. By early January, Mrs. Ciano had agreed to allow him to photograph the five volumes of her late husband's diaries. He was to sneak into her room at the Swiss mental hospital where she was staying. Barnes's first foray into espionage was very nearly a disaster. His photographic equipment blew all the fuses in the sanatorium, throwing the place into darkness and the patients into confusion. Barnes got out in time, and later smuggled Mrs. Ciano and her diaries out to a neutral safe house, where the job was completed.[16]

Barnes was a figure of fascination, and some bemusement, to the rest of Dulles's staff. "We called him Golden Boy," said Cordelia Dodson Hood, an operative on Dulles's staff. "He had those Yale good looks and he was athletic and charming. He was teased about being Dulles's boy, but he was easy about it. There was no chip on his shoulder. He saw Dulles for what he was, but he liked him."

Her only reservation about Barnes was that he was "too trusting, from a C-I [counterintelligence] point of view. In C-I, you mistrust everyone. Tracy had everything. He had no reason to mistrust the human race."[17]

Barnes was bored by courting neurotic widows. "If there was any action around, he was going to get in on it. He had no use for bureaucracy or diplomacy or sitting on his tail," said David Crockett, who served with Dulles in Bern. He found action, as well as romance, with Adele Traxler, the wife of a Swiss industrialist and a friend of Allen Dulles's mistress, Valli Toscanini (the daughter of the conductor). Born Countess Camarana, Adele Traxler was blond and slender, with greenish blue eyes. Her husband had volunteered to escort Barnes over the Alps to deliver a radio to some partisans in Italy. "At the last moment, my father got a throat infection," recalled her son, Ambassador Vieri Traxler. "So my mother volunteered." They went through the Bernina Pass in March 1945, a difficult trek in late winter. Barnes, who despite his athleticism was susceptible to respiratory infections, had difficulty breathing at the high altitudes. Once, he lost his footing and, clawing at the ice with his pick, nearly slid into a crevasse. The radio was delivered to the partisans, and Barnes and Mrs. Traxler went on to Milan, where the body of Mussolini had been strung up in a public square. "He just wanted to see the show," said David Crockett. Years later Barnes told a friend that his time in Italy, with the partisans and Mrs. Traxler, had been the best of his life.[18]

There was one last job to be done by Dulles's OSS team in the spring of 1945: to accept the surrender of German forces in Italy. This was a matter of some urgency: the Russians were stalling, seeking to prolong the war while the Red Army gobbled up larger chunks of Eastern Europe. Dulles was eager to accept the surrender from the German commander, SS General Karl Wolff. Barnes volunteered to fly over the Alps and parachute on top of the German High Command at Bolzano. It was a "brilliant, if dangerous idea," Dulles later wrote in his memoirs, *The Secret Surrender*. "Barnes would parachute in, the surrender terms in his pocket. He would somehow make his way on foot to the German High Command and deliver the papers." "It was a crazy idea," said William Hood, one of Dulles's staffers, "but Tracy was ready to go. He was the least qualified and the most eager. He didn't speak any German or Italian and once he landed, he'd have to walk through three or four kilometers of perimeter defense." Somewhat gingerly, Dulles acknowleged in his book that "there is no use suggesting all the things that could have happened to Barnes before he reached General Vietinghoff [one of the German commanders]." Fortunately, the weather turned too bad to fly. The Germans surrendered without Barnes. In Bern, the spies of all nations formed a conga line and danced through the streets, as the Swiss looked on in disapproval.[19]

Tracy stopped off in Paris on the way home. He had no idea what he would do when he got back. "He talked about staying in intelligence, although he was rather nebulous about it. Also, politics," said Henry Hyde, an OSSer with aristocratic French roots who had befriended Barnes. "Tracy was anything but stuffy. He was very European, like a British lord. He bored easily, and he wanted adventure." He wasn't sure how he was going to find it back in the United States.[20]

TRACY BARNES's mother, Katharine, was a New York grande dame who favored her elder boy, Courtlandt Jr. She wanted "Courty" to be a classical musician—a higher calling in her mind than the law or banking. To Tracy, her younger son, she taught games. "Courty was his mother's great love. He looked like his mother. He was the favorite. Tracy was on his own," recalled Tracy's widow, Janet Barnes Lawrence. "It quite hurt his feelings, but he never said anything about it."[21]

Tracy's mother loved playing sports, even if she did not value athleticism as a worthy calling. Ironically, Katharine Barnes was "a most unmusical woman," said Janet. She was, however, "a good athlete." There is a photograph in the family albums of Tracy playing mixed doubles with his mother. He is four years old.

Barnes's mother also taught him how to gamble at cards and games. She had been taught, in a sense, by professionals; her father had been a plunger who lost his bank, the Knickerbocker Trust Company, in the Panic of 1907. He had committed suicide ("considered very bad form at that time," wrote Courty Barnes). Barnes relished risk from an early age and played harder with a wager on the outcome.

Yet there was always money to cover his bets. Barnes himself never felt any financial insecurity: his family was protected by its wealthy connections. On the day of the Great Crash in 1929, when

Barnes was a Yale freshman, a messenger came to his father's Wall Street office with a check from his cousin Harry Payne Whitney for $1 million. The message said, "Mr. Whitney thought it might be useful." Barnes sent it back, "but it was a wonderful gesture on Cousin Harry's part," wrote Courty Barnes Jr. In later years Tracy Barnes would be heedless about money, much to the exasperation of the administrative staff at the CIA.[22]

Barnes had been a rebellious child. To discipline him, his parents packed him off to Groton at the age of twelve, to be shaped by the "muscular Christianity" of Endicott Peabody. Barnes constantly tested Peabody's patience. He sent himself a telegram on dance weekend announcing "Boom Boom cannot come" just to have the pleasure of hearing Peabody ask, "Who is Boom Boom?" In a metaphor almost too pat to be true, he was disciplined one winter for disobeying the Rector's warnings and venturing onto thin ice. "We must work together," Peabody wrote Tracy's father after the incident, "to impress on Tracy the necessity of 'playing the game' fairly." Football saved Barnes himself from expulsion when Peabody caught him reading a dirty book. The Rector did not want to lose his star quarterback before the St. Mark's game.[23]

To his classmates Barnes embodied that schoolboy virtue, effortless grace. Appearing relaxed at all times is hard work. "He had a pretty good idea he was attractive," said a schoolmate, Charles Devens. "Otherwise, he wouldn't have been so attractive." He was so competitive that before football games he vomited. Playing against larger boys as quarterback in a losing effort against St. Mark's his fifth form year, he could not hold back his tears in the huddle. His teammates thought he was in physical pain from the pounding he was taking. Actually, he was just mad about losing.*

After Groton, Yale was a lark for Barnes. Janet Barnes Lawrence, whom Barnes began courting while he was still an undergraduate, remembered "whizzing down the Merritt Parkway in Tracy's Packard. He loved the risk, speeding. We'd go to Harlem and dance." (Tracy, she noted, "was only good at the steps he invented.") "Why is it that those drunken college moments stand out so vividly in our minds?" Marshall Dodge wrote to his clubmates in Tracy's senior society, Scroll and Key, shortly after Tracy died.

---

* One of his afflictors was Desmond FitzGerald, a six-foot, 180-pound tackle for St. Mark's.

A friend of Tracy Barnes remembered watching him emerge from a fraternity on a football weekend with Janet, a Garbo-esque beauty, on his arm, looking glamorous, genial, utterly assured, "like something out of F. Scott Fitzgerald." Though he was too well mannered to show it, Barnes knew perfectly well where he stood in the world. Society in prewar America had a national following. The popular authors of the day, Fitzgerald, Marquand, and O'Hara, wrote obsessively about the upper class (the theme was usually the desire to belong). This was an era when a debutante appeared on the cover of *Life* and all the New York papers covered Tap Day at Yale. Such attention could make a man careless or cruel. In *The Great Gatsby,* Fitzgerald describes Tom Buchanan, who "had been one of the most powerful ends that ever played football at New Haven—a national figure in a way, one of those men who reach such acute limited excellence at twenty-one that everything after savors of anti-climax."

Barnes was never a user like Tom Buchanan, though he could be careless. He was earnest about the duty to serve. Barnes was the sort to step in and rescue a freshman from a senior class bully (as he did on at least one occasion). In an essay delivered to his brothers in Scroll and Key during his last year at Yale, Barnes wrote, "It sounds as if my day was pretty full of doing nice things for other people, but don't think I mind. I love it; it makes me realize that I am attaining the ambition of my boyhood, devoting my life to service."[24]

WHEN BARNES returned from the war in the summer of 1945, he was thirty-four years old, but not ready for civilian life. "He missed the war," said his wife, Janet. He talked about becoming a test pilot or going off to China with an OSS group that was being organized to fight with the Chinese Nationalists. "We've all got to stick together," he tried to explain to Janet. "You better stick to home," she replied.

Barnes practiced law for a time, without much enthusiasm. As a Wall Street lawyer at Carter Ledyard in the 1930s, he had come to know Frank Wisner. Wisner began working on Barnes to rejoin his old OSS mates in Washington. The outbreak of the Korean War in June 1950 finally did the trick.[25]

Barnes's first job at the CIA was as the number-two man to the director of the Psychological Strategy Board, Gordon Gray, another friend and Carter Ledyard partner. The PSB was very much a creature of its time. This was the era of NSC 68, the Cold War blueprint drafted by Paul Nitze that called for a national crusade against global communism. The PSB was supposed to draft a massive psywar strategy. The PSB "grew to be a monster, out of control," said Townsend Hoopes, an aide to the secretary of defense. "They even had a psywar plan for France."[26]

The PSB itself bored Barnes. It was mostly a talk shop, without any operational responsibility. He was relieved, in October 1952, when Dulles and Wisner made him head of the CIA's newly created "PP" staff—psychological and paramilitary warfare. Barnes was now free to propose actual operations. He welcomed getting back in on the action. One day when Barnes was acting DD/P while Wisner was abroad, he told Tom Braden, the chief of the International Organizations Division, "If war breaks out, you'll be a brigadier general. Sorry I can't give you more than that." Braden asked if he was serious. "Sure," replied Barnes, "if war comes, we'll all be generals."[27]

Barnes, at that stage of his career, was a very popular figure among some of the top brass in the agency. "He got on well with Wisner," said Braden. "He was gung ho, and he never questioned anything." Barnes was also "a hero to the young guys. He looked the part of the dashing parachutist." He was "personable, engaging, and a strong believer in ops," said Arthur Cox, who worked for him on the "PP" staff. "He had the trust of Allen Dulles as much as anyone; he was very smooth and graceful and he could encourage people, build their egos. He was a very elegant dresser, even on weekends in the office, but he never gave the impression of being a snob."

The old OSOers, with their emphasis on careful espionage and wariness of noisy covert action, were less enthusiastic. "Tracy was a wonderful guy, but his thinking was fuzzy and naive," said Carleton Swift. "When Tracy said, 'I've got an op, let's do it,' my heart went in my mouth. On the PP staff, he encouraged the wildest ideas he could think of." Bedell Smith had driven off most of the jokers on the psywar staff, including its head, Joe Bryan, but some of the lampoon spirit lived on. The old psywar plan to drive Russian women wild by dropping huge American condoms in their midst had become no more than an office joke. But plans cooked up by Barnes's staff were only slightly less zany. Among them was a plan to fill balloon baskets with safety razors and other superior Western toiletries and let them drift downwind into communist zones where the standard of living was less comfortable.[28]

Along with the college boys on Barnes's staff were some spookier figures. One of them was E. Howard Hunt, better known in later years as one of the Watergate burglars. Hunt "thought black"—he looked for devious solutions, even if more straightforward ones would do. In 1953, Hunt was working with the Southeast Europe Division, looking for turncoats who (in addition to Philby) might have betrayed the Albania operation. He strongly suspected one of Wisner's émigré warriors, a former bodyguard for Albania's deposed King Zog. Hunt later claimed that he asked Barnes for advice on how to "dispose" of this double agent, and Barnes sent him to see a Colonel Boris Pash, who was on the PP staff.

Pash, a White Russian émigré, had run the Alsos Mission for Army intelligence at the end of World War II to help capture and find German scientists knowledgeable about chemical and nuclear warfare. After he joined OPC in 1949, Colonel Pash was put in charge of a unit called PB-7, set up to handle "wet affairs"—kidnappings and assassinations. There is no record that Pash ever carried out any, and he denied ever having done so before congressional investigators in 1975. But in 1953, encouraged by Barnes, Hunt sought out Pash as a solution to the problem of the traitorous Albanian émigré. Hunt later testified that Pash seemed slightly surprised by Hunt's approach and showed no interest in helping him. According to Hunt, Pash's real purpose seemed to be sitting in his office "drawing his salary and drinking coffee."[29]

If Pash showed restraint, it was self-imposed. Barnes, his colleagues said, was willing to try just about anything. There was little to hold the CIA back. Congress provided almost no operational oversight, while handing out what amounted to a blank check of unrestricted funds. The press was docile, caught up in the thinking that to quibble would be unpatriotic. During the early days of the Cold War, most reporters believed they were teammates, not the adversaries, of the officials they covered, at least in the national security arena. Eisenhower's White House wanted to cut back on defense expenditures, swollen by the Korean War, and the president viewed the CIA as a tool to wage a cold war on the cheap. At the State Department, John Foster Dulles did not trust his own bureaucracy. It was easier to pick up the phone and call his brother, Allen, over at the CIA if he wanted anything done.

Initiative—daring—was a quality prized during the Dulles era at the CIA. Bedell Smith had curbed the appetites and excesses of Frank Wisner's OPC, but under Dulles boldness came back as a virtue to be prized. Barnes's dash and physical courage were one way of showing boldness. Intellectual self-confidence was another. The most confident intellectual in Washington, most insiders would agree, was Tracy Barnes's old schoolmate, Richard M. Bissell.

Chapter Six

A MIND OF HIS OWN

"You do it to fight Providence."

RICHARD BISSELL'S COLLEAGUES would call him the "smartest man in Washington" and mean it. He was unknown to the public and famous to the inner circle of diplomats and foreign policy makers for his work organizing the Marshall Plan to help rescue postwar Europe. In 1953 he was working at the Ford Foundation, then very much in the vanguard of Cold War thinking. There, Bissell met often with CIA officials looking for new ideas. Almost any idea was worth considering: at one meeting Allen Dulles suggested that the Ford Foundation finance a "beachhead university" in Germany to further the battle for men's minds.

In the summer of 1953, Bissell was approached by the CIA to do a study of ways to roll back the Iron Curtain without using force. Setting up shop in one of the old "tempos" where the CIA was headquartered down on the Mall, Bissell spent hours listening to Frank Wisner hold forth on the power of psychological warfare.

Bissell knew Wisner from the Georgetown social scene. He had found him "very pleasant and genial," though a bit "suspicious." Wisner had visited Bissell in an official capacity in 1949, when Bissell was running the Marshall Plan in Washington and Wisner was running OPC. "In carefully chosen language," Bissell recalled, he learned from Wisner that President Truman had given the OPC head access to the Marshall Plan counterpart funds. "I was not to ask any further questions," Bissell said, although he soon figured out the money was making its way into the pockets of European politicians and labor leaders. Wisner did not discourage Bissell's curiosity about OPC. "You should think about joining us," he told Bissell.

Wisner continued to try to recruit Bissell as they debated the effectiveness of psychological warfare in the summer of 1953. "Frank was fascinated by the Russians' ability to put a mob on the street anywhere they chose, anytime they chose. He wanted us to be able to do the same." Bissell was doubtful that the power of ideas, however strong, could be effective against tank divisions. Yet covert action intrigued him. While he was reviewing the CIA's planning documents, he came across a particularly outlandish scheme to liberate Albania with a force of CIA-backed émigrés based in Italy. The plan was preposterous; it would have been impossible to support half-a-world away from the United States, and it was much too large to stay covert. "It would have put the Bay of Pigs in the shade," Bissell remarked years later. Still, the sheer audacity of the concept piqued his interest. He liked the idea of a *coup de main*, and his active mind was engaged by the complexity of planning such an operation.

Bissell began to think more seriously about joining the agency. He liked Wisner and Des FitzGerald, whom he had gotten to know at dinner parties in Georgetown. He also felt comfortable with Tracy Barnes, who had been a class behind him at Groton and Yale. What Bissell especially liked about these men, he said, was that they were "doers."[1]

DICK BISSELL and Tracy Barnes went to school together for nine years. Yet during that time they hardly spoke to each other. Trying to explain this distance, given their close friendship in later years, Bissell struggled a little. He noted that the two men had been "a year apart" and observed that they had "different temperaments." But the larger reason, he acknowledged, was that Barnes was at the top of the strict social hierarchy while he, in the beginning at least, was at the bottom. "I didn't see anything of Tracy at school," said Bissell. "He was an easy going athlete, a success. I was shy and non-athletic." Bissell "couldn't step on a playing field without breaking his leg," said Barnes's classmate John Bross. While painfully insecure, he was at the same time intellectually domineering, though no one in those early years would listen to him. Instead, he was ostracized.[2]

Bissell's only friend when he arrived at Groton in the fall of 1922 was Joseph Alsop, whose family was close to Bissell's in Hartford, Connecticut. He lost that friend when Alsop accused him of putting a stink bomb in his cubicle one night. Alsop's fate for ratting, for breaking the schoolboy code, was to be silenced, cut off by his schoolmates. "A Groton winter term is grim under the best of circumstances," writes Alsop in his memoirs. "A Groton winter term without human company was grim beyond imagining." Alsop seriously contemplated suicide. Bissell just "laid low" and was "desperately homesick."[3]

In his house in Hartford hung a portrait of his mother, Marie, holding Bissell as a young boy. Mrs. Bissell is very beautiful, with sad, luminous eyes; her child is plain. Until he was eight years old, Bissell had crossed eyes. The painter uncrossed his eyes for the portrait, but a difficult operation was required to correct his vision. "I was an outcast, shy and timid, a perfect foil for teasing," recalled Bissell. "My mother was my refuge from the cruel world." As a teenager, mother and son were companions, shopping and traveling, reading in the evening together (" 'Take up the white man's burden.' I still read it," said Bissell). Bissell was a volatile little boy, imperious and prone to tantrums. Once on an Atlantic crossing with his parents, he flung his teddy bear off the fantail into the wake of the ocean liner. "Get it," he commanded his nurse. But his mother taught him self-control. All his life Bissell had impeccable manners, even when he was seething inside.

Marie Bissell herself was a rebel, within the confines of Hartford society. She shocked her peers by driving a yellow roadster and producing a play by Gertrude Stein. The social event of 1936 was her Paper Ball, for which she decorated the Great Court of the Athenaeum entirely with papier-mâché. "It was a wild party," recalled Beth Kent, a friend of the Bissells. "For someone who was married to the head of the Hartford Fire Insurance Company, it was also a risky business, all that paper."

During the Groton winters Bissell dreamed of summer, when he could join the family pilgrimage to Isleboro, Maine. As a little boy taking the train north, he slept in the same bunk as his mother; he would keep her up all night asking questions. At Isleboro, Marie Bissell taught her son how to sail. Sailing in Maine is to sailing as Groton is to normal schooling. In Penobscot Bay, young Bissell had to contend with rocks, thick fog, strong winds, and tremendous tides, but in a glorious setting that made the test seem heroic.

Bissell and his mother sailed in a seventeen-foot Herschoff dinghy with a keel. His mother taught him that a sturdy boat with a lead keel, even a small boat, could heel way over in the wind, take green water into the cockpit over the lee rail, and still not capsize. She taught her son to take risks—calculated perhaps, but still close to the edge.[4]

As a form of self-protection, perhaps, Bissell learned to carry within him a private sense of grandeur. His life before Groton's privations had been grand indeed. Bissell's father was "an elegant man who liked to live well," recalled Bissell. "On the SS *France*, when we were sailing to Europe, my father saw a bucket of caviar in the dining saloon. He exclaimed, 'We will have that and we will have it every night!' " Bissell's parents took him to Europe a half dozen times before he went to college, including a winter in Rome and spring in a villa (with a dozen servants) outside Florence.[5]

At Groton, Bissell's hobby, which he pursued almost obsessively, was to memorize train timetables between distant cities. The bullying boys mocked him for his eccentric interest in railroading: only little boys played with trains. What they could not appreciate was that Bissell was not just playing with trains in his mind, he was building entire railroads. In the library he studied train lines and topography with a critical eye. He would imagine that he was the president of the railroad (not a great leap: his mother's father was president of the Delaware, Lackawanna and Western Railroad and took Bissell for trips in his private railway car, the Anthracite) and decide how he would do things differently. He would tunnel through that mountain, not go around it. He would build vast linkages, empires of rail. They would be better designed, more efficient, faster—superior. The planning and design of transportation networks helped ward off the blues on winter afternoons at Groton. And it would come in handy in a few years, when Bissell was in charge of all Allied shipping during World War II.[6]

Among his schoolmates, Bissell, like his fellow outcasts Joe Alsop and Louis Auchincloss, found a way to grudging respectability by winning good grades. When Alsop's mother worried that her son was too bookish, Peabody reassured her, "That's all right, Corinne, we'll soon knock all that out of him." Grades weren't as important as athletics or manly grace at Groton, but they counted for something. Bissell showed off his intellectual prowess (and his taste for the covert) by outdebating Joe Alsop in a mock trial of Napoleon for committing war crimes. Bissell was the prosecutor; Alsop defended Napoleon. According to the 1928 yearbook, Napoleon was convicted by the schoolboy jury of "having done more harm than good." It was a victory for morality and virtue, except that Bissell, the yearbook recorded, "stole the defense's papers and references before trial, made accurate copies, and returned only part of the stolen property."[7]

It is peculiar, perhaps, that a significant number of Grotonians went on to become senior officials in the CIA. Peabody, after all, was straightforward, utterly lacking in guile. Groton's masters were puzzled and troubled when they learned of some of the tricks their old boys had been up to. "Peabody would have been shocked by the CIA," said Paul Wright, who arrived as a teacher at Groton in Tracy Barnes's last year, 1928, and taught several generations, including Bundys and Roosevelts, until he retired in 1973.

The answer lies partly in the school's Anglophilia. Groton is modeled after an English public school like Eton or Harrow, and British history, as studied by Groton boys, is one vast tapestry of moral relativism. "The Brits were the most bloodthirsty of all," said Henry Breck, Groton '54, a CIA case officer in India in the 1960s. "Of course, if you're in a real war you must fight hard—and the upper classes fight the hardest. They have the most to lose." Paul Nitze, a statesman who advised every president from Roosevelt to Reagan and was the drafter of NSC 68, the so-called blueprint of the Cold War, sent his sons to Groton. He did not send them there to be made meek. "In history, every religion has greatly honored those members who destroyed the enemy. The Koran, Greek mythology, the Old Testament. Groton boys were taught that," said Nitze. "Doing in the enemy is the right thing to do. Of course, there are some restraints on ends and means. If you go back to Greek culture and read Thucydides, there are limits to what you can do to other Greeks, who are part of your culture. But there are no limits on what you can do to a Persian. He's a barbarian. The communists," Nitze concluded, "were barbarians."[8]

AT YALE, Bissell mocked the urge to conform. In his junior year he became the editor of a subversive publication called the *Harkness Hoot*, publishing such screeds as "Universities and Parasites: An

Apology for Tax-Exempt Country Clubs" and "Senior Societies Must Go." The *Hoot* was "most notorious and widely discussed," the 1932 yearbook declared, taking pride that the Hoot had been "the subject of eight editorials in New York papers."[9]

What agitated him the most about Yale was the senior societies, which he thought were elitist, anti-intellectual, and full of mumbo jumbo. On Tap Day every spring, five hundred or so Yale juniors would herd like sheep into a college courtyard to learn if they were among the ninety lucky ones chosen by Yale's half dozen secret clubs for seniors, each with its own "tomb," or windowless club-house. (Tracy Barnes had naturally glided into Scroll and Key, the most genial of the societies.)

Bissell refused to go to Tap Day, though he was hardly indifferent. Secretly, he had calculated the odds that he would get tapped (one in four, he figured). Skull and Bones, the most self-serious of the societies, periodically demonstrated its grandeur by tapping a rebel, so when Harkness Tower struck five on Tap Day in April 1931 there was a knock on Bissell's door. The custom at the time was for the society man to whack the chosen on the back and shout, "Go to your room!" This made sense if he was standing with the rest of the sheep out in the courtyard. But it didn't make much sense when the man from Skull and Bones lurched across Bissell's room, slapped him on the back, and cried, "Go to your room!" Bissell would later regret that he did not have the presence to calmly respond, "I'm in my room." Instead, he mumbled his rejection. The decision pained him. "I felt a little depressed for a while. It meant I was out of a lot of things I wanted to be in on." A year later his friend Eugene Rostow showed up in Bissell's room full of angst, afraid that he would be the first Jew tapped by Skull and Bones, and not sure he could resist the temptation. Bissell saved him from this fate by driving him out of town on Tap Day.

To fill those lonely evenings when other seniors were off in their society tombs, Bissell and his friends borrowed an Oxbridge tradition called roof climbing. Donning sneakers, smearing their faces with black greasepaint like commandos (so as not to reflect the streetlights), the roof climbers would go out a window, said Bissell, "grapple hands on a balustrade and walk up the slate roof to the roof tree. We'd feel along the peak of the roof" and drop down to the window of a friend—for drinks. "It was dangerous, criminally dangerous and potentially fatal," said Bissell. But clambering around steep-pitched roofs in the dead of night satisfied his love of risk. "Bissell was gleeful about evading the campus police," said a fellow climber, Fritz Liebert.

In spite of, or perhaps because of, his lack of social ease, Bissell had enormous intellectual self-confidence. In his senior year Bissell and Rostow published what they called the Yale Economic Plan. This plan for national economic revival was especially ambitious considering that Bissell had never taken any economics. To remedy this after graduation in 1932, Bissell went to the London School of Economics, where he rebelled against orthodoxy by becoming a Keynesian.

Bissell continued to play the renegade when he returned to Yale in 1934 to teach economics. He enjoyed the subversiveness of teaching a "black market seminar" on Thursday evening to a group of undergraduates whom he had handpicked. "He was open, clear, fast, smart, and marvelously irreverent. He espoused economic theories that the graybeards couldn't even understand," said McGeorge Bundy, one of his young stars. "He was a great expositor," said Walt Rostow, who would succeed Bundy as Lyndon Johnson's national security adviser. "My regular ec professor was the freshman football coach. With Bissell, you had the sense you were dealing with a virtuoso." Bissell had time to toss off his Ph.D. thesis, "The Theory of Capital Under Static and Dynamic Conditions," which he "dictated and drafted at the rate of 20 pages a day," according to his memoirs.[10]

Bissell moved on from roof climbing to even more dangerous rock climbing in the hills around New Haven. This time he pushed too far. Climbing a steep cliff on Rattlesnake Mountain without any safety rope, he fell fifty feet and landed on a rocky slope at the bottom. His head was cut, he was bleeding badly, and he had torn his collarbone loose from the sternum. Taken to the hospital in shock, he needed several months to convalesce. When he felt recovered, he went right back to Rattlesnake Mountain. There, alone and again unroped, without telling anyone, he made the same climb. His hands "were shaking"; he knew the climb was "incredibly foolish." But he made it, a triumph of the will that reinforced his stubborn drive to overcome the odds, even if that meant taking great and sometimes reckless chances.[11]

In 1936, Bissell bought a fifty-seven-foot yawl, the *Sea Witch*, to test his love of sailing. "He wanted to stand up against the sea and fight it," said Fritz Liebert, who often sailed with him. "You do it to fight Providence. It was like roof climbing." And at times almost as risky. Though Bissell was an expert navigator, according to Liebert, he did bounce the *Sea Witch* off some rocks in the fog and once stove in her side.[12]

To debate the great issues of the day, Bissell joined a group of faculty, known around campus as "the State Department," that dined together once a week. In 1938 the group launched a seminar called "Where Is the World Going?" The answer, as they all knew, was to war. At Yale the interventionists were led by McGeorge Bundy, who uttered his beliefs with the certitude worthy of the Rector: "Let me put my whole proposition in one sentence. I believe in the dignity of the individual, in government by law, in respect for the truth, and in a good God; these beliefs are worth my life and more; they are not shared by Adolph Hitler," Bundy wrote in a 1940 book of essays, *Zero Hour*. The leader of the isolationists was Bissell. He had been overwhelmed by the devastation he saw on a trip to northern France in 1919. World War I had been a "cataclysm," he believed. To be antiwar also suited Bissell's rebellious streak, since all the "right-thinking" men, like Mac Bundy, wanted to charge up San Juan Hill like Teddy Roosevelt. Bissell shared Teddy Roosevelt's love of the wilds, but not his bellicosity. "He thought Teddy Roosevelt was a figure of fun, ridiculous," said Eugene Rostow.

Bissell's isolationism had been rooted more in contrariness than ideology. "After Pearl Harbor, all bets were off," he said. "I didn't worry about what I had been thinking."[13]

BISSELL WANTED to join the war effort, but he knew he would be a liability in the trenches. Organizing for victory was more his calling. With his macroeconomic training, Bissell could see early on that the generals and fighters would get the glory, but that the war would be won by mobilizing America's industrial strength and bringing it to bear against the Germans and Japanese.

In Washington, Bissell found a dreary-sounding (but draftproof) job with the Shipping Adjustment Board. Within a year he was recognized as a main cog in the war machine. All that daydreaming about train timetables paid off. "I got up a system to forecast ships to be loaded each month," said Bissell. "I had a lady from Census, and we set up a card file, a weekly document with the positions of every ship listed. I developed crude, unsophisticated formulas for predicting when a ship in a given convoy would be back in the

United States, repaired, and ready to load. I could predict three months in advance with a 5 percent margin of error. No one else," he said, "could do this."

Bissell's card file "became the system. I was the American merchant shipping planner," said Bissell. His fussy attention to time-tables, once the object of derision, became a source of marvel. "He knew just where they could pick up one vessel in the South Atlantic, two in the Red Sea and so on," recalled a colleague, Robert Amory. "His mind could just tick off their names and do the mental arithmetic: at 11½ knots, you could be in Tunis and Carthage at such-and-such." The only catch was the military, which was not as logical as Bissell's mind. "There were a lot of snafus," recalled Bissell. "Merchant ships would get to the unloading area and be held for three months. The military wouldn't get them into dock. This, at a time when shipping was in the tightest supply and we were pouring scarce steel! There was colossal wastage." Four decades later Bissell became riled when he recalled the military's incompetence. "We constantly talked to the military about this. The Mediterranean theater was superb, but in the Northern European theater there was a perverse chief of supply—he would get Liberty ships into dock and use them as warehouses. So ships, exceedingly scarce, were used as warehouses," said Bissell, his ire rising as he remembered balky colonels and thick-headed admirals. "It was a control problem. Calcutta was good—a one-week turnaround. The worst was the Southwest Pacific. God! Just a huge fleet sitting around and waiting to be unloaded."[14]

For Bissell, the end of the war in 1945 would be only a pause. Within three years he was back in Washington to fight the Cold War, helping to manage the enormous effort to rebuild Western Europe. Teaching at MIT and consulting with U.S. Steel held his attention only briefly. In July 1947 he was recruited by Averell Harriman to run a citizen's committee to lobby for an economic recovery plan for Europe. The committee's report was extremely influential; it put the establishment stamp on a rescue program for Europe and won editorial endorsements all over the country. In Bissell's rather high-handed fashion, he finished the report at the last possible moment in November 1947 and did not show it to the committee members for their review before releasing it to the press. This was "unavoidable," Bissell wrote. So too was the need to "pull some numbers out of the air" to support the report's conclusions. Within two days of passage of the Marshall Plan in the winter of 1948, Bissell received a phone call from Paul Hoffman, the head of the Economic Cooperation Administration set up to run the Marshall Plan. "He said, 'I want you here as soon as you can get here,' " recalled Bissell. "This was on a Wednesday. I said, 'How about Monday?' He said, 'No, this afternoon.' " Bissell arrived at midnight, unable to get a hotel. He slept in the other bed of Hoffman's hotel room and began work over breakfast at seven.[15]

Bissell spent his first six months essentially writing the plan, operating on his own authority without much regard for the bureaucracy. "I was visited by a Treasury official several years later," Bissell recollected, with some relish. "He told me I owed the federal government $6 to $8 million. I asked why. It appeared that a number of voyages shipping coal from South Africa had been made on my authority. The man asked, what authority did you have? He finally wandered away, unsatisfied. But he couldn't do anything."

Bissell spent hours testifying before Congress about the plan, but his job, as he saw it, wasn't selling; it was telling. Cajoling politicians was for others. Paul Hoffman would handle the senators, but when the questions got complicated he'd turn to Bissell to explain. His grasp gave him immense power. "Bissell relished the complexity," said his deputy, Harlan Cleveland. "It was an intellectual game. He'd be annoyed when a senator would act according to his ego. He'd say, 'Why is he reacting like this? The substance is so clear.' " After a hearing the senators would crowd around Hoffman, and Bissell would stand off to the side, alone. "Bissell didn't envy Hoffman," said Cleveland. "He pitied him for not understanding the substance."

Bissell had "complete contempt for stupid bureaucrats and even senior people who were slow and stodgy," said Paul Nitze, who worked with him at the State Department. "He would express himself in vigorous and biting terms about all these troglodytes wandering around. He was a revolutionary, but he was very bright, and by and large he was right. He made enemies, but fewer than I would have expected because he was so entertaining. In a war situation, people with energy get responsibility to take it away from the troglodytes."

A sinus sufferer, Bissell would inhale through his nose very noisily from time to time. "I always wondered if this was a conscious mannerism," said Cleveland. "It wasn't a snort exactly, but he'd do it when someone was trying to explain something and didn't get it fast enough or told him something he already knew."[16]

Critical to the success of the Marshall Plan, Bissell believed, was its secrecy and independence. The Economic Cooperation Administration, set up to implement aid to Europe, worked apart from the State Department, which it held in some disdain. Bissell and his men, he later wrote, worked "out of the limelight and away from the media's eye so that European leaders were able to accept strong measures, confident that their actions would be supported by ECA financing without seeming to have been unduly influenced by the United States." This was exactly the model for the CIA—a small, elite group, privately manipulating the world with American funds and power.[17]

Chapter Seven

RUNNING THE WORLD

"Dools, Dools, do you take us for fools?"

IN LATE AUGUST 1953, just after Bissell had finished advising Frank Wisner and the CIA on how it might "roll back" communism in Eastern Europe, he had an experience that made him want to join the agency full-time. Taking a few weeks off from the Ford Foundation, he went cruising in Maine on his yawl, the *Sea Witch*, with Tom Braden and his wife, Joan. Braden was the head of the International Organizations Division at the CIA, in charge of running anticommunist front groups in Western Europe.

The *Sea Witch* was anchored in a harbor in Penobscot Bay when Braden received an urgent message informing him that the McCarthyites had discovered a Red at the CIA. The man in question was Braden's deputy, Cord Meyer, a young war hero from St. Paul's and Yale, who had lost an eye in combat in the Pacific. The Bradens immediately abandoned their vacation and drove through the night back to Washington to stand by young Meyer. The FBI was unwilling to give him a security clearance, although typically refusing to say why. Dulles, Wisner, and other top agency officials refused to permit an FBI interrogation of Meyer. Eventually, they forced the FBI to reveal the charges against Meyer, which were flimsy at best (he had once appeared on the same speaking platform as a leftist professor and joined liberal groups deemed subversive by the Justice Department). In fact, Meyer was a staunch anticommunist. After some procedural foot-dragging, he was cleared just before Thanksgiving and allowed to keep his job.

Bissell was impressed and heartened. What Dean Acheson referred to as "the Attack of the Primitives" had been raging for several years in Washington. Senator Joe McCarthy of Wisconsin and other Red hunters were waving phony lists of subversives and hounding government agencies to cut loose their "security risks," no matter how trivial their "leftist" associations. The State Department under John Foster Dulles was particularly craven; Dulles had hired one of McCarthy's henchmen to help him sweep out subversives. To Bissell, for a secretary of state to cavil before a politician was despicable. Secretive, elitist, and seemingly above partisan politics, the CIA seemed to be the kind of organization made for an independent spirit like Bissell. "There was a feeling of esprit," he said, "a sense that you could accomplish things."[1]

That Christmastime, at a dinner party at Stew Alsop's, Bissell walked Allen Dulles to the door as they were leaving. Dulles casually mentioned that he had heard from their friend Frank Wisner that Bissell might be looking for a job. If so, would Bissell stop by Dulles's office? Bissell was interested, of course, and Dulles quickly offered to make him his special assistant, a kind of minister without portfolio. Bissell accepted, and that January he went to work for the agency.[2]

HE WAS JOINING more than an organization. By the early 1950s, there had grown up in Georgetown a kind of elite within the elite, a group of lively and like-minded families who shared friendships and common backgrounds and a certain *joie de vivre*. There was the Sunday Night Supper crowd, the Wisners and Alsops and Bohlens, the Nitzes and Phil and Kay Graham (who owned the *Washington Post*). They tended to be well-to-do liberal Democrats. Interestingly, they did not regard themselves as the upper crust or the establishment, but rather as informal, even a little scruffy, and fun-loving. They were not "cave dwellers," old Washington society, and they were not in the inner circles of the administration, which after 1953 was Republican. In their own minds they were outsiders. But they were very bright, and they took care of their own, all of which made them very attractive to Richard Bissell.

In a way Joe McCarthy had brought them together. At first, the junior senator from Wisconsin had seemed like a figure of ridicule. "Tail Gunner Joe" looked like a blowhard who would run out of gas before he could do too much damage. The laughter in Georgetown quieted, though, when McCarthy began attacking the natives. One of the keys to McCarthy's success was his brazenness. Using the "big lie" technique of earlier mass manipulators, he turned on the same people who had first warned against the threat of international communism, by accusing them of being "soft." This was a ludicrous thing to say about men like Acheson and Paul Nitze, who were hawks. In the spring of 1953, McCarthy had targeted Chip Bohlen and Charles Thayer, two of the top Kremlin watchers who were also brothers-in-law. McCarthy did not quite say what he had on Bohlen and Thayer, though he intimated that the damaging information was of a sexual nature. He hoped to intimidate John Foster Dulles and President Eisenhower into sacking the two highly regarded foreign service officers. Dulles wavered shamefully on Bohlen, nearly withdrawing his nomination to be ambassador to the Soviet Union, but Bohlen managed to slip by. Thayer was not so lucky; his career at the State Department was ruined and he was forced to resign.[3]

McCarthy's next target was the CIA. The attack had come in the summer of 1953, shortly before Cord Meyer had been targeted as a "security risk." McCarthy had announced that the agency was a sinkhole of communists, "the worst yet," and that he was going to root out a hundred of them. He had chosen badly, however, on the first. William Bundy seemed tempting—he was Acheson's son-in-law, and he had donated $400 to the Alger Hiss defense fund (a prima facie case in that age of suspicion). But he was upright and exceedingly clean. Allen Dulles told his chief of security, Sheffield Edwards, to check out Bundy's past, and Edwards reported back, "I've never had a case before where someone didn't at least say, 'Well, he drinks too much.' " When McCarthy demanded that Bundy appear on the Hill to testify before his Red-hunting subcommittee, Allen Dulles refused. McCarthy, for once, backed down. It was a heroic moment at the CIA, and it gave the agency heart to fight back in other cases. McCarthy tried to probe the CIA by blackmail: his henchmen would call an official and threaten to expose some terrible thing from his past—an old girlfriend, a drinking problem—unless the official agreed to meet with McCarthy's investigators and tell all. Dulles shrewdly created an informal committee to run what amounted to a counterintelligence operation. Using wiretaps and plants of disinformation, the committee tracked McCarthy's probes and kept agency employees from becoming McCarthyite moles. Most were saved—the top CIA officials at least, like Cord Meyer, who had become a kind of liberal icon through his writings on behalf of "world federalism."[4]

The CIA's defiance of McCarthy was the beginning of the end for the demagogue; a few months later, in the spring of 1954, he would self-destruct when he took on the U.S. Army and was exposed as a malevolent drunk in nationally televised congressional hearings. For the Georgetown crowd, McCarthy's fall was triumphant. They felt that they had stood fast where others had caved in.

They would never be caught boasting about their defiance, however. The tone was determinedly light and self-effacing, especially in the dark moments. The wives mocked John Foster Dulles for his cowardice. At lunch the friends of Avis Bohlen sang a little ditty, "Dools, Dools, do you take us for fools?," a rhyme that inevitably made its way back to the State Department and did not enhance Bohlen's career. (In 1956, Dulles shuffled Bohlen from Moscow, where he belonged, to the Philippines.)[5]

John Foster Dulles's shabbiness toward Chip Bohlen and his brother-in-law Charles Thayer, along with Eisenhower's notable silence on the subject, had drawn a "we-they" divide between the Georgetown group and the new administration. The Republicans, with some exceptions, like Nelson Rockefeller at the White House, were regarded as dull, earnest, and midwestern. A clear distinction was drawn between the Dulles brothers: Allen, jaunty and bold; John Foster, maladroit and pusillanimous. In Georgetown, Adlai Stevenson was popular, at least among the wives.* "We huddled together and made terrible jokes and behaved rather badly," said Evangeline Bruce. "We didn't think Eisenhower was very bright," said Jean Friendly, who with her husband, Alfred, the managing editor of the *Washington Post*, was part of the circle. Few worried about getting left off the White House invitation

---

* In a letter to her husband, Susan Mary Alsop describes going to a party for the "inner circle of the Stevenson group" at a "charming house" on Prospect Avenue following a Jackson Day dinner in April 1955. The big dinner, in a hotel downtown, had been ghastly; "Evangeline [Bruce] dealt digestive tablets" to the thirty or forty members of the crowd who gathered for a private séance with Adlai Stevenson. "There were decorative blonds, there were two real beauties, Marietta [Tree, FitzGerald's ex-wife] and Evangeline, who seemed automatically to be expected to play the role of senior duchesses in this realm. . . ." "You see," Mrs. Alsop wrote, "the New Democratic Party is not too afraid of public opinion to be dressed by Mainbocher, and very nice, too. . . ."[6]

list. "No one gave a damn about the White House," said Oatsie Charles, a well-known Georgetown hostess and bon vivant. "Bess Truman? Mamie Eisenhower?"

The feel among the Georgetown families was tight, almost clannish, but not narrow or smug, the jokes notwithstanding. On Sundays (the men, workaholics all, would be in the office most Saturdays), "We'd all walk like mad up and down the [Chesapeake and Ohio] canal after lunch with children and the dogs. Bunches of us. All the dogs fought, and the children loved it because they saw their fathers," said Tracy's widow, Janet Barnes Lawrence.

The Georgetown crowd strived to appear carefree. Cautioned against talking about their work, the men referred to the CIA as "the Pickle Factory." "We felt very rebellious. None of us had much money, and the administration was so dull. They believed that government should be straitlaced," said Tish Alsop. The most memorable evening for many was a dance known as "the Bankruptcy Ball," held at the F Street Club in the summer of 1954.

The name of the party was taken from the financial straits claimed by the various hosts, pinched by the cost of the dance band and the liquor bills. Since the hosts included families that were quite well off, like the Grahams and Wisners, the name was a bit of a conceit. Still, wealth is a relative term. It is true that the young families by and large did not have to live on government salaries. Frank Wisner's secretary found a stack of his paychecks, unopened, in his desk. But the less well-to-do families, like the Bohlens, felt strapped, despite their servants, oriental rugs on the floor, and private school educations for their children. Some of the Georgetown crowd grew up in grander establishments. To them, wealthy meant really rich—grand tours of Europe, butlers in the dining room as well as cooks in the kitchen, houses for each "season" from South Carolina to Maine.

The group was elitist, but not snobbish. Real snobs, they believed, belonged to the Chevy Chase Club, an exclusive country club just over the Maryland border. "My parents' friends made fun of Chevy Chase," said Avis Bohlen, who made a perceptive distinction about the Georgetown crowd of the early 1950s: "They were terrible snobs in a way. Not about social background— rather, they were snobs about snobs. They liked people who they thought were gay and funny and sophisticated—like them. They were intolerant of self-importance or heavy-handedness or narrow-mindedness."

Snobs, they believed, were insecure, clinging to their place in the world by scorning those below. The Georgetown crowd, by contrast, projected tremendous confidence. "They ran the world," said Oatsie Charles. "Nothing was beyond them. It wasn't self-conscious; it was just there." Such confidence bred optimism. "We were all full of optimism and enthusiasm about the cause," said Bissell. "You can say we were naive, and that our efforts were not advancing the cause, or that our cause was no good. But our state of mind was one of optimism and enthusiasm, even when things were going badly."

The group was fiercely competitive. "They all loved betting, they all loved games, they loved to do each other in," said Ella Burling. ("I think they saw the CIA as a game, don't you?" she asked. "Like chess. Or bridge.") Many of them, like Barnes and FitzGerald, were sports car buffs. "They all had Jaguars and their Jaguars would never start. You'd see them cursing at them in the morning," said Mrs. Burling. Dancing was a favorite sport. It would take very little—a few drinks would do—to inspire a dinner party to push back the furniture and start dancing, usually to big band music on the phonograph. "Everyone loved to dance," said Jean Friendly, "at charity balls, at home, in the garden, in the salon, at the Shoreham, after dinner. And play charades. It was a giddy life. Nobody seemed to need sleep in those days, for some reason." Nurses and nannies helped, and hangovers did not seem to deter. "I never went to a Sunday Night Supper when someone didn't get embarrassingly drunk," said Tom Braden. "Just to unwind. It wasn't maudlin. No one threw up. We just drank a hell of a lot. A martini was like a glass of water is now."

With all the liquor, unwinding, and gaiety there was also bound to be what the hostesses of the day referred to as "naughtiness." "We all laughed about how the wife of a British diplomat awoke naked in a sleeping bag on the tennis court," said Jean Friendly. "She couldn't remember how she got there." Mrs. Friendly said that she ran the "Wives Protection Association" in the summer when all the families moved to Maine or the mountains and the husbands "bached" in Washington. "I kept an eye on them," said Mrs. Friendly, who did not join the summer exodus with the other wives. There were the inevitable affairs and indiscretions. But the high jinks never became a bacchanal, and the arguments, while boisterous, did not turn mean.[7]

It was not all frivolity, of course. Friendship did mix with policymaking; serious issues were discussed passionately, and the men who sat at the Georgetown dinner parties sometimes made use of the information they gleaned there. The subtle interplay, a mixture of trust, patriotism, and mutual manipulation, can be seen in the relationship of the CIA men to the Alsop brothers, Joe and Stewart.

The Alsops wrote a well-informed, very influential, sometimes strident column that appeared in the *New York Herald Tribune* as well as several hundred papers around the country. Stewart was witty and urbane, a "gent," though perhaps more complicated than he appeared. Joe made no effort to hide his opinions or strong tastes.

Joe Alsop was a kind of keeper of the gate in Georgetown. It was he who decided who should be let in—who set the standards, made the rules, and broke them when he felt like it.[8] For a man schooled in the social graces, Alsop could be unpleasantly argumentative, and he did not disguise his arbiter's power. But Alsop had a great capacity for friendship; he made it his occupation, and his friends learned to forgive his occasional cruelties. His dinners were undeniably entertaining, though perhaps not to the meek. "They would seem relaxed," said Susan Mary Alsop, who was married to Alsop for a time in the 1960s, "the guests would be talking from right to left, but Joe hated it. He knew it had to be done, but he wanted 'gen con'—general conversation. Halfway through dinner, after a lot of wine, Joe would scream down the table, 'Wisner! Frank! What are they saying about this new movement in Cairo?' The table would silence. The women were trained for it. They would stop talking about the trouble with the new kitchen maid. Joe would go on, 'That's what you think, Wisner,' and he would turn to another guest, 'But what about you? You were in Moscow last week. What about you?' More wine would be poured. Fights would break out. Chip would stalk out. 'I'm not staying in this room another minute! Come on, Avis, we're going home. The next day, Joe would write a note to Avis, 'looking forward to seeing you next Thursday.' Some people were put off by Joe's outbursts, but it was really rather thrilling, if you see what I mean."

The dinners were "planned," said Mrs. Alsop. "He'd look for a subject. It was taken for granted that it was all off the record. He was careful; the information was to inform his judgment."[9] His guests sometimes accused him of revealing more than opinion in the column he wrote with his brother Stewart. Angered that Alsop had printed the contents of a sensitive cable, Paul Nitze exploded, "You're not the Alsop brothers! You're the Hiss brothers!" This allusion to alleged treason got Nitze thrown out of Alsop's house, to be readmitted soon thereafter.[10]

The Alsops knew not to inquire too hard, but they were clever, and by using public sources and their intuition, they could use their CIA friends to guide them toward scoops. "The Alsops were fairly discreet in what they asked," said Richard Bissell, "but I was not as discreet as I should have been. They could usually guess." On one famous occasion in 1955, Stewart Alsop guessed correctly that the CIA was worried about the possibility of a Soviet satellite. As it happened, a National Security Council meeting had been discussing the Soviet space threat the day before Alsop's column appeared. The White House was furious. Allen Dulles had to take the unusual step of forbidding Frank Wisner and Bissell to spend the weekend with the Alsop brothers at Wisner's farm in Maryland. Joe Alsop caused a big scene in Dulles's office, pounding on the table about freedom of the press. "It was pretty funny," said Bissell. "A tempest in a teapot." Bissell regarded the Alsops as somehow different from ordinary journalists. At the end of his life, Bissell told Jonathan Lewis, who was helping arrange his memoirs, that he disapproved of leaking to the press and never did. Lewis asked, But what about your friend Joe Alsop? "Oh well," Bissell replied, "I did talk to Joe."

Wisner actively courted the Alsops, along with a few other newsmen he regarded as suitable outlets. When Lansdale was manipulating electoral politics in the Philippines in 1953, Wisner asked Joe Alsop to write some columns warning the Filipinos not to steal the election from Magsaysay. Alsop was happy to comply, though he doubted his columns would have much impact on the Huks. After the West German counterintelligence chief, Otto John, defected to the Soviet Union in 1954, Wisner fed Alsop a story that the West German spymaster had been kidnapped by the KGB. Alsop dutifully printed the story, which may or may not have been true.[11]

Alsop had no qualms about being used in this way: he was a believer—in the work of the agency and its anticommunist cause. To cooperate with the CIA from time to time was not cozy but rather patriotic. Alsop knew many of the station chiefs around the world; they informed and improved his reporting. Wisner was not able to help, however, when Alsop foolishly allowed himself to be caught in a honey trap by the KGB on a trip to Moscow in 1957. The Russians took photos of Alsop in the midst of a homosexual act with a KGB agent and tried to blackmail him into becoming an agent. Indomitable, Alsop refused and continued to write his anticommunist screeds, though he was haunted by the incident, especially when J. Edgar Hoover learned of it and added it to his secret FBI files.[12]

Alsop was not the only journalist in Washington to play along with the CIA. Jean Friendly's husband, *Washington Post* managing editor Alfred Friendly, "never told secrets," she said. The CIA "trusted him." James Reston, the all-powerful Washington bureau chief of the *New York Times*, kept some distance from the Georgetown cocktail circuit, but he spent hours talking to Wisner, and his next-door neighbor, with whom he talked through a hole in the fence, was Paul Nitze. When the occasional journalist dared to cross the national security establishment, he was cut off. Drew Pearson, a muckraking columnist, was struck from the guest list of the Bankruptcy Ball because he had written something critical about Paul Nitze. Many reporters, like the Alsops, knew about CIA plots to overthrow the governments of Iran and Guatemala, but they did not print a word. It is no wonder that men like Richard Bissell believed they could try ever-more ambitious operations without fear of damaging leaks.[13]

Chapter Eight

COUP

*"How are you going
to keep this a secret?"*

IN THE DULLES years, the CIA shifted its focus. The target for most covert action enthusiasts (with the significant exception of Frank Wisner) was no longer liberating the East Bloc, but rather stopping the dominoes from falling in other parts of the world—the Middle East, Asia, Africa, Latin America.

Two critical events in the summer of 1953 signaled that change. One was an outbreak of rioting in East Berlin. In June anticommunist demonstrators took to the streets in the Soviet sector of Berlin. At first, Wisner was excited: Could this be the first spark of a greater conflagration? But he had been reined in by John Bross, Tracy Barnes's old prefect at Groton who was running the Eastern Europe Division at the CIA. Bross was a man of uncommonly good judgment, not as flashy as Bissell and Barnes, but over the long run wiser. Bross convinced Wisner, who really did not need much persuading, that there was nothing the CIA could do. The Berlin station chief clambered for arms to hand out to the rioters, but Washington instructed him to offer only moral support—no weapons. The Soviets were going to crack down hard, and some smuggled Sten guns would only prolong the bloodshed.[1]

The other event was a coup d'etat in Iran. The Iranian coup was the agency's first great success at overthrowing a foreign government, and it was the example, if not the model, for numerous other attempts over the next two decades.

The story of the Iranian coup, Operation AJAX, is one of romantic intrigue, timing, and luck. In 1951 a fervent nationalist,

Mohammed Mossadegh, had come to power in Iran, undercutting the weak Shah, who had been installed by the British. Mossadegh caused unease in Western capitals by legalizing the Tudeh, the Iranian Communist Party. In fact, he hated London much more than he loved Moscow; still, the British and Americans worried that he would become a communist stooge. The British were particularly eager to get rid of Mossadegh after he nationalized the Anglo-Iranian Oil Company, which had been controlled by the British and fueled the Royal Navy's warships. As they had in Albania, the British Secret Intelligence Service approached their "cousins" at the CIA to join in a covert operation.[2]

Here was an opportunity to do something to turn back the communist tide before it reached the beach, as well as a chance to please an ally, and perhaps most important, keep the oil flowing. Nonetheless, at first the CIA was reluctant to conspire with the British in Iran, according to John Bruce Lockhart, the SIS liaison in Washington. Frank Wisner was lukewarm, and Allen Dulles said he would go along only if his brother, Foster, the secretary of state, agreed. In 1953 the CIA was still feeling a little burned by Kim Philby. Nonetheless, the Dulles brothers signed on; Iran was a strategic prize. To work with the British, Wisner and Dulles assigned their best Middle East operative, Kermit "Kim" Roosevelt.

Roosevelt was an Oyster Bay Roosevelt, grandson of President Theodore. He was well acquainted with the Sunday Night Supper crowd, and he had been a few years behind Bissell and Barnes at Groton. Yet he was warier, less trusting than the "typical" Groton boy, which may be why he was more successful at covert work. He steered clear of the Georgetown set. "At the CIA, people resented the Groton clique, but I was not part of that gang," he recalled. As a Roosevelt he felt no need to identify with any particular institution. Along with his cousins Archie and Cornelius, Kim Roosevelt formed a kind of cell-within-the-cell inside the CIA. When, in those early years, Archie Roosevelt's Lebanese-American wife, Selwa, worried whether she was doing the socially "right" thing, Archie cut her off. "Look," he said. "What we do is right."[3]

Roosevelt had been recruited by Wisner in 1950 after teaching at Harvard and working for the OSS in the Middle East, but the working relationship was not close. "Wisner was a frenetic sort of person, both in an effective and a pejorative sense," said Roosevelt. "He bit off more than he could chew and it wore him down. He was opinionated, but I had no confidence in his judgment. He was too enthusiastic, and congenitally inclined to see things his way." Roosevelt disapproved of Wisner's "hangers-on" like Carmel Offie, "an oily little jerk who talked oddly and did odd things." Wisner "browbeat" his hangers-on, said Roosevelt, but he "never browbeat me. He tried, but he gave up."

A loner in every sense, Roosevelt was left essentially free to work his territory, the Middle East. It was here, far from the front lines of the Cold War, that the CIA scored its first big coup.

Hiding underneath a blanket on the floor of an unmarked car, Roosevelt was slipped into the Shah's palace in Tehran in June 1953 to convince young Reza Pahlavi to stand up to the bullying Mossadegh. His first task was to persuade the Shah that Mossadegh was not an American agent (the Shah was suspicious because Mossedegh had been *Time* magazine's "Man of the Year" in 1952). With the right help from the palace, Roosevelt told the Shah, the Americans and British could drive Mossadegh from power. Roosevelt won a promise from the Shah to call for Mossadegh's dismissal from the national assembly. But riots broke out first, and the Shah fled to Rome. Roosevelt was disgusted. "The Shah," he later scoffed, "was a wimp." An anxious wait ensued; Roosevelt holed up in a safe house, drinking lime rickeys and listening to the Broadway show tune "Luck Be a Lady Tonight" on his Victrola. In Washington, Dulles and Wisner assumed the plot had failed. They sent a cable to Roosevelt telling him to flee Tehran "at the earliest moment" for his safety. Washington headquarters, according to the agency's in-house history of the operation, "spent a day featured by depression and despair."

But then the plotters got a break. A small street demonstration backing the Shah became a full-blown riot, fueled in part by $10,000 that Roosevelt had passed around to street goons and some musclemen from the circus. Mossadegh fled over his garden wall. The Shah, eating breakfast in the dining room of the Excelsior Hotel in Rome, learned that he was Shah again. "I always knew the people loved me," he told his shocked wife.

Roosevelt became an instant secret hero, a kind of masterspy miracle worker. At a private dinner at the palace, the Shah looked at the CIA man and offered a toast: "I owe my throne to God, my people, my army—and you!" In London, Winston Churchill insisted on having a congratulatory cognac with Roosevelt. In Washington, President Eisenhower summoned Roosevelt for a personal briefing at the White House. As Roosevelt stood there at the easel pointing at the map of Tehran, the location of the army barracks, the path of the rioters, and Mossadegh's escape route, he noticed Secretary of State John Foster Dulles leaning back in his chair. He thought for a moment that the secretary was bored or dozing off. Then he looked more closely and noticed that Dulles's "eyes were gleaming. He seemed to be purring like a giant cat."[4]

The contentment emanating from the president and secretary of state reflected more than pleasure over restoring the Western oil monopoly in Iran. Artful, quick, inexpensive coups d'etat: here was a role for the CIA that really worked. At the time Eisenhower was trying to cut back his military budget, bloated by the Korean War. The Republican platform had made some grand statements about liberating the "slave states" of Eastern Europe, but Eisenhower and Dulles had no desire at all to go to war to deliver on this promise. As a military man President Eisenhower had a healthy sense of reality about what the military could and could not accomplish. In government, only civilians talk about "surgical strikes." Experienced commanders think about the collateral damage and the iron rule of battle, that whatever can go wrong will go wrong. "Eisenhower didn't trust the military," said historian Arthur Schlesinger. "He knew too much about it." The CIA beckoned as a promising alternative. It was small, relatively cheap, elite, nonbureaucratic, and best of all for a political leader, deniable.[5]

John Foster Dulles had made the most noise about rolling back the Iron Curtain, but he did not really believe his own rhetoric. He was content to contain communism, which seemed a large enough task in 1953. The place it was growing fastest was in the Third World, where colonialism was giving way to chaos. Dulles saw the CIA as a convenient tool that could stop the Red stain from spreading on the map. It was his personal action arm: all Foster Dulles needed to do was call his brother, Allen.

So the new battleground would be back alleys and restless barracks from Cairo to Havana. The Third World beckoned as an easier place to operate than the East Bloc. The communists were the insurgents, not the government. The Kremlin had long tentacles, but they became attenuated; local communist movements were easier to penetrate than ones close to Moscow Center. Third World strongmen were already dependent on American and British companies to run their economies, and the services of many public servants south of the border and east of the Levant were for sale. By judiciously dispensing cash and favors, an American CIA station chief could gain the kind of power enjoyed by a colonial proconsul.

The odds for intervention seemed so encouraging that the men who ran the CIA overlooked one shortcoming: the fact that they knew almost nothing about the so-called developing world.[6]

SOME HISTORIANS use a corporate conspiracy theory to explain why the CIA overthrew the government of Guatemala. The story, as it is usually told, begins in 1936 on Wall Street with a deal set up by John Foster Dulles, then a lawyer with Sullivan and Cromwell, to create a banana monopoly in Guatemala for his client, United Fruit Company. In 1952, Jacobo Arbenz, Guatemala's reform-minded president, appropriated United Fruit's holdings. To get his company's land back, Sam "The Banana Man" Zemurray, the head of United Fruit, hired the Washington lobbyist Thomas "Tommy the Cork" Corcoran. With his usual energy and skill, Corcoran beseeched the U.S. government to overthrow Arbenz. His case was sympathetically heard, in part because just about everyone in a position to do something about Guatemala was, in one way or another, on United Fruit's payroll. Both Secretary of State John Foster Dulles and his brother, Allen, the CIA director, had sat on the board of United Fruit's partner in the banana monopoly, the Schroder Banking Corporation. The assistant secretary of state for inter-American affairs, John Moors Cabot, owned stock in United Fruit. (His brother Thomas had served as president of the company.) U.N. Ambassador Henry Cabot Lodge was a stockholder and had been a strong defender of United Fruit while a U.S. senator. Anne Whitman, Eisenhower's personal secretary, was the wife of Edmund Whitman, United Fruit's public relations director. Bedell Smith, the undersecretary of state, was actively seeking a job with United Fruit and later sat on the company's board.

Against this capitalist juggernaut, the story goes, stood Arbenz, an idealistic reformer who wanted only to help the downtrodden peasants of his country. He posed no national security risk to the United States. His badly equipped, poorly led army of 6,500 men was incapable of threatening its neighbors, much less the colossus to the north. Arbenz was a leftist, but not really a communist, and he wasn't working for Moscow or trying to subvert other countries. His only crime was to threaten the profits of United Fruit.[7]

There is some truth behind this explanation of the Guatemala coup, but it is not the whole story. For one thing, Arbenz "considered himself a communist, and with his few confidants, he spoke like one," writes historian Piero Gleijeses. Guatemala was the one country in Central America willing to harbor communists, and agrarian land reform did pose an ideological threat to its neighbors.[8]

Certainly, the top policymakers in Washington believed that Arbenz was a communist, or close to it, and that he posed a threat to the hemisphere. With or without United Fruit, Guatemala was a likely target for American intervention in the early 1950s. The prevailing view in Washington was succinctly stated by Tracy Barnes when he signed up David Phillips, a CIA operative, to join the Guatemala operation. In his agency memoirs, *The Night Watch*, Phillips quotes Barnes's recruiting pitch:

> "It's not just a question of Arbenz," he said. "Nor of Guatemala. We have solid intelligence that the Soviets intend to throw substantial support to Arbenz. . . . Given Soviet backing, that spells trouble in all of Central America. An easily expandable beachhead, if you want to use the current term."[9]

Barnes believed what he was saying; he was not being cynical about the "expandable beachhead." After churning out pages of urgent warnings about global communism for the Psychological Strategy Board in 1952, he had convinced himself; his views were generally shared by his friends and colleagues. "Tracy and I were not concerned with an ideological debate over whether to do it," said Bissell, who also took part in the operation. "Just how to do it." Barnes and Bissell were activists, and overthrowing a foreign government was action on a dramatic scale. "Tracy was so relieved he could actually do something," said his wife, Janet.[10]

Barnes and Bissell were not Allen Dulles's first choice to run the Guatemala operation. After the Iranian coup Dulles asked Kermit Roosevelt to reprise his feat in Central America. But independent as ever, Roosevelt demurred. For a coup to be successful, Roosevelt told Dulles, the army and the people have to "want what we want." He doubted that the Guatemalan peasants wanted what United Fruit wanted.[11]

In later years the CIA's engineering of a coup in Guatemala would be regarded as a model of tactical success, of agency cunning and mastery of covert action. To the participants at the time, however, it was a near disaster saved by good fortune, the willingness to take risks, and the cravenness of the opposition.

The CIA had tried and failed to lure Arbenz out of power by offering him a Swiss bank account. The agency also considered assassinating Arbenz, but didn't want to make him a martyr.[12] If they couldn't bribe Arbenz or kill him, perhaps they could scare him out of office. The CIA's records do not disclose who first suggested the idea, but the concept that Wisner, Dulles, and Barnes first contemplated in the fall of 1953 closely mirrors Barnes's own experiences in World War II. Barnes's exploit was psychological warfare at its most daring. Attacking along with only one other commando, he had convinced a garrison of Germans holding a little town in Brittany that they were under siege from a superior force. Barnes accomplished this trick by racing about on the outskirts of the village firing weapons, setting off explosions, and generally making a ruckus. The frightened Germans had fled.

In Guatemala, the CIA set about to play essentially the same trick on a grander scale. The agency would recruit a small force of exiles to invade Guatemala from Honduras. They would pretend to be the vanguard of a much larger army seeking to "liberate" their homeland from the Marxists. By radio broadcasts and other propaganda, the insurgents would signal a broad popular uprising. Fearing a revolution, Arbenz would throw up his hands like the frightened Germans and flee.

The key to shocking Arbenz, Barnes and his "PP" staff believed, was airpower. The Guatemalan Air Force consisted of a few light training planes and three hundred men. If the insurgents could get control of the skies and bomb Guatemala City, they could create panic. Barnes set about creating a small pirate air force to bomb Arbenz into submission. An odd-lot fleet—six aging P-47 Thunderbolts, three P-51 fighter bombers, a Cessna 180, a PBY naval patrol bomber, and a P-38 fighter—were smuggled into neighboring Nicaragua under the cover of military aid to the regime of Anastasio Somoza, an American ally. To fly these planes, the CIA recruited soldiers of fortune like Jerry DeLarm, a former skywriter who owned an automobile dealership in Guatemala City and who liked to put a .45-caliber pistol before him on the table when he spoke to a stranger.

This entire operation was supposed to be highly secret—deniable by the U.S. government. But Gilbert Greenway, an old friend of Frank Wisner's assigned to help locate air crews for the operation, recalled that "Tracy was very lax on security. We were going to hire crews with very little cover. He was in such a hurry that he wanted to hire people without any security checks, a flagrant security violation. He just wanted to get going." Greenway balked, but Barnes insisted. "Oh, go ahead," he urged Greenway. "Sell Wiz on it. You're a friend." Wisner, while eager for the operation to succeed, was more cautious than Barnes, far more concerned about leaks and blown cover. Wisner threw Greenway out of his office, telling him that Barnes's hiring methods were "stupid" and "ridiculous." In the end, the cover for the pilots was pretty flimsy: many of them were hired from a Florida flight school owned by Greenway's brother-in-law.

Greenway regarded Barnes as a marvelous fellow but a poor judge of the people he hired. "Some of them were out-and-out flakes. He thought they were hot stuff. He was a bad judge of character, period."[13]

One of Barnes's recruits for the Guatemala operation was E. Howard Hunt. Hunt would work for Barnes for most of his CIA career, at times to Barnes's detriment. A graduate of Brown, Hunt regarded himself as Barnes's social peer. But David Phillips immediately saw a difference between Barnes and Hunt when the two men approached him about working on the Guatemala operation: "[Barnes] wore a subdued plaid sports jacket, a button-down shirt and old school tie, and gray flannel slacks and loafers. He was very urbane with an easy confidence. . . I liked him instantly." Hunt, fiddling with his pipe, "exuded urbaneness but not with Barnes's quiet flair. He was dressed less conservatively and wore a tropical straw hat with the brim snapped down over his eyes."[14]

Hunt had a flair for the dramatic. He successfully moonlighted as a part-time author of spy thrillers; he wrote forty-five of them, under various pseudonyms, and one, *Bimini Run*, was made into a movie in 1948. Barnes signed him up to be chief of propaganda for the Guatemala operation.[15]

David Phillips, a charming if unsuccessful actor who had drifted into the CIA when he could not make it on Broadway, was put in charge of creating a phony radio station to make clandestine broadcasts into Guatemala. It was to be named the Voice of Liberation, and its slogan was *Trabajo, Pan, y Patria* (Work, Bread, and

Country). Phillips hired a couple of Guatemalans—"Pepe" and "Mario"—to write stirring calls to arms. Beginning on May 1, Labor Day in Guatemala, the Voice of Liberation was to prepare the proper psychological climate for the revolution, scheduled to begin on June 18.

Phillips was a smart man—more grounded than Hunt—and he was perceptive about the conflicts roiling below Barnes's unflappable exterior. As he was being recruited by Barnes, Phillips asked him, "What right do we have to help someone to topple his government and throw him out of office?" Barnes "ducked" the question. "For a moment," Phillips writes, "I detected in his face a flicker of concern, a doubt, the reaction of a sensitive man."[16]

To command the operation on the ground, Wisner and Dulles selected Al Haney, a former Army colonel who had run CIA guerrilla operations into Korea. Haney was regarded as resourceful and aggressive, perhaps overly so.[17] Haney immediately bumped up against E. Howard Hunt. "They deserved each other," said Enno Hobbing, Haney's number two. "They were both braggarts with two left feet. Haney, who boasted that he had been the youngest bank vice president in the United States, asked Hunt, 'Do you drive a Cadillac?' Hunt, condescending, answered, 'Yes, for the last eight years.' "[18]

Haney's "field" headquarters was on an abandoned Marine air base in Opa-Locka, Florida, in a suite of offices over a nursery. Wary of Haney almost as soon as he hired him, Wisner did not want his field commander going "in country." Haney was "too physically prepossessing," Wisner explained to Hobbing, who thought Wisner was looking for "any excuse" to keep Haney from blundering about Guatemala. The Berlin station chief, Henry Heckscher, was brought back and sent to Guatemala City disguised as a coffee buyer in a straw hat and dark glasses. He tried, without much success, to penetrate Arbenz's army and turn the officers against the president. He did manage to recruit one member of Arbenz's planning staff, who turned out to be a useful spy.[19]

The rebel "army" of 150 men was trained on one of General Somoza's Nicaraguan plantations by an American soldier of fortune, William "Rip" Robertson. Their commander—the "Liberator"—was a disaffected Guatemalan army officer, Carlos Castillo Armas. Robertson regarded his recruits as "tenth rate" and sarcastically told Hobbing that Armas "might make sergeant in the American army." Tracy Barnes had his doubts about Armas, whom he called a "bold but incompetent man." But he tried to put a brave face on Armas's rag-tag soldiers, calling them "the hornets."

Before the hornets could be set loose, the United States needed some justification to make clear to the world and the Guatemalans that Arbenz was a communist figurehead. The CIA tried to contrive evidence by planting caches of weapons, fraudulently stamped with the Soviet hammer and sickle, along the Guatemalan coast. The discovery does not seem to have caused much of a stir. But then Arbenz played into Washington's hands.

In January, according to the agency's secret history of the operation, a Panamanian double agent revealed the CIA plot to Arbenz. This betrayal might have blown the whole operation, but Arbenz overreacted. Precisely because he feared an attempt by "los Norteamericanos" to overthrow him, the Guatemalan president went shopping for communist reinforcements. Through his spy on Arbenz's staff, Heckscher learned that Arbenz had ordered an entire cargo of weapons from Czechoslovakia to be shipped from Poland aboard the freighter *Alfhem*. The CIA tracked the *Alfhem* all the way to the Guatemalan port of Puerto Barrios, where it docked in mid-May 1954. Wisner was angry that the United States Navy had failed to intercept the freighter, until he realized that the shipment of 2,000 tons of communist weaponry was just the excuse the United States needed to intervene.

Surreptitiously, Rip Robertson and a band of his hornets tried to stop the shipment before it reached Guatemala City. Their plan was to destroy a railroad trestle just as the Guatemalan freight train carrying the weapons rumbled across. With the kind of bad timing that seemed to dog these early CIA paramilitary operations, the dynamite did not explode; a downpour had drenched the fuses.[20]

It did not really matter; the weapons were of limited use to Arbenz. The World War II–vintage machine guns did not work and the antitank weapons had no utility in a region that had no tanks. But they gave the State Department cause to fulminate. The American ambassador to Guatemala, John E. "Jack" Peurifoy, had been handpicked by Wisner to work with the CIA. A flamboyant figure who paraded around the embassy in a jumpsuit with a shoulder holster, sporting a green Borsalino hat with a feather on his head, Peurifoy was not a typical striped-pants diplomat. "I picked him up off the beach," Wisner joked to his colleagues. Peurifoy demanded an audience with Arbenz and cabled home that if the Guatemala leader was not actually a communist, "he'll do until one comes along." The White House denounced Guatemala as a Soviet bastion and the Pentagon shipped fifty tons of small arms to the exile "army" of Castillo Armas.[21]

The American press played along with this charade. They simply ignored Arbenz's cry that the CIA was plotting against him. Most reporters accepted uncritically whatever American officials told them, and if they didn't, their editors did. Dispatches from *Time* magazine reporters in Guatemala, generally sympathetic to Arbenz, were rewritten at the magazine's editorial offices in New York to take a hard line against the Guatemalan government. The editor in chief of Time Inc., Henry Luce, was a friend of Allen Dulles, and the reporters strongly suspected government intervention. The most naked—and successful—attempt to control the press came at the *New York Times*. The dispatches of Sydney Gruson, the *Times* man in Mexico City, seemed overly influenced by the Guatemalan foreign minister. Since the *Times* reporter was taking the wrong line, Wisner suggested to Dulles that the CIA try to silence Gruson. As a "left-leaning" émigré who traveled on a British passport issued in Warsaw, Gruson was a "security risk," Wisner argued. The necessary phone calls were made, and as a patriotic gesture *New York Times* publisher Arthur Hays Sulzberger ordered Gruson to stay out of Guatemala—just as Gruson was about to launch an investigation of Armas's army.[22]

Wisner was able to control the press, but within his own organization, he faced a small civil war. Wisner and Dulles had decided to cut out the Latin American division chief, J. C. King, from active participation in the operation. They felt that King was too closely allied with United Fruit. Jealous and put out, King insisted to Wisner that Al Haney, the ground commander, was trying to start a "Korean War right at our doorstep." Haney, in turn, bitterly resented King's meddling. "We were an agency divided against itself," recalled Haney. Wisner sided with Haney in this dispute, but he, too, worried that Haney was taking excessive risks.

To make peace—and partly to keep an eye on Haney—Wisner sent Tracy Barnes to Opa-Locka to act as "headquarters liaison." To Haney's deputy, Enno Hobbing, it seemed as if Haney resented Barnes's presence, at least at first. "Haney tried to bully Tracy, but Tracy was very civilized. When browbeaten, he would just smile and look attentive," Hobbing recalled. Haney soon came to welcome Barnes's soothing presence, however. "He was the last of the old-school gentlemen, through and through," Haney said. The feuding between Opa-Locka and headquarters stopped. "Tracy was a calming influence. He came in and chatted everyone up," said E. Howard Hunt.[23]

Barnes was accompanied on the trip to Opa-Locka by his old schoolmate, now his CIA colleague, Richard Bissell. In his role as a special assistant to Allen Dulles, Bissell had been dispatched as a kind of "eyes and ears" for the director, to report back to Washington on how this bold and highly sensitive operation was progressing. Bissell was thoroughly impressed. He later recalled that both he and Barnes admired Haney's operation. Neither of them had ever been in a military headquarters on the eve of battle, and their experience with paramilitary operations was entirely theoretical. Here, in a dusty old barracks, determined men moved swiftly, impressive maps and a forty-foot chart lined the walls, phones rang, telexes chattered—it all looked to Bissell and Barnes like a smoothly run, crisply efficient organization.

Wisner, on the other hand, emerges in the CIA's still-secret in-house history of the Guatemala operation as full of doubts. He had initially opposed the creation of a CIA-backed rebel air force—even threatening to resign—for fear that it would blow the agency's cover. In January, after the Panamanian double agent informed Arbenz of the CIA plot, Wisner considered aborting the operation, but Dulles decided that the agency was already committed. In April the agency discovered electronic bugs "similar to the jobs the Russians used"—including a microphone in the chandelier—in the U.S. embassy in Guatemala City. On April 28, Wisner wrote a memo to file, stating that the operation "appears to be rather naked. . . . Several categories of people—hostile, friendly, and 'neutral'—either know or suspect or believe that the U.S. is directly behind this one and, assuming it proceeds to a conclusion, will be able to tell a convincing story." To try to "quiet" the operation, Wisner briefly suspended "black" flights of arms and material to the rebel army.

Bissell was puzzled—both at the time and as he recalled it years later—by Wisner's restless unease. Bissell regarded Wisner as a bold activist, a believer in covert action. Yet he found Wisner surprisingly edgy about his gung-ho field commander. Bissell wasn't exactly sure why. Perhaps it was Wisner's inability to delegate, his feeling that he needed to control every detail, that made him uneasy. Bissell also thought Wisner was overconcerned about leaks. Perhaps, Bissell thought in retrospect, Wisner's agitation could be explained by his incipient mania, which came out under stress. Another explanation—one never really considered by Bissell—was that Wisner was being prudent. He had been burned by painful experience with his failed operations in the East Bloc. It is likely that Wisner looked at Guatemala and saw the shadow of Albania—and Kim Philby.

Bissell and Barnes had no such experience with failure. To them the Guatemala operation was impressive, even thrilling. The two men liked it so much they tried to replicate it six years later in setting up Operation ZAPATA, better known as the Bay of Pigs.[24]

Barnes's diplomacy and Bissell's positive reports helped reassure the decision makers in Washington. On June 15, President Eisenhower authorized the CIA to launch Operation PBSUCCESS, as the attack on Arbenz was called. "I want you all to be damn good and sure you succeed," the president told Allen Dulles. "When you commit the flag, you commit it to win." On June 18, Castillo Armas, dressed in a check shirt and driving his command vehicle, a beat-up old station wagon, pushed across the Guatemalan border with about two hundred hornets, whom Armas had met for the first time a week before. Their aim was to capture Zacapa, a rail junction, and Puerto Barrios, the main port. The invasion got about six miles and stopped without firing a shot.

Barnes's air force went into action. Jerry DeLarm, the former skywriter who was now code-named Rosebinda, dropped leaflets heralding the coming liberation over Guatemala City. A Cessna dropped hand grenades and Coke bottles filled with gasoline out the window over Puerto Barrios, making loud bangs but causing no real damage. Two other planes were shot up by small-arms fire, and another pilot, sent to strafe the city of Cobán, ran out of gas while still airborne. He crash-landed just over the Guatemalan border in Mexico. A pilot sent to knock out the government's radio station blew up the transmitter of some American evangelical missionaries by mistake. In Guatemala City, the CIA's chief of station sent a cable describing the bombing as "pathetic." The Guatemalan people did not rise up.[25]

In early June, Arbenz had cracked down on student dissenters, arresting 480 in the first two weeks. Tracy Barnes noted that the CIA's network of spies had "suffered losses" and suggested to Wisner that it be "reorganized." "But," notes the CIA's history of the operation, "there was nothing left to organize." Instead, Arbenz executed ringleaders, burying seventy-five dissidents in a mass grave. At agency headquarters in Washington and at Haney's base in Opa-Locka, optimism was fading quickly. Only Barnes, with his characteristic buoyancy, remained upbeat. Everyone else feared a disaster in the making. "We were all of us at our wits' end," recalled Bissell. "We talked about calling the whole thing off," said Hobbing. Haney begged Washington to send more airplanes. Wisner was nervous, unsure what to do. It was almost too late to keep the CIA's involvement a secret. James Reston was beginning to hint in the *New York Times* that Washington was behind the "invasion," and a sudden show of force, however thinly disguised, risked exposing the whole operation. Wisner decided to push ahead anyway. "He was almost fatalistic, amenable to putting the actions in motion and letting the cards fall as they may," Bissell recorded in his memoirs.

Allen Dulles, accompanied by Bissell, brought the request for more planes to President Eisenhower. He was opposed by an assistant secretary of state, Henry Holland, who brought an armload of law books to argue that the United States was violating a number of laws and treaties by its increasingly blatant intervention. These were American pilots, he said, bombing a neutral country. Eisenhower listened to Holland and asked Dulles what the odds were of success. Dulles responded that with the planes they were "about 20 percent"; without the planes, zero. The president gave Dulles the planes.

The former commander of the Allied invasion force at Normandy, accustomed as he was to the inflated promises of his fellow officers, appreciated Dulles's honesty. As Dulles left, the president told him, "Allen, the figure of 20 percent was persuasive. If you had told me the chances would be 90 percent, I would have had a much more difficult decision."[26]

Dulles had deputized Bissell to handle logistics for the operation. He knew about Bissell's facility at running the merchant shipping fleet in World War II. Bissell quickly found two war-surplus P-51s; as cover, the CIA gave $150,000 to Nicaragua's Somoza to buy the planes; he in turn leased them back for a dollar. Bissell worked feverishly as the operation headed for an uncertain climax. Fearful that Arbenz would move to crush Armas's tiny force, still sitting just inside the border, Bissell worked out a plan to rescue them with a sea lift and then land them at a different location. Bissell contacted his old wartime friends in the shipping industry to charter what Bissell later called "a few small disreputable ships."[27]

Before Bissell could stage this covert Dunkirk, however, events on the ground dramatically improved. The CIA's psywar experts would later take credit. David Phillips's radio station, the Voice of Liberation, had been broadcasting from "somewhere in Guatemala"—actually, Nicaragua and the roof of the American embassy in Guatemala City—calling on the people to rise up against their communist bosses. The broadcasts were not having much effect on the people, but they helped plant doubt in the conservative Guatemalan officer corps by warning that Arbenz planned to betray the army and arm the peasants. An air force colonel defected, and Phillips's men tried to persuade him to broadcast back an appeal to fellow officers to join him. The colonel refused. But he proceeded to get drunk with the American agents, who coaxed him into giving the speech he would have given. Secret tape recorders captured the fiery diatribe, which was broadcast the next day while the officer slept off his hangover. Worried about losing his tiny air force, Arbenz grounded it.

Once the invasion began, Voice of Liberation broadcast phony bulletins, breathlessly reporting pitched battles and heavy casualties. The CIA front used classic disinformation techniques to start rumors and spread fear. "It is not true that the waters of Lake Atitlán have been poisoned," began one broadcast. "At our command post here in the jungle we are unable to confirm or deny the report that Castillo Armas has an army of 5,000 men." Armas never had more than four hundred men, but the rumors, repeated often enough, took on a life of their own.

The psywar campaign was given credibility when Armas's men finally bestirred themselves to fight a small battle. On June 24 the rebel column dared to advance to Chiquimula, a small town near the border. There they engaged a garrison from the Guatemalan Army in a brief firefight. Richard Bissell later traced the turning point of the operation to the scene of a hospital train arriving in Guatemala City, bearing dozens of wounded soldiers from the front. The two new P-51s sent down by Washington went into action on a seventy-two-hour bombing spree. They didn't do much actual damage, but a large smoke bomb dropped on the parade ground of Fort Matamoros made it look as though the government was under siege. The locals began referring to the bombs as *sulfados* (laxatives) for the effect they were having on Guatemala's leaders. To shut the radio transmitters at the U.S. embassy, Arbenz ordered the power turned off, but the ensuing blackout just caused more panic. From Opa-Locka, Phillips ordered the Voice of Liberation to launch a "final big lie"—that two massive columns of rebel troops were advancing on Guatemala City.

In Washington, Wisner remained anxious. "I was aware of the stress that Frank felt," said Bissell, "though he kept it well concealed. He felt a great sense of tension, worried that it would fail. We all worried about the consequences of failure, the exposure, even though Latins expected us to get involved. Frank did not joke to lighten things up. He grilled the junior types, 'How are you going to keep this a secret? How are you going to do this without blowing U.S. support wide open?' " Wisner was enraged when Rip Robertson, acting on his own authority, sank a British freighter on June 27 by dropping a 500-pound bomb down its smokestack (Robertson mistakenly thought the freighter was delivering fuel to Arbenz for his trucks and planes; this "subincident," as Bissell described it, cost American taxpayers $1.5 million to repay). "Frank was an activist," said Bissell, "but he believed in stern discipline and no freelancing." Bissell himself was not optimistic about the prospects for Operation Success, putting the odds at less than even.

But then Arbenz panicked. The Guatemalan president was exhausted and drinking heavily. He was convinced that if he suppressed the rebel invasion, a greater invasion beckoned—by U.S. Marines. On June 25 he had ordered the distribution of weapons to "the people's organizations and the political parties." This was anathema to the conservative officer corps, whose loyalty was already shaky. As Piero Gleijeses has pointed out, the Guatemalan officers were not so afraid of the small rebel army—or the CIA's radio broadcasts and tiny air force—as they were of Uncle Sam moving in with a full-scale invasion. Pressured by his officers, Arbenz agreed on the evening of June 27 to step aside for a military junta.[28]

The news caught the CIA by "surprise," said Bissell. "We thought we'd lost," said Phillips. In the "war room" inside the CIA's L Building on the Reflecting Pool a few hundred yards from the Lincoln Memorial, glasses were raised and cheering broke out as Arbenz tearfully announced his resignation over the government radio that Sunday night. There was still some cleanup work to be done in Guatemala City, however. The CIA had planned to install Colonel Elfegio Monzón as the caretaker president of Guatemala until Armas could make his triumphant procession into the capital. Ambassador Peurifoy called Monzón his "tame pup"; he had been recruited by the CIA's Guatemala station chief, John Doherty, in the least subtle way: Doherty had knocked on his door one morning and announced, "I'm the CIA's chief of station. I want to talk to you." After Arbenz resigned, Monzón lost his nerve and agreed to serve in a junta under Army Chief of Staff Colonel Carlos Enrique Díaz. The CIA was furious. "We've been double crossed. BOMB!" Enno Hobbing cabled Washington.

Jerry DeLarm took off in a P-47 and dropped two loud bombs on the Fort Matamoros parade ground. Hobbing and Doherty paid a visit to the new junta. When Díaz started arguing about the merits of Arbenz's social reforms, Hobbing was blunt: "Wait a minute, Colonel," he interrupted. "Let me explain something to you. You made a big mistake when you took over the government." He paused for a moment. "Colonel, you're just not convenient for the requirements of American foreign policy." Díaz, who had been nicknamed "the Sad Chicken" by his troops, stammered, "I talked to your ambassador. He gave me his approval."

"Well, Colonel," Hobbing said, "there is diplomacy and then there is reality. Our ambassador represents diplomacy. I represent reality. And the reality is that we don't want you."

Over the next eleven days, five provisional governments formed (Monzón set the record by appearing in four of them) before Castillo Armas took over, with Washington's blessing. The "Liberator" was greeted by 150,000 people in Guatemala City, shooting off firecrackers that had been distributed through the crowd by the CIA.[29]

In Washington on July 4 weekend, John Foster Dulles went on national radio to proclaim "a new and glorious chapter" in the history of the Western Hemisphere. The press played right along. The *New York Times* judiciously noted that the United States had supplied "moral support" to Armas just as Moscow provided "moral support" to Arbenz. With classic newsmagazine equivocation, *Newsweek* wrote: "The United States, aside from whatever gumshoe work the Central Intelligence Agency may or may not have been busy with, had kept strictly hands off." *The New Republic* coyly noted: "It was just our luck that Castillo Armas did come by some second-hand lethal weapons from Heaven knows where."[30]

At the CIA, Dulles and Barnes were giddy, "exuberant," recalled Tom Braden. "Allen was very Rooseveltian. He'd say, 'Bully! Bully! We did it!' He gave Tracy a lot of the credit." Others, like Jake Esterline, the Washington war room chief, credited Wisner with his persistence and attention to detail. Wisner permitted himself a momentary sigh of relief. The operation, he cabled his men in the field, "surpassed even our greatest expectations." Yes, there had been rocky times, but boldness had paid off. The odds were always long in covert action. But the CIA had pulled off an operation that was beyond the ken of the State Department and the Pentagon. At a cost of less than $20 million, the CIA had driven communism back into the sea in the Western Hemisphere. Gratified and proud, President Eisenhower summoned the CIA men of Operation Success for a formal briefing at the White House, with slides and charts. "How many men did Castillo Armas lose?" Eisenhower asked. The answer was "only one." Dave Phillips watched as Eisenhower shook his head, remembering, perhaps, the thousands killed at D-Day. "Incredible," said the president.[31]

Tracy Barnes's wife was sitting at home after the briefing when her husband and Frank Wisner burst in. Barnes generally did not discuss his work at home, but he could not resist telling Janet about the Guatemala operation. "Wiz and Tracy were very pleased," she recalled. "They did a little scuffling dance and said, 'We've been to see the Prexy, and it was great!' "

Wisner was more subdued back at the office. "For at least a few weeks after, I noticed that Frank was watching and worrying," said Bissell. "He couldn't let go. He was still worrying that something would blow the U.S. role." The more carefree spirits, however, were already creating myths. Dulles, who liked to extol the virtues of his secret agency in the public prints, fed an article entitled "America's Secret Agents: The Mysterious Doings of the CIA" to the *Saturday Evening Post*. Printed in October, three months after the coup, it offered a glowing and sanitized version of the agency's role.[32]

The war stories began to circulate; the memory of the mistakes began to fade. Phillips regaled agency hands with his brilliant disinformation campaign on the Voice of Liberation. Understandably proud of his role, Haney prepared a dramatic account of the coup for President Eisenhower. ("Al," said Dulles after hearing Haney rehearse it, "I've never heard such crap.") Tracy Barnes recounted how the agency's pet colonel, Monzón, had been dead drunk when the time came for him to assume power; a CIA man had to hold him up in the shower.[33]

This theme, of the hapless Third World stooge being supported —literally—at the critical moment by a cool and all-knowing CIA man was becoming a staple of agency folklore. The Colonel Monzón of the Iranian coup had been General Fazlollah Zahedi. Howard "Rocky" Stone, one of Kim Roosevelt's young operatives and later a legendary figure at the agency, told the story of how he had to button Zahedi's uniform collar on the morning of that successful coup. Zahedi had been too nervous to dress himself. "We're in! We're in!" Zahedi exclaimed to Stone after the coup had made him prime minister. "What do we do now?" Stone went on to another Third World country where he recruited an agent who "happened to be the next prime minister." On the morning after the man's election, Stone was sitting on his bed, shaking him awake. "Come on," commanded the CIA station chief of the hungover prime minister, "we've got a lot of work to do."[34]

These tales were good for esprit, and true enough. But they contained dangerous illusions. The lesson of Guatemala to Richard Bissell was that a Central American strongman can be frightened out of power by the mere thought of American intervention. Bissell later contrasted the way things looked to the CIA with the way they must have looked to Arbenz during the invasion. At the agency, officials fretted over the obstacles to success—just a few planes and some sullen exiles to work with, botched assignments and missed communications, freelancing troublemakers like Rip Robertson. Yet Arbenz, as he drank alone at the presidential palace in Guatemala City and listened to the sound of exploding *sulfados* outside, apparently was seized with doom, fearful that he was about to be crushed by "the government of the north." Lower-ranking officials had the same explanation for the agency's miraculous success. "It should have been a fiasco," said Hobbing, "except for the idiotic Latin attitude that gringos are all powerful."

The American press may have been lulled into playing down American involvement in Guatemala, but the Latins had no doubt. In the week Arbenz fell, there were Yankee-Go-Home riots in Argentina, Brazil, Chile, Colombia, Cuba, Honduras, Mexico, Panama, Peru, Uruguay, and Venezuela. At the time of the coup Cuba's Ernesto "Che" Guevara was in Guatemala studying Arbenz's social reforms. "It was Guatemala," his first wife said, "which finally convinced him of the necessity for armed struggle and for taking the initiative against imperialism." Guevara also learned a practical lesson: that it was necessary to purge the army of all conservatives. Arbenz's revolution failed because it had been too moderate.

For Guatemala, the coup ushered in several decades of repression. The "Liberator" canceled Arbenz's land reform, gave United Fruit back its holdings, banned "subversive" books like *Les Misérables*, and restored the secret police. José Linares, the police chief, gave electric baths to suspects and employed a skullcap designed to "pry loose secrets and crush improper thoughts." Exiled, Arbenz himself died of drugs and alcohol in Mexico in 1971. A CIA official noted that "he was his own person, he was not a Soviet agent. He didn't go to the Soviet Union and become a colonel in the KGB."

In later years Barnes and Bissell would regret the outcome of the Guatemala coup. Bissell would blame "poor follow-up" by the White House and State Department. But in 1954, Operation Success ensured that their CIA careers would take off. For his role, Barnes was awarded the Distinguished Intelligence Medal, the agency's second-highest honor (the Distinguished Intelligence Cross is usually awarded posthumously), in a secret ceremony. "After Guatemala," said Janet Barnes Lawrence, "it was, 'You can have any job you want! You can own the world!' "[35]

Chapter Nine

THE SPY WAR

"Jesus Christ, it's been blown!"

TRACY BARNES'S REWARD was Germany: command of the CIA's largest and most important operations on the front line of the Cold War. By the time Barnes arrived at CIA headquarters in Frankfurt in November 1954, his predecessor, General Lucian Truscott, had cleaned up the most outrageous OPC operations and packed home the more amateur operators. Barnes's gentility would be welcome after Truscott, who was a commanding presence but abusive when he was drinking. During a last argument with Mike Burke, a flamboyant OPC operative who was leaving the agency, Truscott poured a pitcher of water over his head as the two men stood by the bar at a cocktail party—"to cool him off," Truscott explained.

Truscott strongly objected to the choice of Barnes as his successor running the German Mission. He regarded Barnes as a callow Ivy Leaguer who would be likely to undertake risky, insecure operations—just the kinds of projects that Truscott had spent the last three years trying to shut down. But Allen Dulles insisted on Barnes. "It was the mutual protection association," said Thomas Polgar, Truscott's top aide, who was, like his boss, suspicious of old-boy networks. "Dulles was partial to people of a certain social milieu."[1]

Although slimmed down from its Korean War peak, the CIA station that Barnes inherited was vast. There were over a thousand men and women working for the CIA in Germany in 1954. They were engaged in a daily spy versus spy war against the communists, with often frustrating results.

To the Western intelligence community, the East Bloc remained a void in the early 1950s. It is remarkable, given all the spying that went on, how little the West actually knew about its enemy. The SIS and CIA had little useful "signals intelligence" (electronic intercepts), no aerial photography of the Soviet Union, and no completely reliable agents behind the Iron Curtain. Lacking any hard information about either Soviet intentions or capabilities, the Joint Chiefs of Staff feared a surprise mass tank attack by the Soviet Union.

Under tremendous pressure to create some kind of early-warning system, the CIA and the British Secret Intelligence Service looked for a way to tap into Soviet communications. Once again it was the British who came up with the basic idea. In 1951 the British had successfully tunneled under and tapped Soviet telephone landlines in Vienna in a program called Operation Silver. In 1953 they proposed a grander variation—Operation Gold—in Berlin. An East German agent operated by the SIS had located a phone cable containing 350 lines between Berlin and Soviet military bases all over the East Bloc. The line lay only about two hundred yards inside the East Zone, underneath a highway running from a Soviet air base to the city proper. The British proposed digging a 500-yard tunnel—right underneath the feet of the East German border guards—to tap the line.

It was an enormous and expensive undertaking, costing about $20 million. The U.S. Corps of Engineers built a semi-underground warehouse that could accommodate 3,100 tons of dirt excavated—very quietly—by a secret team of diggers. The 1,476-foot tunnel was air-conditioned (so the heat from all machinery below would not melt the ice above) and lined with 125 tons of steel plates that had been sprayed with a rubber solution to keep them from clanking while under construction. To record the tapped phone lines required 600 tape recorders operating 1,200 hours a day using 800 reels of tape. To translate and process the "take" in Washington fifty CIA officers fluent in German and Russian worked in a prefab hut near Memorial Bridge called the "Hosiery Mill" because of the web of electronic cables snaking through it.

Intelligence analysts on the receiving end were underwhelmed with the fruits of all this labor. "Allen Dulles kept asking me, 'Is there anything interesting?' But there never was anything interesting," said Gordon Stewart, the chief of the "FI" (Foreign Intelligence) Staff. Nothing interesting, that is, in the sense of

Fraternities and Literary Societies of the University of Virginia 1931

Frank Wisner (*front row, center*) as captain of the University of Virginia track team. At the CIA, Wisner's men admired his energy, deferred to his power, and laughed at his long and often ribald stories. But they were worn out by him.

Courtesy of the Wisner family

Courtesy of the Wisner family

At her salon in Georgetown, Polly Wisner entertained top officials and her own social set of diplomats, spies, and journalists.

Wisner aboard Bissell's yawl, the *Sea Witch*. Wisner created America's covert action arm after World War II; his war against the KGB was a highly personal crusade.

Courtesy of the Wisner family

Wisner as station chief in London in 1960. Wisner was a manic-depressive whose energy masked his illness. His breaking point was the failure of the Hungarian Revolution in 1956.

Courtesy of the FitzGerald family

Enlisting as a thirty-one-year-old private, Desmond FitzGerald longed for combat in World War II. He learned how to eat monkey brains fighting with the Chinese in Burma. As the CIA's top spymaster for the Far East, he later ran secret armies in Tibet and Laos.

Courtesy of the FitzGerald family

FitzGerald married Marietta Peabody in 1939 (they were divorced after the war). He had "the imagination and dash," said a CIA colleague, "of a Renaissance soldier of fortune."

In 1948 FitzGerald married Barbara Lawrence. Although he could be stuffy, he had a great sense of curiosity and whimsy; he often quoted *Alice's Adventures in Wonderland* at CIA staff meetings.

Courtesy of the FitzGerald family

FitzGerald brought esprit and high standards to the clandestine service. He wanted his spies to be at once intellectual and macho. His idea of perfection, said one of his case officers, was a Harvard Ph.D. who could handle himself in a bar fight.

Courtesy of the FitzGerald family

Tracy Barnes won the Silver Star in World War II for a secret mission behind German lines. With his high cheekbones and royal nose, he looked to one daughter "like Sitting Bull."

Courtesy of the Barnes family

Janet and Tracy Barnes were the most glamorous couple on the Yale campus in 1932.

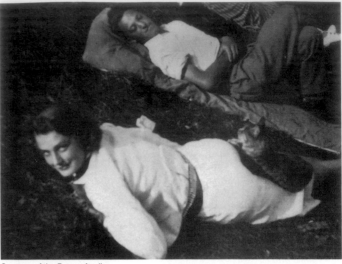

Courtesy of the Barnes family

Barnes escorts his daughter Jane at her debut in the late fifties. A natural athlete, Tracy did not walk; he glided.

Barnes's official CIA portrait, taken after the Bay of Pigs in 1961. Once the agency's "Golden Boy," and the favorite of Director Allen Dulles after the Guatemala coup, he fell from favor and was dismissed in 1966.

Courtesy of the Barnes family

Central Intelligence Agency

Richard Bissell was regarded as the smartest man in Washington, the true brains behind the Marshall Plan and the creator of the U-2 spy plane. But he had no knowledge of spy trade craft and little experience with covert action when he became the CIA's top spymaster in 1959.

Courtesy of the Bissell family

Courtesy of the Bissell family

Bissell's mother, Marie, was a society rebel who taught Bissell perfect manners and a love of risk.

Bissell launched the CIA on a campaign of assassination. In 1960, he hired the Mafia to try to "eliminate" Fidel Castro.

Courtesy of the Bissell family

Courtesy of the White House

Bissell was awarded the Medal of Freedom in 1961 by President John F. Kennedy. Kennedy had already fired Bissell for his role in the Bay of Pigs. The President could not understand how someone so smart had led him to do something "so stupid." The debacle overshadowed his earlier triumph with the U-2 spy plane.

learning about some imminent secret Russian move against the West. The CIA did learn that the Soviets were not preparing to attack. In this anxious era, when the American military establishment believed that Russian tanks were ready to roll, no news was good news. In fact, the Kremlin couldn't attack even if it wanted to: information picked up by the taps revealed the chaotic state of the East German rail system—necessary to any massed Soviet assault against the West.[2]

The tunnel was finished in February 1955, three months after Barnes arrived in Germany. It was exposed by the Russians a little over a year later. Barnes was in Switzerland with Janet and one of his operatives, Jim Critchfield, when word reached him that Russian soldiers had broken in through the roof, sending the agency's listeners scurrying down the tube to safety. At 3 A.M. on April 22, 1956, Barnes knocked on Critchfield's hotel room door. "Jesus Christ, it's been blown!" Barnes said. "Tracy was wild," recalled Janet Barnes Lawrence. "He woke me and said, 'This is serious' and roared off to Bonn to tell the ambassador," who had been kept in the dark about the operation. Barnes, who refused to use a chauffeur because he liked to drive fast, drove his Mercedes over a hundred miles an hour down the autobahn to the West German capital. The American ambassador, James Bryant Conant, told Barnes, "I like cops and robbers, but I don't like getting caught."[3]

At first, the discovery of the tunnel was regarded as a terrible blow. But it turned out to be a public relations coup for the West. On May 1 the *Washington Post* ran an editorial entitled "The Tunnel of Love," which hailed "Yankee ingenuity" and saw the whole exercise as a tremendous morale boost to the West Germans, who were hungry for any signs of fighting back against Moscow. WONDERFUL TUNNEL was the headline in *Time*. CIA officers who claimed to know nothing about the tunnel were greeted with winks, guffaws, and slaps on the back.[4]

The Russians appeared to have stumbled on the tunnel by chance while making routine repairs on the phone line. It is likely, however, that they were tipped off to its existence by yet another Soviet mole in the SIS, George Blake, who had served as notetaker at planning sessions for the tunnel in London. There is a dispute in the intelligence community over why the Russians waited a year to blow the operation. The Kremlin may have been perfectly happy to overwhelm the West with relatively useless information—indeed, it took the CIA over two years to catch up with the backlog of tapes flooding the "Hosiery Mill." More likely, the KGB did not want to risk exposing Blake's cover, preferring to save him for greater things.[5]

As station chief for all Germany, Barnes was not directly involved in carrying out operations, which were run by base chiefs and case officers. But he presided eagerly over his empire, touring the agency's various outposts, reviewing plans, and trying to offer advice.

He was not always listened to. Barnes had little professional experience with espionage, and he was not temperamentally well suited for it. His closest friends in intelligence, though they loved and admired Barnes, saw a basic blind spot. "He was gallant, cavalier, relaxed, imaginative, a charmer without effort," said John Bruce Lockhart, who worked with Barnes as SIS liaison in Washington and then as head of SIS European operations. But Barnes "didn't really understand" what Lockhart called "Secrets," with a capital "S." "He disliked the mastery of detail, the inevitable period of quietly waiting, the maintaining of careful records, the imposition of irritatingly strict security discipline—all of which are alas part of secret operations."

Barnes's CIA colleagues in Germany spotted his weaknesses right away. "Tracy was awful with secret documents. He needed a keeper. He was a candidate for real disaster," said Jim Critchfield, the CIA base chief in Pullach. Barnes was regarded as warm and genial, good at his liaison role with the ambassador, the military, and the German government, but gullible and a virgin at tradecraft. "Nobody got mad at Tracy, but some people made fun of him," said Peter Jessup, a case officer.

The fact that Allen Dulles seemed to dote on Barnes was a source of embarrassment. At a meeting of all European station chiefs in the winter of 1955, Dulles announced that he had some "good news." He had gone to the budget office and wrangled bonuses for the most deserving officials. "The first person to get one," Dulles proudly declared, "is C. Tracy Barnes." The others watched as Barnes "practically slid under the table," said Bill Hood, a senior operative in Vienna.[6]

Barnes's antithesis was William Harvey, the head of the Berlin operations base. As well as having a drinking problem, Harvey was short, fat, and hideous looking; he had bulging eyes, attributed to a thyroid condition, and a froglike voice. His agents called him "the Pear." Harvey was a memorably bizarre figure, out of place in any kind of normal world yet at home among double agents. He serves as a kind of template against which to measure Barnes, if only to show that Barnes, so pleasing and genial in most circumstances, was equally out of place in Harvey's world, the secret spy war of the 1950s.

Postwar Berlin was a natural habitat for Harvey. Divided into zones of occupation by the Russians, Americans, British, and French, Berlin in the mid-1950s was called "kidnap town" by members of its large spy population. In his book *Wilderness of Mirrors*, David Martin describes a typical abduction, telling how Dr. Walter Linse, director of a CIA-financed organization that collected intelligence from an underground network of laborers in East Germany, was "wrestled into a taxicab one morning [in 1953] as he emerged from his apartment. Police gave chase as the taxi sped toward the Soviet sector, guns blazing. Linse was never seen again—one of the two-score kidnappings that occurred in Berlin over a two-year period."

Berlin was "a cowboy business," said Tom Parrott, the agency's base chief in Frankfurt in the mid-1950s. "Everyone was a spy and the spies were spying for everyone." William Harvey seemed to delight in the fact that he could trust no one. The walls of his office, writes Martin, "were lined with racks of firearms, and a thermite bomb perched atop each safe, ready for emergency destruction of files in the event of a Russian invasion." Harvey kept three or four firearms in his desk and two on his body at all times. He refused to check them in restaurants or embassies. "Look," he'd say, flashing a pearl-handled revolver in his sweat-stained armpit, "when you need 'em, you need em in a hurry."[7]

Harvey was to many of his colleagues an outsized, if slightly ridiculous figure, a source of constant awe as well as the butt of occasional humor. He claimed to never go a day without "having" a woman. According to a probably apocryphal story, one of Joe Bryan's merry men on the psywar staff, looking into a window one day, spotted Harvey having his way with his secretary on a desktop. The prankster picked up the phone and dialed Harvey's number. Still rutting, Harvey picked up the receiver. "This is God," said the psywar operative. "Aren't you ashamed?" Lunch at Harvey's house, a fortresslike white stucco villa in a Berlin suburb, was served at 4 P.M.; guests were invited at noon and fed martinis until they "were plastered," said Parrott. "We called it trial by firewater."[8]

The combat veterans from World War II rolled their eyes at Harvey's gun play. Parrott was drinking in a beer hall with Harvey when the waitress approached and politely inquired, "Sir, I believe this belongs to you?" She handed him a pistol that had fallen out of his pants onto the floor. "He didn't need a gun. It was all nonsense," said Parrott, given the unwritten agreement between the CIA and KGB not to kill each other's spies.

But Harvey was a very competent spymaster. "He was an incredibly good case officer," said Carleton Swift. "He was disciplined and superb at making ops. He thought out every detail." Familiar with sin, he understood temptation and planned accordingly. He insisted that the cleaning ladies in the CIA's safe houses be old and ugly so they wouldn't sleep with the agents and betray them to the Russians. Harvey was street-smart in a way that Tracy Barnes could never be. Among his agents in Berlin were a string of prostitutes. "The Groton guys wouldn't have been able to do that," said Swift. A former FBI agent, Harvey had figured out that Philby was a Soviet agent while the CIA men were still inviting the British SIS man to lunch at the Metropolitan Club.[9]

The son of a small town lawyer in Indiana, Harvey was "anti-elitist," said Swift. He disliked and resented the Ivy Leaguers in the agency. "He ruined several people's careers just because they were polite Yale boys," said Parrott. Harvey had developed a theory to explain why wellborn men like Kim Philby and Alger Hiss betrayed their country. "He believed that the elite had a guilty conscience," said Swift. "Guilt was the upper-class pathology. Actually, he was envious as hell. He wanted to be part of the establishment. He knew he wasn't, so he hated it."

Barnes touched off all of these conflicting feelings in Harvey. "To his face, Harvey would suck up to him," said Parrott. "Behind his back, he'd say what the hell good is he? Just a Yale boy."

Barnes, who was proud of Harvey and his ilk and fascinated by them, chose not to hear the whispering behind his back. "Isn't he a sweet guy?" he'd say about Jim Critchfield, who also regarded Barnes as sweet—but incompetent. Barnes knew that he was a source of resentment. "Tracy was not popular with the troops," said his wife, Janet. "He was a surprise to these people. He was not a company man. They were thugs. I asked Tracy, 'What are these people doing here?' Tracy said, 'Well, no one else will do these jobs.'"

Barnes wasn't quite sure what to make of Harvey. Before he

became station chief, he went on an inspection tour of Berlin with Frank Wisner. Harvey drove them to see the Lord Mayor of West Berlin. Sitting behind the wheel of his armor-plated Cadillac, Harvey told an aide, "Finger the turns," an old FBI expression meaning "point the way." This was the source of sophomoric punning between Barnes and Wisner. "Don't forget to finger the terns," Barnes wrote Wisner. "Or to goose the gulls." Both Wisner and Barnes had a scatological turn of humor that they used to be one of the fellows and sometimes to make fun of them. "Tracy was a little snotty about the gumshoes," said his secretary, Alice McIl-vaine.[10]

At some level Barnes may have understood that he was miscast in the world of espionage, although he could only vaguely articulate his disquiet. During a long Sunday afternoon spent drinking with Tom Parrott in Frankfurt, he seemed to grow moody and introspective. He told Parrott that he wasn't sure what he was—"an operator" or a "philosopher." Parrott did not know what to make of this statement, which Barnes just left hanging. Barnes, who could be maddeningly obscure beneath all the charm, may not have wanted to push this line of thinking, which could have led him to the conclusion that he was neither an operator nor a philosopher.

One of Barnes's stranger evenings of vinous soul-searching came with Critchfield, a South Dakota farm boy and a tough combat veteran of World War II. Drinking in Munich one night, Barnes and Critchfield explored the "culture gap" between them, and then Barnes turned to "self-analysis." He told Critchfield a version of his OSS drop into France that did not much resemble the citation for his Silver Star. After parachuting into Brittany, Barnes told Critchfield, he had been hidden in the attic of a house by the French underground. When an American armored division was heard rumbling toward the town, the German garrison troops fled. Barnes emerged from his hiding place and shot one old soldier in the back with his carbine—an "overage first sergeant." According to Critchfield, Barnes "felt low about it." There was no mention of the mercy killing of the wounded German officers. "I didn't have the feeling I was getting the whole story, he was so modest," said Critchfield. "If he killed fifty SS storm troopers, you wouldn't know about it. He offered this story in contrast to me—to my real combat experience. He was all self-deprecation, self-mocking, 'Let me tell you how I killed a German.' "

Barnes's self-deprecation, while part of the gentlemanly code, could be so extreme that one wonders if it didn't reveal something more than well-mannered modesty. Barnes could be oddly downbeat, even as he projected serene self-confidence. This was true of his view of the world at large as well as his self-image. In his occasional trips to Munich, Barnes became friends with Mary Cutler, an attractive woman working for the U.S. State Department who came from a good Boston family and whose uncle Robert Cutler was President Eisenhower's national security adviser. Cutler was charmed by this "swashbuckler macho man" but a little surprised to hear how gloomy he was about the fate of the world. "He thought evil would triumph over good," she said. "He was getting to the point where he thought people were no damn good."

Barnes's experience with the maquis in France had introduced him to the moral vagaries of war. He got a refresher course supervising spies in the secret war. At the CIA base in Frankfurt, Barnes had to deal with a case of torture by American agents. The Swedes had given the Frankfurt base a pair of Estonian defectors, a man and his wife. The woman confessed to being a Soviet spy but later recanted and said she had confessed under duress. In Washington, the counterintelligence staff sent over a specialist to get the truth out of the two Estonians. The woman was made to strip down and testify in her slip. The man was forced into a steaming bath, where liniment was poured on his testicles. Screaming in pain, he ripped a bath fixture right out of the wall.[11]

Pressed by some outraged subordinates, Barnes finally stepped in and put a stop to the inquisition. "He was a fairly moral guy," said Parrott. But it was hard to know where morality fit in for a CIA chief of station, or even what the word really meant in the context of the Cold War. The Russians do it, so we must too. That was the code that men like Bill Harvey lived by. It was even enshrined in a secret study evaluating the agency's covert activities, the Doolittle Report, commissioned by President Eisenhower in the summer of 1954:

> It is now clear that we are facing an implacable enemy whose avowed objective is world domination by whatever means and at whatever cost. There are no rules in such a game. Hitherto acceptable norms of human conduct do not apply. If the United States is to survive, long-standing American concepts of "fair-play" must be reconsidered. We must develop effective espionage and counterespionage services and must learn to subvert, sabotage and destroy our enemies by more

clever, more sophisticated and more effective methods than those used against us.[12]

Barnes subscribed to this hard-nosed theory in principle, but he sometimes had trouble putting it into practice. He was torn between his deeply ingrained sense of "fair play" and his equally deep belief in the cause he was engaged in. Because the rhetoric of the day, like that employed by the drafters of the Doolittle Report, was so lurid, it is tempting not to take it very seriously. "Global domination" starts to sound like a quaint paranoia, especially considering the shambles that the Soviet Union became. It is true that political leaders hyped the Red Menace to get elected or wring more money out of Congress for the military-industrial complex. But for men like Barnes who actually had to "do battle" with the KGB on a day-to-day basis, the threat did not seem at all contrived. "Every morning," said Janet Barnes Lawrence, "Tracy got up and went to war." Because it is necessarily secretive and insular, the world of intelligence can become a kind of echo chamber in which the sounds are amplified and made more frightening. A small incident, recounted by his daughter Jane, is revealing, and of a piece with the gloom Barnes showed to Mary Cutler. On the morning of March 6, 1953, young Jane, then in her early teens, saw a huge headline in the paper announcing STALIN DEAD! She raced up the stairs to find her father toiling away on an exercise bicycle. "Daddy, Daddy, Stalin's dead!" cried Jane. Barnes barely looked up. He, of course, already knew the Kremlin leader was dead. His only response was, "Maybe we'll get someone worse." Jane was chilled by the scene. "I could see," she said, "that his thankless work was the most important thing on earth."[13]

IF BARNES felt passionately about the Russian threat, Frank Wisner felt even more so. It was not an abstraction to him. He had seen the boxcars roll out of Bucharest and heard the cries of innocent people being carried off to Stalin's labor camps in 1945. The setbacks experienced by OPC had not dimmed that picture. In 1956 he felt more strongly than ever an obligation—not just a national duty but a personal obligation—to liberate those people enslaved by communism.

Wisner was not wholly unrealistic about the chances for "rollback." He had refused to hand out weapons to the rioting East

Berliners in 1953, lest the bloodshed be worsened. He understood that many of the operations begun in haste and innocence by OPC needed to be scaled down or junked. Indeed, he was surprised to find some of those operations still in place in the mid-1950s, long after their usefulness had been called into question. In 1955, as he flipped through a sheaf of status reports at a meeting of European station chiefs in Vienna, Wisner remarked, "For Christ sakes, will you look at these things we started as emergency, temporary ops and then got stuck with?"[14]

There was one operation, however, that Wisner wished to keep alive. In the towns around the old postwar displaced persons (DP) camps in Germany lived a corps of East European émigrés who had volunteered to serve as a secret CIA paramilitary force. The idea, which Wisner conceived even before the creation of the OPC, was to use the émigrés to infiltrate Eastern Europe if and when the day of liberation came. This émigré army was to be the shock force of revolution.

By the mid-1950s, it was a pretty seedy group. Some of the refugees still served as guards imprisoning Nazis who had been convicted of war crimes. This was a rough, if undisciplined bunch. One doctor treating a company of Albanian prison guards told the CIA's Peter Jessup that he had never before seen 130 cases of VD in 100 men. But more of the troops had drifted into civilian life and lost whatever martial bearing they once had. John Mapother, a CIA officer based in Vienna, saw them hanging around the PXs of military bases in Germany. "I figured if the balloon went up, they'd knock off the cash register and head for Paris," he recalled. Another CIA official looking into the files of a paramilitary group in Frankfurt about 1956 found that the men were "perfectly decent enthusiasts, but they all had wives and kids and jobs at the local garage. It wasn't a paramilitary group at all. It was a social club." Even so, as chief of station in Germany, Tracy Barnes tried to keep the paramilitary groups going. "He still believed in rollback," said Critchfield. "There was no gap between Tracy and Wiz. Tracy tried to keep the émigré force alive while he was in Germany."[15]

The day when it might actually be needed seemed to draw a little closer in the winter of 1956. In Moscow, Nikita Khrushchev, the new Kremlin boss, gave a secret speech to the Twentieth Party Congress denouncing the crimes of Stalinism. Allen Dulles was very eager to get the full text of the speech. Its propaganda potential was immense: here was the head of the Communist Party decrying the excesses of communism. Frank Wisner exhorted his operatives to spare no effort to secure a copy of the speech, and within two months they produced one.[16]

Wisner did not wish to simply release the speech. He wanted to "exploit" it—to feed it out slowly, piecemeal, perhaps salted with disinformation, all through the East Bloc. He reasoned, correctly, that the speech would stir unrest among the captives of the "slave states," but he wanted to be able to control the timing and, if possible, the degree and nature of the unrest. The CIA's Radio Free Europe, with a staff of 1,400, had introduced "saturation broadcasting" to counter Soviet jamming techniques. It could be heard from Gdańsk to Sofia. Khrushchev's secret speech was the best sheet of music that Wisner had ever obtained for his Mighty Wurlitzer, and he wanted to play it at his own pace and in his own way.[17]

Dulles puffed on his pipe, listened to Wisner's arguments, and then rejected them. He released the entire speech to the *New York Times* on June 2. As predicted, rioting began. In Poznań, Poland, workers went on a militant strike on June 28 and forty-four were killed before it was suppressed. By October there was a state of political crisis throughout the East Bloc, stirred by a general ex- pectation that the Soviet Union would loosen its grip on the East Bloc as the Kremlin moderated Stalinism at home. This view, shared by Wisner, proved to be a dangerous illusion.[18]

Wisner had trouble accepting Dulles's decisions. His annual fit- ness reports, otherwise unblemished, noted that he was "oversen- sitive to criticism." Wisner was having increasing difficulty making it all look easy. He was still sociable, in a mannered, courtly way. Like the rest of his crowd, Wisner was comforted by his cocktails. "Oatsie," he said one evening to Oatsie Charles as he cradled his martini glass, "doesn't it just put its little hand in yours?" But as time went on, his gaiety seemed increasingly manic. "He would carry it on a little too far," said Jane Thompson, whose husband, Ambassador Llewellyn "Tommy" Thompson, was a Soviet expert and close friend of the Bohlens. "He would joke about the Venu- tians, little red-bearded people with long pointed fingers. It was just a beat too far."

Social life for Wisner was, as ever, work. "For Tracy Barnes, a party was a party," said Fisher Howe, a foreign service officer and social friend. "But for Wiz, it was, what can be achieved?" Some thought that Wisner never got over feeling like an outsider among the Groton-Yale-Harvard crowd.[19]

Wisner's insecurities were not merely or primarily social. The forces eating at him were much more profound in the early 1950s. Wisner had been trying to stand up against the communist threat before others knew there was such a threat—to create a spy network to combat the Kremlin when Tracy Barnes was footnoting railroad cases for his law firm and Des FitzGerald was trying to figure out how to legally wiretap the bosses of Tammany Hall. The strain of standing up to the communists was both relentless and deeply personal. Wisner had the feeling that he was fighting on a number of fronts, and that his rear guard was being constantly attacked. There were bureaucratic wars that made enemies out of the Pentagon and State, as well as bitter contests within the CIA. There was Philby's betrayal, particularly galling for an Anglophile. McCarthyism just ratcheted up the pressure in a way that was very uncomfortable for Wisner.

When Bohlen and Thayer had come under McCarthy's attack, Wisner made a public stand in their defense. While other government officials scrambled for cover, Wisner and his wife, Polly, took the opposite tack: they insisted that both Bohlen and Thayer stay at their house on P Street.[20] Within the Georgetown set, Wisner was hailed for his steadfastness. What few realized, however, was that he himself had become a target for blackmail.

Princess Caradja was McCarthy's weapon. After Wisner left Bucharest, she had divorced her husband, the wealthy brewer, and married an American pilot. When the communists forced the pilot to leave Romania in 1947, she followed him to Vienna a few months later. But at the American embassy there she was interrogated and accused of spying for the communists.* Her file was sent to Washington, where it made its way into the hands of J. Edgar Hoover. The FBI chief saw the potential to work mischief. Hoover hated Wisner, whom he regarded as a rival. Hoover would "just go into orbit" because Wisner's "gang of weirdos" was operating in the United States, an FBI veteran told author Mark Riebling. Hoover routinely fed raw intelligence files to McCarthy to fuel his witch-hunts. Now McCarthy and Hoover had a file they could use to try to threaten Wisner. How would it look if the head

---

* Caradja strongly denied the charge to the author in 1993.

of the CIA's clandestine service had had a wartime dalliance with a woman who had allegedly become a communist agent?

McCarthy and Hoover never went public with the file on Princess Caradja. Wisner had too many friends in the press, and the charges were flimsy, even by McCarthyite standards. On at least three occasions between 1952 and 1954, Hoover probed the agency, seeking new information on Wisner and Caradja, but Allen Dulles was steadfast in resisting. Wisner had been the subject of "vicious rumors" from Romanian émigrés, Dulles wrote Hoover on April 19, 1954, but he stood by an earlier "Eyes Only" report that the CIA's own investigation "discloses no association with Mr. Wisner since approximately 1945 nor any indication that he had any knowledge of espionage activities on the part of Tanda Caragea [Caragea is the original Romanian spelling]." Even so, the existence of such a file was a source of anxiety for a man already overburdened with cares. His wife, for one, would not want a scandal over her husband's wartime fling, and Wisner could never be sure what use Hoover would make of this indiscretion in the years ahead.[21]

Wisner's insecurities were compounded by the uneasy nature of his relationship with Allen Dulles. There was mutual respect among the old OSS comrades, but their styles and personalities were different. Dulles found Wisner dogmatic, excitable, and thin-skinned; Wisner felt that Dulles was a little careless and vain. Dulles was a PR man. Wisner preferred to operate in the shadows, while Dulles liked to see his picture in the papers. Dulles was, if anything, a worse administrator than Wisner, and he was constantly calling down the chain of command. Wisner hated being circumvented in this way. Wisner felt slighted in another way: he could see how much Dulles doted on his new recruits, Barnes and Bissell. Wisner did more work and had much more responsibility, but felt he earned less respect. Wisner was fond of Bissell and Barnes, but he could not help feeling a touch of envy and resentment.[22]

WISNER'S ONE refuge was his farm on the Eastern Shore of Maryland, about two and a half hours from Washington. He had always wanted a farm and had bought this one in 1947, in the little town of Galena, while he and Polly were still renting a house in Georgetown. As a suburbanite living outside New York in the 1930s, Wisner had owned a sheep, which he liked to talk to and feed cigarettes. On his farm in the flat countryside of eastern Maryland, Wisner planted okra and squash and liked to work in the soil. His son Ellis remembers him happily rooting in his garden, sweat dripping from his nose.

Wisner was a warm, distant, and magnificent figure to his children. "He seemed to be only half with us, always pondering some insoluble riddle," said his youngest son, Graham. "Nonetheless, he dominated every conversation with an extraordinary mixture of wit, charm, humor, and southern power." Wisner loved to tell elaborate and spooky ghost stories and spin out puns and word games ("What is similar between a piece of paper and a lazy dog? A piece of paper is an ink-lined plane and an inclined plane is a slope up and a slow pup is a lazy dog"). He would read aloud—*David Copperfield* and his favorite spy book, *Kim*, about the Great Game in India. He organized constant games and races—three-legged races, relay races, sack races, races between his mud pond yachts, the *Gargantua* and the *Pantagruel*. Other children noticed his warmth too. Georgetown was a very grown-up world—there was no talk of children at table—but "in a forest of gray flannel knees, Frank Wisner was the one who would bend down to talk to you," said Barbara Lawrence, Des FitzGerald's stepdaughter. Wisner was especially good with children who felt lost as teenagers. He would listen in a way others would not.

To his children, Wisner seemed more content in rural Maryland than in downtown Washington. "My sense was that he was not entirely comfortable in the world of preppy bankers," said Wendy Hazard, his daughter. He disapproved of country clubs. The children at Chevy Chase had a "chit mentality," he told his kids, whom he put to work shoveling silage and picking corn. In long (and sometimes long-winded) conversations he taught his children a strict code of honor and truth and really seemed to mean it. In later years they wondered how their father could reconcile that code with the moral ambiguities of his job. The answer, of course, was that he could not.

Galena was a break from work, but not much of one. He would arrive, bone weary, often late on Saturday afternoon and have to return the next day after lunch. There was never time to really unwind and lie back; there was too much to be done.[23]

In the summer of 1956, Wisner's old boss at the State Department, Charles Saltzman, stayed one night at the Wisners' while in Washington on business. It was a brutally hot night in August, and

Saltzman recalled the two men "panting" as they drank a late glass of milk in Wisner's kitchen after attending a dinner at Joe Alsop's. Wisner told Saltzman he was "feeling hurt because of something Allen Dulles had done." Saltzman was surprised. "It was unlike Frank. He was the last person to feel sorry for himself."[24]

The strain was showing. That same summer Gilbert Greenway was staying with Wisner in Washington while their families escaped the heat. Greenway recalled watching Wisner march James Reston of the *New York Times* around and around the garden on P Street, emphatically lecturing the journalist. Yet when Reston then made use of the information in his column, Wisner was furious. He couldn't seem to pace himself. On a long flight that summer to visit the Far East, Wisner "stayed up until the stewardess refused to serve us any more drinks," recalled Larry Houston, the CIA general counsel. When he returned, Houston went to see Gordon Gray, Wisner's friend from boarding school and Wall Street who was working at the Pentagon as an assistant secretary of defense. "I've been bothered by Frank," Houston said to Gray. "He's full of odd ideas." Gray looked at Houston and replied, "I think Frank is in real trouble."[25]

Chapter Ten

COLLAPSE

"SOS SOS SOS . . . THE FIGHTING IS
VERY CLOSE NOW. . . ."

THE HUNGARIAN REVOLUTION, which would cost 30,000 lives including, some would say, Frank Wisner's, began with rioting on October 23, 1956. A mass demonstration of 300,000 people marched on the parliament building in Budapest, demanding open elections and the withdrawal of Soviet troops. A pair of workers with acetylene torches stoked the mob by cutting off a giant bronze statue of Stalin at the knees, leaving a pair of empty boots. The Hungarian secret police opened up with machine guns, but the army sided with the people, handing out arms to students.

On its powerful transmitters in Munich, Radio Free Europe began rebroadcasting calls to arms picked up from a dozen low-power radio stations scattered throughout Hungary. RFE had been cautious during the Polish riots, warning the workers against suicidal action. But in Hungary, the people heard the broadcasts on the CIA's secretly funded radio station and believed that the hour had arrived, that the West would intervene to save them.[1]

In mid-October, shortly before the Hungarian uprising, Wisner and Al Ulmer, another senior official in the clandestine service, had walked about Wisner's farm on the Eastern Shore of Maryland, debating what, if anything, the agency could do if revolution broke out behind the Iron Curtain. Wisner was wrought up, but not overwrought, according to Ulmer. Both men knew that direct intervention by the United States was unlikely and that the émigré battalions supported by the CIA were probably not up to facing Soviet tanks. But the CIA might send in arms—"lots of arms," Wisner told Richard Bissell when he returned to Washington after the weekend.[2]

On the day the Hungarians revolted, Wisner was beginning a long-scheduled tour of CIA stations in Europe. It was supposed to be a routine trip, a whirlwind tour of pressing the flesh and listening to the gripes and plans of his operatives across the continent. Wisner had made a dozen such trips before.

At his first stop, London, on October 24, Wisner called on the Secret Intelligence Service. It was arranged that Wisner would dine with Sir Patrick Dean, the head of the U.S./British Joint Intelligence Committee, a clandestine arm of the "special relationship." John Bruce Lockhart, the former SIS liaison who had remained close to Wisner (he helped arrange for Wisner's son Frank Jr. to attend his old school, Rugby), described an evening that was all downhill. The plan, said Lockhart, was to meet at "Pat's flat, that the ladies should withdraw early, and that there should be good gossip over the port." Unexpectedly, Dean was called away to Paris. He was supposed to return by six, but he got hung up and was incommunicado. "We met for dinner at seven-thirty—no Pat. By eight-thirty, Frank was becoming visibly agitated. By nine, Patricia [Dean] suggested we eat. It was a grim meal, but we did what we could. By eleven Frank could hardly contain his sense of outrage and he left. . . . Pat contacted Frank early the next morning to explain as best he could, as I did." Wisner was "absolutely convinced" that the British were snubbing him on purpose. He left London the next afternoon, "angry, frustrated, and insulted," said Lockhart.[3]

Four days later, on October 29, Great Britain caught the CIA by surprise by starting a war in the Middle East. In a last gasp of empire, the British and French sponsored an Israeli attack on Egypt to recapture the Suez Canal, the old colonial gateway to the East. Dean had been unable to meet with Wisner in London on the twenty-fourth because he had been in Paris, plotting with the French. The affair was a debacle; a week after it began the United States stopped the proxy war by threatening to use its economic power to ruin the British currency, and the government of Prime Minister Anthony Eden fell.

Wisner was furious. He knew that Suez would distract and divide the allies, opening the way for the Kremlin to crack down on

Hungary and crush the revolt. He felt betrayed by his British friends, not for the first time, and mortified that the CIA had failed to see what was coming.[4]

While the Suez crisis raged, the situation continued to deteriorate in Hungary. On November 4 the Soviets invaded their satellite with 200,000 men and 2,500 armored vehicles. Red Army tanks pounded blocks of Budapest into rubble. Leather-jacketed teenage boys, called Yobos, tied sticks of industrial dynamite around their waists and threw themselves under the treads. Soviet troops went house-to-house, slaughtering insurrectionaries and their families. The ring leaders were shot or thrown into boxcars, to be hauled off to the gulag.

Wisner was reported by a CIA official to be "somber and quiet" when he attended some NATO briefings in Paris after leaving London. When he arrived in Germany on November 5 to stay at Tracy Barnes's villa in Frankfurt, he was strung out, unable to sleep, and beginning to ramble. "He made no sense. He was in awful shape," said Janet. Wisner's bag carrier from the agency made an odd request of Mrs. Barnes. Were there any electric trains in the house? Slightly taken aback, Janet answered that Tracy Jr. had a set upstairs. Wisner went up to play with the trains, trying to calm down. Janet and Tracy, desperately worried about their dear friend, stayed up the night of November 6, supposedly listening to the American election returns (Eisenhower in a landslide), but actually just keeping Wisner company.[5]

On November 7, Wisner arrived in Vienna, which was as close as he could get to Hungary. The newspaper teletype lines chattering into the Associated Press office in Vienna described, in heartbreaking cablese, what was happening in Budapest:

"RUSSIAN GANGSTERS HAVE BETRAYED US; THEY ARE OPENING FIRE ON ALL OF BUDAPEST. PLEASE INFORM EUROPE AND THE AUSTRIAN GOVERNMENT . . . WE ARE UNDER HEAVY MACHINE GUN FIRE . . . HAVE YOU INFORMATION YOU CAN PASS ON . . . TELL ME, URGENT, URGENT."

There was a pause.

"ANY NEWS ABOUT HELP? QUICKLY, QUICKLY. WE HAVE NO TIME TO LOSE. NO TIME TO LOSE."

The connection broke. Another line began to chatter:

"SOS SOS SOS . . . THE FIGHTING IS VERY CLOSE NOW AND WE HAVEN'T ENOUGH TOMMY GUNS IN THE BUILDING. . . . I DON'T KNOW HOW LONG WE CAN RESIST . . . HEAVY SHELLS ARE EXPLODING NEARBY. . . .

"WHAT IS THE UNITED NATIONS DOING? GIVE US A LITTLE ENCOURAGE-MENT.

"THEY'VE JUST BROUGHT A RUMOR THAT AMERICAN TROOPS WILL BE HERE WITHIN ONE OR TWO HOURS . . .

"GOODBYE FRIENDS. GOODBYE FRIENDS. GOD SAVE OUR SOULS. THE RUS-SIANS ARE TOO NEAR."

The line went dead. On November 8, the resistance crushed, Budapest fell to the Red Army.[6]

In Vienna, Wisner borrowed a bed, in which he was unable to sleep, at the residence of his friend Llewellyn Thompson, the U.S. ambassador to Austria. The Thompsons were close friends from Georgetown. Together the Thompsons and Wisner listened on the radio to the United Nations debate what to do about Hungary (ultimately, nothing). "We were all disgusted," said Jane Thompson. "It was just disgusting. The whole world was distracted by Suez and the Austrians didn't want to lose their neutrality by sending in arms."

In conversations with junior officers in the embassy, Wisner seemed strangely obsessed with the notion that a large number of Mongolian troops were in the Soviet units sent to suppress the rebellion. He regarded this "oriental" force as sinister. Talking on too long and too fast, he conjured up an assault on European culture from the Eastern hordes. "It was, 'Here come the Huns,' primitive and uncivilized, plundering the great institutions of Europe," recalled John Mapother, an intelligence officer in Vienna, who was baffled because as far as he knew, there were no Mongolian troops with the Russians.

Wisner was eager to establish a battlefield command post. He was "really wound up," said William Hood, a senior official in the CIA's Vienna station who dined with him the first night at the Thompsons'. "He told me he wanted to see all the cable traffic. I said all of it? He insisted, so I took it all out to the residence." Wisner had converted the embassy library into his bunker. The clandestine chief rifled through the reams of paper, demanding, "What's this? What does it say?" But it was "all routine stuff," said Hood—background checks on low-level agents, rumors and raw gossip. Wisner "colored as he read. There was very little traffic on the revolution. He felt isolated, out of the loop. He was drowning in junk, in useless cable traffic."[7]

For Wisner, who wanted to control everything, this was an

unbearable state of affairs. Here he was, the CIA's director of clandestine operations at the most crucial moment of the Cold War, only a few miles from the revolution he had wished to foment, and he had no power to do anything to help. The decisions were all being made back in Washington. He began sending back cables beseeching Eisenhower and the Dulles brothers to do something to exploit the opportunity.

In fact, the CIA could do very little. There was some talk among the CIA case officers in Vienna of sending weapons into Hungary. But, according to the agency's in-house history of the uprising, "there were no weapons handy enough to commandeer hurriedly, we knew too little, we had absolutely no picture at all of who needed weapons, when, what kind, where. . . ." There weren't even any Hungarian speakers among the case officers sent to Vienna.

In Washington, Allen Dulles had been initially disposed toward action. On October 27 he had cabled Wisner, still in London at the time, that "these are dramatic days and we must carefully weigh all our actions. However, I'm not one of those who believes we should be hindered by Undue Caution." But when the Russians cracked down a few days later, Dulles and his brother, John Foster, became more cautious. For all their talk of rollback, they did not want to start World War III. On November 11, Dulles cabled Wisner, "Headquarters advising station that CIA tentative thinking is not to incite to action."[8]

In Vienna, Wisner "was profoundly moved, distressed, depressed. He saw it so close, he was right there, it was happening under his nose," said Richard Bissell. "He felt this was the first big break of the Cold War, the first clear crack in the monolithic defense. Frank believed that the agency was created to take advantage of this situation. It was why we had covert operations."

Unable to sit still, Wisner went to the Austro-Hungarian border and saw thousands of refugees, many of them bloodied, streaming across. "He met with resistance leaders and had to say no to their requests," said Bissell, who was reading the cable traffic back in Washington. "It was an intensely emotional moment for him. He felt we had done a lot to inspire and encourage the event."

In Washington, the agency was caught in a moral dilemma. "Either you give assistance and get bloody results, or you don't and appear weak and mislead your friends," said Bissell. "I don't remember any lucid conversations. I remember a lot of hand-wringing. No one had thought it through. I think Frank thought it was better to have a little bloodletting, and give the Russians a header."[9]

The Kremlin publicly blamed the CIA for inciting the Hungarian revolution. A number of commissions in the United States and Europe studied the question and dutifully pronounced the United States innocent in the affair.[10] Most CIA men, however, scoff at a whitewash. "Sure, we never said rise up and revolt," said Thomas Polgar, "but there was a lot of propaganda that led the Hungarians to believe that we would help." Interviewed by reporters and relief officials as they fled Hungary, many of the partisans said that they had been encouraged by the radio to believe that reinforcements were on the way. Wisner heard the complaints; on November 12 he cabled Dulles that "discussion with refugees shows some criticism of RFE broadcasts into Hungary."[11]

As the slaughter crested in Hungary, Wisner's behavior became increasingly erratic, and he was not always able to contain his feelings. After he had returned from the border on the evening of November 11—and received Dulles's cable saying that Washington had decided not to "incite to action" in Hungary—Wisner joined with a pair of old friends, Walter and Marie Ridder of Knight-Ridder newspapers. They, too, had gone up to the border to witness the flood of refugees. During tea at the American embassy, Wisner suggested that they all go out to dinner at a Hungarian restaurant. In the restaurant a radio was broadcasting a report from a British journalist who claimed (erroneously) that Russian tanks were pushing over the border. Panic broke out in the restaurant. Walter Ridder got up on a chair to say that he had just returned from the border and seen no tanks, that the broadcast was just sensationalism.

The crowd quieted, but Wisner just seemed to get riled up. He began talking, almost shouting, about how the American government was letting Hungary down. He said that he himself felt personally betrayed, that he felt disgraced. He began talking about how much money the Americans had spent on Radio Free Europe "to get these people to revolt." The Ridders watched with growing dismay. Walter Ridder began concentrating on how to get Wisner out of the restaurant and into a taxi.[12]

Still on his tour of CIA stations, Wisner pushed on to Rome. William Colby, a senior CIA officer in Rome, recalled that Wisner "was rambling and raving all through dinner, totally out of control.

He kept saying, all these people are getting killed and we weren't doing anything, we were ignoring it." Wisner paid a visit to Clare Boothe Luce, the American ambassador to Italy, who was sick in bed. As Wisner spoke to her, he became increasingly distraught until, finally, he broke down and wept.[13]

IN GREECE, at the last stop on his exhausting tour of CIA outposts, Wisner ate a plate of bad clams that gave him hepatitis. The virus incubated for a month before it struck; in the meantime, Wisner careered along, manic and barely in control. The reports of his shaky behavior in Europe began to circulate through the corridors of the L Building, the headquarters of the Directorate of Plans down on the Washington Mall. The rumors intensified as people watched Wisner perform at meetings. Author Tom Powers relates the story of Wisner constantly interrupting one of his aides, who was trying to report to the other DD/P chiefs on Wisner's trip, with various interjections, including a "long, detailed, thoroughly scatological story which involved some Russians, a confusion between the men's room and the women's room, and a great deal of toilet paper."[14]

Wisner returned to Washington to discover that he was being attacked from the rear—by one of his own circle of friends. Although Eisenhower fancied the agency as his "action arm," he was shrewd enough to sense its potential for getting out of hand, and in early 1956 he had created the President's Board of Consultants on Foreign Intelligence Activities (PBCFIA). The board had no authority over the CIA or even much knowledge of its activities. It could have been just another honorific commission. But one of its members, David K. E. Bruce, was an unusually commanding figure, as well as knowledgeable about intelligence. Bruce had run OSS operations in London during the war, and he and his wife, Evangeline, were part of the Georgetown set. In a variety of high-level jobs—ambassador to Germany, France, and England and undersecretary of state—Bruce was a charming, courtly diplomat with a hard head. He was very suspicious about what the CIA was up to.

As a senior State Department official in the Truman administration, he had blocked an earlier attempt by the CIA to overthrow the government of Guatemala in 1952. After learning of the plot, Bruce went to Secretary of State Dean Acheson, and together the two diplomats persuaded President Truman that overthrowing the duly elected government of a Central American country would do more harm than good. Bruce's objections had been swept away when Eisenhower and the Dulles brothers came to power in 1953, but Bruce, who had gone off to be ambassador to Paris, maintained his skepticism. When Eisenhower appointed Bruce as a member of PBCFIA in early 1956, Bruce took the job seriously and began trying to look into agency activities.

What he learned confirmed his doubts. Because he shared the same background (a wellborn Virginian, he was Princeton and OSS), Bruce understood the type of operator recruited by Wisner and the temptation of a young American Galahad to play king-maker. In a PBCFIA report to the president, Bruce was caustic about the "busy, monied and privileged" young men of the CIA who went about "mingling in the affairs of other nations." He noted the seductive quality of covert actions like the Guatemala coup, and scoffed that while the agency was busily ringing up " 'successes'—no charge is made for 'failures' "—the CIA was neglecting the harder, more tedious work of collecting intelligence. Approval for "almost any action" was "pro forma" at informal lunch meetings of the "Operations Coordinating Board," a toothless oversight panel set up by the National Security Council. According to Robert Lovett, who also served on PBCFIA, Bruce's attitude was, "what right have we to go barging around in other countries buying newspapers and handing money to opposition parties or supporting a candidate for this, that, or the other office?" The PBCFIA report concluded that the CIA's covert actions were "responsible in great measure for stirring up the turmoil and raising the doubts about us that exist in many countries in the world today. . . . Where will we be tomorrow?"[15]

It is not clear whether Wisner knew precisely what tack Bruce would take in his report, which was due at the end of the year. But in October, just before he left on his tour of European stations, Wisner had sensed that the president's board was not going to rubber-stamp his activities. His files show him trying to reassure Lovett and Bruce that "informality does not mean irresponsibility," and warning Dulles that the PBCFIA "is hearing complaints from ambassadors kept in the dark" about CIA covert action. The mere existence of an outside commission second-guessing his work was enough to make him anxious. This was particularly true after the collapse of the Hungarian revolution, when there was a great deal of high-level muttering around Washington that the CIA had helped inspire the revolution and then abandoned it. In December 1956, Wisner's characteristic feeling of being under siege was not a paranoid reaction.

Bruce's report was formally presented to President Eisenhower on December 20. Just a few days before, on December 16, Wisner had been suddenly struck by a chill as he climbed out of his car in Georgetown after a weekend of duck hunting on his farm in Maryland. The hepatitis "hit me right on the end of the nose without any preliminaries whatsoever," Wisner later wrote in a medical report to the CIA. The attack was so severe that he barely made it inside the house. In the next few days his fever spiked to 106 degrees, and Wisner found himself "partially be-fogged in my mind and not in a position to make clear judgments or discriminating decisions."[16]

In later years Wisner's hepatitis would be blamed by some of his friends and family for his mental illness.[17] Wisner's medical form indicated that he was suffering from viral infectious hepatitis, which is not as severe as the amoebic variety. It appears that Wisner was subjected to heavy dosages of cortisone, a then-experimental drug that can cause severe mood swings. But it is unlikely that his emotional problems were caused by the disease.

Wisner was not diagnosed with his deeper ailment—manic depression—at this time. Not much was known about manic depression in the late 1950s; it was a decade before medical science fully appreciated that manic depression is caused by a chemical imbalance in the brain. Men of Wisner's kind had an aversion to admitting to any long-term mental disability. It was permissible to have a "nervous breakdown," but after a suitable period of rest one was expected to rejoin the world. Hepatitis became a convenient excuse that allowed Wisner to rest for a few months while his "liver" recovered.[18]

During his absence Wisner had been covered by his chief of operations, Richard Helms. Helms was the embodiment of what Stewart Alsop called the "Prudent Professionals"—the careful, patient intelligence gatherers who were wary of the more glamorous, more reckless political activists, or the "Bold Easterners," as Alsop dubbed them. Helms had been in OSS in Germany with Allen Dulles and Frank Wisner at the end of the war, but he had stayed in intelligence and gone to work for OSO. Like the other "Prudent Professionals" in OSO, he had looked askance at the swashbucklers in OPC. Helms was extremely well organized, a clean deskman, the perfect "number two," though there were doubts, at least in the beginning, that he would make a number one.[19]

Helms was a great bureaucratic survivor. He had good judgment and a shrewd sense of character. He rose by making the machinery work and staying away from trouble, not easy to do in an organization that prided itself on risk-takers. When OSO and OPC were merged by Bedell Smith, Helms became the chief of operations of the clandestine service, reporting to the DD/P, Frank Wisner. Helms did not hide his distaste for big, showy covert actions, but he did not advertise it either. In the weeks before the Guatemala operation, when the talk turned to the progress on the upcoming coup at Wisner's morning staff meeting, Helms would quietly get up and absent himself. He was not in the chain of command; he had no need to know and no real desire to. Because Helms's name never seemed to attach to big "flaps"—and increasingly, Frank Wisner's did—the wags in the clandestine service began crudely joking about "Frank the fucker and Dick the ducker."[20]

Actually, the two men were quite close. Though Helms's social credentials were perfectly presentable—he spent a year at a posh Swiss boarding school, Le Rosey; graduated from Williams; and played tennis on Sunday mornings wearing long white flannel trousers at the Chevy Chase Club—he was not really comfortable in the Georgetown crowd. His wife was considered to be dull, and Helms, while he could be sardonic, was not thought to be much fun. But he was loyal to Wisner, and Polly, who valued loyalty, trusted him to protect her husband.

He did it discreetly. Increasingly, even after Wisner returned from sick leave, Helms ran the clandestine service, not just the day-to-day routine, but many of the larger operations as well. Many officials at the upper level realized that Wisner was not "right," but they kept him propped up, hoping that his erratic behavior would prove to be a case of exhaustion, and that in time he would recover. In the meantime, Helms was a steady hand. He reached for power in a subtle, low-key way, careful not to offend Wisner, who was sensitive to slights, but at the same time making clear where the real control lay. "When I first realized Frank had a problem, it was by a gesture," said Gordon Stewart, the chief of the Foreign Intelligence Staff. "I wanted to run a project by Wisner, and Helms just pointed over his shoulder at the wall separating their offices. Helms was saying, don't bother to go to Frank anymore."

Slowly, Helms weeded out or shut down the least promising projects and brought some order and a standard of care to the Directorate of Plans. He was joined in this task by General Truscott, who had been brought back by President Eisenhower after Hungary to quietly dismantle "rollback." The émigré paramilitary force was finally junked, the labor battalions were disbanded, the secret arms caches scrapped. The "radios" were put under tighter control. There was no more talk of liberation or revolt in the East Bloc.

Wisner himself had a hard time giving up. It seems remarkable, given the Hungarian tragedy, but when he returned full-time to work in the spring of 1957, Wisner started agitating for an operation to free Czechoslovakia from the Kremlin's grip. The idea never got much beyond the talking stage. At least as far as rolling back the Iron Curtain was concerned, "no one was listening to Wisner by then," said Jim Critchfield, who had returned from Germany to be head of the East European Division. "He was pretty sick."[21]

Chapter Eleven

BROTHER'S KEEPER

"If you knew what you'd done to me . . ."

DESMOND FITZGERALD WAS regarded as a "comer" at the CIA, a good bet to rise in the ranks. He had the requisite drive, intelligence, flair, and social connections. What he lacked was experience in the field. Like Tracy Barnes, his rough equivalent in stature in the agency, FitzGerald wanted a tour of duty in the front lines. For FitzGerald, who by 1954 had risen to become acting head of the Far East Division, that meant Asia. Going into the field was a way for him to become more credible among the covert action operators who sometimes sneered at the innocence of their bosses in Washington. And it was a way to satisfy his deep curiosity about the Far East, to continue the education begun as an Army major in the Burma-China theater in World War II. In the fall of 1954, just as Barnes was leaving Washington to run the German Mission, FitzGerald was sent by Allen Dulles and Frank Wisner to the Far East, to run the CIA's China Mission.

The goal of the China Mission was to penetrate and, if possible, destabilize Red China. It started out as a group of old hands from the OSS who never left the Far East after World War II. Driven from China after the fall of Shanghai in 1949, the China Mission wound up in Japan, at a naval station in Yokosuka. From Yokosuka, the China Mission tried to gather intelligence on Red China. This was a very difficult task against the Maoists, whose security was as tight as the Kremlin's. The mission's officers had scored a few successes, most notably stealing the Shanghai police files as they fled in 1949, but they had experienced more failures trying to crack the "denied area." Just as OPC had been scammed by East European refugees selling phony intelligence out of the East Bloc, the China Mission was used by "paper mills" in Hong Kong, Saigon, and Singapore.[1]

In one among a number of depressing examples, an agent code-named LFBOOKLET claimed to run a network of clandestine radio operators out of Saigon. He offered information about mainland China in exchange for financial support. For two years the agency funneled millions of dollars to LFBOOKLET's operations. The China Mission gradually became suspicious, however, when agency radio monitors were never able to actually pick up any of the transmissions he claimed. It eventually turned out that there were no transmissions; the agent clipped Chinese newspapers that had made their way to Saigon, embellished on the information in them, and sold the "take" as the authentic intelligence of his many non-existent agents.[2]

FitzGerald knew nothing of this fraud until after he arrived in Yokosuka in the autumn of 1954. "He came in on top of all these cowboys, many of whom hadn't gone to college," said Jim Lilley, a case officer in the Far East Division. "He thought the China Mission was really going to work, but it turned out to be an irrelevant buffer between Washington and the field."

FitzGerald was a determined but slightly out-of-touch leader of agents in the field. He memorized a "face book" of names and photographs so he would know his troops and went skeet shooting to bond with some of the old China hands. Inevitably, his subordinates twitted him for his formality, but they regarded him with a mixture of respect and envy. "He had very fancy shotguns but he was not a good shot," said Charles Whitehurst, an old OSO China deskman. "He was too concerned with how he looked, and it made him tight. He would pick up his head. I teased him about being stiff."

FitzGerald had a sense of humor, even about himself, and he smiled at the teasing. He had the ability to stand back and observe the ironies of his trade. His colleagues were amused by his observations about the peculiar nature of the CIA and the style of leadership exercised by Allen Dulles, who loved to play the spy. He remarked that Dulles organized the agency so that every function was covered by someone other than himself. The arrangement left

Dulles time and opportunity to meddle in any activity he chose. This, FitzGerald drily observed, was "good administration."[3]

CIA officials lived like shoguns in Japan in the 1950s. FitzGerald occupied a house "built for a Japanese prince by a German architect in a Tudor style," said Barbara Lawrence, his stepdaughter. The house came with a "cook, housekeeper, nurse, driver, and a gardener, all for under $200 a year, plus people flitting about the garden. I am not sure what they are doing but they are always there," wrote FitzGerald's wife, Barbara, to his sister, Eleanor. The staff would line up outside the toilet in the morning and bow when FitzGerald emerged. With his family, FitzGerald would take long walks around the rocky coastline; he would poke at the ground with his walking stick, looking for mines left over from the war.[4]

After a year FitzGerald and the China Mission moved to Subic Bay in the Philippines, to the new Navy base there. Subic, with its row on row of military housing and rank consciousness, was a less pleasant environment for the FitzGeralds. Barbara FitzGerald was a loving and dutiful wife, but it bothered her that she could not tell anyone what her husband did.[5] FitzGerald tried to keep up morale. He arranged to have a fire truck run over a python that had crawled out of the jungle after a typhoon. He then announced to his staff that there were no more snakes, prompting someone to leave the carcass of another python on his desk.

Some staffers were biting about FitzGerald. E. Howard Hunt, transferred out to Asia after Guatemala, recalled seeing FitzGerald "sit on the verandah while the peons toiled in a river of mud. It was symbolic of his life. He was condescending to all hands. We called him the Instant Enthusiast. He'd have an idea, someone would work it up, but then he'd lose interest. 'Where did you get the terrible idea?' he'd ask." Hunt's bitterness may have been colored by his own insecurity; he undoubtedly sensed that FitzGerald had little regard for him.[6]

Nothing happened on FitzGerald's watch to get him mentioned in dispatches to Washington. The China Mission was a "loser," said Lilley. FitzGerald and his boss, Al Ulmer, traveled to Taiwan in the fall of 1955. "We were dropping Chinese agents into China— two a month—but we weren't getting much," Ulmer recalled. "Des wanted out. He had no use for the Chinese Nationalists. [Generalissimo] Chiang [Kai-shek] tried to ply us with women and song at a big banquet. Des said to him, 'You don't understand, Al and I are fairies.' This was his way of keeping his distance from Chiang. I thought Des was a realist. Maybe he was a little lax—he allowed ops to keep going after they had turned sour. But he had nothing else going." Like Tracy Barnes, said Ulmer, FitzGerald had little interest in "FI," in intelligence gathering. His real interest was in political action, in trying to subvert or stop communist insurgencies.[7]

Increasingly, FitzGerald looked south and east in Asia. Korea had been a bust, China was impregnable, Taiwan was corrupt. The tragic death of Magsaysay in an airplane crash in 1957 threatened to undo Lansdale's work in the Philippines. The more promising battlefields were in Malaysia, Thailand, Laos, and Vietnam, where communist insurgencies were picking up support.

FitzGerald was particularly interested in the counterinsurgency work of the British in Malaya. To him, the British were a model. He was careful not to be too overtly Anglophile—after Philby, excessive regard for the "cousins" was frowned upon at the CIA. But the British had a deep expertise at running colonies. Some of the Colonel Blimps out of the colonial office were clumsy racists, but the better British intelligence officers were sophisticated about native cultures, and they showed a willingness to be uncompromising—brutal if necessary—when it came down to combating terrorists and native insurrectionists.

FitzGerald appreciated that the key to counterinsurgency was penetration and control. The British had succeeded in getting inside the local insurgencies with their agents and then subverting them. "You've got to recruit them, penetrate them, don't trust anyone. You establish control, you bring in the polygraph," said Lilley. FitzGerald had learned from his mistakes. "In Korea and Burma, we had flown blind. Everything had been doubled. Des saw it happen again and again," said Lilley. FitzGerald wanted to be the dealer, not the chump. He explored devious new tactics, like "false flag recruitment," setting up a fake Communist Party to sting the Red Chinese, who were always trying to recruit throughout Southeast Asia.[8]

FitzGerald was eager to try new tricks, but the station chiefs in Southeast Asia were not willing to see him try in their territory. He was left to churn paper in Subic. In early 1956 he got an idea of how irrelevant the China Mission was. Ralph McGehee, a midlevel official at Subic who later became an agency renegade, described FitzGerald angrily demanding to know what had happened to a top-secret document that Washington had sent to Subic some weeks before. The document was finally traced to a safe where it sat with a stack of other top-secret documents that the code clerk, for some reason, had never bothered to distribute. No one in Washington sending out these missives had even noticed the lack of response from the China Mission. In the summer of 1956 the China Mission was shut down. (A few months earlier a harsh secret report by the CIA's Inspection and Review Staff in Washington had declared that the China Mission "represented a waste of operations and manpower.") FitzGerald and his family came home, and FitzGerald was given a staff job until Allen Dulles could find more useful work for him. In the meantime, FitzGerald devoted much of his energy to watching over and worrying about Frank Wisner.[9]

WISNER'S OWN interest in Asia was sporadic. Stretched too thin, he had devoted most of his energies to Eastern Europe in the months before he got sick in December 1956. But in 1957 his attentions were increasingly consumed by Indonesia, and a concerted effort by the Unites States government to oust the Southeast Asian archipelago's troublesome strongman, Achmed Sukarno.

Sukarno's crime was neutralism. Like a number of postcolonial strongmen—U Nu of Burma, Nehru of India, Nasser of Egypt—Sukarno did not want to owe allegiance to either Moscow or Washington. In 1955 he had organized a conference of "nonaligned" nations at Bandung, a meeting referred to by some at the State Department as the "Darktown Strutters' Ball." To John Foster Dulles, neutralism was intolerable; you were either on the side of the forces of light—the United States—or darkness—the Soviet Union. Sukarno preferred a shadowy middle ground. A nationalist, he had fought in the resistance against the Dutch before they abandoned their East Asian colony, but in 1949 he had also outlawed—for a time—the Communist Party. He was a great orator, but his vision was vague. He said he favored "guided democracy," which sounded to the State Department like the road to communism but actually resembled something closer to the city hall in Chicago or New York—government by cronyism.

Foster Dulles, a deeply prudish Presbyterian, found Sukarno

personally offensive—"disgusting," according to the American ambassador to Indonesia, John Allison. Sukarno claimed to be descended from an Indian Brahmin and a Javanese sultan, but the
Dutch believed him to be the illegitimate son of a coffee planter.
He was renowned for his sexual appetite. "As an artist," Sukarno
explained, "I gravitate naturally toward what pleases the
senses."[10]

The CIA spent a million dollars to try to influence the Indonesian elections in 1955, but much of the money was wasted or stolen,
and Sukarno grew stronger, while the Communist Party (no longer
illegal) polled a surprising six million votes. When Sukarno visited
Red China and the Soviet Union in 1956 and the Soviet foreign
minister toured Indonesia in the spring of 1957, Washington decided that stronger measures were in order.

Wisner had his usual—and justified—apprehensions about a full-
scale paramilitary operation against the Sukarno regime. He had
shown bravado at first. "I think it's time we held Sukarno's feet to
the fire," Frank Wisner had told Al Ulmer, the head of the CIA's
Far East Division, in the fall of 1956, shortly before leaving on his
ill-starred trip to Europe.[11] But after Wisner returned from sick
leave in the winter of 1957, he cautioned the Dulles brothers that
the CIA could not guarantee success. At a meeting of the National
Security Council on August 1, 1957, Wisner warned that "absolute
control [of the rebellion] could not be guaranteed . . . that explosive results were always possible, that U.S. officials must be
braced for allegations of covert U.S. activities." The warnings
were not heeded; the Dulleses were determined. In the fall of 1957,
Wisner hand-carried to Allen Dulles's office a voucher giving the
DD/P the authority to spend $10 million to back a revolution in the
Indonesian archipelago. Dulles signed the voucher "with a little
flourish," according to one witness. Wisner did not tell Ambassador Allison about the covert action because, as he put it, the plans
"might elicit an adverse reaction from the ambassador." Instead,
Allison was transferred to Czechoslovakia.[12]

The CIA's basic approach was similar to PBSUCCESS in Guatemala. The United States had made common cause with a band of
restless colonels in Sumatra who in February 1958 declared themselves an independent government. Once again the agency looked
to psychological warfare to undermine the regime. The agency
began to spread the rumor that Sukarno had been seduced by a

good-looking blond airline stewardess who worked for the KGB. To document this seduction, the CIA commissioned a blue movie to be made of a Sukarno look-alike in the amorous embrace of a porn actress posing as the Russian spy. To play Sukarno, the moviemakers (Bing Crosby and his brother) chose a bald Chicano wearing a latex face mask. The CIA wanted the model to be bald because Sukarno was vain about his own baldness and always wore a skullcap, except, presumably, in bed.[13]

The colonels were not much better than the movie. The CIA set up an air supply operation with its front airline, Civil Air Transport, but on at least one occasion the rebel troops waiting for an airdrop broke and ran at the sound of approaching planes, which they feared were Sukarno's. Because the State Department did not want "too many white faces" associated with the rebel army, the CIA had been permitted to provide only a single case officer and a radio operator to the Sumatran colonels. Sukarno, on the other hand, enjoyed a more efficient and loyal military than Guatemala's Arbenz. Sukarno had a real navy, an air force, and paratroopers, and he used all of them to methodically suppress the revolt throughout the Indonesian archipelago. Too late, the CIA sent in two more teams of agents and unleashed its private air force of aging B-26s to bomb and strafe.

Frank Wisner was scheduled to go on a tour of CIA stations in the Far East after the uprising began, and once again he headed for the front, arriving in Singapore demanding to be briefed on the progress of the operation. The reports were all bad: on May 18 a B-26 flown by a CIA operative, Allen Lawrence Pope, was shot down just as he accidentally dropped a stick of bombs on a local church, killing most of the congregation. Pope was captured and his identity revealed; he was foolishly carrying papers, including his PX card from Clark Air Force Base in the Philippines. The agency's cover was blown, though John Foster Dulles continued to maintain that Pope was a "soldier of fortune," and the press, docile as usual, for the most part played along with plausible deniability. It eventually cost the United States government 37,000 tons of rice and a shipment of arms to get Pope freed, as well as the promise of pressure on the Dutch to decolonize Western New Guinea. At CIA headquarters a few days after Pope was shot down, Dulles ordered the Indonesia operation to "disengage." "This is the most difficult message I have ever sent," he cabled his two field officers. They hiked out of the jungle to be picked up by a waiting boat. Within Indonesia, the populace assumed CIA involvement and applauded Sukarno for his defiance.[14]

IN THE spring of 1958, as the Indonesia operation was failing, Wisner was collapsing emotionally. On his tour of the Far East, he visited Manila and stayed with Chip Bohlen, then ambassador to the Philippines. "Wisner was so depressed about how the world was going," said Chip's daughter, Avis. "Everything was going against us. Hungary was still eating at him. He felt we were losing the Cold War."[15]

Sam Halpern, the executive assistant to the chief of the Far East Division, met Wisner at the airport upon his return to Washington in June. He had been sending Wisner cables every day on developments at headquarters. "I could tell he was in bad shape, talking too fast," said Halpern.

Des FitzGerald saw the deterioration right away. From his new post as head of the Psychological and Paramilitary Warfare Staff ("PP"), FitzGerald had worked closely with Wisner throughout 1957 and into 1958. FitzGerald had been a skeptic about the Indonesia operation (in later years, old hands would say they knew the Indonesian op was doomed when he began doubting; he was such an enthusiast for covert operations that if he had doubts, then the operation must be a real disaster).[16] FitzGerald had also seen Wisner socially, and he and President Eisenhower's national security adviser, Gordon Gray, had begun talking about Wisner's shaky condition.

Because FitzGerald could be intimidating and remote, he was regarded by some as insensitive. But he was perceptive and loyal. Colleagues began to notice that FitzGerald was spending more and more time with Wisner. Most CIA officials were avoiding Wisner by then. "His eyes would glaze and he'd talk right past you," said William Crowley, a CIA officer based in Washington. Increasingly, FitzGerald and Dick Helms covered for the chief of the clandestine service.[17]

Wisner's friends in Georgetown did not want to believe that he was mentally ill, but it was getting harder to ignore the symptoms. Every Fourth of July the Paul Nitzes threw a big party for their friends out at their farm in southern Maryland along the Potomac. There were the usual free-flowing cocktails and high jinks, races and games and fireworks. Tracy Barnes in particular liked the fireworks. "He was always in the trenches shooting them off," said Janet Barnes Lawrence. "They would have battles. I sort of dreaded the whole thing; I thought someone would get rooked." Frank Wisner was usually at the center of the fun, organizing the races and challenging the men to footraces (the former Olympic hopeful would handicap himself by running backwards).

Des FitzGerald's stepdaughter, Barbara, who was then fourteen, watched Wisner as he joined in the children's games of tennis and hop, skip, and jump and follow-the-leader. "At first, I thought it was wonderful." Like many children, she had a special affection for Wisner, who was more attentive to children than most of her parents' friends. "But at some point it struck me as a little strange. He seemed sort of frenzied. I asked my mother, but she blew me off."

Sitting around the pool, Dick Bissell watched as Wisner waxed on about some elegant silks he had brought back from Thailand. There seemed to be something too insistent and dramatic about his manner. Paul Nitze was taken aback when Wisner got worked up as he excoriated a *New York Times* editor; nothing new there, but Wisner must have known that the man was a friend of Nitze's. All of them had seen Wisner be manic before, and this was an occasion that called for hilarity, but even by the standards of the Georgetown crowd at play Wisner was flying.[18]

It was worse at the office. Wisner's secretary, Billie Marone, was a no-nonsense gatekeeper who could generally handle her boss. She was the one who noticed that Wisner had let his paychecks pile up. ("Here," she deadpanned, handing her boss his uncashed bounty. "Go buy yourself an Oldsmobile.") But during the sultry months of the summer of 1958, Wisner became increasingly irrational, even abusive with her. In late July, Sam Halpern was called to Wisner's office for a meeting on CIA-SIS liaison in Southeast Asia. He found Billie Marone in tears. "She motioned me over and said that Wisner had blasted her. He kept talking at her, not to her, and then just dismissed her," said Halpern. Entering Wisner's office, Halpern found the chief of the clandestine service babbling. "None of it made sense," Halpern recalled. "It was like he couldn't stop. I didn't know what the hell was going on." When Halpern, shaken, returned to his office, he told FitzGerald what he had seen. "It's getting towards the end," said FitzGerald.

FitzGerald got Wisner out of his office and sent him home to rest. Wisner moved out to his farm in Galena, but his condition continued to worsen. Deeply worried, his wife, Polly, called Fitz-Gerald and Gordon Gray and asked them to help. They brought a team of in-house psychiatrists from the CIA.[19]

Paul Nitze, Wisner's old friend, was interviewed by the psychiatrists, looking for some clue. "They asked me if there were sexual problems in his childhood or marriage. I said no, just stress and exhaustion and hepatitis," Nitze recalled. He dismissed the idea of some deeper psychological disorder.[20] But FitzGerald knew that his friend needed institutional help. He persuaded Wisner to go to the Sheppard-Pratt Institute, a private psychiatric hospital near Baltimore, which Wisner entered on September 12, 1958. The doctors there diagnosed him as suffering from psychotic mania.

Wisner had almost surely been sick for years. Manic depression usually sets in early in life, often in the teenage years. It is now fairly obvious, in hindsight, that Wisner's grandiosity, his fervent attention to detail, his long-windedness, were symptoms of a disease. The highs of manic depression can be a spur to greatness. History's list of manics is long: Alexander the Great may have been one; Lincoln, with his dark depressions, and Churchill, with his "black dog," showed many of the symptoms. Mania may have helped give Wisner the drive to establish America's covert operations capability after the war. But the disease also consumed him.

The treatment the doctors at Sheppard-Pratt prescribed was psychoanalysis and shock therapy, the standard treatment for manic depression in 1958; but it did not help much, and in some cases it made the patient suffer more.[21] Electroconvulsive treatment (ECT), otherwise known as shock therapy, is familiar to readers of Ken Kesey's *One Flew Over the Cuckoo's Nest* as a somewhat barbaric procedure. Shocking the brain—inducing a seizure—can end a depression, but it cannot stop depression from recurring, as it always does in a manic depressive. The convulsion can be a terrible experience. It apparently was for Wisner. He never talked about his six months in Sheppard-Pratt, except to say to FitzGerald, "Des, if you knew what you'd done to me, you could never live with yourself."[22]

Tracy and Janet Barnes and Chip and Avis Bohlen were waiting at the Wisners' to welcome Frank when he came home from the hospital. At the age of forty-eight, Wisner was a robust man, barrel-chested and taut, even after he had put on weight. His eyes were wide and piercing. But when he walked in the door of his house on P Street, "he looked so sad and diminished, you wanted to cry," said Janet Barnes Lawrence. To break the painful silence, to find something to do, Bohlen suggested that they play a little game, putting a golf ball on the living room rug. Wisner stirred slightly, but sat back and stared vacantly.[23]

Chapter Twelve

HIGH FLIER

"Was it really wise to do that the first time?"

FOR ALL ITS stresses, the life of secrets was addictive, and even as he lay shocked and careworn in a psychiatric hospital Wisner did not want to give it up. While he was still convalescing in Sheppard-Pratt in the fall of 1958, Wisner had been visited by his old friend and aide Gilbert Greenway. Wisner "seemed desperate," said Greenway. "He was scared to death he'd be let go by Allen Dulles. The life he had been living would be gone." Wisner was obviously too sick to continue as head of the clandestine service. Still, Dulles gave him the title of "special assistant," and in September 1959 he would find a place for him as chief of station in London, a post that was more ceremonial and diplomatic than operational. Dulles was hopeful that Wisner could handle the more relaxed pace; others, more familiar with the increased frequency and oscillation of Wisner's highs and lows, were less sanguine.[1]

The logical and popular choice within the agency to succeed Wisner as DD/P was Richard Helms. In effect, he already was DD/P, and had been ever since Wisner's deterioration became obvious nearly two years before. Helms was a first-rate administrator, and he enjoyed the confidence of his troops, or at least most of them.

Unfortunately for Helms, Allen Dulles did not care much about clean desks and efficient management. Dulles was a poor administrator himself. Fascinated by operations and bored by budget lines and flowcharts, the "Great White Case Officer" routinely ignored the chain of command and called upon agents in the field. A man's connections, not his GS grade, were what really counted to the CIA director. At one of his frequent stag dinners at the Alibi Club, Dulles leaned over to Lloyd Emerson, a junior staffer in the DD/P, and asked, in a conspiratorial voice, "Do you read the society pages? Young man, that's where I get a lot of valuable information. You should read it every day, to get the beginning of things."

Almost boyish in his love of the spy trade, Dulles prized boldness and panache. His romantic predilections were well known, which may be why few in the upper ranks of the CIA were shocked in the fall of 1958 when Dulles passed over the stolid Richard Helms. They were a little surprised, however, when Dulles ignored all the other contenders in the clandestine service and reached out to make Richard Bissell the DD/P.

Bissell, after all, had no experience as a spy or running covert operations on the ground. But what he had been doing for the past four years was, in a tangible way, the most important accomplishment of the agency since its inception in 1947. Beginning in late 1954, Bissell had been in charge of developing and operating the U-2 spy plane.

Dulles had given Bissell the job after a White House commission chaired by MIT President James Killian concluded in the fall of 1954 that the United States needed some way to warn against a Soviet surprise attack. Bissell was ideally suited for the task. Building a state-of-the-art plane—from scratch, and as quickly as possible—was an immense logistical undertaking that required a technical grasp and a willingness to push the boundaries of innovation, while cutting through the usual red tape that binds even the most high priority and secretive government operations.

The fact that Bissell knew nothing about reconnaissance, airplanes, or cameras only made the challenge more interesting to him. Early in the development of the U-2, Gordon Stewart, the chief of the Foreign Intelligence Staff, accompanied Bissell to an Air Force base to inspect aerial reconnaissance planes. As Stewart cooled his heels standing around on the tarmac, Bissell spent hours in the cockpits of various airplanes, quizzing the crews and technicians and educating himself. "He was excited and geared up," said Stewart. Here was the chance to leap over the waiting and uncertainties of human intelligence—Stewart's job—with a technological solution. When Allen Dulles had first briefed Eisenhower about the U-2 and the Berlin Tunnel, he had equated them by joking about a pair of new projects, "one very high, one very low." Bissell understood from the outset that the U-2 would be the Berlin Tunnel times a thousand.[2]

First came some bureaucratic skirmishing. Creating his own small, tightly held Development Projects Staff, Bissell wrested control of the plane from the Air Force in a "moderately bloody affair," as Bissell put it. Bissell had to defy General Curtis LeMay, the cigar-puffing warrior who ran the Strategic Air Command. LeMay was so aggressive about interservice turf battles that he once adorned his office with the model of a Polaris submarine affixed with the seal of the Strategic Air Command, just to irk Navy visitors. Bissell was able to ignore LeMay's bluster because of what he had—money—and what he didn't have—bureaucracy. Bissell could draw $22 million from the CIA's "reserve fund" without having to get congressional approval, crucial if the operation was to avoid leaks that would give the Soviet Union a head start on developing an air defense system that could shoot the plane down. Without teams of colonels writing plans and more plans, Bissell's Development Projects Staff was able to move with astonishing speed: eighty-eight days to a prototype, eight months to a test flight, eighteen months to fully operational airplanes.

The plane was developed in a hangar with blacked-out windows—called the "Skunk Works," after Li'l Abner—at Lockheed Corporation in Burbank, California. The designer was Kelly Johnson, a genius described by historian Michael Beschloss as a "taller, sober version of W. C. Fields" whose earlier achievements included the P-38 and the F-104 fighter planes. Johnson proposed to develop a plane that was light but strong enough to fly at an altitude of 70,000 feet over a range of 4,000 miles. "Angel," as the plane was nicknamed by the agency, was essentially a glider with a jet engine. It was so frail looking that pilots joked about the first "disposable airplane." The formal name was the U-2: the "U" stood for "utility," an intentionally dull name for an engineering feat that was as much a utility airplane as Joe DiMaggio was a utility outfielder.

Bissell was able to build a revolutionary aircraft in less time than it usually takes the Pentagon to write procurement specifications for a pair of boots by "throwing the procurement book out the window," said Bob King, his special assistant. "He ignored the lowest bid stuff. It took too long and you got a bad product."

Instead Bissell went right to the best: Johnson of Lockheed to design the plane; Edwin Land, the creator of the Land camera for Polaroid, to design the film; Pratt and Whitney to build the engine. Through the intervention of General Jimmy Doolittle, who was on the board of Shell Oil, Bissell got a petroleum company to concoct a special fuel without knowing what it would be used for. The total cost of the plane: $19 million, $3 million under budget.[3]

To test the plane in complete secrecy, Bissell persuaded the Atomic Energy Commission to annex a dry lakebed in Nevada as an atomic testing ground. An airfield was built, and only the jackrabbits and lizards observed the spidery black craft going through its paces. Bissell had to scramble at least once to preserve the veil. On a long test flight over the southern United States, the U-2 suffered a flame-out. Alerted in his Washington office, Bissell called the commander of Kirkland Air Force Base in Albuquerque, New Mexico, who mustered his troops just in time to screen off the area where the pilot made his dead stick landing.[4]

By the summer of 1956, Bissell was ready to begin overflights of the Soviet Union. From Anthony Eden, the British prime minister, Bissell received permission to base his planes in Britain. The cover story was weather reconnaissance; "the First Provisional Weather Reconnaissance Squadron" arrived at Lakenheath in June; the pilots had been "sheep-dipped"—secretly re-assigned— from the Air Force. They were given poison-coated pins to stick themselves with if captured, and each plane was equipped with a self-destruct charge if shot down. President Eisenhower was assured that there would be no identifiable wreckage and no survivors, but he was still nervous about penetrating Soviet airspace.

On July 2, Eisenhower gave Bissell authorization to fly over the Soviet Union for a period of ten days. "That's ten flying days," pressed Bissell. No, he was told, ten days, period. On July 4, Bissell walked into Dulles's office. "Well, Allen, we're out and running."

"Where is it flying?" the CIA director asked.

"It's flying first over Moscow, then over Leningrad," Bissell replied.

Dulles visibly paled, according to Bissell. "Was it really wise to do that the first time?" Bissell assured Dulles that the first time was the safest.

The Soviets picked up the flight on radar, but they couldn't do anything about it. They protested, but quietly within diplomatic channels; they did not want to call the world's attention to the fact that the United States had just built a plane that could fly directly over Moscow, and that the leaders inside the Kremlin were powerless to do anything more than shake their fists.

Bissell was shrewd about playing to the White House. The photos he brought to show the president were not of rail yards or airplane hangars, but detailed peeks into the courtyards of the Kremlin in Moscow and the Winter Palace in Leningrad—the inner sanctums of leaders. Eisenhower had no trouble seeing the power of his new tool, but he was still anxious about the Soviet response. Would the Soviets move against Berlin in retaliation? He told Bissell that he wanted to personally approve each flight. Bissell sensed immediately that permission would come sparingly.[5]

Bissell's own superiors did not quite understand the import of what had dropped in their lap. After the first flight Bissell took a photograph of a Soviet airfield to Allen Dulles and Frank Wisner. Dulles leaned over to Wisner. "How much would you give for the intelligence in these photos?" he asked his chief spymaster. "Oh, about a million dollars," Wisner replied. "The one-million-dollar photo," Dulles marveled. Yet Wisner and Dulles "didn't understand technical intelligence," said Dino Brugiani, one of a team of photo analysts put together under Bissell. "Dulles measured things in terms of espionage—how much would it cost? How hard would it be to steal? He didn't see what the photo was really telling us—that the bomber gap didn't exist."[6] Once, while he was being briefed on a highly technical collection method, Dulles said sadly to the briefer, "You're taking all the fun out of intelligence."[7]

Bissell was impatient with slow students, even ones sitting at the head of the class. In a remarkable act of lese majesty, he contrived a means to circumvent President Eisenhower to get permission for U-2 overflights. Bissell approached the British SIS and Royal Air Force with a plan to undertake U-2 missions of their own. Bissell described his thinking to historian John Ranelagh in a way that captures his mix of cunning and gall:

My theory was to set up a system whereby there would be another chief of state who could give consent, namely the British prime minister. So I approached the RAF, and, needless to say, they were eager to be in on the act. My real problem was this—it was a very difficult negotiation—they said, "If we're partners in this, that will require the approval of the prime minister and the President." I said, "Not at all. That's not the play. We're not going to call it that kind of partnership. There will be missions that the United States will run and missions that the United Kingdom will run. And I want it to be perfectly clear that the United Kingdom can run missions without detail from Washington and Washington can run missions without detail from London." The RAF got the point, and we got it set up.[8]

Bissell next approached President Charles de Gaulle of France—without telling anyone at State, the White House, or even the CIA. "Much to my surprise," Bissell later wrote, "he wanted no part of the operation. Although this outcome was disappointing, it may have been a very fortunate turn of events. After returning to Washington and explaining the nature of my trip and the surprising French reaction, virtually none of my colleagues thought that this had been a good idea. Evidently, the French were held in lower esteem as intelligence partners than I realized, and had de Gaulle accepted my proposal, not only would I have had to face a fight back at the Agency, but I would have created a potential diplomatic problem if an agreement had been reached and then had to be broken."[9]

Bissell had become a kind of independent contractor, peddling his magic eye-in-the-sky, the president be damned. Little wonder that the Air Force pilots "sheep-dipped" to the CIA began to joke that they flew for the RBAF—the Richard Bissell Air Force. Bissell took advantage of compartmentation and secrecy to create a separate fiefdom within the CIA. He moved out of the CIA headquarters down on the Mall and into offices on L Street. His doings were strictly Eyes Only: of his staff of 225, thirty handled security. Bissell had his own highly restricted cable traffic; he later said that he doubted Dulles was aware of much of it.[10]

Able to fly across the Soviet Union above the range of antiaircraft fire or Soviet warplanes, the oddly graceful craft, with its thin body and wide floppy wings, represented a revolution in intelligence gathering. Long a "denied area" (in Moscow, even the phone book was classified), the Soviet Union was now open for inspection by cameras so powerful that they could read a stop sign from 70,000 feet. By 1958, Bissell estimated, 90 percent of all hard intelligence about the Soviet Union coming into the CIA was funneled through the lens of the U-2's aerial cameras. With one technological breakthrough, Bissell had been able to accomplish a goal that all the human spies ever run by Richard Helms had not come close to achieving. By photographing air bases, navy yards, rail lines, tank factories, and missile launch sites, the U-2 could measure the destructive capability of the Soviet Union.

The information was crucial; it brought stability to a situation that was fraught with uncertainty. The Pentagon's ignorance of its adversary had bred something approaching paranoia. This was the era when the generals first warned darkly of the "bomber gap" and then the "missile gap," predicting that the Kremlin would, within a few years, have the power to wipe out the United States with a surprise attack. The estimates were based on guesswork and fragmentary evidence—a flyby of Soviet bombers over Moscow on May Day—hyped in the cause of fatter defense budgets. Still the "gaps" had great popular currency. Pentagon chiefs "shudder," reported the Alsop brothers, when they think of the bomber gap.

The aerial photographs taken by the U-2 proved that the bomber and missile gaps existed—but in favor of the West, not the Soviet Union. The United States remained well ahead of its global rival in producing weapons of destruction. President Eisenhower was unable to publicly disparage the popular myth of Soviet military omnipotence without revealing the existence of the CIA's top-secret spy plane, so the politicians continued to rail (the "missile gap" was an important factor in John F. Kennedy's defeat of Richard Nixon in 1960). But the knowledge that Khrushchev was lying when he boasted that the Soviet Union was building rockets "like sausages" allowed Eisenhower to control defense spending. More importantly, it kept the United States from overreacting in international crises—perhaps the most valuable service an intelligence agency can perform in peacetime.[11]

Most of the top CIA officials who had some dim awareness of what Bissell was up to—certainly the ones who saw the flood of intelligence provided by the U-2 after so many years of drought—were impressed. Only Richard Helms remained a skeptic. Gadgets are all very fine, he said, but you can't ignore the human side of intelligence. Someone has to evaluate what it really means.[12]

Helms was right, of course, but he was out of phase in the late 1950s. This was the great age of the American technocrat. The economy was booming along on good old American know-how; no other country could come close to American engineering and manufacturing skills in the 1950s. A decade after World War II, Germany and Japan had barely finished sweeping up the rubble. American technological superiority was so overwhelming that managers became drunk with it. Executives like Robert McNamara at the Ford Motor Company were looking for ways to make workers into ever-more efficient—and unthinking—cogs in the assembly line. This management philosophy has been rejected since: by the 1980s, American managers were trying to mimic the Japanese with their emphasis on worker skills, initiative, and quality. But in 1958 the goal of a manager in Detroit was, in effect, to dehumanize the process—to remove messy feelings, beliefs, intuitions, and emotions, and substitute mechanical efficiency.[13]

Though his top-secret work kept him in the shadows, Bissell was the greatest of all technocrats, greater than the captains of industry whose faces adorned the covers of *Fortune* or *Time*. It suited Bissell to think that human weakness could be factored out of the equation. He liked to be able to quantify. What were the chances he would get into Skull and Bones? One in four. What were the chances the Guatemala coup would succeed? Forty percent. There was a bloodless quality to Bissell that his subordinates all noticed. He was extremely courteous and courtly, a gentleman. But the body language all said stay away. "Toughness" was an adjective much in vogue among the generation that had survived World War II. Bissell, who had survived being unpopular at Groton, wanted to be known as tough, and he was. "Dickie Bissell was tough, tougher than the others," said Eleanor Dulles, the sister of Allen and John Foster.[14]

The irony was that Bissell was actually full of passion. When he described the U-2 project almost forty years later, he lit up like a schoolboy at the dessert tray. The experience had been exhilarating, he said, the most gratifying of his life. And for all his calculation of the odds, he was forever trying to beat them, from climbing the steep slate roofs of Yale to testing the probability that one day the Soviet Union would build a missile that could shoot down the U-2.

If Bissell was even aware of his inclination to tempt fate, it is not likely he dwelled on it much in 1958. He was a man of action; like his friends he lived by doing, and in 1958 there was much to do. As soon as the U-2 was winging over the Soviet Union, Bissell began to build a second spy plane—the SR-71—that could fly higher and faster. "The U-2 was state of the art," he said. "The SR-71," which could fly two and a half times the speed of sound at 85,000 feet, "was a little beyond state of the art."[15]

IN THE autumn of 1958, Bissell hesitated for a week before he accepted Allen Dulles's offer to replace Wisner as head of the clandestine service. It wasn't because of his lack of experience at running covert operations. Bissell figured he could learn quickly enough. Rather, he wondered if there wasn't something more ambitious that he could aspire to. Since the DD/P was sometimes called the "second most powerful man in government" by CIA operatives, Bissell was perhaps being immodest. But many years later he explained, "I was, let's face it, rather spoiled in matters of employment." Though few newspaper readers would recognize his name, Bissell had been, through his work on the Marshall Plan and the U-2, one of the sub rosa champions of Cold War Washington.[16]

Bissell did not like having a deputy or a chief of staff; he felt he was perfectly capable of running his own shop, no matter how large it had become. He was, however, shrewd enough to know that he needed a "salesman" who could help promote his ideas and represent his interests to the government bureaucracy and within the agency itself. He needed to be able to trust this man, to count on his discretion and loyalty, as well as his ability to charm others. The perfect choice, he thought, was Tracy Barnes.

Barnes was languishing in London that fall. He had been moved from Germany to England in December 1956, right after Suez, by Allen Dulles in an attempt to patch the badly torn "special relationship" between the United States and Great Britain. John Hay "Jock" Whitney, Barnes's cousin and old friend, was going over to London as ambassador, and the Dulleses had figured that the wellborn pair would be soothing to the British. As the CIA's "special representative," Barnes proved to be a very successful liaison to the SIS. With his democratic touch, he was equally adept dining with Tory peers and Labour Party MPs. He became a lifelong friend of Maurice Oldfield, the chief of MI-6 (in the British secret service, espionage and counterintelligence abroad were handled by MI-6, subversion and counterintelligence at home by MI-5). "Maurice loved to dance," said Janet Barnes. "In the summers, he would come visit us in Rhode Island and dance under the trees at night"—an incongruous picture of the mysterious figure known to British SIS officers as "C" and to the readers of Ian Fleming's

James Bond thrillers as "M." Barnes was struck by the deep cyn-
icism and world weariness of the British, shorn of empire and
humiliated by Suez. "All of this is a lot of shit," Leslie Mitchell, a
senior MI-6 man, told Barnes. "We're just playing games."[17]

Barnes was eager to get back to the center of things. One
evening before Christmas 1958, Janet noticed Tracy standing by
the fireplace in their little house on Gloucester Square, "conspir-
ing" with Richard Bissell, who had just flown in from Washington. "It was clear to me they were working out some kind of
arrangement," she recalled. The arrangement was for Barnes to
return to Washington as Bissell's ADD/P/A—assistant deputy di-
rector/plans for action. Barnes would not really be the number
two in the clandestine service, but a special kind of deputy to
Bissell. He would have no day-to-day operational responsibilities.
Rather, he would be Bissell's liaison to the Pentagon, State, and
the White House, and his troubleshooter on sensitive assignments.

Bissell had picked Barnes partly at the urging of Allen Dulles,
who remained fond of his gallant protégé. Dulles and Barnes often
played golf together, "a good game for spies, they can talk," said
Janet. Bissell regarded his relationship with Barnes as "comfortable," but it was also complicated. For so many of their school
years together, Barnes had stood at the top of the schoolboy pyr-
amid and Bissell at the bottom. Bissell was aware of the "role
reversal" between them, but, he said, "we never talked about it."
Although the two old schoolmates spent a great deal of time in
each other's adjoining offices at the CIA, they rarely had personal
or deeply reflective conversations. They were bound by a code of
shared background and values that existed in a kind of natural
equipoise—of "toughness" rounded by good manners, of noblesse
made less haughty by oblige, of daring restrained often (but not
often enough) by sound judgment. Above all, Bissell felt he could
trust Barnes, which in most senses he could, although not always
to do the wise thing.[18]

To THEIR own children, Tracy Barnes and Richard Bissell were at
once remote and endlessly fascinating. Children are not always the
most reliable sources about the character or actions of their parents, but they sometimes see things adults do not, and their in-
sights can open a window worth looking through. Barnes, as

pictured by his own children, was a more complex man than he appeared to his charmed contemporaries.

In an unpublished short story written in 1993, Jane Barnes describes the way her father looked to her when she was an insecure teenager and he was a baron of the CIA in the late 1950s: "With his hair combed flat against his head, his high cheek bones, and his large, elegant nose, he looked like a great Indian chief. He could have been Sitting Bull, gazing out at a field where Custer awaited him."

"He was royalty," she said. "You had to admire his swish, his sense of privilege." In later years, as his children looked back, they sensed that he was perhaps more rigid and driven than genuinely self-confident. "You couldn't tell him anything, he was so sensitive," said Jane. "He didn't want to hear bad things. He denied they existed. He wanted to be an optimist." Barnes's son Tracy Jr. observed that his father's "defenses were rigid. He had to have things his way." He was deeply self-effacing toward the outside world, but not always at home. "He hated the cult of personality," said Tracy Jr., "but he loved being the center of attention."

His vanity showed through. At his father's direction, Barnes as a schoolboy had abandoned Brooks Brothers because the off-the-rack suits were too boxy; Barnes's suits were tailored by Bernard Wetherill in New York, with nipped waists and broad shoulders. Though he was not a snob, Barnes preferred first class: he rooted for the New York Yankees and bought only the best brand-name equipment. "There were his Arnold Palmer golf clubs, his Nikon camera, and his Head tennis racket. He drove an MG; we drove Buicks," said Jane Barnes. "You could never touch his stuff. It was his territory. He was very generous, but with an outrageous sense of himself. He gave presents he wanted to be given. You could be a teenager and get a rotisserie cooker for your birthday." Barnes was an early enthusiast about mail-order catalogues. "He loved to spend money on things like chain saws," said his neighbor Ben Sturges, "though he was not at all mechanical. He once nailed a Christmas tree to a parquet floor in his New York apartment. He got impatient."

Personal feelings were not to be spoken of at Barnes's dining room table. "Meals were exciting but terrifying events," said Tracy Jr. "You entered the conversation at your own risk. It was like playing Wimbledon verbally. He did not tolerate failure; he'd slice and dice you." The tennis court was equally demanding. "He wanted to engage you in an intense activity. The only place he showed his emotion was on the tennis court, the golf course, or with his dogs. On the tennis court, he could come close to tantrums. He created an atmosphere that was so tense it became unpleasant. In public, he'd keep it together, but with the family it was pretty intense."

Barnes hated the "idleness of resort life." He shunned the swells of Newport, across Narragansett Bay from his summer home in Saunderstown. His own house was an old barn that Janet had transformed. Its picture windows offered sweeping views of the bay; after dinner Janet would push back the furniture and create a large dance floor. Every year she would hold square dances "and make everyone do the hokey-pokey," said John Casey, Barnes's former son-in-law. Barnes enjoyed the gay social life; he was "always welcoming," said Casey, though he observed that Barnes's good cheer required self-discipline. "He'd sit relaxed at parties, but you'd see his foot jiggle slightly. Afterward, he'd erupt, 'That idiot!' " Barnes wanted to be able to escape from time to time. When the barn was being redesigned, Barnes asked (in all seriousness) if the architect could hang a bosun's chair from the cathedral ceiling so the man of the house could haul himself up and be free with his thoughts.

Janet and Tracy had a long and in many ways close and successful marriage. "They were not bored by each other," said John Casey. "There were fights, but a lot of eros." Tracy and Janet "spoke of each other romantically and lovingly," said Jane. She recalled Barnes driving the children up to Rhode Island in the summer of 1959, "waxing on about how wonderful Mummy was, how lucky he was to have her." There were tensions, however. Barnes had an eye for the ladies, who returned his attentions. Janet "didn't go to college, and she felt intellectually inadequate. He could argue circles around her. At dinner, Daddy would be crushingly smart and she would be foolishly challenging," recalled Jane. Janet liked high jinks—squirt gun fights after a picnic lunch. But, like him, she was "extremely uncomfortable, squeamish, about raw emotion." She could not talk to him about his life at the CIA; it had to remain secret.[19]

BISSELL'S CHILDREN strike the same note of awe describing their father and his life in the late 1950s. "The house was always full of men and women who loved to laugh and have a wonderful time. There was a lot of tension, a lot of edges, and a lot of brain power," said Ann Bissell, his daughter. The Bissells gave black-tie dinner parties about twice a month; the guests often included the Alsops (Stewart and Tish were his closest friends), the Nitzes, the Barneses, the Brosses, and the Rostows. "On Sundays," said Ann, "there would be lots of drinking, lots of Bloody Marys, lots of gin, and hours and hours of raucous policy planning with all kinds of people."

Kelly Johnson, the designer of the U-2, was often in the house, "jolly and warm and fun with kids." Bissell and Johnson would chortle over their plane. "We can photograph a grapefruit with it," Bissell exclaimed to his children, a bit indiscreetly perhaps. To learn more, Bissell's eldest child, Richard III, dangled a microphone down the chimney so he could electronically eavesdrop on the adult conversation. Bissell was "not pleased," said Ann. To protect security, the house was "full of safes and different-colored telephones."

Bissell was a warm and courteous man, with a seemingly innate gentility. He could also be rigid and self-absorbed. To his children he was a confusing figure. "He was a wonderful parent," said Ann. "He was very apologetic when things were grave and distracting and he had to be away at night and on the weekends. What little time he had at home he wanted to spend with us, walking on the canal or on a little island he bought in the Potomac." After some reflection she added, however, that "there were lots of weekends at the Nitzes', Alsops', and Wisners' farms, so we didn't really have him to ourselves. Even at home the men would continue with their rituals." As a father, "he didn't really participate in your life. I was a good athlete and he never came to a single game I played in, nor did he take my brothers canoeing. And my mother hated walking on the island. She was afraid of snakes."

Mrs. Bissell—"Annie"—is a warm and generous woman, earthy and motherly, "absolutely without pretension or prejudice or rough edges," said her daughter. Like Janet Barnes, she was insecure about her lack of a college education; like almost everyone who dealt with Bissell, she was intimidated by his intellect. But she was game, a quality much valued and honored by the men of her class and time. Sailing "absolutely terrified her," said her daughter, Ann. Yet she never complained about the Bissells' summer cruises off the coast of Maine, even when, in one storm, she became tangled in her lifeline after she was swept to leeward by a wave. Trapped under the green water surging over the lee rail, she nearly drowned in the scuppers. "Mrs. Bissell took sailing as a curse of life," said Fritz Liebert, Bissell's longtime sailing friend. "It was something she had to live with."

Bissell's yawl, the *Sea Witch*, was his mistress, thrilling and consoling. "I had many scrapes aboard her, but no matter how scary, they were better than the bureaucratic fights," said Bissell. At fifty-seven feet, with a ten-foot-deep keel, the *Sea Witch* was roughly twice as long and drew twice as much as a typical cruising boat. Bissell, so eager to conquer the frontiers of high tech in aerial reconnaissance, was practically a Luddite when it came to sailing. The *Sea Witch* had no radar or radio direction finder to navigate through the fog that shrouds the Maine coast and no depth finder for the many shoals and sandbars of the New England littoral; Bissell preferred using an old-fashioned lead line. To keep track of distances traveled, he trailed a log line that became fouled in the propeller from time to time. He did keep flares on board and had to use them during his periodic brushes with disaster.

Bissell avoided the familiar cruising grounds around Martha's Vineyard and Nantucket. In Maine, he preferred to sail east of Penobscot Bay, into cold and remote waters where a boat can sail all day and not see another, and the anchorages are empty at night. He was happiest when the wind was roaring or the fog was closing in. The self-appointed navigator on all cruises, he liked to sail by dead reckoning. Nothing thrilled him more than to sail out of the deep fog at night into a narrow passageway marked by a single unlit buoy. He accomplished this time and again. He also bounced off a few rocks, once nearly sank, and twice lost a mast. The first dismasting was in a nor'easter. The second came when he guessed wrong on the height of a drawbridge at Saybrook, Connecticut. "He didn't want to wait," said Fritz Liebert. "He had a will of steel and if he thought this was the course to be taken, he was committed. God help anyone who got in his way. He'd turn ice cold and grit his teeth."

On shore visits Bissell liked "a good four-to-seven-mile hike up Mount Sergeant" near Northeast Harbor, Maine. Bissell never got seasick, though his family and guests were not so fortunate. During one nor'easter the *Sea Witch* lost every sail save one, the engine fouled, and she began taking water. Annie Bissell tied down the Bissell children on deck as best she could.

Bissell's other pleasure was music. He went to the symphony

every week during the Washington season, often to the Metropolitan Opera in New York, and never missed an annual Bach festival in Bethlehem, Pennsylvania. He preferred the baroque over the romantic. Every Sunday afternoon he listened to Bach's Mass in B Minor. "He liked the variety, the emotional intensity, the complexity, and the richness," said his daughter, Ann.

The Bissells lived simply, if that word can apply to someone who owned a fifty-seven-foot yacht. The Bissell house in Cleveland Park near the Washington Cathedral was frumpy and cluttered, though the threadbare rugs were Aubussons. Guests coming across the porch had to step over muddy boots, bundled newspapers, and old clothes put out for the Goodwill. There were no live-in domestics; Annie Bissell wanted none. Though the heir to a considerable fortune, Bissell tried to support his family on his government salary.

He was unable to, in part because William, his fourth child, was retarded and needed to be institutionalized. The baby had been born jaundiced, a condition easily treated now but one that could cause severe brain damage in the late 1940s, when the child was born. For more than ten years, the Bissells tried to keep William at home as much as possible, until his presence became too much of a strain on the family. "It was such a low and despairing time in their lives," said Beth Kent, a family friend. "They tried so hard to get through to him. They studied and went to lectures. It was the only time I saw Dick completely down. They tried to keep him out of an institution, and the struggle was horrible." William gradually spent more and more time away from his home, until he was institutionalized full-time in 1959. "It was a slow struggle of giving him up," said Ann. "It took a toll on my mother, who felt guilty. They would go to group therapy once a week, but they hated it. They would lace themselves with a couple of cocktails beforehand."

Bissell withdrew into his work. The loss of William "seemed to have no effect on my father," said Ann. "He was lost and absorbed in what he was doing." Like Barnes, Bissell could not talk to his wife about work, which in 1959 was becoming almost maniacally intense.[20]

Chapter Thirteen

A CLANDESTINE WORLD

"I took to covert action like a duck to water."

As a young boy touring Europe with his parents, Bissell had stood in the Colosseum in Rome, dreaming of lost glories. The experience, he recalled, "gave me an early interest in empire." At Groton and Yale, Bissell's academic interest had been in empires, particularly those of Rome and Britain. At the CIA, he would often think of that history as he surveyed his own domain.

Shortly after Bissell assumed control of the clandestine service in January 1959, he flew in the back seat of an Air Force T-2 jet from a secret U-2 base in Turkey to Athens, to meet with agents there. Swooping along the Turkish coast, Bissell asked if he could take a closer look at the isle of Rhodes. As the plane circled, he gazed down at the harbor where the Colossus was said to have stood. The covert action chief proceeded to give the pilot a history course, pointing out the landmarks of antiquity scattered across the Aegean. To Bissell, the line to Pax Americana was long, but direct.

In the winter of 1959, Bissell was just beginning to discover the subterranean empire he had inherited from Frank Wisner: more than fifty undercover stations around the world, hundreds of covert action programs up and running at any given time, a "reserve fund" of at least $100 million in unvouchered funds at his disposal. "I was surprised by the extent of it," Bissell said. As he rummaged through the "Eyes Only" files kept in a safe in Wisner's old office, an unadorned and slightly shabby room with peeling linoleum and dingy posterboard walls in a corner of the L Building, Bissell pieced together a vast and intricate puzzle. "I kept running into new pieces," said Bissell. The mind that had memorized railroad timetables as a boy and assembled the Marshall Plan after the war was captivated by the complexity and ambition of Wisner's legacy.[1]

The reach of the clandestine service was especially great in the so-called developing world. The CIA had not enjoyed much luck penetrating the "denied areas" of the East Bloc and Red China, but it had made great inroads in the "nonaligned" nations. The late 1950s were the high age of the CIA station chief. In countries all throughout Asia, the head of state was close to the CIA chief of station, if not actually on his payroll. The same was true throughout Latin America and the Middle East. "The number of top people who were at the time CIA assets is astonishing," said Donald Gregg, a Far East hand who later became chief of station in South Korea, another habitual friend of the agency.

CIA men uniformly say that they did not make policy; the president did. The CIA merely executed the chief executive's policy. In practice, however, the agency did make policy, whether or not it meant to. Covert actions were recommended by the CIA based on intelligence that was also developed by the CIA. Station chiefs and division heads who were eager for action had built-in conflicts of interest. They recommended a course of action and then developed the intelligence to justify it. In this role they were not merely the president's "action arm" in the world arena; they were a self-generating pitching machine.[2]

The final collapse of colonialism after World War II had set off a competition between the United States and the Soviet Union to influence, if not control, the newly "emerging nations." The Kremlin spent billions fomenting communist insurgencies all over the Third World to fight "wars of national liberation." There is a tendency among revisionist historians of the 1960s and 1970s to accuse the agency of hyping the communist threat, and it is true that the more zealous policymakers in Washington sometimes mistook a nationalist for a communist. But it is also true that the Kremlin and to a significant though lesser extent the Red Chinese were aggressively engaged all over the world in exporting revolution. Since President Eisenhower was reluctant to commit overt military force to resist communist expansionism, the CIA was called upon to resist through covert means.

A principal weapon in this struggle was cash. As the colonial empires broke up, the new rulers often had their hands out to both Washington and Moscow. Ideology was for the most part less important than lucre. "The Africans did not know how racist the Russians were, and some of them believed in the socialist utopia," said Ed Welles, a station chief in the CIA's Africa Division. "But the real incentive was money, not ideology. The Africans would take money from anyone."[3]

The CIA had no shortage of money to spread around. "There basically wasn't a limit," said Lyman Kirkpatrick, the CIA inspector general from 1952 to 1963. About two-thirds of the CIA's overall budget went for covert operations in those days (versus about 5 percent in the 1990s). "We got what we asked for," said Kirkpatrick. "It was a war, and Congress couldn't say no." As Allen Dulles's special assistant, Bissell had accompanied the DCI up to Capitol Hill at budget time to make the CIA's request for funds. Dulles, who would regale the Hill barons with old spy stories, did not need to sell very hard to lawmakers, who regarded the agency as a cheap and effective way of fighting the Cold War. On one occasion Bissell heard Clarence Cannon, the chairman of the House Appropriations Committee, ask, "Mr. Dulles, are you sure you're asking for enough money?"[4]

Western politicians were not above accepting a tip or a retainer from the CIA from time to time. In Italy, William Colby ran a $25 million a year operation. An OSS veteran from Princeton and a Roman Catholic, he was an idealistic believer in political action: he wanted to be "for a democratic Italy, not just against a Communist one," he declared. Although he was up against a formidable foe— the Soviets pumped up to $50 million a year into the Italian Communist Party—Colby did not wish to unduly corrupt the country he was trying to save. A moral man, he favored funding front groups—labor, students, intellectuals—over cash bribes.[5]

In the developing world, the politics were a little more crude, the payments more direct. "We admired the British model," said Carleton Swift, an operative in Asia and Iraq in the 1950s. "The Brits believed that you only need two agents: the chief of police and the head of state. If you had them, you didn't need all those big political action ops." Allen Dulles had his own retinue of "million-dollar agents," government officials in the Middle East who received six-figure subsidies from the CIA. Jim Critchfield, the newly appointed head of the CIA's Near East Division, was infu-

riated in 1959 when one of these "million-dollar agents" ordered
Critchfield to drive him to the airport. Kim Roosevelt dispensed
bags of gold all through the Middle East, although the money did
not always go where it was intended. Roosevelt gave $12 million to
General Bey Naguib in Egypt to facilitate the overthrow of King
Farouk, but after the revolution Gamal Nasser put Naguib under
house arrest—and stole his American booty. Part of the $12 million
was used to build the Cairo Tower, a skyscraper also known as the
CIA Monument and, among CIA officials back in Washington, as
"Roosevelt's Erection."*6

Most government officials could be had for much less than a
million. "It wasn't that expensive. It's when you get into gadgets
and covert action that the costs go up. Buying a newspaper editor
is inexpensive, and chiefs of police generally went for less than
$50,000," said Sam Halpern. Money, said Halpern, was actually
less important as a persuader than other inducements. "Medical
aid was big. You get a lifelong friend and it doesn't cost much."
The CIA's Office of Medical Services had an operational unit that
tended to the illnesses and accidents of Third World leaders and
their dependents. "We would fly them back to the United States
for treatment and cut through the red tape," said Halpern.[7]

The CIA also made friends with heads of state by training their
police forces. The agency bought an old parking garage in Georgetown and turned it into a training facility for foreign police officers.
The CIA may not have taught these knucklebreakers to read suspects their constitutional rights, but the visiting policemen were
told that torture is generally an ineffective means of interrogation.
The visitors were also given tours of democratic institutions. Tour-
ists would occasionally see Georgetown matrons in print dresses
escorting men wearing shades and speaking with Latin accents
on guided tours of the Capitol, Supreme Court, and Library of
Congress.[8]

The most effective tool of recruitment was not cash or thumb-
screws or blackmail or ideology—but simple friendship. Sam Halpern recalled the genuine gratitude of an ousted Thai prime
minister (the agency worked the "outs" as well as the "ins") when
Halpern presented him with a bronze Buddha's head. "It only cost

---

* In 1959, when the CIA became opposed to Nasser while the State Department
supported him, the CIA "gave some thought to blowing the tower up," according
to Ted Atkins, a CIA operative in the Middle East.

$100, but you would have thought I'd given him the world. He liked it even better than the Thunderbird we gave him," said Halpern.[9]

The really effective station chiefs were often bluff, charismatic men who were adept at befriending their "penetration hard targets." Howard "Rocky" Stone was vilified by the Soviets as a dangerous "masterspy" and rewarded by the CIA with the Distinguished Intelligence Medal, its highest career award. But he was effective in Asia and the Middle East because he was determined and likable, not because he was sinister or dashing. In a *Wall Street Journal* piece in 1979, David Ignatius describes Stone as not at all the James Bond type: round-faced, with his hair combed neatly over a bald spot, chronically hard of hearing, drinking beer in his basement as he tells of his exploits in a good-humored way. It had been Stone who, after the overthrow of Iran's Mossadegh in 1953, buttoned the uniform of General Zahedi, the Shah's man who was literally undone by the prospect of becoming prime minister. Stone had recruited "a high-level official at a key government ministry of a Third World country" by spending months figuring out "what this man really wanted out of life." It turned out that the man was abused by a domineering wife and worried about affording the tuition payments to educate his young child at boarding school. Stone and his wife played "marriage counselor," showing what a really loving family life could be like (the CIA paid the child's tuition). The man gratefully opened up and volunteered a "flood" of information.[10]

Sometimes simple companionship, albeit well lubricated, was enough to win over a lonely leader. Ray Cline, the agency's station chief in Taiwan in the late 1950s, often drank late into the night with Chiang Ching-kuo, the eldest son of Chiang Kai-shek, to maintain the agency's ties to the regime. Robert "Red" Jantzen, the CIA's station chief in Thailand in the late 1950s and early 1960s, played the role of indulgent big brother to various Thai political leaders. A large, redheaded backslapper, he liked to tell the story of how a few drinks with Praphat Charusathien, the number-two man in the government, turned into a friendly wrestling match that became less friendly when Jantzen, who was six-four, began to get the upper hand over the short, fat Thai. Diplomatically, Jantzen allowed himself to be pinned. He carried a secret tape recorder on him to drinking bouts with the top Thai officials so he wouldn't have to remember what had transpired the night before.

The conviviality paid off when Jantzen persuaded the Thai premier, Field Marshal Sarit Thanarat, to call off a planned invasion of Cambodia in 1959. Desmond FitzGerald, Jantzen's boss at the time, pronounced him "the greatest single asset the United States has in Southeast Asia."[11]

Ambassadors were supposed to be the official representatives of the United States; the CIA station chief was usually under cover in some lower diplomatic rank. But the CIA men handed out the gold, and they often had a more direct line of communication to the White House than the ambassador, whose cables had to filter through layers of bureaucracy. CIA station chiefs had a more expansive view of their role than most ambassadors. "The ambassador's job was to get along with the host country's foreign office. We saw the broader interests—the real interests. The ambassador's job was reporting, ours was to support and move forward American foreign policy," said Carleton Swift, station chief in Baghdad in 1957–58. "The State Department disliked this. A foreign service officer said to me, 'Everything you do should be divided into two baskets—things the Department of State should do, and things that shouldn't be done at all. We looked where the real power lies. That's why the deputy chief of the army was on my payroll." Ambassadors were "always furious in Southeast Asia," said George Holmes, a CIA operative. "The police and the military, not the foreign office, controlled the country, and the CIA had bought the police and military."[12]

The inevitable friction between State and the CIA generated what were generally called "pissing contests": crossed cables, mixed signals, bureaucratic one-upsmanship. Not infrequently, the overt policies of the United States were subverted by covert policies. It is not unusual for governments to run on "two tracks"— talking softly while waving a big stick, and State and the CIA were natural "good cop, bad cop" partners. But in the 1950s the balance between the two was uneven. The ambassador usually had the grander office; everything else about him counted for less.[13]

A formal procedure existed for vetting the CIA's covert actions. Worried that the agency was getting out of control, Eisenhower in 1955 set up a committee consisting of the national security adviser, the CIA director, and the deputy secretaries at State and Defense. Known as the 5412 Committee (after the national security order defining its role, NSC 5412/2), these top officials were supposed to decide whether covert actions were "proper" and in the national interest. As a practical matter, however, the procedure was "somewhat cloudy," according to internal CIA documents cited by the Church Committee, "and based on value judgments by the DCI." To maintain "plausible deniability," the CIA director sometimes bypassed the 5412 Committee—or as it was later called, the Special Group—and went directly to the president. Or the director simply acted on his own initiative. The more "sensitive" the operation, the less likely Allen Dulles was to tell the Special Group about it.[14]

Congressional participation in this process was little to none. Senator Richard Russell of Georgia and Senator Leverett Saltonstall of Massachusetts played an informal oversight role, but there was much they chose not to see. They accepted the notion that they should be protected from the agency's darker actions so they would never have to lie about them, or, on the other hand, be blamed for them. Before one of his private sessions with Richard Russell's Senate Armed Services Committee, Allen Dulles told an aide, "I'll tell the truth to Dick. I always do." Then he chuckled. "That is, if Dick wants to know!"[15]

Dulles himself kept a very high profile. He was bored by administration (and poor at it), but he continued to be fascinated by covert action. As time went on he was less involved in the operational details and more a spokesman for the idea of an aggressive intelligence agency. Puffing on his pipe, telling old war stories, he entertained a steady stream of dignitaries to his office. When the CIA's new headquarters in Langley, Virginia, was designed in the late 1950s, Dulles asked to have a series of different waiting rooms outside his office, so his visitors couldn't see one another or any undercover men who happened to be passing through. He made speeches, planted stories in the press, and cultivated reporters. On Dulles's around-the-world tours, station chiefs, who were supposed to be under cover, would stand sheepishly with newspaper reporters and photographers at the airport, waiting for the "Great White Case Officer" to land in his specially outfitted plane. Each New Year's Day, Dulles gave a party for the CBS News staff at the Alibi Club (the CIA picked up the bill). "It was a terribly nice party," William Bundy, who was an agency analyst in the 1950s, told Leonard Mosley. "We had a CIA man next to each CBS [man], and there was general table conversation, very useful in giving the feeling of Allen's thinking without giving them secret material. . . . It was a very warm and relaxed occasion."[16]

Dulles "did little to discourage the notion that he was a commander on the front lines of the Cold War who could change hostile regimes, frustrate the KGB, pierce the Iron Curtain and do other minor miracles of daring and skill," writes Michael Beschloss. Dulles counseled a reporter to think of the CIA as the "State Department for unfriendly nations" and was thrilled to be called "the most dangerous man in the world, far more dangerous than John Foster Dulles" by Soviet propagandists. If the CIA man ever forced his way into heaven, the Kremlin ranted, "he would be found mining the clouds, shooting up the stars, and slaughtering the angels."[17]

No wonder, in that more credulous era, that "the Agency had enjoyed a reputation with the public not a whit less than golden," writes William Colby in his memoirs. "After all, we were the derring-do boys who parachuted behind enemy lines, the cream of the academic and social aristocracy, devoted to the nation's service, the point men and women in the fight against totalitarian aggression, matching fire with fire in an endless round of thrilling adventures like those of the scenarios in James Bond films." Ian Fleming's James Bond novels had begun appearing in the late 1950s in the United States. With no evidence to the contrary, and plenty of hints from Allen Dulles that he was master to a whole crew of Agents 007, the public wanted to believe this myth. In 1958, at a time when J. Edgar Hoover was still a national hero, there was no reason for the public to believe that the CIA was any less noble.[18]

"I TOOK to covert action," said Bissell, "like a duck to water." He was aware of its limitations, the potential for an embarrassing "flap" if an operation was blown. By 1959, as he watched Guatemala sink back into feudal repression, he understood that even if successful, covert action "didn't settle anything for very long. We should have been better about stepping in after a success like that [the 1954 coup] to make the gains enduring." Even so, covert action appealed to Bissell's zest for doing. "At least it gave the government the opportunity to do something," he said. The fact that the government was doing it in secret meant more autonomy for the deputy director/plans.[19]

Bissell was eager to rationalize the clandestine service, to impose some kind of system that would allow him to weigh priorities and resources. He regarded the system set up by Wisner as "dated

and inefficient"—really, no system at all, just a maze of compartmented and overlapping operations. Confident that every problem
has a solution, Bissell appointed John Bross, his old Groton schoolmate, as his "planning officer" and devoted hours to what he called
"capital formation"—improving the organization. "He spent his
Saturdays dictating letters tackling management problems," said
Jim Flannery, one of Bissell's three special assistants. "He said it's
amazing the DD/P has gotten as far as it has. It's like a boat
dragging behind its anchor."[20]

Bissell did make some improvements. Declaring that the DD/P
was overstaffed and "not up to snuff," he set up a system to get out
the lowest 5 to 10 percent, "the OSS hangovers and former FBI
gumshoes," said Flannery. He terminated Miles Copeland's contract and shuffled aside Hans Tofte, the Korean War guerrilla
specialist whose claims were not matched by his exploits. At a
meeting of Asian station chiefs in Manila in 1959, he heard Peter
Sichel, the Hong Kong station chief, argue against the practice of
dropping Chinese nationalist "boy scouts into China to blow up
railway cars." Sichel called the airdrops of the ChiNats—who almost never returned—"a complete waste of life. We may as well
just shoot them." Bissell was "willing to listen," said Sichel, "and
afterwards, we did less of it." At a meeting with European and
Middle Eastern station chiefs in Greece the same year, "he was
wonderful," said Edgar Applewhite, the Beirut station chief. "He
said, 'I'm not interested in general complaints. I only want to hear
specific complaints.' He said it with absolute assurance. He was
much better than Wisner, who was hard to brief because he did all
the talking."[21]

Bissell could hold forth with great reason and lucidity on the
management problems facing the DD/P and articulate a host of
correctives. Then an hour later, as Thomas Powers writes, "he'd
go out and break every one of his own rules."[22] Part of the problem
was Bissell's love of tinkering—he couldn't leave anything alone.
But his deeper problem was his need to control things. Bissell
frowned on the practice, commonplace in the DD/P as well as other
large bureaucracies, of sending out cables drafted by subordinates
in the name of the director. He believed, not unreasonably, that he
could do things better than most people. He had already accomplished a great deal without widely delegating. In World War II,
Bissell had ordered all of Allied shipping and managed to organize
the entire Marshall Plan without losing track of anything, except

perhaps the load of South African coal that the timid Treasury official had come to see him about a few years later.

Bissell's aides in the DD/P were amazed by how much knowledge he could retain, especially since so much was new and unfamiliar. Bissell was "bored by Africa," but he called on Flannery in early 1959 when the African independence movement was growing and told his assistant that he wanted to be briefed for a half hour. Flannery summoned the chief of the Africa Division and his deputies, but before they could begin Bissell said, "Look, to save a little time, let me tell you what I think I know." Bissell "talked for ten minutes and covered everything they would have. He took the wind out of their sails," said Flannery. Bissell was blessed with a photographic mind; he was able to glance at documents and commit them to memory.[23]

Bissell was "frightening" to work for, said Flannery, but also fascinating. He was always in a hurry. "You can't run as fast as he could walk," said Bob King, his chief assistant. "Doris [Mirage, his secretary] had to trot behind him. We called him the 'mad stork' because none of his limbs were connected exactly right. The effect was slightly comic, a *Reader's Digest* 'most unforgettable character I've ever met.' " Bissell was chronically late and—dangerous for the chief of the clandestine service—sloppy about keeping track of paper. "His desk was a mess, and he was careless about taking home top-secret documents. We finally had to put a safe in his house," said King. "The security people were still afraid he'd have an accident and top-secret stuff would be strewn all over the highway."[24]

His staff treated him with respect: "He was a lousy manager," said King, "but a great leader." King had worked for Bissell at the U-2 operations center. "When he arrived, there would be this wave of 'Here comes Mr. Bissell!' He imbued you with idealism, that you were doing something very important." But King and the others were amused, and slightly baffled, by his high WASP customs and habits. They could not quite understand why he drove old cars until they fell apart (he occasionally showed up at work with a distributor cap in the pocket of his English suit). Though his suits were expensively made, King was under the impression that he had only two of them, and neither had ever been pressed. "He kept a dirty Kleenex in his pocket," said King, and constantly snorted on an inhaler to clear his sinuses. Bissell was friendly and sometimes charming with the staff, whom he teased ("surrounded as I am by boobs and incompetents") but rarely invited to his home. King did go once and couldn't comprehend why a man with so much money lived so modestly—as King saw it, almost shabbily. "There was laundry piled high and the dog was tied to the stove. On the stairs to the third floor there was a sign saying 'Parents only!' and in the living room there were some threadbare rugs and grandes dames holding court." At Christmas, Bissell made a "wicked milk punch" and joked with the staff, "but the body language was standoffish," said King.[25]

His aides were very sensitive to the class differences between them. "He thought it very uncouth that we ate before 1 P.M.," said Jim Flannery, a combat infantry veteran from World War II. "We ate at eleven because we were in the office reading cables at seven. I told him in Texas we eat when we get hungry. He grinned." Flannery felt that Bissell had in him "a great deal of warmth, but he didn't let it out easily. He was an understanding guy who had led a protected life." Bissell was calm and controlled during crises, almost eerily so. But "every once in a while he'd blow," said Flannery, "and it was magnificent when he did." A small thing, some tiny loss of control—a misplaced paperweight was enough—could unleash an eruption, a tantrum at once infantile and Vesuvian. Unlike the Ivy Leaguers who had learned how to swear by being around enlisted men in wartime, Bissell did not cuss much. "Sweet Jesus" was about as profane as he got, but he could say it with real emphasis: "Swe-e-et JEEsus!"

Bissell was still suspicious of the military, whose bureaucracy he found impenetrable ("Bissell distrusted all bureaucracies," said King, "including his own"). Bissell once lost patience with Flannery's slowness in arranging for an Army officer to be "sheep-dipped" (loaned) to the CIA. " 'I can't understand why you can't get that guy out!' he yelled at me. I said, 'Have you ever been in the military, Mr. Bissell?' He calmed down. But he'd rant and rave and throw his newspapers on the desk." Bissell was equally hard on the State Department. For all his scientific exactitude, Bissell loved conversational hyperbole. "All secretaries of state are treasonous," he would declare, meaning that he disagreed with their policies and found them habitually timid. He also would assert, "All economists should be hanged," which, his aides felt, he really did mean.

Bissell was extremely impatient. Though he himself was often late, he could not tolerate tardiness in others. Cord Meyer, who was the head of the International Organizations Division, was a little too independent for Bissell's taste, and he had an annoying habit of giving Bissell voluminous recommendations for action only moments before they were due in Allen Dulles's office. Bissell's aides could hear him shouting at Meyer over the phone after the delivery of one such memo before an imminent deadline, "I'm going to tear it up! I'm going to tear it up!" He put down the phone. "I just tore it up!" he yelled. He sent Meyer the pieces in an envelope.

Bissell's approach to annoying impediments was to ignore them. He would calculate the risk and then push ahead. Driving his secretary to an office party, he dismissed her warnings that he was driving the wrong way down a one-way street. "Goddamn it, I'm only going one block," he said. Bissell took a bigger risk when he failed to pay heed to the intelligence analysts at the CIA, as he did from time to time when he did not like what they were saying. The CIA had an entire directorate of analysts who were supposed to assess intelligence, the DD/I (Deputy Directorate/Intelligence), as well as Bissell's operations directorate, the DD/P (Deputy Directorate/Plans). "The covert action people under Bissell would just ignore the DD/I estimates if they didn't like them. The covert action staff would produce its own estimate instead," said Lloyd Emerson, one of Bissell's assistants. "This was a very fallible system."

Bissell was confident that he could calculate the odds better than the analysts or his own subordinates in the DD/P, but he did not always guess right. In Cambodia in 1959, some colonels planned a coup against Prince Sihanouk. "Bissell ordered me to send a radio operator with the coup plotters," said Charles Whitehurst, who ran the Cambodia desk. "I argued against it. But Bissell wanted the information right away. He was always pressing, always in a big hurry." When the coup collapsed, the CIA man was captured and exposed. Sihanouk denounced the United States for plotting against him and began to turn more to the Red Chinese. It was a serious flap, with unfortunate long-term consequences. "Bissell didn't listen," said Whitehurst. "He told me to do things with an agent that couldn't be done and it backfired."[26]

Lacking any background in tradecraft or much in covert action, Bissell naturally stirred up resentment when he arrived. "He came out to Japan too cocksure, very hardline," said Donald Gregg, who was under cover in Tokyo in the late 1950s. "I had a feeling, here's a hard-charging bureaucrat who needs to get out into the field." "A lot of old hands thought he was the worst thing since Stalin," said Flannery. "He was stirring the pot, and people had gotten comfortable with the way things were." Some were vocal in their opposition: after lunch one day Bissell was set upon in the men's room by a drunken GS-18, an old OSSer, for "ruining" the clandestine service.[27]

Others kept their feelings to themselves. The person who most resented Bissell was Richard Helms, though he was too much of a gentleman to show it, at least at the outset. The two men were set apart by a basic philosophical difference: "Bissell didn't mind rocking the boat, and Helms did," said Flannery. But beyond that was a question of pride. It was bad enough to be passed over in favor of Bissell, but Bissell salted the wound by failing to consult with Helms. He barely spoke to him outside the morning meeting, even though Helms remained chief of operations for the DD/P. Equally significant, he took away the cable traffic from Helms, who had handled it for Wisner. Bissell wanted to see the cables himself. Helms, who had been at the center of everything, found himself out of the loop, demeaned by his ignorance. Tom Powers, Helms's biographer, tells the story of Helms asking a counterintelligence man, in a purely conversational way, "What's new?" The CI man was amused; after all, Helms was chief of ops. "You mean you don't know?" he teased. Helms raised his hands and said in German, "Aber keiner sagt mir was!" ("No one tells me anything!")[28]

Cutting out Helms was a very big mistake, one that troubled Bissell later in life. In many ways, Bissell realized too late, Helms could have been the perfect complement: he knew the clandestine service and he was a superb administrator. As he was leaving punctually at six, his own affairs in order, Helms would sometimes clean up a neighbor's desk if classified papers were lying about. But Bissell's desk was both out of bounds and beyond hope.

Bissell did leave Helms in charge of the DD/P's espionage operations, but only because he wasn't much interested in espionage. "The thing we need," he said sarcastically to Bob King, "is more spies." Bissell thought the spies exposed themselves to great danger for little return. Technical means—the U-2, communications intercepts—were much more efficient and productive. Bissell was dismissive of the best spy the CIA and SIS ever recruited, Oleg Penkovsky, who turned over thousands of pages of Soviet military documents—personal histories of leading generals, operations manuals for the latest missiles. "How do we know this guy is on the level?" Bissell asked Soviet Division chief Jack Maury, who was incredulous: Penkovsky had long since proved his bona fides.[29]

Helms's way of dealing with Bissell might be described as passive aggressive. One Friday, the Saturday duty officer asked Helms what he should tell Bissell about Penkovsky if Bissell happened to ask him. Helms leaned across his desk. "Not a fucking thing," he said. If Bissell wasn't going to consult with Helms, Helms wasn't going to consult with Bissell. When a particularly dicey covert action came up at the morning meeting, Helms would simply remain silent. "You might call it an accommodation," said Lloyd Emerson. "Bissell left spies to Helms. And Helms left the Bay of Pigs to Bissell."[30]

THE DIVISION chiefs in the clandestine service were sometimes called the "barons," in part because they saw themselves as independent fiefdoms. The Far East Division ("FE") belonged to Des FitzGerald, who took over in the summer of 1958 after the bungled Indonesia revolt demanded a housecleaning. He was largely left alone to run the division as he saw fit. Allen Dulles trusted Fitz-Gerald and admired his dash; so, too, did Richard Bissell, who was busy on other fronts. By the late 1950s, FitzGerald felt well steeped in Asian politics and the art of covert action. His approach, to use a favorite expression of the day, was "forward leaning." FitzGerald's tour of duty is remembered as a time of tremendous activity, of earnest attempts at "nation building" and counterinsurgency against a ubiquitous and subversive foe.[31] William Colby, the Rome political action operative who transferred to "FE" in the fall of 1958, describes, a little breathlessly, the glamour of coming to work for FitzGerald:

> Desmond FitzGerald had just become chief of the division, and his spirit permeated it. . . . With a lovely Georgetown house and a country residence in Virginia, he was well connected throughout Washington, where his romantic activism produced great dinner talk. In the Far East Division and at its stations in Asia, he had a rich stable of immensely colorful characters from "ugly Americans" like Lansdale, swashbucklers accustomed to danger, to quiet students steeped in the culture of the Orient. . . . They were a brilliant corps of officers, unparalleled in their ability to operate in the special Asian environment,

accustomed to the unrelenting presence of open and secret violence and conspiracy there. . . .[32]

FitzGerald liked to view himself as a simple civil servant in the British tradition, carrying out—but never making—the policies of his government. This was to some extent a comfortable fiction. "He was making policy, not just carrying it out," said Chester Cooper, the CIA liaison to the National Security Council staff. "Allen Dulles would say, 'What should we do?' and we'd tell him." John Horton, an old FE hand, said that "FitzGerald loved policy. He'd be changing the world at the morning meeting." FitzGerald was too self-effacing to say it, but he may have felt, not without reason, that he knew more and was better qualified to make policy decisions than the policymakers he worked for. He always wanted to have a leg up on the State Department. He insisted that a station chief should always be better informed than the ambassador, whom he usually regarded as a target to be controlled and manipulated. "Your first recruit," he told Bill Colby, before sending him out to be station chief in Saigon in 1960, "should be the ambassador."

FitzGerald was too sophisticated to be an ideologue. He did not regard communism as monolithic, and while he was wary at first of a bluff he soon recognized that the Sino-Soviet split was profound. There was, however, some tension between his worldliness—his acceptance and even delight in cultural and ethnic differences—and his need to force events. He did not think that neutralists could run a country, as if neutralism was somehow a sign of dangerous passivity in a leader.

Chastened by the blunders of the Korean War, FitzGerald espoused a fairly cagey philosophy of covert action. He was wary of big, splashy paramilitary operations, believing that the CIA too easily lost control (as he had failed to control Li Mi's ChiNat army in Burma in 1951–53). He favored political action over paramilitary operations, arguing that the kind of "nation-building" counterinsurgencies run by Lansdale in the Philippines and the British in Malaya was the way to turn back communism in the Far East. He had no faith at all in the Pentagon's ability to intervene with force majeure in Asia. FitzGerald counseled patience, arguing that the way to win was over the long term by carefully building secure intelligence networks and winning the hearts and minds of the people.

Unfortunately, however, FitzGerald, like Richard Bissell, did not always obey his own rules. He could be disciplined and shrewd, but he could also be headstrong and impulsive. James Lilley, a veteran CIA operator and station chief in the Far East who became ambassador to Korea and China under Reagan and Bush, saw a basic conflict at work in FitzGerald. "Des talked about being patient, but he didn't apply the same rules to himself," said Lilley.

This tension—between a careful, highly sophisticated approach to tradecraft and a hubristic penchant for action and risk—played all through FitzGerald's career. In some cases he allowed prudence and wisdom to dictate, but in others he was unable to resist the temptation to plunge headlong.

FitzGerald was given to sayings, two of which he repeated like mantras. "We are not here to monitor communism, we are here to destroy it," he would instruct his operatives. To the more cautious types like Richard Helms, FitzGerald would argue that information was useless as long as it was locked in a safe. "Des was basically a guy interested in political action, not espionage, and I don't think he ever understood counterespionage. He felt he had to get something visible done. Collecting intelligence was passive. The only reason to collect it was to use it. He understood about tradecraft and security, but really he cared more about using the stuff," said Sam Halpern, his executive assistant. "Des couldn't have cared less about espionage," said John Horton, who was station chief in Hong Kong, an important listening post on China but not a base for much political action. "I told him, 'You only come to Hong Kong to buy a new pipe.' "

Like Bissell, Wisner, and Barnes, FitzGerald had no use for military chains of command or tables of organization. "What he cared about was getting the right person to do the job," said Halpern. "The idea, right out of World War II, was to get something done and to hell with the paperwork."

In the nineteenth century England had extended and protected its empire with a class of brave young men known as "thrusters"— forward thrusters who could travel alone into the mountains of Afghanistan armed with little more than an Eton education and somehow persuade the local chieftains to take sides against Russia in the "Great Game" for Central Asia. FitzGerald wanted to create a cadre of modern "thrusters." His ideal, said Jim Lilley, was "the intellectual activist." FitzGerald wanted "a guy with street smarts with a Ph.D. from Harvard who could write up an analysis of the

Communist Party and then go out and get drunk." The number of
bar-fighting Harvard Ph.D.s being in short supply, FitzGerald usually got either brains or brawn, a mandarin or a wiseguy. Still, he
was resourceful and flexible in his approach to getting the right
person for the job. "You need all kinds," he told Halpern. "Guys
who can burgle safes and guys who can drink tea without rattling
the cup."

Two of his more memorable operatives were Tony Poshepny and
Campbell James.[99] The two men could not have been more differ
ent, except that neither would have survived long in the ordered
worlds of the military or the foreign service. Campbell James was
by anyone's definition a fop. Poshepny was known in clandestine
service parlance as a knuckledragger. Both played critical roles for
the CIA in the violent intrigue of Southeast Asia in the late 1950s.

James, heir to a Standard Oil fortune, was educated at Groton
and Yale. (His nickname was "Zup" or "Zoop"; his colleagues mistakenly assumed his money came from Campbell Soup.) James had
run guerrillas into China from the coastal islands in the early 1950s.
"He had a wine cellar on Quemoy that was as good as any in
Washington," said Chester Cooper. A bon vivant out of Graham
Greene, James dressed the part in linen suits and a floppy hat
holed by a bullet. In later years he sported a monocle, and his key
chain "looked like something you'd put on a fence with a padlock.
It had all sorts of things on it, like a swizzle stick and a gold
toothpick," said Cooper, not to mention a wine thermometer and a
caviar taster. James also carried at all times a half pint of brandy
in the hollow of his walking stick. He entertained visitors to the
CIA outpost on Quemoy by inviting them to listen to the Chinese
Nationalists scream obscenities over a loudspeaker at the Red
Chinese across the channel. James would then dramatically an-
nounce, "We have thirty seconds to get to the caves!" and lead a
chase down into the mountain bunker before the first artillery shell
came crashing down.

In Laos, where James was sent in 1957, FitzGerald used him to
penetrate the effete, Frenchified court society and get close to
Prince Souvanna Phouma. Though a slightly cartoonish figure—old
FE hands tended to roll their eyes when his name came up—James
was imaginative and quite brave. "He was there when the chips
were down, crawling house to house in the battle of Vientiane,"
said David Laux, an operative in Laos and Cambodia.

"In eccentric operating situations, Des found people who could offer nonbook responses. He gave us a lot of leeway," said James, who "knew Des through Mike Peabody [Marietta's brother] at Groton. In my cables, I was very blunt. I'd say of a Thai agent, 'In short, he's a dilettante fanatic.' Des would purr. He loved that kind of description. He disliked people with furrowed brows, seriousness. He called them Heathcliffs. When we shot down a Russian supply plane over the Plaine des Jarres, we worried that we had gone too far. Des just cabled back, 'Good shot, Red Baron.' "

Tony Poshepny—"Tony Poe" as he was called—was a paramilitary expert. A former Marine who fought in the Pacific in World War II, Tony Poe ran secret armies for the CIA. In 1956 he trained Khamba tribesmen in Tibet for guerrilla warfare against the Chinese communists; he was one of the CIA's paramilitary advisers to the failed colonels' revolt in Indonesia, and he would go on to become a kind of warlord with the Hmong tribesmen in Laos. Faintly resembling Marlon Brando in middle age, he was sometimes said to be the real-life version of the mad Colonel Kurtz of *Apocalypse Now*, but even after he went native in Laos and began consuming a bottle of local white lightning every day, he was a very effective fighter. He was fearless; he seemed at home with violence (on R&R, he always carried a boxer's mouthpiece in case he got into a bar fight). Wounded several times, Poe had a claw for a hand, maimed by a jungle booby trap. He had some odd habits: for a time, he paid Laotian irregulars to bring back the ears of their enemy dead—a dollar per ear. Once, when headquarters questioned a body count, he mailed in a fresh batch of bloody ears. He desisted in the custom when he ran into a Laotian boy who was missing his ears. The boy explained that his father had chopped off his ears to sell to the Americans.[34]

FitzGerald was at once fascinated and amused by characters like Zup James and Tony Poe, and he liked to come visit them in the field as often as possible. FitzGerald was a collector of exotica. His office was decorated with such curios as a flintlock musket used by the Hmong tribesmen of Laos and an autographed photo of Mata Hari. "He would look forward to these trips and he would come back with suitcases full of wonderful things," said his stepdaughter, Barbara (although a Hong Kong tailor monogrammed some of his shirts with Chinese characters that translated "smelling slightly of dead fish"). FitzGerald had a full set of safari suits made by Abercrombie & Fitch and a specially designed CIA bag with all

sorts of straps, loops, and secret compartments. Peter Sichel recalled him tramping around the subtropics, somewhat stiffly, in a
pith helmet and white gloves (to protect his skin, which never got
over its sensitivity to the sun from his Burma days in World War
II). He was adventurous and ever-curious; with David Laux, he
insisted on being taken to Chinese movies in a seedy district of
Phnom Penh; "he wanted to wallow in it, to get a feel for the
culture," said Laux.

When he first came out to the Far East on a trip with Frank
Wisner during the Korean War, the two men stood in a corner at
a CIA cocktail party in Tokyo, whispering and summoning people
over for private audiences. "They were important, powerful, significant, and rude," said John Horton. FitzGerald was more genuinely commanding by the time he went to the Far East as division
chief in 1959. At a station chiefs' meeting up in the hills of northern
Luzon, FitzGerald gave an impressive overview of the CIA's ambitious mission in the Far East, "nothing ideological—nothing so
vulgar—but high concept," said Horton.

By most accounts, FitzGerald was willing to listen, and always
open to new ideas. But he was hard to argue with, especially for
aides who felt not only outranked but also socially inferior. Sam
Halpern would be FitzGerald's loyal and admiring executive assistant in several different assignments over seven years; "I loved
working for the guy," said Halpern, who wept when FitzGerald
died. "I was a kid from Brooklyn. My father had been a tailor who
went bust in the Depression. I wasn't on his social level. I didn't go
to his fancy parties."

FitzGerald's operatives were generally admiring, even if they
occasionally poked fun, and they tended to defer to his judgment.
"We were so glad to have such a presence, someone so stylish, we
didn't care what he did," said Horton. "He was out of a movie, a
great image, confidence inspiring," said Donald Gregg, who later
became ambassador to South Korea. FitzGerald was not above
manipulating his juniors with "tradecraft in the office," said
Chester Cooper. "He'd place your chair so that sunlight would
stream into your eyes while you were talking to him." To keep
subordinates on their toes, he would quiz them on minute geo-
graphical detail. "He spoke eloquently and sometimes delphically,"
said Horton. "He would say things like, 'Buenos Aires has one of
the three best meat restaurants in the world.' We'd wonder, what

are the other two?" He could also be arch. "I told him one of my sources was secretary of Chinese affairs in Hong Kong. Des asked, 'What other affairs are there?' "

Literate and ironic, he had a well-developed sense of whimsy, demonstrated by his fondness for Alice in Wonderland as a metaphor for the spy business. "I had to keep a copy on my reference shelf," said Halpern. "I had the whole series. He'd refer to phrases in *Alice's Adventures in Wonderland* and it would drive us all whacky. What the hell is the boss talking about? Only after you got the allusion could you fathom him. It was a way of getting the upper hand, of creating space—a ploy to keep other people off balance. He did it with everyone."

FitzGerald's literary allusions were more likely a way for him to maintain some detachment from his work. Intelligence work is so insular and involving that it tends to consume its practitioners over time. FitzGerald wanted to be able to keep his distance from a world that was becoming "curiouser and curiouser," though his romanticism made it hard not to succumb.

There was, at the same time, a gloomy streak in FitzGerald. For all their esprit, the men who ran the clandestine service had a morose side that would emerge from time to time, usually in apocalyptic remarks about the course of world events. Tracy Barnes, usually sunny and upbeat, had surprised his friend Mary Cutler in Germany by predicting in 1956 that "evil" would triumph over "good." Frank Wisner, weighed down by his illness, had shocked Chip and Avis Bohlen with his global despair on a trip to the Philippines in 1958. Desmond FitzGerald, normally so jaunty and bold, shared this periodic foreboding. From Japan in 1955 he wrote his daughter Frances, who was fourteen at the time:

> I must say that the world is a dark and dangerous place and the dehumanization of man has made terrible progress. I see the worst of it from where I am—nations of blind warrior ants in the making and the world of morality and reason being slowly forced back. I am afraid that I am a bit gloomy these days as I cannot see the answer to these problems nor find a guarantee of the most important thing in the world to me—that there will be the right kind of world for you to live in.

FitzGerald's angst may have been just a case of the blues. He did not like being so far away from his daughter from his first marriage ("I miss you very badly, Frankie, and always will when we are away from each other," he ended the same letter). But FitzGerald's low estimation of the world was also influenced by his own private but deeply felt yearning for an idealized lost age.

To FitzGerald and his kind, the Cold War was not an ideological abstraction. It was a real, if shadowy struggle, fought through surrogates but sometimes face-to-face, and the outcome was not foreordained. CIA operatives saw communist expansionism up close: in cables back to Washington, they may have exaggerated the money, discipline, and zeal of the opposition, but not always or by much. To Third World peoples throwing off colonialism, the communists had a seductive story to tell. The more clever Marxists were skillful at cloaking themselves as nationalists and stirring up anti-West, anti-American hatred.

In Romania at the end of the war, Frank Wisner had seen how the Soviets swallowed a country whole. FitzGerald had not had such a vivid personal experience, but in the Far East he watched nations of "blind warrior ants" being manipulated by Marxist dogma and repression. He "felt the communists had the upper hand and had no intention of stopping until they took over all of Southeast Asia," said Charles Whitehurst, who monitored activities in Laos for the CIA.

During his tour of duty running the CIA's China Mission in the mid-1950s, FitzGerald had been chilled by fragmentary reports about Mao's attempts to modernize China. Red China was largely sealed off, and the CIA had little good firsthand intelligence. But the CIA's agents in Hong Kong and Taiwan heard stories of forced mass relocations, "reeducation camps," and massive famine caused by Chairman Mao's brutal progress toward the millennium. Some of these reports were discounted; the CIA was getting so much bad intelligence from fabricators and paper mills that it could not know what to believe. But FitzGerald, with his dread of dehumanizing mass movements, thought he was witnessing, however distantly, an end to civilization. At a time when panicky Americans were beginning to build fallout shelters in their basements and backyards, FitzGerald refused to be a mere "stone axe," as he had described himself and his men when he first learned about the atom bomb in August 1945. He harbored a faith—romantic, perhaps, but central to the identity of the CIA in the 1950s—that individuals could make a difference, that it was possible to push back against tyrants who wielded nuclear weapons, and certainly necessary to try.[35]

FITZGERALD'S WIFE, Barbara, would be "terrified and proud" when her husband went off on his secret missions, said his stepdaughter, Barbara Lawrence. On his return he would describe what it was like to live in a cave on Quemoy or on a mountaintop in Laos, but he couldn't discuss what the CIA was up to there, except in the most general terms. His family had to accept that FitzGerald was lost to them most of the time; they could tell it was Saturday if he wore a sport jacket, instead of a suit, to work. On Sundays and at night the (secure) phone rang constantly with reports from duty officers, and the house had to be swept every six months for electronic bugs.

"My mother was complaining one day about the household staff," said Barbara Lawrence. "Desie cut in, 'Do you realize that I have four men on a hill in China with very little hope of getting them back?' " The outburst was unusual, out of character. He normally kept his frustrations to himself. There were only limited outlets for stress; his busy social life, of course, was partly work. "He liked going out, he 'liked the talk,' " said his daughter Frances Fitz-Gerald. "He was a good dancer, though he refused to do anything Latin. He said North American men weren't built to do it." Manly pleasures—guns (he owned a skeet gun with a specially curved stock) and cars—entertained him: like Tracy Barnes he drove too fast and grumbled because his Jaguar was always in the shop. Religion offered no comfort. He had tried to talk to a Jesuit priest about Catholicism after his divorce in 1947, but the conversation was more intellectual than spiritual; FitzGerald could appreciate the idea of the leap of faith, but he could not make the jump himself.

He tried to be optimistic and enthusiastic, and usually he was. He would blow up occasionally, but his temper would quickly pass. His stepdaughter, Barbara, theorized that his lonely childhood made him comfortable in the secret world. "He liked having secrets, he liked knowing things other people did not." She said that he enjoyed feeding disinformation to his old friend, columnist Joe Alsop. At breakfast he'd amuse himself reading the papers to see if Alsop had taken the bait.

His children were in awe of his stoicism. Joan Denny recalled a driving lesson with her father out at their farm in The Plains, Virginia:

> I was driving a small jeep, and my father was trying to teach me how to accelerate around a curve. We turned right down a dirt road. I thought, Oh, I'll show him. We skidded right towards a stone wall. My father's face remained absolutely impassive, his pipe clenched in his mouth. He remained immobile as we were about to crash. He never flinched. His profile was perfect, the teeth clenched, the jaw slightly more pronounced. . . .

Returning home from the country one Sunday, he closed the garage door on his finger. His son, Desmond Jr., found him standing silently, his finger crushed in the door hinge, sweat pouring from his brow. "He was trying to remain calm and unemotional," said the younger Desmond.

Closed to his own emotions, he did not like to talk to his children about theirs. "He thought a lot about his children, but he was not one for intimate conversations," said Frances. Driving home with his wife and children from the country one evening, he announced, "Let's have a talk," and proceeded to talk for an hour on the mechanics of the internal combustion engine, from fuel injection through the turn of the wheel.

FitzGerald's distance from his offspring was hardly exceptional in that less child-centric era, and he could make time for activities he enjoyed. "We did grenade launch together," Des Jr. said. "I remember sitting behind a stone wall out in the country shooting at snapping turtles with hollowed-out bullets. He had brought out from the CIA a prototype assault weapon, with clips of tracers and dummy grenades. We laid waste to those snapping turtles."

Barbara FitzGerald teased her husband, "deflated some of his pomposity, spoofed him," said Joan Denny. A warm, fetching woman, Barbara was very much admired by friends and her children for her light and steady touch. She had survived the London blitz during the war, and few noticed that she had been left half deaf by a bomb blast (she could read lips across a room). "She never demanded attention. She was a good sport, a good Brit," said Joan. "When the chips were down, you wanted her down in the shelter with you, breaking into a cockney song."

Her children said that she played very much the dutiful wife with FitzGerald. "She'd go to Elizabeth Arden and she'd model for him," said Barbara Lawrence. "He'd sit there, picking and choosing. My mother had no taste of her own. She'd twirl around in her evening dresses, some for at home, some for on the town, always very elegant and conservative."

Her husband adored her, even if he couldn't say it. "He told me he loved her, but he didn't tell her," said his stepdaughter, Barbara. "He knew he was bad about it. She felt underappreciated and complained to her mother." On one occasion her children heard her cry, "Just once won't you say you love me?" FitzGerald was "silent," said Des Jr., but, he added, "they slept in the same bed." Like Barnes, Bissell, and Wisner, FitzGerald "couldn't talk shop" with his wife. "She couldn't very well say, 'How did your meeting with the spy go, dear? Did you snuff him?' " said Joan, with a slight edge in her voice. Her father's profession was hard on her and her mother and her siblings, and hard on FitzGerald, too, though he almost never complained.[36]

Chapter Fourteen

PLOTS

*"We thought of Daddy
as James Bond."*

"THERE WILL BE no communist government in Latin America while I am DD/P," Bissell declared to the Western Hemisphere (WH) Division shortly after he became head of the clandestine service in the winter of 1959. He had not figured on Fidel Castro's Cuba.

At first, Castro didn't look like a communist. In April 1959, four months after Cuban dictator Fulgencio Batista fled Havana, Castro paid a triumphant visit to the United States, where he laid wreaths on the memorials of Jefferson and Lincoln and said on NBC's *Meet the Press* that he opposed communism. *Time* magazine noted, however, that he was not a democrat: there had been twenty-eight executions in Cuba the week before, bringing the total to 521 since he had taken power. The magazine quoted Senator George Smathers of Florida to the effect that Castro's government was "peppered" with communists. For once the Lucepress was not exaggerating the communist threat.

Advised by Ernesto "Che" Guevara, who had witnessed first-hand the fall of Arbenz, Castro was determined not to repeat the mistake of Guatemala. He made sure that the army and the press were under his tight control, even if it meant purging and alienating the middle class. He turned instead to the local Communist Party for support, in large part because it was effective at organizing the labor unions. He nationalized the sugar plantations, making him a true communist in the eyes of American businessmen, and began to receive weapons from the Soviet Union. Ominously to the CIA, he also dispatched clandestine teams to stir revolt in Cuba's Caribbean neighbors, the Dominican Republic, Panama, Haiti, and Nicaragua. Castro became intolerable to the top policymakers in Washington; he had to go. The only question was how the CIA was going to get rid of him.[1]

Bissell did not have to look hard for a model. In the winter of 1959–60, he dusted off what DD/P veterans called "the Guatemala scenario." By early March 1960, the DD/P had drafted a top-secret policy paper, "A Program of Covert Action Against the Castro Regime." It called for the creation of an exile government, a "powerful propaganda offensive," developing resistance groups within Cuba that would provide intelligence and be "responsive" to the exile government, and the establishment of a paramilitary force outside Cuba for "future guerrilla action." It was PBSUCCESS Part II—in essence, a plan to scare Castro out of power, just like Arbenz before him.[2]

Burdened by his other duties as DD/P, as well as by his continuing responsibility for running the U-2 operation, Bissell was not able really to focus on the Cuba project until the autumn of 1960. In the meantime, he did not trust the head of the Western Hemisphere Division, J. C. King, to run the show. King, a West Pointer and former pharmaceutical representative in Buenos Aires and São Paolo, lacked flair. He had been pushed aside during the Guatemala operation by Frank Wisner, and Bissell did the same to him with Cuba. Instead, Bissell asked the assistant DD/P, Tracy Barnes, to help get the Cuba operation up and running. Bissell hoped that Barnes would reprise the role he had played so well in the Guatemalan operation—as a pacifier and mediator, both within the CIA and with its masters in the executive branch.

At Bissell's request, in the winter and spring of 1960, Barnes took on the job of putting together a team to overthrow Castro. The approach, which seemed reasonable at the time, was to reassemble the old Guatemala group.[3] The project director, Jake Esterline, who had run the PBSUCCESS "war room" in Washington, was competent. A former guerrilla fighter with the OSS's Detachment 101 in Burma during World War II, he looked like a linebacker, though he loved opera; he was at once deferential and uncomfortable around "the Yalies," as he referred to Bissell and Barnes. The propaganda chief was again David Phillips, the smooth ex-actor whose Voice of Liberation and artful disinformation campaign had apparently fooled the Guatemalans. But after these two, mediocrity set in. Dick Drain, Esterline's number two, had studied economics under Bissell at Yale, but he knew nothing about paramilitary action. The forty or so officers working for them were often castoffs from division chiefs who, as Bissell later ruefully recognized, "cried crocodile tears to lose them."

The two men chosen by Barnes to act as political officers, charged with setting up the Cuban government-in-exile, were unpromising. Gerry Droller, a German who chain-smoked cheap cigars in closed rooms and dined on liverwurst sandwiches, chose to be a steel tycoon as his cover in Miami; he treated the Cubans like peons and bragged, "I carry the counterrevolution in my checkbook." A former Swiss desk officer, he could not speak a word of Spanish. His sidekick was E. Howard Hunt. After the Guatemala operation Hunt had served as station chief in Uruguay. Told that he was being sent back to Washington, Hunt had enlisted the president of Uruguay to lobby the president of the United States to let him stay on; Eisenhower was embarrassed and Hunt was yanked back from Montevideo. As ever, Hunt had a fertile, if not always practical imagination. One of his schemes, never implemented, was to send a white-painted "flight of truth" on a tour of Latin America bringing a "Billy Graham–type operation—the message of Castro's betrayal of the Cuban Revolution."

At his first meeting with the top officers on the Cuban operation in March, Phillips noticed that while "Barnes spoke frequently . . . Dick Helms listened carefully, often inspecting his carefully manicured fingernails, but said nothing. It was the first time," Phillips observed, "I had seen the usually articulate Chief of Operations so reserved."

In his passive way Helms had been opposed to the operation from the beginning. After Bissell first informed him about the plan in the winter of 1960, Helms assembled in his office several of his allies, including Bill Harvey, Jim Angleton (the spooky chief of counterintelligence), and Critchfield. "He said, 'You know what His Nibs wants to do?' He told us that Bissell wanted to invade Cuba. There was a lot of eye rolling and scoffing," said Critchfield.[4]

On a trip to Athens in March 1960, Bissell asked Critchfield if he would run the Cuba operation. "He thought he could do it with a bunch of rusty old ships and guys like Tracy," said Critchfield. "I told him I wanted a prior commitment from the military, a carrier with planes off the coast and plenty of backup. Bissell believed a civilian-run paramilitary operation would work." Critchfield, the former tank commander under Patton, refused the post. Other senior operatives also begged off when they were approached by Bissell or Barnes. Some had been subtly signaled by Helms that joining the Cuba group would not be a wise career move. Offered a top job in the Cuban group, Tom Polgar, a European operative, went to Helms and asked, "What do you think?" Helms replied, "Tom, remember, I've always been your friend. I didn't offer that job to you." "Helms was warning me," recalled Polgar; he turned the job down. "Helms didn't give Tracy the best people," said Al Ulmer, who had been moved from FE to a European station. "But Tracy wouldn't have known them anyway."[5]

Barnes and Bissell plunged ahead. Castro was given a cryptonym: AMTHUG (Che Guevara, a medical doctor, was AMQUACK).[6] A "war room" was set up in Quarters Eye, an old and run-down WAVEs barracks on Ohio Avenue off the Mall. Phillips built a radio station on Swan Island, a pile of guano off Honduras, and began broadcasting. The Guatemalans allowed the CIA to build a camp in the jungle to train guerrillas, mostly idealistic middle-class boys recruited from the exile community in Miami. Droller and Hunt went about trying to establish an exile government, bickering almost as much as the Cubans did. Droller, whose alias was Frank Bender, was liberal; Hunt, whose alias was Eduardo, was arch conservative. Droller called Hunt "Popsy" and "Boychick," which Hunt couldn't abide.[7]

Barnes and Bissell knew it would be at least six months until the guerrilla force was ready to invade ("infiltrate" was the word used at this stage of planning), and Dave Phillips told Bissell that it would take him six months of radio propaganda and leaflet drops to soften up the Cubans, they were "more sophisticated" than the Guatemalans, who had been suckered in six weeks. In the meantime, Barnes began to dream up a psychological warfare campaign that could be aimed at Castro or, as he was popularly known, "the Beard."*[8]

---

* Bissell also used Barnes to help sell the Cuba operation to the Defense and State Departments. In February 1960, a month before the Cuban plan was presented to the Special Group for approval, Barnes went on a hunting trip in South Carolina with Secretary of State Christian Herter and Secretary of Defense Thomas Gates. "It was very cozy," recalled Janet Barnes. "I have a hunch there was a lot of talking down there, in between the shooting, the rum cocktails at lunch, and the martinis at dinner."

Psyching out the enemy—fooling him into believing that he was about to be overwhelmed by a superior force—had won Barnes a Silver Star in World War II. It had worked on a much larger scale in Guatemala, frightening Arbenz out of office. Barnes was eager to try it again on a larger and more formidable target.[9]

TRACY BARNES loved James Bond. At Thanksgiving he laughingly passed out copies of the Ian Fleming spy series to his family. "We thought of Daddy as James Bond," said his daughter Jane. "A man of elegance who knew his martinis. Nefarious, but clean." Barnes's favorite was *From Russia with Love*. "He liked the part about the poison knitting needle," said his wife. "These books must be nonsense," his Rhode Island summer neighbor Sandol Sturges told him. Barnes responded, with apparent sincerity, "On the contrary, they're understated."[10]

In March 1960, just as the Cuba operation was getting started, Ian Fleming, who was working on *Thunderball* at the time, came to Washington. Oatsie Charles (then Oatsie Leiter) took him to a dinner party at Jack and Jacqueline Kennedy's house on N Street in Georgetown on the night of Sunday, March 13. The other guests were the Alsop brothers and John Bross. Over brandy, Senator Kennedy, who was in Washington during a lull in the presidential primaries, asked Fleming what he would do to get rid of Castro. "Ridicule, chiefly," the author replied. He said that the Cubans cared only about money, religion, and sex. He suggested dropping fake dollar bills on Cuba to destabilize their currency and leaflets declaring that Castro was impotent. Or leaflets warning that atomic testing had made the Cuban atmosphere radioactive: radioactivity made men impotent and lingered longest in their beards. Cubans would shave off their beards, losing their virility and the symbol of revolution.

"We all thought it was a little far-fetched," said Oatsie Charles, but the next morning the phone rang at 7:45. "It was Allen Dulles," she said. "He was desperate to find Ian." The CIA director also called Henry Brandon, the London *Times* Washington correspondent (Fleming was the *Times*'s foreign editor). He had heard that Fleming had "developed some interesting ideas of how to deal with Castro" and wanted to hear them personally. It was too late; Fleming had already headed back to London.[11]

It may or may not be a coincidence that at just about this time the CIA began to experiment with a plan to make Castro's beard fall out. The idea was "to destroy Castro's image as 'The Beard,' " according to a "Secret—Eyes Only" internal study conducted by the CIA inspector general in 1967. The plan was to sprinkle thalium powder, a woman's depilatory, in his shoes when they were put out at night to be shined. The drug, which could cause paralysis in large doses, was tested on animals. Castro was scheduled to take a trip to Chile in the spring of 1960, and the CIA hoped to penetrate "the Beard's" hotel. The scheme was called off when Castro canceled his trip.[12]

The thalium-in-the-shoes plot was one of several ideas dreamt up by the CIA in the winter and spring of 1960 to try to embarrass Castro before his people.* The Technical Services Division was ordered to look for other ways and suggested several, including giving Castro a box of his favorite cigars treated with a chemical to induce "temporary disorientation." The hope was that he would smoke one before a speech. According to Esterline, the cigars were never delivered; no one could figure out how to give them to Castro without the danger of "blowback on the Agency." The elves in the Technical Services Division also came up with "a scheme to contaminate the air of the radio station where Castro broadcast his speeches with an aerosal spray of a chemical that produces reactions similar to those of lysergic acid (LSD)." Nothing came of the idea, according to the 1967 IG report, "because the chemical could not be relied on to be effective."[14]

According to Bissell and Esterline, the moving force behind these plots, which became the source of much mirth and head shaking by the press and public after they were revealed by the

---

* A myth has developed that then–Vice President Richard Nixon was a prime mover behind the early Bay of Pigs plotting (including the assassination attempts on Castro). On the Watergate tapes Nixon refers to the damage that could be done by investigating Howard Hunt, whom the White House had hired as a "plumber" after his retirement from the CIA. Investigating Hunt, Nixon said, "would uncover a lot of things" that the agency might prefer to keep secret. "You open that scab, there's a hell of a lot of things." The CIA's in-house history shows that Nixon was briefed by Bissell on March 2, 1960, and told of various psywar plans, including the use of "goon squads" and the possible use of a drug "which if placed in Castro's food, would make him behave in such an irrational manner that a public appearance could have very damaging results for him." But the history concludes that Nixon was not a member of a conspiracy to kill Castro, and "by no stretch of the imagination was Nixon the architect of the Bay of Pigs." Bissell recalled very little involvement by Nixon.[13]

Church Committee in 1975, was Tracy Barnes, along with his propaganda chief, Dave Phillips. "Tracy and Dave Phillips thought up nonlethal means to make Castro look ridiculous," said Esterline. "Phillips and Tracy were on the same wavelength. They sat around and kicked around what to do with cigars to make Castro look foolish, to make his hair fall out. It was a fun thing. But then all of a sudden this grim thing emerged."[15]

The "grim thing" was a plot to assassinate Castro. It emerged, at least as far as Esterline and the line officers in the Cuba operation were concerned, on the morning of July 21, 1960. The night before, the Miami station had sent a cable to Washington, informing headquarters that a Cuban agent working for the CIA expected to come into contact with Raul Castro, Fidel's brother. The agent was an Air Cubana pilot. He told his CIA case officer in Havana that he was leaving at 3 P.M. on July 21 to fly to Prague, Czechoslovakia, to pick up Raul and fly him home. The pilot suggested that perhaps an "accident" could be arranged. He suggested that, on the return flight, he might be able to "ditch" the plane "three hours outside of Havana."

Bissell was away at the time, sailing aboard the *Sea Witch*. As his deputy, Barnes answered the cable. It was nearly midnight on July 20, and the agency's man in Havana needed an immediate answer. "Possible removal top three leaders [the two Castros and Che Guevara] is receiving serious consideration at HQS," Barnes cabled him. The cable inquired whether the agent was sufficiently motivated to risk "arranging an accident" involving Raul Castro. Ten thousand dollars was authorized as payment "after successful completion," but no advance payment was permitted in case the Cuban agent was a double.[16]

The case officer "swallowed hard" when he read the cable from Washington. It was, he later told the Church Committee, "quite a departure" from the agency's normal procedures. This was an understatement. In the history of the CIA, it was the first time an assassination of a foreign leader had ever been authorized by headquarters. There had always been tough talk, of course. Allen Dulles reportedly once made a threat against Egypt's Nasser: "You tell that colonel of yours that if he pushes too hard we'll break him in half." Wisner and other top officials had talked about assassinations—of Stalin in the early 1950s and Arbenz in Guatemala in 1954. But in each case the idea had been rejected as impractical and unwise: it might not work, the target might be replaced by someone worse, the Russians (who were better at this sort of thing) might retaliate. Barnes's cable to the Miami station that July was a first: it launched an era that CIA officials regard as an unfortunate aberration, a period that would muddy the reputation of the CIA without, ironically, ever actually killing a foreign leader.[17]

Despite misgivings, the case officer contacted the Cuban agent and, as they rode in a bus to the airport on the morning of July 21, told him of the proposal. The case officer avoided using the word "assassinate," but spoke instead of "an accident to neutralize" Raul Castro's influence. The pilot agreed to take "a calculated risk" that could pass as an accident. In case he died trying, the Cuban asked that the CIA provide his son with a college education.

When the case officer returned to his base after meeting with the pilot, he received another "operation immediate" cable from Barnes: "Do not pursue ref. Would like to drop matter." But it was too late to "drop the matter," since the pilot had already departed. To the relief of his CIA handlers, the pilot's nerve apparently failed, and he never ditched the plane.

Bissell claimed to have no recollection of this incident. But as Esterline recalled it, Barnes "got himself into a real wringer" by ordering such a drastic act without proper authority. "He was stepped on pretty hard," said Esterline. Apparently, Barnes had jumped the gun. Recklessly, he had seen an opportunity and plowed ahead without first consulting with Bissell or Allen Dulles. Bissell later testified that the order was presumably canceled by Allen Dulles because he considered it "altogether too risky and technically not sufficiently likely of success." He speculated that Dulles thought that "too many innocent people would be killed by crashing a plane" and that, while Raul would be dead, the main target, Fidel Castro, would still be alive.[18]

But Dulles did not countermand Barnes's order because it was wrong or counter to CIA policy. In fact, by July 1960, Bissell had already decided to look for a way to kill Fidel Castro if they couldn't get him out any other way. To a generation that had survived World War II by using severe means, assassination was not an unthinkable act. Still, Bissell did not use the word "assassinate," even in his private conversations. He preferred the term "executive action," by which he meant any covert action aimed at incapacitating a foreign leader, with murder as a last resort.

Bissell's approach to "executive action" was pseudo-scientific.

With the optimistic faith in high-tech characteristic of his era, he had no use for the notion that some problems have no solutions. He was interested in solving problems, by whatever means. Bissell had a "proclivity for technical solutions. He was all for them," said Sidney Gottlieb, who went by the formal title assistant for scientific matters to the clandestine services chief.

By his own description, Gottlieb was one of the "Dr. Strangeloves" of the Technical Services Staff (TSS). Born with a clubfoot and a stutter, he compensated by becoming an expert folk dancer and obtaining a Ph.D. from Cal Tech. A pleasant man who lived on a farm with his wife, Gottlieb drank only goat's milk and grew Christmas trees, which he sold at a roadside stand. The CIA's Technical Services Staff was mostly concerned with electronic eavesdropping and surveillance, building more ingenious bugs and taps, cameras, and recorders. But Gottlieb's end, the Chemical Division, was concerned with something more exotic in the early 1950s: mind control.

Gottlieb ran a top-secret project code-named MKULTRA. The project grew out of a concern, almost a panic, that the Russians had somehow developed a drug or technology for controlling men's minds. At show trials in Eastern Europe in the late 1940s, defendants with glazed eyes had confessed to crimes they didn't commit. In the Korean War, there were reports of brainwashed prisoners (transformed into assassins in the popular novel and movie, *The Manchurian Candidate*). In Berlin in 1951, George Kennan, the U.S. ambassador to the Soviet Union, had made some inexplicably undiplomatic remarks at a press conference and was declared persona non grata by the Kremlin. Had Kennan's brain somehow been zapped or drugged?

At CIA headquarters in 1951, Bedell Smith and Frank Wisner had anxiously tried to figure out why all their agents were being rolled up in Albania. They wondered if the agency had been somehow penetrated by a secret signal that could read minds. When Philby and the Cambridge spy ring were exposed, and Wisner learned that he had been betrayed by the British SIS men, the mystery was not solved but rather deepened: Had the Russians somehow brainwashed these misguided aristocrats?

To bridge the "mind-control gap," Dr. Gottlieb was ordered to begin experimenting—to see if it was possible to create, in effect, a human robot. Many of the early experiments were with the drug LSD. "I started them when we got an intelligence report that the

Soviets were trying to buy up the world's stock of LSD," recalled Gottlieb. The intelligence was wrong, but Project MKULTRA went ahead anyway. All through the 1950s the CIA covertly tested LSD on unwitting subjects, usually drug addicts and johns. The agency ran whorehouses in Greenwich Village and San Francisco where the customers were slipped walloping mickeys, and the case officers, watching through one-way mirrors, joked about "Operation Midnight Climax." At the Addiction Research Center in Lexington, Kentucky, one group of seven volunteers was kept on LSD for seventy-seven days, a brain-frying trip for the most hardened acidheads. Most of the subjects were black men, although a white Army civilian scientist, Frank Olson, who worked with Gottlieb, also experimented with LSD and fell to his death from the window of a New York hotel in November 1953.[19]

As head of the DD/P, Frank Wisner had "signed off on these experiments, but he was hardly interested," said Gottlieb. "He was an arts and letters man, as nontechnical as you could be. One day we were showing him how you send a radio signal to blow up a charge. Instead of a load of dynamite, we had a little squib that made a pop. Wisner pressed the button and the squib popped. Wisner said, 'What in hell would that little pop do to anyone?' I thought, My God, he's hopeless."

Bissell, on the other hand, was "more open-minded," said Gottlieb. He had, of course, worked closely with the Technical Services Staff developing the U-2. When he became DD/P in 1959, "he was very interested in MKULTRA," said Gottlieb. "He fancied himself a technological promoter and entrepreneur. He wanted to understand what the farthest reach could be. He wanted to know, could you assassinate someone without anyone ever finding out about it?"

At first it was all "speculative," recalled Bissell. But the concept interested him. If one of the obstacles to assassination was what agency officials called blowback, perhaps there was a technical solution. "I wanted to see if there was a way to make it look like a natural occurrence. This would be the best way to preserve security. You'd shut off curiosity."

Bissell was hoping ultimately for some kind of death ray, an undetectable beam that could be aimed from long distances at the target. The Technical Services Staff never came very close. The agency experimented with the idea of turning an animal into a walking bomb (a hit man who couldn't talk or be stricken by conscience), even going so far as to sew up a battery-driven guidance system inside a cat (his tail was the antenna). On its first remote-control outing, the cat wandered off and was run over by a taxi. The drug experiments were no more successful. The human mind turned out to be resistant to control, and it was hard to get the dosage right: they could make a man forget a crime, but he was likely to forget everything else as well.

Still, even failures could get Bissell to thinking. In his very first study of covert action, back when he was a consultant at the Ford Foundation in 1953, he had decided that "rollback" was probably a hopeless exercise. Yet there was something about the plan to invade Albania that captured his imagination; he was still turning it over in his mind when he planned the Bay of Pigs in 1960.[20]

Executive action held the same allure. Removing a dangerous demagogue was in the interests of the United States. Wars were destructive, and coups were expensive and hard to stage. But a simple decapitation was a low-cost way to execute foreign policy, if only a way could be found to accomplish the task without, as it were, any fingerprints.

Bissell dated his first consideration of executive action to 1959, the year he took over as DD/P. The target discussed was President Sukarno of Indonesia. Bissell told the Church Committee in 1975 that the assassination of Sukarno had been "contemplated," but that "planning had proceeded no farther than identifying an 'asset' who it was believed might be recruited to kill Sukarno." Bissell was guarded and spoke "circumlocutiously" to the author about this matter in 1992 and 1993. "We felt that if Sukarno could be biologically immobilized, it would be a tremendous gain," he said. According to Bissell, the originator of the idea was Desmond FitzGerald, who as chief of the Far East Division "ran a few ops" to see if an agent could get close enough to deliver the blow. "One involved a female associate of the target," said Bissell. "Nothing ever came of it, nor was much said about it."

Asked about this plot, Bob King, Bissell's special assistant, said, "It was common knowledge that Sukarno was insatiable. He took a great many airline stewardesses, one after another. So the thought was, Hey, let's give him a dose of the clap. We did find a stewardess whose job was to keep him happy, but even at our worst, we couldn't do it." King said that he himself was not involved in the planning and had no direct knowledge of the details.

Told what his former assistant had said, Bissell was cryptic. He chuckled and said, "Ah, yes, the stewardesses," but he would make no other comment except to say, "It never got crystallized, not even as a proposal." He would not go into any detail about whether they were looking for a woman who was already infected with "the clap," or whether they planned to give a stewardess some stronger germ from Dr. Gottlieb's laboratories to "biologically immobilize" Sukarno. Sacrificing an airline stewardess to "immobilize" a communist-sympathizer dictator in Southeast Asia and experimenting on unwitting subjects just to observe the effects of an hallucinogenic drug were not unthinkable acts by the CIA in 1959.[21]

Bissell claimed to have no memory at all of the agency's next, less tentative foray into executive action. In February 1960, a month before the Cuba project was up and running, the Near East Division asked for the approval of what was euphemistically called "the Health Alteration Committee" for a proposed operation to "incapacitate" one of the new rulers of Iraq, a Colonel Mahdawi. After taking power in a coup in 1958, a junta under Abdul Karim Kassem had butchered the royal family and many other friends of the CIA, restored diplomatic relations with the Soviet Union, and lifted a ban on the local Communist Party. The Near East Division wanted to put Colonel Mahdawi, who ran a notorious kangaroo court that sentenced to death hundreds of foes of the regime, out of action for at least three months. "We do not consciously seek subject's permanent removal from the scene; we also do not object should this complication develop," stated the proposal.

Tracy Barnes signed off on the operation on behalf of Bissell in April 1960. "Bissell knew about it," said Gottlieb. The operation was to mail the colonel a monogrammed handkerchief that had been dipped in poison. "We weren't trying to kill him," said Gottlieb. "Just put him on his back and make him sick." The handkerchief was apparently never received. With the black humor sometimes typical of covert operators, an internal CIA memo notes that Colonel Mahdawi "suffered a terminal illness before a firing squad (an event we had nothing to do with) not very long after our handkerchief proposal was considered."*[22]

---

* The hankie may have been lost in the mail. Mahdawi was shot in his office by rivals in February 1962. According to Ted Atkins, a Middle East operative for the agency, he was targeted because several levels of review boards at the CIA determined that he had "no redeeming social value."

Bissell did vaguely remember Tracy Barnes pushing him to approve psychological warfare operations against Castro, like the scheme to make his beard fall out. Gottlieb recalled that the "first overtures" for technical assistance on the psywar campaign came from Barnes, at Bissell's suggestion. "Bissell said to Barnes, 'These are smart guys in the TSS. Why don't you bother them to help us out?' That's when the discussion of the beard began. They were screwy ideas, and we didn't have the operational assets to put them in place." There would be more and deadlier ideas.

Chapter Fifteen

SHOOT-DOWN

"Beware the lesson of Icarus. . . ."

BISSELL HAD ALWAYS known that the U-2 would eventually come within the range of Soviet air defenses. In the spring of 1960 he had already been at work for two years on a spy satellite to replace the U-2. Unlike the U-2, however, the satellite project, code name Corona, had been a flop.

A spy satellite posed a difficult technical challenge: once the satellite was up in space, how did the film get back to earth? Bissell's team proposed an ingenious solution: the satellite would eject canisters of film, which would fall through the atmosphere until they were caught by an Air Force transport plane towing a big net. Not surprisingly, there were glitches. Thirteen of the first fifteen tries were failures: *Discoverer 2* was launched successfully in February 1959, but its photographic capsule landed in Norway by mistake (where it may have been found by the Russians). *Discoverers 3* and *4* failed to reach orbit, and *Discoverer 5* ejected its photographic capsule farther into space.

"It was a heartbreaking business," said Bissell. An airplane can be looked over and adjusted after a test flight; the pilot can report on what worked and what didn't. But with a satellite, "you fire the damn thing off and you never get it back. There is no pilot, of course, and you've got no hardware, and you never see it again. So you have to infer from telemetry what went wrong. Then you make a fix, and if it fails again you know you've inferred wrong. In the case of Corona it went on and on."[1]

Bissell felt a great sense of urgency. The U-2 spy plane was looking increasingly vulnerable. The U-2 pilots were reporting that the MiGs sent up to chase them were climbing higher and higher; they could see their guns winking below, the arc of the shells drawing nearer. To intercept a U-2 flight in early April 1960, the Soviets had scrambled fifty-seven MiGs. Bissell knew that the Russians, who had launched *Sputnik* three years before, were developing an antiaircraft missile that could knock down the spy plane. The Air Force warned Bissell that the Soviets had developed a missile that could intercept a U-2 at 70,000 feet. Bissell chose to disregard the warning because the SAM was inaccurate over 60,000 feet, 5,000 feet below the U-2's cruising altitude. "The Russians could get the SAM up, but they couldn't control or bring it in for a kill, or so we believed," Bissell recalled.[2]

If the Soviets got to the U-2 before the Corona was ready to take its place, the United States would go blind at a critical moment. The Soviets were just beginning to install their intercontinental ballistic missiles, and with all the politicians clamoring about the "missile gap," it was especially important to know the true nature of the threat. Bissell was determined to keep the U-2 flying as long as possible. In April 1960 a U-2 spotted what appeared to be an ICBM launch site under construction at Tyuratam. The CIA needed at least one more flight to see what the Soviets were up to. The United States could not afford to wait, Bissell counseled President Eisenhower. A few months would give the Russians time to camouflage their rockets.

Eisenhower had reason to be wary of more U-2 overflights. As his second presidential term came to a close, he was trying to forge a détente with the Soviet Union. His counterpart, Nikita Khrushchev, seemed similarly inclined, and the two superpower leaders had scheduled a summit meeting in Paris for mid-May. If a U-2 was shot down before then and the pilot captured, "peaceful coexistence" might be strangled at birth. Perhaps this was the moment "to beware the lesson of Icarus and Daedalus," writes historian Michael Beschloss in *Mayday*, his account of the U-2 affair.[3]

Calculating the odds in his usual fashion, Bissell reassured Eisenhower that there was only "one chance in a million" that a U-2 pilot could survive a shoot-down. The flimsy plane would disintegrate when hit; if not, the pilot was ordered to pull a switch detonating a time-delayed bomb under his seat. The pilot himself was not likely to survive a parachute jump from 70,000 feet; if he did, he could use a poison pin coated with lethal shellfish toxin from Dr. Gottlieb's lab to silence himself.[4]

Eisenhower hesitated, but he, too, wanted the intelligence promised by the spy plane. Significantly, the U-2 mission in early April had flown over 4,500 miles of rail lines in the Volga valley without spotting a single ICBM launch site. The CIA's own intelligence estimates had predicted that by the end of 1965 the Soviets would have thirty-five missiles in launchers. Where were they? Eisenhower was eager to prove that the "missile gap" was phony, to silence the press and the hawks on Capitol Hill who were suggesting that there was one and accusing his administration of weakness. He wanted a flight over Plesetsk, where the CIA thought it might find an SS-6 site, as well as the flight over Tyuratam, where the Soviets showed signs of developing a second-generation ICBM. Finally, the president gave the go-ahead: the U-2 could fly until May 1, two weeks before the summit.[5]

The flight plan, writes Bissell, was "the most daring yet. Up to this time, the U-2 had never voyaged more than half-way across the Soviet Union. It would fly that far and then turn around for the journey home." On this mission the U-2 would traverse the Soviet Union for the first time. Bissell, who loved to sail in the roughest weather, gave the mission the code name Operation Grand Slam. He failed to consider that May 1—the day the U-2 mission finally flew—was May Day. Soviet airspace was virtually empty on the national holiday. The Soviets picked up the U-2 the moment it crossed the border.[6]

On that Sunday morning, May 1, Bob King was jolted awake by an anxious duty officer repeating the code words, "Billy Bailey didn't come home." On its overflight from Peshawar, Pakistan, to Bodø, Norway, the U-2 had gone down near Sverdlovsk, Russia's main atom test center, in the Ural Mountains. When King got to the U-2 operations room in an office building at 17th and H Streets (known by its staff as "the Bissell Center"), "people were running around like chickens with their heads cut off," King recalled. "Bissell arrived, looking like it was just another Monday afternoon staff meeting. 'Good afternoon, everybody,' he said. Everyone cooled down. An inordinate calm settled over the room." Bissell was hiding his emotions. He felt "a sense of disaster," he later recalled, "that the program would probably be terminated."[7]

Bissell's staff put out the cover story, prepared years before, that a NASA weather plane had strayed off course and been shot down. Bissell assumed the pilot was dead, but he was wrong: having failed to press the self-destruct button in the plane as it hurtled earthward or prick himself with the poison pin after he landed, Francis Gary Powers was sitting in a cell in Lubyanka Prison, a prize pawn in the superpower game.

The Soviets waited a few days to allow Washington to lie indignantly about the innocent weather plane so brutally attacked. Then the Kremlin pounced. On May 7, Nikita Khrushchev rose to the podium in the Supreme Soviet and declared, "Comrades, I must let you in on a secret. . . . We have the remnants of the plane—and we also have the pilot, who is quite alive and kicking!" Khrushchev held aloft Powers's unused poison pin—"the latest achievement of American technology for killing their own people"—to cries of "Shame! Shame! Shame!" Khrushchev noted the outrage of American congressmen that the Soviet Union should have downed an American plane. "Perhaps these outraged people would rather seek that answer from Allen Dulles," Khrushchev mocked. "The whole world knows that Allen Dulles is no great weatherman!"[8]

The State Department was forced to admit the truth. "U.S. CONCEDES FLIGHT OVER SOVIET, DEFENDS SEARCH FOR INTELLIGENCE," said the *New York Times*. "MORAL LEADERSHIP OF U.S. HARMED," wrote the *San Francisco Chronicle*. "The Americans have made fools of themselves," wrote the London *News Chronicle*. "We have violated the eleventh Commandment—Thou Shall Not Get Caught," said Senator Hugh Scott of Pennsylvania. From Washington, James Reston wrote in the *New York Times*, "This was a sad and perplexed capital tonight, caught in a swirl of charges of clumsy administration, bad judgment and bad faith. It was depressed and humiliated by the United States having been caught spying over the Soviet Union and trying to cover up its activities in a series of misleading official statements."[9] Only Joe Alsop seemed happy. In a column entitled "The Wonderful News," Bissell's friend looked on the bright side, that the United States had been keeping close track of Soviet ICBM development. At the White House, President Eisenhower arrived at the Oval Office "very depressed," according to his secretary, Anne Whitman. "I would like to resign," he said.[10]

Eisenhower knew that "because of this stupid U-2 mess" his hopes for détente had been dashed. The Paris summit was canceled. In Moscow, the hardliners gained, and Khrushchev, for all his bluster, began to lose his grip on power. Khrushchev took the U-2 flights "almost as a personal insult," said Chip Bohlen, who had been ambassador to the Soviet Union. "More than that, I think it made him out a fool. He'd been telling obviously all the other leaders that Eisenhower was a good, solid guy and you could trust him, and then—*whambo*—this plane comes over, and this shook a lot of Khrushchev's authority in the Soviet Union." The U-2 episode, George Kennan later wrote, led to "the shattering of the political career of the only Soviet statesman of the post-Stalin period with whom we might conceivably have worked out a firmer sort of coexistence."[11]

For Bissell and the doctrine of plausible deniability, the U-2 incident should have been a cautionary experience. Because information about the spy plane was so tightly held, Eisenhower was wholly dependent on Bissell's judgment. Bissell had guessed wrong and his wrong guess had backfired. And the incident had damaged the credibility and policies of the president.*

Bissell was not one to look back. He took risks, but he was willing to accept the consequences and move on. If anything, after the U-2 affair he began to press harder and take more risks.

IN THE summer and fall of 1960, in the wake of the U-2 disaster, Bissell ran no fewer than three "executive action" operations, all at once: against Trujillo of the Dominican Republic, Patrice Lumumba of the Congo, and Castro. He regarded them as "chance-y, with a low probability of success," but nonetheless as worthwhile experiments driven by necessity.

The plotting against Rafael Trujillo was born partly of a liberal impulse. The agency was eager to show that it opposed dictators of the right as well as the left. During his thirty-year rule, Trujillo had come to own 70 percent of the land that grew the Dominican Republic's only big export crop, sugar. He had disposed of thousands of political enemies by tossing them into an inlet near Santo Domingo—known as "the swimming pool"—where they were devoured by sharks. Other enemies were hanged by meat hooks in cold storage vaults. Just as the repressive Batista regime had led to Castro, the CIA and the State Department feared that Trujillo's brutality would give way to communism. The CIA and the State Department began to look for the right kind of dissidents to back.

In the spring of 1960 the U.S. ambassador, Joseph Farland, had

---

* After a show trial, the U-2 pilot, Francis Gary Powers, was swapped in 1962 for a Soviet spy who had been imprisoned by the West.

made contact with a group regarded as "moderate, pro–United States, and desirous of establishing a democratic form of government." In June the dissidents asked for twelve "sterile" (untraceable) rifles with telescopic sights, with five hundred rounds of ammunition. The CIA agreed to airdrop them for what Bissell described as "targeted use" against the Trujillo regime. Perhaps contemplating a dip in Trujillo's "swimming pool" if they failed, the dissidents lost their enthusiasm; the rifles were not delivered. But then in September came a new request for two hundred rifles followed by another hesitation—then three hundred rifles in October. Back and forth the cables and secret messages went into the winter of 1961, but Trujillo remained unscathed, at least for the time being.[12]

Delay and indecision also dogged the plot against Lumumba, but in this case the hesitancy was on the part of Bissell's own operatives. Patrice Lumumba was a product of the rush to decolonize Africa. Belgium had let go of the Congo in the spring of 1960, and the new republic was one of sixteen African nations to emerge that year. The Congo was not ready for self-rule; only twenty Congolese had any kind of higher education. Within a couple of weeks of "liberation," the army went on a rampage, slaughtering Congolese and Europeans alike. To the Cold Warriors in Washington, the Congo seemed like a good place to take a stand. Katanga Province in the Congo was rich with minerals, and the Soviet Union was clearly making a bid to control the new nation. Policymakers could see the rest of Africa slipping away.[13]

Lumumba was the prime minister of the three-week-old Republic of the Congo when he arrived in Washington seeking economic aid in late July 1960. He did not make a good impression: "He would never look you in the eye," said Undersecretary of State C. Douglas Dillon. "He looked up at the sky. And a tremendous flow of words came out. . . . You had a feeling that he was a person that was gripped with this fervor that I can only characterize as Messianic." The United States lost its willingness to help Lumumba after these meetings, said Dillon. Distaste turned to revulsion when Lumumba demanded that a white prostitute be sent to him at Blair House, the presidential guest house where he was staying. Lumumba was "impossible to deal with," said Dillon, a friend and Groton schoolmate of Bissell's. Bissell, for his part, regarded Lumumba as a "mad dog."[14]

At a National Security Council meeting on July 21, 1960, Allen

Dulles described Lumumba as "a Castro or worse" and stated that it was safe to assume that he had been "bought by the communists." The minutes of the meeting of the Special Group on August 25, 1960, come as close as anything ever written to explicit presidential authorization of an assassination attempt. The words are veiled and conditional, but to Bissell their real meaning was perfectly clear. At the meeting Gordon Gray, the president's national security adviser, stated that Eisenhower "had expressed extremely strong feelings on the necessity for very straightforward action in this situation, and he wondered if the plans outlined were sufficient to accomplish this." The Special Group "finally agreed that planning for the Congo would not necessarily rule out 'consideration' of any particular kind of activity."

The next day Allen Dulles sent a cable to the CIA station chief in Leopoldville, Lawrence Devlin:

IN HIGH QUARTERS HERE IT IS THE CLEAR-CUT CONCLUSION THAT IF [LUMUMBA] CONTINUES TO HOLD HIGH OFFICE, THE INEVITABLE RESULT WILL AT BEST BE CHAOS AND AT WORST PAVE THE WAY TO COMMUNIST TAKEOVER OF THE CONGO WITH DISASTROUS CONSEQUENCES FOR THE PRESTIGE OF THE UN AND FOR THE INTERESTS OF THE FREE WORLD GENERALLY. CONSEQUENTLY WE CONCLUDE THAT HIS REMOVAL MUST BE AN URGENT AND PRIME OBJECTIVE AND THAT UNDER EXISTING CONDITIONS THIS SHOULD BE A HIGH PRIORITY OF OUR COVERT ACTION.[15]

Bissell was once again sailing on the *Sea Witch* the day Dulles sent this cable, but he understood that "removal" by the Congo station meant "kill" and "consideration" by the Special Group meant "do it now." The fact that Lumumba was driven from power by his rivals in early September and into the protection of United Nations troops did not slow up Bissell as he began preparations to execute the "mad dog." With his messianic appeal and loyal "goon squads," Lumumba was still considered a threat to make the Congo a Soviet client state. In "late summer or early fall," Dr. Gottlieb recalled, Bissell asked him to pick out a poison to be used against an "unspecified African leader." Bissell told Gottlieb that the assignment had been approved by "the highest authority," which Gottlieb took to mean the president. Gottlieb gave Bissell a choice of rabbit fever, undulant fever, tuberculosis, anthrax, smallpox, and sleeping sickness. They settled on one "that was supposed to be indigenous to that area [of Africa] and that could be fatal," according to Gottlieb. The CIA scientist put together a package of "accessory materials"—hypodermic needles, rubber gloves, and gauze masks—"that would be used in handling this pretty danger-ous material."

Bissell cabled Lawrence Devlin and told him to expect a visit from "Joe from Paris," who would "explain his assignment to you." Traveling under the alias Joseph Braun, Gottlieb arrived in the Congo in late September. He explained the assassination plot to Devlin, who later testified that he had "an emotional reaction of great surprise." He explained that he had brought a vial of poison to be injected into Lumumba's "food or toothpaste." Devlin was "sober and grim" about this assignment, but he began to look for an agent to carry it out.

Devlin later testified that he "looked on it as a pretty wild scheme . . . I did not think that it was practical professionally, certainly, in so short a time, if you were going to keep the U.S. out of it . . . I explored it, but I doubt that I ever really expected to carry it out." The cable traffic makes Devlin look like a willing warrior, but his old colleagues say that he intentionally stalled.[16]

Impatient with Devlin's lack of progress, Bissell turned to William Harvey. Harvey had been transferred from Berlin back to Washington to run "Staff D," a supersecret outfit involved in code breaking—"crypt ops." About a half dozen "assets" utilized by Harvey were "second story men," said Sam Halpern, the execu-tive assistant to the Far East Division chief. According to the CIA's 1967 inspector general's report, they were recruited to "break into safes and kidnap couriers." They were a very rough bunch, with strong ties to (if not full-fledged membership in) the underworld. "We had to keep the FBI informed when one of them traveled," said Halpern. Bill Harvey knew where to find men of this caliber.[17]

Harvey loaned Bissell his deputy, Justin O'Donnell. Bissell asked O'Donnell to go to the Congo to "eliminate" Lumumba. To Bissell's surprise, he refused. A Roman Catholic, O'Donnell be-lieved that "murder corrupts." He became both pious and legalistic with Bissell. O'Donnell raised the possibility that a "conspiracy to commit murder being done in the District of Columbia might be in violation of federal law." Bissell "airily dismissed" this prospect, said O'Donnell, but he did not try to force the issue. "In hindsight, I was an idiot to even ask him," said Bissell. From his usual perch on the fence, Richard Helms told O'Donnell that he was "abso-lutely right" to refuse the assassination assignment from Bissell, though Helms made no other effort to get involved.

O'Donnell was not, however, a saint. In somewhat Jesuitical fashion, he was willing to run an operation to lure Lumumba out of the protection of the United Nations so he could be captured and "tried by a jury of his peers." O'Donnell understood perfectly well that if Lumumba was seized by his political foes in the Congo, he would likely be executed. "I am not opposed to capital punishment," O'Donnell later testified.[18]

When O'Donnell arrived in Léopoldville on November 3, station chief Devlin told him that there was "a virus in the safe," a goodie bag of sorts left by Dr. Gottlieb. "I knew it wasn't for somebody to get his polio shot up to date," said O'Donnell. To help "neutralize" Lumumba, O'Donnell brought along an "asset" code-named QJWIN, identified in the Church Committee report as a "foreign citizen with a criminal background." Another CIA memo describes him as a "Bureau of Narcotics informant" recruited in Frankfurt, in Harvey's old territory. Described by O'Donnell as "not a man of many scruples," QJWIN's job was to try to penetrate Lumumba's guards and abduct him.

What came next was dark comedy. Another CIA "asset," WIROGUE, tried to recruit QJWIN to join an "execution squad" to kill Lumumba. WIROGUE, "an essentially stateless soldier of fortune," was the sort of figure associated with the CIA in B movies. He was described by his Africa Division superiors as a "man who learns quickly and carries out any assignment without regard to danger." He had been recommended by Washington to the Léopoldville station chief under these terms:

> He is indeed aware of the precepts of right and wrong, but if he is given an assignment which may be morally wrong in the eyes of the world, but necessary because his case officer has ordered him to carry it out, then it is right, and he will dutifully undertake appropriate action for its execution without pangs of conscience. In other words, he can rationalize all actions.[19]

WIROGUE may have been a professional killer, but he was also a maverick: he had not been authorized to kill Lumumba. He worked for Devlin as a "utility" agent helping with surveillance and agent recruitment. WIROGUE tried to recruit QJWIN without knowing (thanks to compartmentation) that QJWIN was already working for the CIA. They met because they were staying at the same hotel.

While the agency's deadly assets were circling each other in the hotel bar, Lumumba gave the slip to his U.N. guardians in December. The CIA was caught by surprise. Lumumba was immediately seized by his rivals and shipped to Katanga Province. The CIA's base chief in Elisabethville, the Katangan capital, archly cabled to his colleagues back in Léopoldville, "Thanks for Patrice. If we had known he was coming we would have baked a snake." The CIA man reported from his "sources" that the Congolese government had no plan to liquidate Lumumba. The CIA was behind again; by the time the cable was sent, Lumumba had already been executed. The agency never did find out by whom or how. When he heard the news of Lumumba's death, Devlin took Dr. Gottlieb's package—poison vial, syringes, and all—and threw them into the Congo River.[20]

ALSO BY the summer of 1960, the CIA had turned from trying to make Castro look bad to trying to kill him. In June, Bissell asked Dr. Gottlieb to make an inventory of toxic agents that could be used to "incapacitate or eliminate" a man. A new box of Castro's favorite cigars was procured and treated, only this time the chemical was not intended to make Castro "disoriented" but rather dead. A box of fifty cigars was contaminated with botulinum toxin, a virulent poison that "produces a fatal illness some hours after it is ingested," according to the CIA's 1967 inspector general's report.[21]

Bissell had the lethal intent and the poison, but he still needed a delivery vehicle. The CIA lacked the "operational assets" willing or able to kill Castro. Just as he had reached out to the Technical Services Staff to help him find the right poison, now he reached out to a different division, the Office of Security, to find the right assassin.

In August, Bissell began a series of conversations with its head, Sheffield Edwards. The Office of Security was, just as the name implies, a glorified Pinkerton service for the CIA; its job was to physically protect the agency's secrets by tracking down leaks and enforcing security rules. The men who worked for the Office of Security would never be found at a Georgetown cocktail party, and Bissell remarked that "you can see their lips move when they read," but some of them, former FBI agents who had chafed under Mr. Hoover (or been fired by him), had excellent contacts in the underworld. This is what Bissell was looking for, though he credited Sheff Edwards for first suggesting, sometime in August or September 1960, that the CIA hire the Mafia to kill Fidel Castro.[22]

The story of the CIA's relationship to the Mafia is a tragicomedy. The long-term ramifications were far greater than those created by the bungled attempt on Lumumba—not for the target, Fidel Castro, who remained unharmed, but for the CIA, which was ultimately humiliated.

Sheff Edwards told Bissell that he knew just the man for the job. Along with James P. O'Connell, a former FBI agent who was Edwards's operations chief, Edwards had met a mobster, Johnny Rosselli, at a clambake given by Robert Maheu in the summer of 1959. Rosselli was a medium-level hood (he had the concession for the ice-making machines on the Strip in Las Vegas, as well as a number of less legitimate interests in the gambling world). Maheu was a former FBI agent who had done contract work for the CIA (most notably in 1958 arranging for the production of the blue movie of Sukarno and the Russian airline stewardess). Edwards asked Maheu to approach Rosselli about eliminating Castro. The chain of "cut-outs" was intended to distance the CIA: Maheu's cover story was supposed to be that he represented some rich businessmen who saw killing Castro as a first step toward recovering their investments in Cuba.

At lunch with Rosselli at the Brown Derby in Hollywood, Maheu promptly shed his cover and told the gangster that he was working for the CIA. At first Rosselli expressed shock. He couldn't understand why the U.S. government would want him to help. "Me?" he asked. "You want me to get involved with Uncle Sam? The Feds are tailing me wherever I go." Rosselli at the time was under investigation for income tax evasion.

Maheu later wrote that Rosselli agreed to help for "patriotic reasons." Rosselli himself testified before the Church Committee in 1975 that he had "felt an obligation to my government." A more plausible explanation is that Rosselli saw an opportunity to collect a marker. If he was being tailed by the Feds, what could be more useful than to be able to throw his patriotic duty right back at the prosecutor? Maheu told Rosselli that the CIA would pay $150,000 for the job. Rosselli graciously offered to do it for free.

Rosselli set out to recruit more patriots to help dispose of Castro. On September 14, O'Connell, Edwards's number two, met at the Plaza Hotel in New York with a gangster who introduced

himself as Sam Gold. "Sam Gold" was actually Sam "Mo Mo" Giancana, the boss of Chicago, heir to Al Capone's empire. Giancana
told the CIA official, who was posing as a businessman, that he had
contacts in Cuban gambling syndicates who could arrange to eliminate the Cuban leader. At the Fontainebleau Hotel in Miami later
that month, Giancana introduced Maheu to "Joe," the "courier"
who would handle arrangements in Havana. Joe was Santos Trafficante, the Mafia chieftain of Cuba, who was, like Giancana, one of
the ten most powerful dons in the Cosa Nostra.[23]

Only after these meetings did Bissell go to Allen Dulles and
inform him of the plot to kill Castro. The conversation was circumlocutious. Instead of names, Bissell and Edwards referred to a
chain of "A" to "B" to "C" (for Edwards to Maheu to Rosselli).
They did not mention the Mafia or say "assassination" or even
"executive action." Rather they referred to an "intelligence operation." The CIA director asked no questions. He merely nodded.
Nonetheless, Bissell later insisted that Dulles understood he was
authorizing an assassination attempt. He "assumed" that Dulles
later cleared it with Eisenhower.[24]

While Bissell and Dulles were tiptoeing about, trying to avoid
the use of what Bissell called "bad words," Giancana was mouthing
off to his friends. On October 18, 1960, Bissell received a memorandum from FBI Director J. Edgar Hoover informing him that
Giancana had told "several people" that he was involved in a plot
to assassinate Castro. The memo did not mention the CIA's role,
but it was enough to give Bissell a start. Hoover was decidedly not
a friend of the CIA, and if mobsters were bragging about knocking
off Castro, Bissell could forget about his hopes of maintaining plausible deniability. Bissell had to try to plug the leak, but his agents
blundered and drew the CIA in deeper.[25]

O'Connell, the CIA man who was acting as Maheu's case officer,
later described the incident as "a Keystone Comedy Act." As they
sat around the pool in Miami, eating caviar that the mobster ordered flown in every day from New York, Giancana complained to
Maheu that he was being two-timed by his girlfriend, singer Phyllis McGuire, who was back in Las Vegas. Giancana was upset
about the infidelity, and he threatened to go back to Vegas. Maheu
was determined to keep the mobster in Miami, where his presence
was required to set up the Castro hit. Maheu offered to bug the
hotel room of the man who was imprudently "dating" the gangster's moll, comedian Dan Rowan (later of Rowan and Martin's

Laugh-In). The CIA approved the bug in the hopes that it would also determine whether Giancana had told his girlfriend about the Castro plot, and whether she was spreading it around town.

The private investigator hired by Maheu to put in the bug in Rowan's room at The Sands got caught by the hotel maid. (When Giancana heard of this, he began laughing so hard he "almost swallowed his cigar.") To avoid prosecution, Maheu had to invoke "national security" and tell the U.S. attorney he was working for the CIA. The secret held—for the time being—but the circle was being widened, and Bissell was on notice that his secret was a shaky one.

Still, he did not pull back. He was preoccupied with trying to figure out exactly how to kill Castro. He had hoped, naively, that the Mafia could carry out a traditional gangland slaying, gunning down Castro in a restaurant or on the street. Giancana rejected the idea out of hand: too messy, and too hard for the hit men to escape. He wanted something with more finesse.

Bissell turned to Cornelius Roosevelt, the head of Technical Services (and cousin of Archie and Kim), to provide the appropriate poison. (Bissell alternated between Roosevelt and Gottlieb for scientific advice, not always telling the one he was talking to the other.) Roosevelt offered up four choices: (1) something highly toxic, like the shellfish poison on the pin that Francis Gary Powers had failed to use; (2) bacterial material in liquid form; (3) bacterial treatment of a cigarette or cigar; and (4) a handkerchief treated with bacteria, like the one mailed (unsuccessfully) to Colonel Mahdawi of Iraq. Roosevelt recommended liquid bacteria.

Giancana demanded pills. Roosevelt went to work, making up a batch of botulin pills that would dissolve in Castro's drink. The development was difficult; the first batch failed to dissolve, and another batch failed to kill guinea pigs. The changeover from the Eisenhower to the Kennedy administration occurred in January without any pause in Roosevelt's work. Finally, in February, he got the formula right. The pills were delivered to the mob in a tube disguised as a pencil.

The next problem was finding someone close enough to Castro to drop the pills in his drink. Trafficante chose a senior official in Castro's government. According to a CIA report, the official was close to the mob, and he seemed to have a good motive: he was bitter because he had been deprived of kickbacks ever since Castro closed the Havana casinos to Cubans.

Sometime in late February or early March, the official returned the pills, unused, to the mob. Rosselli explained to the CIA's Edwards that the man had gotten "cold feet." In fact, he was no longer in a position to use the pills, and the mob knew it. He had fallen out of favor and lost his job in Castro's government at the end of January, before he was enlisted by the mob. Rosselli and Trafficante next suggested a man in the Cuban exile government in Miami who might be able to get the job done. Their choice, Tony Varona, was said by a CIA report to be motivated by his hope of securing the gambling, prostitution, and dope monopolies in the event that Castro was overthrown. Perhaps he could find someone in Havana to administer the pills. Varona wanted $50,000 for expenses and told his Mafia handlers that he had lined up a waiter in a restaurant. A little later he, too, reported failure: Castro no longer visited the restaurant where the waiter worked.

Despite the supposed cover that Edwards and O'Connell were "businessmen," Rosselli made no attempt to hide the fact that he knew they actually worked for the CIA. Not to worry, though, he reassured them; he would never divulge a thing.[26]

Bissell watched this charade from afar with a growing sense of resignation. He had never been particularly confident of success in the executive action department, he later recalled. To him the assassination plots amounted to a calculated gamble, a worthwhile risk that, if it paid off, might obviate the need for more drastic military action against the Castro regime. "As the failures occurred, my estimate of the likelihood of success began to sink," he said. In March 1961 he knew time was running out. By then, the main thrust against Castro—the invasion of Cuba by a CIA-backed exile army—was nearly ready. It was scheduled for early April on a beach in the Bahía de Cochinas, the Bay of Pigs.[27]

Chapter Sixteen

PLAUSIBLE DENIABILITY

"They were mad dogs."

IN 1975, WHEN the CIA was forced to publicly admit to the assassination plots, the senators on the Select Committee to Study Governmental Operations with Respect to Intelligence Activities (the Church Committee) were never able to resolve the question of who, if anyone, authorized the CIA to attempt assassinations. Was the CIA acting alone—a "rogue elephant," as Senator Frank Church at first described the agency? Or was the CIA merely carrying out the orders of the president and his National Security Council? At the hearings officials from the executive branch indignantly swore that neither they nor Presidents Eisenhower and Kennedy would have tolerated, much less authorized, such immoral acts. The CIA officials looked pained and exasperated; they were good soldiers, they weren't going to point any fingers, but really, how could the senators be so naive? The CIA executed policy; it did not make it. Of course, the CIA had obtained authorization. But such things are never written down, nor are they to be ever acknowledged. That is why presidents have secret intelligence services: to perform secret acts that are supposed to be kept secret.[1]

Without hard evidence it is impossible to know whether Presidents Eisenhower and Kennedy authorized the CIA to try to kill Castro. But it is clear from Bissell's own words that he did not need much authorization to order an "executive action." As a general matter, Bissell insisted, he was confident that he was always acting with presidential authority. But when he described how he received that authorization, the links in the chain of command begin to look rather tenuous, and Bissell's own initiative looms larger. No president ever gave the order directly to Bissell. Allen Dulles did approve of Bissell's plans, but, as noted, they were conveyed in the most "circumlocutious" fashion. Dulles never told Bissell that he had been given authorization from the president. Bissell just "assumed" it, since Dulles made no objection to Bissell's plan. "I think the president knew, but I don't know if he knew, and Dulles is dead," said Bissell. "I just have to assume that Dulles had authority. He didn't say it." Eisenhower's national security adviser, Gordon Gray, strongly denied that the president ever authorized an assassination and insisted that Eisenhower was not the sort of man to engage in "circumlocutions."[2]

Eisenhower did press Dulles for "drastic" action against Castro, which may have been code for assassination. And most CIA veterans take it on faith that Bissell was merely carrying out the wishes of the president. But some who knew him and watched him in action are not so sure. "The CIA had an awfully long leash," said Chester Cooper, a senior official in the DD/I who became the agency's liaison to the national security staff in the Kennedy administration. He believes Bissell saw authorization in a double negative: "I think the fact that Eisenhower didn't say 'don't do it' was enough for Bissell." Thomas Parrott was the CIA officer assigned to the Special Group. Among his jobs was to record all approvals and authorizations given the CIA by the executive branch. "Bissell couldn't have cared less what the Special Group talked about. He was bored by it," said Parrott. "I don't think he ever even read the minutes." Parrott believes that Bissell launched the initial assassination attempts against Castro on his own initiative, without presidential authorization. So does Lyman Kirkpatrick, the CIA's inspector general in the late 1950s and early 1960s. F.A.O. Schwarz Jr., the general counsel of the Church Committee, said that while the committee was never able to resolve the question of authorization one way or the other, his "personal guess" is that "Eisenhower didn't know. He never had a conversation with Dulles."

Allen Dulles, who died in 1969, before the revelation in 1975 of the CIA's "family jewels," as the assassination plots and other "dirty tricks" were known, is a mysterious figure in this debate. It is clear that he felt assassination was morally acceptable, along with just about everything else the CIA did. In the OSS, Dulles had tried to help the plotters against Hitler, and in a speech after the war he declared that "assassination may be the only means left of overthrowing modern tyranny." Nonetheless, the general view of Dulles in the period 1959–61 is of a man beginning to fade. The death of his brother, John Foster, in 1959 was a personal blow, and it broke the cozy connection between the president's senior foreign policy adviser and the CIA director. He was weary after running the CIA for six years, his health was beginning to decline, and he was simply less of a force than he had been in earlier days. He had always prized bold activists; his instinct was to give them plenty of freedom to act. After 1959, Dulles passed to Bissell "effective leadership of the CIA," writes Peter Grose, "reserving for himself the tasks he most enjoyed and could do best: avuncular and nostalgic meetings, in a haze of pipe smoke, with officers from the field, the intelligence briefings to the National Security Council, and public speeches to secure the image of the CIA."[3] It is unlikely that Bissell failed to tell Dulles of his activities, but by Bissell's own description and the other available evidence, it appears that Bissell did not tell Dulles very much about what he was doing. Without question, Bissell was the driving force behind the assassination plots. Dulles's role was to acquiesce. "Dulles had great respect for Bissell's judgment," said Bob King, Bissell's executive assistant. "Bissell was hyperactive and Dulles was laid-back. Dulles basically gave Bissell his head. It was, tell me if there's anything horrible; otherwise, I don't want to hear about it."[4]

Bissell was an articulate defender of the rationale behind plausible deniability. Looked at more cynically, however, plausible deniability became a convenient excuse for Bissell to do whatever he wanted. By not telling his masters, Bissell convinced himself, he was protecting them.

Like Dulles, Bissell believed in 1960—and right up to his death in 1994—that assassination is, under the proper circumstances, a moral act. The generals' plot to kill Hitler in 1944 was moral, Bissell believed; had it succeeded, the Germans would have sued for peace and perhaps hundreds of thousands of lives would have been spared.

It seems improbable now to equate Castro or the other Third World strongmen targeted by the CIA in 1959–60 with Adolf Hitler. But in 1992, Bissell still maintained, "Lumumba and Sukarno were two of the worst people in public life I've ever heard of. They were mad dogs. Castro I saw not as a mad dog but as a purposeful antagonist. I believed that they were dangerous to the United States. There was a widespread belief that societies in the noncommunist world were exceedingly fragile, susceptible to being destroyed by these demagogues."

But he conceded that "our judgment was wrong." In retrospect, he realized that these Third World demagogues were "not dangerous." Over the years, as he reflected on his time at the CIA, he came to believe that the assassination plots showed "bad judgment." Still, he hastened to add, "not bad morality." He was regretful because the plots failed and then they became public, not because they were morally wrong.

The assassination plots all failed, in part, because the CIA was not clever. "I was flummoxed by the stuff not working," said Bissell. "It wasn't for lack of trying, it was just technical failures." Perhaps the CIA was just unlucky. But one wonders if the CIA really knew what it was doing. The staff of the Church Committee had a mocking code name for the agency: The Gang That Couldn't Shoot Straight.[5]

The American upper class, like the British upper class it wished to emulate, was brave, but not always shrewd. The wellborn in war have a certain tendency to blunder, to order the Light Brigade to charge. In the Great War, the British upper class was willing to die in extraordinary numbers; about a thousand names, roughly four full classes, are etched in the wall of the main courtyard at Eton. Many of them fell because they were marched straight into machine guns. The American WASPs who ran the CIA a generation later were willing to take risks, but they weren't always very street-smart.

The image of Richard Bissell, blinking behind his glasses, plotting to use Sicilian mobsters to carry out U.S. policy, seems from the realm of fiction. Bissell thought he was being practical. The Mafia are professional killers, after all, and they know how to keep secrets. But the mob routinely botches its own executions, and the code of omertà applies only among mafiosi, not to dealings with the U.S. government. There is a view among some former Justice Department officials and FBI agents that the Mafia's involvement in the assassination plots was always a big scam: the mob never really intended to bump off Castro; they just wanted to pick up an IOU from the government, an insurance policy against prosecution. The Chicago mob boss Sam "Mo Mo" Giancana invoked his

CIA service when the FBI was "crowding him" in 1963, according to the CIA's 1967 inspector general's report.[6]

Bissell said the CIA assassinations did not fail for "lack of heart." But one wonders whether his heart really was in it. Along with stoicism, Bissell picked up a moral sensibility at Groton. In my own conversations with him, he was not nearly so bloodless as he appears on the pages of *Alleged Assassination Plots Involving Foreign Leaders,* the Church Committee report that is, along with the CIA's 1967 inspector general's report, the core document on assassinations. He could be lively and full of passion on subjects ranging from sailing to the quality of friendship. It was only when he began discussing assassinations that his tone changed. He became ponderous and formal, as if he were testifying. The skilled expositor, the famously clear briefer who had been so reflective and candid on most subjects, suddenly became fuzzy, opaque, and muddled. He began to sound like the type of bureaucrat he routinely mocked.

It is possible, of course, that Bissell was, out of duty or habit, still practicing plausible deniability. Like a good soldier, he may have been protecting his superiors and colleagues long after they had gone to their graves. But that seems unlikely. The Cold War was over when I talked to him, and the CIA's "family jewels" had long since been exposed. Bissell seemed quite open about most "secret" matters. My own strong suspicion is that he spoke so guardedly about assassination plots in order to protect himself, not from history's judgment—it was too late for that—but from his own sense of guilt. "In a subliminal sense, maybe he and Tracy were afraid of the subject," said Bob King. His secretary, Doris Mirage, recalled that "Bissell got calls from the Mafia, but he wouldn't take them. I don't even know how they got his inside number." In early 1961, Bissell received a written proposal from a mobster, Joe Bonano, offering to assassinate Castro. The paper just sat for days in Bissell's "in box." "He wouldn't touch it," said Mirage. "Somebody delivered this piece of yellow paper; it was not mailed to him. He just didn't want any part of it. I think, at heart, assassination was very disagreeable to Bissell," she said. "You needed to be a different sort of person for this kind of thing."[7]

Significantly, the assassination plots were never seriously discussed as a policy change. The reason, Bissell said, was that they were "too sensitive." That explains why they were not discussed at the White House or State Department. But Bissell went on to say that he never discussed the plots with Dulles or Barnes except in the most cursory fashion. This seems hard to believe. It obviously was an enormous step to assassinate a head of state, no matter how disreputable. How could they not have discussed the consequences?

The answer lies partly in the CIA's culture of secrecy. "Their instincts were to protect themselves, to protect each other," said Eleanor Dulles, the sister of John Foster and Allen Dulles. "They used the same idiom, the same language." Top agency officials spoke "circumlocutiously" even among themselves while they were sitting in secure rooms. There was a certain amount of joking that the ratty old offices of the CIA down on the Mall could never be made secure, but it is doubtful that the fear of KGB bugs made the CIA men avoid what they called "bad words" like assassination. Of course, the habit of secrecy is important for an intelligence official. People are naturally talkative, and spies have to condition themselves to keep secrets from their friends and mates. But over time the practice of keeping secrets at the agency passed from prudence to obsession. Some senior officials came to prefer speaking in code. Dulles especially liked to use code words, even when their meaning was fairly obvious. His associates found it childishly spooky, as if he were playing at being a spy.

Behind the culture of the CIA is another reason Bissell never really discussed assassination with his colleagues. Denial is a common-enough defense. For men of Barnes and Bissell's time and class, it was virtually a code of conduct. It is embodied in all the clichés about cold showers, keeping a stiff upper lip, "never complain, never explain." Perhaps because it offended their Puritan roots, the New England rich feared indolence. To compensate for the "softness" of wealth, boys learned to be tough. Hiring the Mafia may have been a crazy idea, certainly in retrospect, but it was tough.[8]

THE DEMANDS of toughness began to quietly eat at Tracy Barnes. He was, like Bissell, ambivalent about assassination. According to his secretary, Alice McIlvaine, Barnes at first objected when the director of the Technical Services Staff, Cornelius Roosevelt, demonstrated to him a way to kill Castro early in 1960. Roosevelt, another Grotonian who, with his rosy cheeks and bright bow ties, made an unlikely Dr. Strangelove, had worked up a poison to be put in the hatband of Castro's fatigue cap. "Tracy got indignant," said McIlvaine. "He said, 'We're not in that business, no way. We have absolutely no authority to kill anyone.' " Yet shortly thereafter Barnes signed an order to arrange an "accident" for Raul Castro—which he withdrew the next day.

At home, Barnes's children began noticing a subtle change in their all-powerful father. The man who once ruled the dinner table with his sharp, sarcastic wit began "talking gobbledygook," recalled his daughter, Jane. "He had always set an acid example of getting to the point. Now he beat around the bush." Barnes, who had made law review at Harvard, was capable of analytical thinking. But at the CIA his colleagues began noticing that his conversations meandered. "He assumed a lot of knowledge and was discursive. He was hard to sit next to at dinner," said Chester Cooper. "My wife was never quite sure what he was saying."

His inarticulateness was a symptom. As he traveled into the secret world and was forced to betray his own values, he gradually lost his bearings. Years later, in a letter to the author, Jane Barnes sought to defend her father's essential goodness. He was ardent, graceful, and brave, but, as she acknowledged, "he embodied the poetic illusions of his class more than its power." Lacking the defenses of the shrewder, tougher Cold Warriors, Barnes showed, before the others, signs of the demoralization that would afflict many of them over time. He was, his daughter wrote, "the canary in the coal mine. As he descended into darkness, he was subtly afflicted by the air, quick to register its malaise, yet too undermined to realize how poisonous the environment was to him."[9]

Chapter Seventeen

INVASION

"He was building a tar baby."

IN FEBRUARY 1961 the CIA welcomed the Kennedy administration with a private dinner at the Alibi Club, a small (fifty-member) men's club housed in a narrow brick building a few blocks from the White House. Allen Dulles often used the Alibi, with its cozy, old-world feel, for CIA dinners. On this evening Dulles had invited the top men of the new administration to meet the upper echelon of the CIA. The purpose was to have a good dinner, tell spy stories and, as Bob Amory, the deputy director/intelligence, put it, "to get a head start on the State Department." Each CIA official was supposed to prepare a *"New Yorker*-ish précis" of what he did.

The evening began with three martinis all around (except for White House speechwriter Ted Sorensen, a teetotaler) and ended well after 1 A.M. Des FitzGerald spoke of his work against the communists in the Far East, and Tracy Barnes went on a bit about the CIA's secret war against Castro, though he was circumspect, and said nothing about assassinations. The White House men found Barnes charming, if a little vague.

The star of the evening was Richard Bissell. He seemed like an incongruous spymaster—tall, slightly stooped, a little clumsy. But no one doubted his force of personality or intellect. "I am," he announced, "a man-eating shark." There was laughter across the thicket of glasses. It was just the right touch, a mix of bravado and self-mockery.[1]

BISSELL, IN turn, was delighted by the new administration. The young men around President Kennedy were action-oriented, and they seemed equally impatient with bureaucracy. The CIA was the place to go for quick results, President Kennedy told his friend journalist Charles Bartlett. The State Department just dithered. "They're not queer at State, but . . . ," said JFK. "Well, they're sort of like Adlai. . . ."[2]

Bissell contrasted JFK and Adlai Stevenson from his perspective as a student of empire. A liberal Democrat, Bissell had voted twice for the Illinois governor, "but I understood Kennedy's attitude towards Stevenson," he said. "Stevenson hadn't been tested by tough decisions. If you were going to be an effective Cold Warrior, you had to be a good orator in the Roman sense. Stevenson was. But you also had to be ready to make huge and ruthless decisions. Stevenson was about Cicero. Cicero spoke a good war against the Catilines, but he didn't do much. Kennedy," said Bissell, "was Caesar."[3]

Kennedy made clear that he had no use for the elaborate executive branch infrastructure; he called cabinet meetings "a waste of time" and felt the same way about the National Security Council. The CIA men wasted no time filling the void. "They thought they had Kennedy's number already," Richard Reeves writes in his biography *President Kennedy*. "They were calling this White House 'the floating crap game.' No regular meetings meant that all the action went with the President; if he was not looking, there was no system and no guarantee that anyone was checking for him. Kennedy was at the center, but he was alone there—and Bissell was going ahead on his own. . . ."[4]

Kennedy's lieutenants seemed at once easy with the CIA—youthful, vigorous, and like-minded—and a little in awe. When Richard Goodwin, a young White House aide, was briefed by an agency man who hinted "at vast and wondrous operations still unrevealed," he felt "the first stirrings of that seductive power—the invisible child wandering unseen through the grown-up world: 'Who knows? The Shadow knows.' . . ."[5]

Within the CIA some officials on the analytical side, the DD/I, worried that the New Frontiersmen were too easily seduced by the gamesmen of the DD/P. "Barnes and FitzGerald would think up operations over lunch. It might start in jest, but about halfway through, they'd begin to believe they could work it out," said Chester Cooper. "Not just derring-do, but manipulation. Someone would know someone's cousin. 'We can get him,' they would say."

At the State Department, senior officials were wary. "[Secretary of State Dean] Rusk and I regarded these people as slightly immature," said Undersecretary George Ball. "It was fun and games. Rusk thought covert action was something for youngsters to play with. He treated it with scorn." Chester Bowles, the undersecretary of state for political affairs, had to be replaced on a special task force on counterinsurgency (a subject of particular fascination to the Kennedys) because he disapproved of all clandestine interventions. That was fine with the CIA; giving Bowles authority over covert actions, said Des FitzGerald, was like entrusting a ship to a captain who hated the sea.[6]

While the Stevensonians in the State Department looked askance at the CIA's covert actions, they nonetheless hugely admired the man who ran them. It is a real measure of Richard Bissell's stature in the government in early 1961 that Bowles asked Kennedy if Bissell could come over to Foggy Bottom to be his deputy undersecretary. Bowles was a Yale acquaintance who had chartered the *Sea Witch* from Bissell for summer cruises, and while not modest himself, he bowed before Bissell's intellect and accomplishments. Bissell was actually tempted by Bowles's invitation; he thought he might get a crack at making foreign policy if he went to State. Bissell fairly assumed that he would quickly upstage Rusk, Ball, and Bowles. This assumption was shared by National Security Adviser McGeorge Bundy, who thought that Bissell would inject imagination and decisiveness into State.

But Kennedy said no to moving Bissell. "You can't have him," said the president.

"Why not?" asked Bowles.

"He's going to take Allen Dulles's job on July 1."[7]

ALLEN DULLES had been one of John F. Kennedy's first two appointments after the election. The other was J. Edgar Hoover of the FBI. Both men were "legends," explained Kennedy, better left undisturbed. His deference may have been encouraged by the knowledge that the CIA and FBI had thick files on the president-elect's past, including his brief affair with a German spy during World War II. The family patriarch, Joseph Kennedy, had urged his son to play it safe by reappointing Hoover and Dulles.[8]

But Allen Dulles was fading in 1961. He had been director of Central Intelligence for eight years; his chronic gout was forcing him to pad around in bedroom slippers; he missed his brother, John

Foster. He had barely been involved in the planning for Cuba. The Havana station chief, returning to brief Dulles in 1960, had found him "pretty foggy about the whole thing."[9]

Dulles had always been an admirer of Bissell's and inclined to give him his head. By January 1961, the DCI was leaning on Bissell for support. That month Dulles told Bissell that he would recommend him as his successor. He added that he would like to stay on as DCI "a bit longer." Bissell realized, he later recalled, "that this was a question to me. Would I press the President to appoint me as Allen's successor quite soon and leave Allen in honorable retirement?"

Dulles was correct in assuming that Bissell had more clout with the Kennedys than he did. John Kennedy had been impressed by Bissell at a dinner party given by Joe Alsop in August 1960. Alsop had praised Bissell to Kennedy for his toughness and brilliance. Kennedy figured that if Bissell could be so highly praised by a hardline hawk like Alsop and a Stevenson dove like Bowles, he must be about right. Before Kennedy's inauguration a member of his transition team had asked, "There must be someone you really trust within the intelligence community. Who is that?" Kennedy answered, "Richard Bissell."*

Admired and deferred to, Bissell could hardly be blamed for feelings of omnipotence in the winter of 1961. Years later he said that he realized that he was only at "the beginning of wisdom" in 1961. "I was beginning to learn there was a lot I didn't know." But, he added, "It dawned on me too late."[11]

Bissell's only real detractors were inside the CIA—the core of "Prudent Professionals" around Richard Helms, the DD/P's chief of operations. Helms was no longer hiding his disdain for Bissell or the ambitious plans he had been working on for the past year to overthrow Castro. Helms had taken to sardonically referring to Bissell as "Wonder Boy."[12]

Bissell, along with Tracy Barnes, had become more hostile toward Helms. Barnes called Helms "Rubber Stamp," to mock him as a paper shuffler, and both men sometimes referred to Helms,

---

* About a month before the election, Bissell recalls in his memoirs, he met privately with Kennedy (Alsop was again the matchmaker). "I made it clear to Kennedy that I was still working for Eisenhower and therefore couldn't do anything of an active nature for him, but I also told him truthfully (although perhaps a little inappropriately since I was still part of the current Administration) that I agreed with most of his philosophy."[10]

who slicked back his hair, as "the Eminence Grease." By January 1961, the name-calling had escalated into a showdown. Bissell and Barnes went to Allen Dulles and tried to get Helms transferred to London, out of headquarters where he had spent his entire CIA career, and into a relatively meaningless post in the field. Dulles generally went along with Bissell, but in this case he wisely demurred.[13]

THE CIA's plan to invade Cuba, code-named JMARC, landed on John Kennedy's desk before he was sworn in as president.* Bissell and Dulles had briefed the president-elect on the project at his father's winter home in Palm Beach on November 18. Bissell had set up maps and charts on a large table by the swimming pool. The CIA men stressed to the president that there was "not much time" to act. The Soviets were sending Castro MiG fighters and training the Cubans to fly them. Without command of the air, an invasion would be impossible. Bissell was struck by Kennedy's impassiveness. He seemed neither for nor against the operation. He expressed surprise only at the scale of it.[14]

The operation had grown over the past few months. What had begun in the spring of 1960 as a plan to infiltrate a few dozen commandos to slip into the jungle and join the resistance had become by November a full-scale invasion—several hundred men storming a beachhead, backed up by air support. The original budget and staff—$4.4 million, forty operators—had multiplied ten times. The escalation had come about not because things were going well, but rather because they were going badly.[15]

For months the CIA had been trying to drop weapons and supplies to the Cuban resistance. The first mission, on September 28, 1960, was inauspicious. It was to drop an "arms pack" for a hundred men to an agent waiting on the ground. The air crew missed the drop zone by seven miles and landed the weapons on top of a dam, where Castro's forces scooped them up. The agent was caught and shot. The plane got lost on the way to Guatemala and landed in Mexico. "It is still there," caustically notes a CIA inspector general's report written a year later. Of thirty missions flown by the CIA, four were rated a success, but even this scorecard

---

* The operation became publicly known by its Pentagon code name, Operation ZAPATA.

may have been generous.[16] Pilots missed their targets, or the Cuban farmers who made up the tiny (and frightened) anti-Castro underground could not find their way to the drop sites. The pleas from the resistance became increasingly desperate: "Impossible to fight. . . Either the drops increase or we die . . . men without arms and equipment. God help us." Infiltrators were usually "picked up within days," said Bissell. "Our model was the French resistance in World War II. There you had devoted people and tight security." The true precedent was Albania. Security was poor; Miami was full of Castro's agents. "Cubans don't know how to keep secrets," said Bissell.[17]

It was clear that infiltration would not work. But like a driver who speeds up approaching a yellow light, Bissell ordered his aides to look for a more direct approach—a World War II–style amphibious landing. The operation's senior military adviser was a Marine colonel, Jack Hawkins, who had landed at Iwo Jima. Barnes and Hawkins were an unfortunate match. Hawkins, while brave, was unimaginative and narrowly focused. He was accustomed to the military's enormous logistical and supply "tail" and unfamiliar with the CIA's more informal ways. Barnes, also brave, was perhaps too freewheeling and somewhat careless about logistics. ("Tracy Barnes seemed to have a great deal more to say than was warranted by his knowledge and apparent understanding of the planned action," notes the CIA's secret in-house history of JMARC.) Still, at Bissell's prodding, plans for an invasion kept escalating, from a force of 200 men in October, to 600 men in December, to 1,200 men in April.[18]

Recruited from the exile community in Miami, the men of "La Brigada" were being trained on a banana plantation in Guatemala by CIA paramilitary experts of the Tony Poe variety. One was William "Rip" Robertson, who ordered the bomb dropped down the smokestack of a British freighter during PBSUCCESS. Banished for a time, he had been rehabilitated for this operation but told to stay out of combat (an order he was to ignore). Some of the CIA men had trained Wisner's shadow émigré army in Germany. Speaking no Spanish, they startled the Cuban boys by shouting Hungarian and Russian obscenities at them. The Americans tended to refer to their charges as either "fucking Cubans" or "tame Cubans," but they gradually came to admire their spirit if not their military proficiency. At a nearby airfield, pilots "sheep-dipped" from the Alabama National Guard taught Cubans how to fly a fleet of thirty war-surplus B-26s scrounged up by Tracy Barnes.[19]

Though daring and a little racy, Barnes was Victorian about discussing sex, especially at the dinner table. He looked pained when the Guatemala station chief told Barnes and Bissell over dinner in Washington one night in the summer of 1960 that the CIA needed to provide whores to keep the Cubans from getting restless at their training base. Insisting that this would be an improper use of taxpayer funds, Barnes got up and left the dining room table for several minutes. Bissell just chuckled and told the station chief, "I don't want to hear anything more about it. Your job is to get things done down there."[20]

In the Florida Keys in January 1961, the CIA was loading two old LCIs (landing craft/infantry) with enough weapons to support the invasion as well as the popular uprising that was supposed to follow. The locals laughed at the cover story that the ships were to be used for hydrographic and geological research. In Miami, E. Howard Hunt and Gerry Droller continued to quarrel with each other and with the Frente, the Cuban exile leaders, who also squabbled among themselves. The CIA was sloppy about security. One of Hunt's couriers managed to lose a suitcase full of top-secret documents in Mexico City, while Droller's plotting was overheard through the thin walls of his motel—and embarrassingly fed to the FBI. These leaks were among many. Photographers recorded the recruits lining up in Miami to enlist in La Brigada and spectators began showing up at Opa-Locka to watch blacked-out flights take off for Guatemala every night. In the fall and winter of 1960, the *Miami Herald*, the *Nation*, the *St. Louis Post-Dispatch*, the *Los Angeles Times*, *U.S. News & World Report*, and the *Washington Post* had reported bits and pieces of the story. In January 1961 the *New York Times* came right out and reported that the United States was training an exile army in Guatemala to invade Cuba.

Curiously, there was little public reaction. Congressmen did not stand up and demand to know what the administration was up to; editorial writers did not question American adventurism. In part, people were perfectly content with the idea that the government was plotting against Castro; and few, in any case, questioned the covert activities of the CIA.[21]

The CIA's masters in the executive branch were equally quiescent. Eisenhower, serving out his last of eight years in office, had shown little enthusiasm for the Cuban operation. "Boys," he told

Dulles and Bissell after the project had been delayed in the summer of 1960, "if you don't intend to go through with this, let's stop talking about it." But in August, Eisenhower had authorized $13 million to pay for the project, and in January he had encouraged President-elect Kennedy to push ahead. The dramatic escalation of the operation—from infiltration to invasion—appears not to have been vigorously debated in the Special Group. Both Secretary of Defense Thomas Gates and Undersecretary of State Douglas Dillon later said that they had qualms about the operation, but if they raised them at the time with the CIA's liaison, Tracy Barnes, Barnes said nothing about it to Bissell. Bissell did not read the minutes of the Special Group.[22]

After he took office, Kennedy did ask the Joint Chiefs of Staff to vet the project. A committee of colonels was sent over to the CIA's "war room" in Quarters Eye, expecting to be handed a thick document with the usual charts and timetables. Instead, they were given a "verbal rundown." The colonels retreated to the Pentagon and, working from feverishly scribbled notes, tried to write their own plan. They had been told that in March, La Brigada planned to land in the town of Trinidad, supposedly a hotbed of opposition to Castro. Within four days the invasion force was supposed to recruit enough local volunteers to double in size. Airborne troops would secure the roads leading to the town, and a force of guerrillas would be waiting in the nearby Escambray Mountains.

The Pentagon colonels decided that the Brigade could last up to four days if—and this was a crucial if—it had complete air supremacy. The enemy could not be allowed to have "any airplanes, period." The ultimate success of the invasion would rest with the size of the popular uprising, which was impossible to estimate. The Pentagon concluded that the personnel and logistical support for the invasion were "marginal at best." Pressed to give an overall rating of success, the colonels said "fair," by which they meant 30 percent.

When it came time to brief President Kennedy on the Pentagon's findings in late February, Richard Bissell—not the Pentagon—handled it. Bissell, who had read the colonels' executive summary but only skimmed the more pessimistic main report, neglected to mention that a "fair" chance of success meant less than one in three. The Joint Chiefs stood to the side. The CIA would be held responsible for its operation.[23]

"Bissell wanted backing, but he didn't want a lot of advice," said

Bob King. "He had a lot of confidence." So did the man appointed by Kennedy to coordinate his national security policy, McGeorge Bundy. The former Harvard dean was regarded as intellectually confident to the point of arrogance. One of the curiosities of the Bay of Pigs is why Bundy, who as national security adviser was supposed to be a kind of "honest broker," did not do more to ride herd on Bissell or clear up a series of ruinous misunderstandings between the CIA and the White House. Bundy had inklings of Bissell's flaws: "if Dick has a fault," Bundy wrote JFK in February, "it is that he does not look at all sides of the question." But Bundy, too, was a little enthralled by his old Yale professor. He fell for the glamour of covert action, he admitted years later. "It was the stupidity of freshmen on our part, and the stupidity on their part of being wrapped in their own illusions."[24]

Bissell "made no attempt to pull wool over your eyes, except to the degree he pulled it over his own," said Bundy. This is not entirely true; Bissell was guilty of at least being disingenuous with his old friend and college protégé on the sensitive question of assassinating foreign leaders.

In the winter of 1961, Bissell told Bundy that he was setting up an "executive action capability." It was not operational, merely a "standby" tool. Bundy made no objection. He later testified that he thought Bissell was "testing my reaction," not "asking my authority." At the time Bissell made no mention of the fact that the CIA was already enagaged in an assassination operation against Castro. When Bissell instructed William Harvey to set up the "executive action capability"—code name ZRRIFLE—he said that he had been "twice urged by the White House" to do so. Bissell was dissembling; he had not yet talked to Bundy. F.A.O. Schwarz, the chief counsel of the Church Committee, later concluded that Bissell was playing a game, looking for "implied authority" for the assassination projects already in the works.[25]

By April 1961, Bundy would realize that the president's dislike of bureaucracy and his penchant for an ad hoc approach to crises—form a task force and attack!—had serious drawbacks. On April 5, Bundy wrote a memo to Kennedy under the title "Crisis Commanders in Washington" arguing that the task-force system had left no one truly in charge, no one to take long-term responsibility.[26] But that was less than two weeks before the invasion of Cuba, too late to change the system that had allowed it to go forward. And in the case of Cuba, there was very definitely someone in charge—Richard Bissell. By using secrecy—his old cloak of plausible deniability—and cleverly playing the White House, Bissell had tried to make the Cuban operation virtually a one-man show.

In the end, of course, Bissell knew that he could not order the invasion of Cuba on his own. He had to get the final approval of President Kennedy. In the final six weeks before the invasion, his relationship with Kennedy, a man he much liked and admired, would be a case study in indecision and misunderstanding.

JOHN F. KENNEDY was deeply ambivalent about the Cuban operation. He could very well see the risk of failure. His fledgling Alliance for Progress with Central and South America, a liberal response to years of Yankee-Go-Home resentment, would get off to a poor start if a CIA-backed force was pushed into the sea by Castro—or even if it succceeded and the American involvement was widely known. And he was worried that if the United States went after Castro, Khrushchev would go after Berlin. On the other hand, he didn't want to get blamed by the Republicans for "chickening out" or going soft on communism. In his own mind, the president made a calculus: the less the military risk, the greater the political risk, and vice versa. It was a foolish calculus because it invited the president to take half measures in an all-or-nothing situation.[27]

Bissell came to brief the White House on the details of the plan on March 11. The briefing was a full-dress performance in the Cabinet Room: the president was there, as were the Joint Chiefs, Bundy, Defense Secretary Robert McNamara, and Secretary of State Dean Rusk. Bissell laid out the plan to put 750 men on a beach near the port of Trinidad on the south coast of Cuba. The model, he said, was the Anzio landing in World War II (not the best precedent, perhaps; the Allied invaders had been pinned down on the beachhead for four months). Kennedy interrupted after a few minutes:

"Too spectacular," he said. "It sounds like D-Day. You have to reduce the noise level of this thing."

Bissell tried to lecture Kennedy. "You have to understand . . . ," he began. The president said he understood perfectly, but that there were political considerations. He wanted the least possible political risk, even if that meant more military risk. There was to be no overt American military action, and he wanted to be able to deny—plausibly—the CIA's covert role. He sent Bissell back to draft a new plan, one with a more remote landing site and less "noise."[28]

This was a moment that demanded hard thinking and honest debate. The fact is that the invasion needed to be "noisy" to succeed. There was no way that 1,000 men were going to overwhelm Castro's army and militia—some 200,000 men. The success of the operation depended on stirring up a revolt in Cuba, and there needed to be plenty of commotion to do that. The plan was not to defeat Castro by force of arms but to scare him out of office. The model was supposed to be Arbenz in Guatemala in 1954. The Guatemalan president had not been driven out by the sham force under Castillo Armas, stalled on the Nicaraguan border, or even by the CIA's clever disinformation campaign on the Voice of Liberation. Arbenz had been afraid of Uncle Sam—of the Marines coming ashore.

But Bissell never discussed this point in his meetings at the White House. Bissell, along with his boss, Allen Dulles, incorrectly assumed that in the end, Kennedy, like Eisenhower, would commit himself wholeheartedly to the mission. Before Guatemala, Bissell had heard Eisenhower tell Allen Dulles that "if you commit the American flag, you commit it to win." Dulles had basically stayed out of the planning of the Cuban operation, deferring to Bissell (who later regretted, "I was too prepared to run it as a single-handed operation. I was impatient if Dulles raised too many questions"). Dulles had been willing to let Bissell run the show in part because he had confidence in him, but also because the Guatemala experience had made him (unrealistically) confident about Cuba. He had not worried unduly, he later wrote, because he remembered Eisenhower approving more planes just in time to salvage the faltering Guatemala coup. The CIA expected the same from Kennedy: "We felt that when the chips were down, when the crisis arose in reality, any action required for success would be authorized rather than permit the enterprise to fail," Dulles later wrote in notes that were never published but found in his personal papers after he died.[29]

"It never occurred to Bissell that if push came to shove, Kennedy wouldn't put in his stack," said Mac Bundy. "He never said, 'Do you really mean it? If we get the beachhead, will you back us up?' These worries were covered up. Once engaged, Bissell believed,

Kennedy wouldn't allow it to fail." Bundy or Kennedy himself should have pressed Bissell to own up to his real expectations and intentions. It is the job, particularly, of the national security adviser to prevent misunderstandings between the president and his foreign policy advisers. But Bundy was a little too trusting and admiring of Bissell, as was the president. And Bissell was too sure of himself and his plan to fully seek their advice as well as consent. The cheerful, damn-the-bureaucrats bond between the CIA and the New Frontiersmen was a curse.[30]

Back at Quarters Eye, Colonel Hawkins and Jake Esterline, the project director, worked through the night to produce a plan for the White House that was less "noisy." A few days later Dave Phillips, the propaganda chief, walked into the war room and noticed that someone had scrawled a large red "X" over the town of Trinidad. "There's been a change in the plan," said Colonel Hawkins. "Trinidad is out. Now we are going to land here." He pointed to an area on the coast a hundred miles to the west. Phillips laughed when he saw the name. "Bahía de Cochinos? How can we have a victorious landing force wading ashore at a place with that name? How can propagandists persuade Cubans to join the Brigade at the Bay of Pigs?"

Phillips squinted at the map. "It's too far from the mountains," he said. The invaders were supposed to be able to "melt into the mountains." Now the Escambray Mountains were eighty miles away—across an impenetrable swamp. "How will the Brigade take the beach and hold it?" he asked Hawkins.

"The first ships to land will carry tanks."

"Tanks!" Phillips was "stunned," he writes in his memoirs, *The Night Watch*. "We're going to mount a secret operation in the Caribbean with tanks?"

"That's right," said the colonel. "A company. Three platoons of five each, with two command tanks."[31]

It is hard to see how the addition of tanks made the operation "less noisy." But the loss of the "guerrilla option" was a serious change in the plans. Without the ability to "melt into the mountains," the invaders had to secure and hold the beachhead—or be pushed back into the sea. There was no fallback plan. Bissell never told Kennedy. "I did not deliberately mislead the president," he said. "I didn't take the trouble to say to him that if we shift from Trinidad to the Bay of Pigs, the fallback plan becomes totally different. The guerrilla option was not an option. In a guilty mood,

I have to take the blame for not calling that move from one locale to another a radically altered fallback." The new "fallback" was no fallback at all. By removing the option of making for the mountains, Bissell had created a choice of win-or-die.[32]

Naturally, the suspicion arises that Bissell kept quiet intentionally. Some old CIA hands believe that Bissell was setting a trap to force U.S. intervention. "He was building a tar baby," said Edgar Applewhite, a former deputy inspector general. Right after the invasion several of the Cuban exiles leading the Brigade made a sensational allegation to newspaper reporter Haynes Johnson. They claimed that they had been secretly advised by their CIA handlers to stage a fake "mutiny" if they received last-minute word from Washington canceling the invasion. The Cubans were to disregard the order and proceed to the beaches. The Cubans believed these instructions came from Bissell himself.

As the Cubans described it, the CIA feared that Kennedy would flinch in the final moments and try to call off the invasion. But it would be an incredible act of lese majesty, even for Bissell, to concoct such a plot. Jake Esterline, his chief of operations, said he had always assumed that "we couldn't stop the Cubans even if we wanted to," but he insisted "flat out" that Bissell never tried to go around the president in this way. Bissell did say that he never warned Kennedy that there was no middle way, no guerrilla option, because he was afraid the president would call off the whole operation. "I was confident it would work," Bissell said. "I was eager for the plan to go forward." He denied, however, any "conspiracy" to trick the president into a situation where he would have to commit U.S. forces to win.[33]

In the recriminations that followed the Bay of Pigs, the CIA would be accused of misleading the White House about the prospects of instigating a popular revolt. The CIA had mixed intelligence on the loyalty of the Cuban people. In his effort to maintain secrecy—and control—Bissell had cut out the analytical side of the CIA and thereby deprived himself of experts who might have cautioned him against being too optimistic.[34] In an informal brainstorming session a couple of months before the invasion, Tracy Barnes was told by the analysts that Castro's army was likely to remain loyal to "the Beard." This was a critical question—in Guatemala, Arbenz had given up when his army turned against him. But Barnes apparently ignored the analysis, and in any case it was never formally presented to Bissell. Bissell himself paid no heed to an analysis prepared by his friend of twenty-six years, Sherman Kent. In a memo to Dulles entitled "Is Time on Our Side in Cuba?" Kent predicted that Castro's position would grow stronger rather than weaker over time. Although Kent was not "witting" of the coming invasion, he was effectively predicting that an internal revolt was unlikely. Bissell was able to take more heart from the intelligence reports prepared by his own staff, which offered such evidence as a "private survey that showed that less than 30 percent of the population is still with Fidel. In this 30 percent are included the Negroes who have always followed the strong men in Cuba but will not fight."[35]

In later years Bissell's men argued that they never put much faith in a spontaneous uprising in Cuba, and they never promised the White House that one would occur. If anything, they had been cautioned by Allen Dulles to downplay the chances of success. He had told them one of his favorite war stories from Guatemala, of the time Eisenhower had asked him what the odds of victory were, and Dulles had answered "about 20 percent." The president had told Dulles that if he had blithely promised victory, he never would have authorized the extra planes that turned the day.[36]

The record is murky on just what Bissell predicted to Kennedy about a popular revolt, but the debate begs a larger question. Assuming that the old CIA hands are right, that they never predicted an immediate uprising, just exactly how did they plan to win? Bissell uncharacteristically struggled a little bit as he addressed this question thirty years later. Unlike Colonel Hawkins, he never thought, he said, that the invaders would march victoriously on Havana. He said that his real hope had been that the Brigade would secure a beachhead—and he had felt confident they would. Their initial success, he had hoped, would sow "turmoil and confusion," especially since the exiles' (CIA-run) air force of B-26s would be flying up and down the island, bombing army installations and electrical grids, and knocking out Castro's phones. Linked by a microwave system, Cuba's phones could be silenced by bombing a few transmission towers. Castro, like Arbenz, would become anxious, fearing American intervention. "The United States would step in"—not necessarily with overt military force, but by asking for a meeting of the Organization of American States to call for a cease-fire.

Bissell did not sound entirely convinced himself that this plan could have worked—the OAS was a weak reed to lean on—and he admitted to a certain failure to "think things through." The implausibility of Operation ZAPATA, as the new landing plan was called by the Defense Department, has led some historians to wonder if Bissell didn't have another card up his sleeve. Was he counting on the success of "Track II"—the assassination plot against Castro?[37] Bissell did have some hope initially that the invasion would be made easier—or unnecessary—by decapitating Cuba's leader. But that winter, as he got back reports that the Mafia had failed to deliver on its contract to kill Castro, "my estimation of the likelihood of success began to sink," he recalled.

Why, then, didn't Bissell just call the whole thing off? Increasingly, as March turned to April, and the deadline for the invasion was set, then postponed, then postponed again—first April 5, then April 15, then finally, April 17—logic and reason gave way to hubris, momentum, and fatalism.

McGEORGE BUNDY noticed a change in the president when he returned from Easter weekend in Palm Beach. Before Kennedy left, he had seemed dubious about the Bay of Pigs invasion. ("What do you think about this damned invasion?" White House aide Arthur Schlesinger asked on March 28. "I think about it as little as possible," answered Kennedy.) But he came back from the family compound resolved to go ahead. Bundy wondered what had happened over golf and cocktails. Schlesinger, who opposed the operation, suspected that Kennedy had been talking to his father, his mentor in the school of hit-'em-again-harder. All through his life, when John Kennedy saw his father, he would make a fist. Joe Kennedy would wrap his hand around it.[38]

At 6 P.M. on Monday, April 3, the day Kennedy flew back to Washington, he met secretly with a dozen of his top advisers, including Bissell. The time had come to make a final decision on Operation ZAPATA. Apparently on a last-minute whim, Kennedy had brought along Senator William Fulbright, the chairman of the Senate Foreign Relations Committee. Fulbright made a moral argument against the United States sponsoring secret invasions of other countries. His argument irritated others in the room, who thought that the time for moral arguments had long since passed. Some, like Paul Nitze, the assistant secretary of defense for international security affairs, found themselves voting for the invasion, not because they really believed in it, but because they were irked at Fulbright. Others felt pressure to rally round. Pressed for a yes-no answer, A. A. Berle, a tough old New Dealer and State Department specialist on Latin America, cried out, "I say, let 'er rip!" Assistant Secretary of State William Bundy, watching the president's advisers argue uncomfortably, uncertain of the facts, thought the whole meeting was a "charade."[39]

Bissell was encouraged by the meeting. He felt he had finally been given approval, although Kennedy reserved the right to make a final decision on the eve of the invasion. Bissell's staff, however, was in a state of near revolt. They were demoralized by what they regarded as Kennedy's constant trimming, his demand that the invasion be made less "noisy." Kennedy had insisted that the landing occur at night—quieter, but more dangerous to a force that had never landed anywhere before, day or night. The loss of the guerrilla option was a serious setback, and they were upset by the president's insistence that U.S. forces would not intervene militarily in Cuba. Howard Hunt thought the president was engaging in disinformation, but others in Quarters Eye feared the president actually meant what he said.

On Saturday, April 8, Esterline and Hawkins, the two top-line officers, came out to Bissell's house in Cleveland Park. They told him they wanted to resign. The project was out of control, and they could not go on with it.

If Bissell was shocked, he gave no sign. He was sympathetic; he shared many of their concerns. But he asked them not to quit. The reason he gave was personal loyalty. He asked them to hang on. The project was too far along; if they quit it would be hard for Bissell, but it would not stop the landing. He asked them to be good soldiers; reluctantly, they agreed.[40]

Bissell had always been calm in a crisis—almost eerily so. Over time he had learned that he enjoyed this feeling of mastery. He recalled how his mother had taught him that a boat with a sturdy keel will not capsize, no matter how far it heels. He had taken intellectual and physical risks, and he had defied them. He was no longer the nearsighted, woefully uncoordinated boy who had failed at football. He was the spymaster, the chief of all covert operations—he could laugh—a man-eating shark!

And yet . . . the pressure on him was overwhelming. Bissell was planning an invasion while trying to preserve not only secrecy beforehand but also deniability after the fact—all while running the clandestine service with its intricate web of operations around the world. Remarkably, Bissell was simultaneously supervising the development of the SR-71 spy plane that winter and spring of 1961, and unlike the U-2, the SR-71 was moving slowly off the drawing boards. Bissell felt vexed, impatient. The president was meddling with his Cuba plan, his crew was mutinous, and the whole enterprise was in danger of foundering. Aboard the *Sea Witch*, while he was navigating in heavy weather, Bissell would become rigid, determined, utterly fixed on his course. So he became about the invasion of Cuba.[41]

Two days after he calmed his lieutenants, Bissell briefed the president's brother, Attorney General Robert Kennedy, on the operation. He rated the odds of success at two out of three, and assured RFK that even in the worst case the invaders could turn guerrilla and remain a dangerous nuisance to Castro. RFK had his doubts. "I hope you're right," he told Bissell. But he was also the type to push ahead in the hard going. Young Kennedy became Bissell's moral enforcer. He told Schlesinger he was "performing a disservice" in raising his objection with the president and that henceforth he "should remain quiet." When RFK saw Chester Bowles in the White House, according to a story that later made the rounds, he jammed three fingers into the undersecretary's soft stomach and told him in an even voice that "he, Bowles, was for the invasion, remember that, he was for it, they all were for it." President Kennedy cut off conversation with his speechwriter Ted Sorensen by saying, "I know everyone is grabbing for their nuts on this."[42]

On April 14, President Kennedy read a cable from Colonel Hawkins, who had visited the Brigade as they prepared to embark from Guatemala. The officers, reported Hawkins, "had a fanatical urge to begin battle." They did not, he added, "expect help from U.S. armed forces." The telegram cheered Kennedy, who had been especially anxious after the *New York Times* reported that the United States was training Cuban exiles for an imminent invasion. The story had been blurred and played down by the publisher, but it still infuriated Kennedy. "I can't believe what I'm reading!" he told his press secretary, Pierre Salinger. "Castro doesn't need agents over here. All he has to do is read our papers!"[43]

The president was still determined to "quiet" the American role. Air strikes were scheduled to begin against Cuba on Saturday, April 15—D-Day minus two. Kennedy asked Bissell how many B-26s were to be sent. "Sixteen," he answered.

"I don't want it on that scale. I want it minimal," said Kennedy.

Bissell cut back the number of sorties to eight. It was, he would later acknowledge, a critical concession. The invasion could not succeed without air cover. Castro had a small air force—a dozen serviceable planes, mostly old Sea Furies and a few T-33 jet trainers (a gift from the United States to Batista) fitted with 20-mm cannons and bomb racks. They all had to be destroyed on the ground or they could sweep the beaches clean. The Brigade's wing of B-26s, based in Nicaragua, lacked the range to patrol the skies for very long over Cuba. It would take time to secure the airfield at the Bay of Pigs where they could land. To ensure air supremacy, two air strikes were planned against Castro's airfields: one on D-minus-2 and another at dawn on the day of the invasion. By cutting back the first raid, Bissell made the second even more critical. He did not know, then, that his old friend Tracy Barnes would make a mistake that would eliminate the margin for error.[44]

BISSELL USED Barnes as his representative to the rest of government partly because he could say as little as possible without causing offense. "Tracy was incapable of going from point A to point B in a direct line. He couldn't give you a blunt assessment of anything. He was too genteel," said Jake Esterline, the gruff project director. Barnes's knack for lulling senior government officials into acquiescence, a useful tool in most cases, backfired when he went to brief Adlai Stevenson, the U.S. ambassador to the United Nations, on April 8, a week before the invasion.

Stevenson had been given the U.N. post as a consolation prize by his political rival, John Kennedy. He had also been awarded cabinet rank and a place on the National Security Council, but these seats didn't mean much in Kennedy's ad hoc government, and Stevenson grumbled about being left out. He was not "witting" of the Cuban operation, although, like most senior officials, he had heard rumors.

By unfortunate coincidence, the United Nations was scheduled to debate Cuban allegations of "various plans of aggression and acts of intervention" on Monday, April 17—D-Day for Operation ZAPATA. Clearly, Stevenson had to be briefed on the upcoming invasion. In the war room in Quarters Eye, the feeling was that Stevenson should get a "cold, hands-on blunt assessment," said Esterline. But when Bissell announced that Barnes would go up to

New York to brief Stevenson, Esterline exchanged nervous glances with his number two, Dick Drain, who had nicknamed Barnes "the soul of vagueness." "We looked at each other and thought, Barnes doesn't have what it takes to tell Stevenson the truth," said Esterline.

Actually, he wasn't really expected to level with the U.N. ambassador. Before Barnes left for the United Nations, Bissell took him aside and said, "Don't be too specific on briefing Adlai." Barnes was supposed to tell Stevenson "enough to shut him up and keep him happy, because Adlai liked to shoot his mouth off," said Bob King, Bissell's assistant. "But Bissell didn't anticipate the mess that Barnes would create."

Barnes took the Eastern Shuttle up to New York on Saturday, April 8, and met with Stevenson at the U.S. Mission to the United Nations. Barnes was on easy terms with Stevenson, an old social friend, as well as with the other members of the U.S. delegation, who were arrayed around the oblong table in the mission's offices at 2 Park Avenue. Stevenson's deputy, Francis T.P. Plimpton, recalled how Barnes had applied for a job with his law firm after Harvard Law School. One of Barnes's wartime roommates in London, Charles P. Noyes, was the mission's minister counselor. Barnes and Noyes had gone to Yale together.

Barnes told his friends that there was indeed a secret operation in the works against Cuba. But he said it was strictly a Cuban affair. The Americans had helped with the financing and the training, but the U.S. role would not be visible. Barnes said nothing about air strikes or about the timing of the invasion. Asked what the "appearance" of the operation would be, he answered that it would appear to be happening from the "inside," with some "outside participation"—but without any "American participation." When he was done Stevenson said, "Look, I don't like this." But it was "Kennedy's show" and he would be a good soldier as long as there was no American participation and nothing happened while the U.N. General Assembly was in session. Barnes genially nodded in assent. Then the men retired to the Century Club for lunch.[45]

Two days before the first air strikes, Kennedy made one last request to "mute" the invasion. The air strikes had to appear to be an inside job—originating from Cuba, not from the CIA's secret air base in Nicaragua. Barnes cooked up an elaborate cover story with the help of Dave Phillips. After the raid a pair of B-26s would land in Florida, piloted by Cubans claiming to be defectors. They would tell newsmen that they had bombed and shot up their own airfields on the flight to freedom. To make the planes look as though they had been through combat, a CIA man pulled out his .45-caliber pistol and plugged a few holes in the wings.

On Saturday morning, April 15, eight B-26s out of Nicaragua, manned by Cuban pilots, bombed three of Castro's airfields. The morning session of the U.N. General Assembly had just been gaveled to order when Dr. Raul Roa, the Cuban foreign minister, demanded the floor to declare that his country had been bombed by U.S. aircraft. The allegation called for a response from Ambassador Stevenson. His staff checked with the State Department, which had been fed the cover story by Barnes: the planes had been flown by Cuban defectors.[46]

In the war room in Quarters Eye, David Phillips and Jim Flannery, one of Bissell's aides, watched on television as Stevenson took the podium. He held up a photograph of one of the planes that had landed in Florida. "It has the markings of Castro's air force on the tail, which everyone can see for himself," he said. "The Cuban star and the initials F.A.R., Fuerza Aerea Revolucionaria, are clearly visible." Phillips watched in fascination. "What a smooth, smooth phony he is!" he thought. Then it occurred to him that Stevenson didn't know the truth. Phillips felt a "chill," he later wrote. He asked Flannery, was it possible that Stevenson had not been briefed?

"It's possible, I guess," said Flannery. He told Phillips that Tracy Barnes had been sent up to brief Stevenson. "But you know Tracy," said Flannery. "He can be charming and urbane and talk around the subject until you don't know what he means to say." Flannery wondered if Barnes had given Stevenson "the flavor but not the facts."[47]

The cover story began to peel away almost immediately. A newsman noticed that the machine guns on the plane of the "defector" still had tape over the gunports. How could these guns have just been fired in combat? Stevenson learned the truth the next day when he asked for more evidence to rebut the Cuban charge and was told that it "wouldn't be worthwhile to pursue that line of inquiry any longer." The ambassador was beside himself. He felt that he had been "deliberately tricked" by his own government. He sent an angry cable to Rusk at State:

I had definite impression from Barnes when he was here that no action would be taken which could give us political difficulty during current U.N. debate . . . I do not understand how we could let such an attack take place two days before debate on Cuban issue in GA [General Assembly]. Nor can I understand, if we could not prevent such an outside attack from taking place at the time, why I could not have been warned. . . . There is gravest risk of another U-2 disaster in such uncoordinated action.[48]

In the war room back at Quarters Eye that Saturday, the atmosphere was oddly jubilant. After all the months of difficult planning, of cutbacks and disappointments, the decisive hour was near. "There was a sudden belief that it would work," writes Phillips. U-2 photographs showed that instead of dispersing the aircraft that had survived the first raid, Castro had foolishly parked them wing tip to wing tip. They would be easy prey for the dawn raid on the morning of the invasion. The Brigade had been told "the skies will be yours." The CIA men felt confident that they could deliver on this promise.

That evening a number of the senior CIA officials had been invited to Tracy Barnes's for dinner. The guests "were on high," recalled Janet Barnes Lawrence. One even came dressed as Castro, in fatigues with a fake beard. But she observed that "Tracy was very unhappy that night. They were all up. But not Tracy."[49]

JOHN F. KENNEDY was also feeling gloomy that weekend. He had gone out to Glen Ora, the weekend place his wife favored in the Virginia hunt country. The first lady rode; the president was bored. He spent the early afternoon driving golf balls into a cow pasture. He was also physically uncomfortable. His chronic venereal disease had flared up again; a specialist would give him a shot of penicillin the next morning. Physical pain was nothing new to Kennedy, who had been sick all his life. More disturbing was the decision he had to make about the Cuban invasion.[50]

Bissell had told the president that the final deadline for a go/no go decision was noon on Sunday, when the invasion fleet would begin closing in on Cuba. Bissell was fretting in his office in the L Building, twisting paper clips and pacing back and forth in his long, ungainly strides. Finally, at 1:45, the phone rang. Without much enthusiasm in his voice, Kennedy simply said, "Go ahead."

Bissell felt a sense of relief. He had slightly misled the president. The true point of no return was 4 P.M.

And so the invasion was on. Over at the war room, General Charles Pearre Cabell stopped by, dressed in his Sunday golfing outfit. General Cabell, the deputy director of the CIA, was a figure of little consequence and some ridicule. Dulles had hired him as a genial greeter. He was always urging agency men to be "headsy" and "forward leaning." Most of his time was spent touring CIA stations, visiting as many countries in as little time as possible. The men in Quarters Eye called Cabell "Old Rice and Beans" because he insisted the airdrops to the Cuban resistance include sacks of rice and beans. Told that the Cubans didn't need the food supplies—that weapons and ammunition were all they wanted— Cabell replied that he didn't want to have to explain to an appropriations committee that the CIA was flying nearly empty planes over Cuba. A leader of the Cuban underground later complained that one of his men had almost been killed by a falling bag of rice.[51]

Cabell was nominally in charge of the CIA on Sunday, April 16, because Allen Dulles was out of town, on a speaking engagement in Puerto Rico. (Bissell had encouraged Dulles to keep the date despite the invasion; his absence would be good cover.) Cabell asked Stan Beerli, the operation's air director, what was happening. Beerli told him about the upcoming raid to hit the half dozen or so of Castro's planes that had been missed in the first raid. Cabell asked if the mission had been approved. Beerli assured him that it had. Just to make sure, Cabell said that he would check with Dean Rusk at the State Department.

Cabell's casual intervention came to be regarded as a fatal accident. Rusk, who had been quietly skeptical about the invasion, was in no mood to approve any more air strikes. Nor was the president's national security adviser, Mac Bundy, who was trying to help Rusk calm down Adlai Stevenson. Stevenson was so angry that Bundy, at the president's request, was preparing to fly to New York to "hold his hand." A second raid would just compound Stevenson's unwitting lie, since the planes could not possibly be seen as coming from Cuba. Bundy and Rusk decided to recommend no more raids until the exiles had seized an airstrip on Cuba that could be legitimately used as a base. Rusk called Kennedy and told him about the second raid, recommending against it. Kennedy had forgotten all about the second raid, thanks to the sloppy staff work. "I'm not signed off on this," the president replied. He was upset that Stevenson had been left hanging at the United Nations. Rusk called Cabell back: the president had said no.[52]

At the CIA's air base in Nicaragua, Major General George Reid Doster, the air commander, threw his cap to the ground in disgust. "There goes the whole fuckin' war," he said. Richard Bissell, who usually never said anything more profane than "Sweet Jesus," said "Fuck Cabell" when he heard what had happened. Barnes was equally upset. "You've got to be kidding," he said to Rusk when the secretary of state told him that the air strike had been canceled. Barnes understood the import of the canceled strike. Just a few days before he had been taken aside by Brigadier General David Gray, who had been loaned to the CIA by the Pentagon to help with the planning. Gray had impressed on Barnes the critical importance of air supremacy as the two men drove to the White House for a briefing on April 12. Gray wanted to know if Barnes, in his liaison role to the executive branch, had arranged to brief the president and his advisers on the need for the air strikes. "Jesus Christ, Tracy, this is the last chance," Gray had implored. Barnes had assured Gray that he would arrange for a full-dress briefing. But he never had. Now Barnes watched helplessly as his failure to warn Stevenson merged with his failure to brief the president on airpower.[53]

Bissell arrived at Rusk's office shortly after 9 P.M., with Cabell in tow, in a last-ditch attempt to change Rusk's mind. The two CIA men got Rusk to call the president and to state the argument for going ahead with the raid. But when he was done, Rusk told Kennedy that he still favored cancellation. Then Rusk, who was trying to be an honest broker, held out the telephone to Bissell. Would Bissell like to talk to the president himself?[54]

Within the CIA, Bissell had long been famous for his willingness to pick up the phone and call the president. On this cool spring evening in 1961, Bissell reached forward to take the phone . . . and hesitated. No, he said. Rusk shrugged and hung up.

Bissell would come to regret his decision not to argue with the president. He recognized that it was out of character. He could not really explain it years later, except to concede that perhaps a kind of fatalism had set in. "I believed the president had made up his mind. There was no point in prolonging the agony. We had to go ahead and make the best of it," he said. He decided not to go home that night. Instead, he climbed up to "the dormitory," a bare room with ten army cots up on the second floor of Quarters Eye, and tried to sleep.[55]

AT MIDNIGHT, as D-Day began, a public relations man, named Lem Jones, got a call from Howard Hunt. "This is it," said Hunt. He began to dictate a message, "Bulletin No. 1," that was to be issued in the name of the Cuban Revolutionary Council: "Before dawn, Cuban patriots began the battle to liberate our homeland from the desperate rule of Fidel Castro. . . ." The Revolutionary Council, the Cuban exile government cobbled together by Tracy Barnes, was being held incommunicado in a safe house in Miami, virtual prisoners of the CIA.

At 3:44 A.M., Radio Swan, Dave Phillips's propaganda arm broadcasting from a tiny island in the Caribbean, called on the Cuban Army to revolt: "Take up strategic positions that control roads and railroads! Take prisoners or shoot those who refuse to obey your orders! . . . All planes must stay on the ground. See that no Fidelista plane takes off. Destroy its radios. Destroy its tail. Break its instruments. Puncture its fuel tanks. . . ." In Cuba, Castro's army mustered instead to defend the "fatherland" from "American mercenaries."

In the dark off the Cuban coast, five rusty freighters (once owned by United Fruit) and two old landing craft carrying 1,543 members of La Brigada slid quietly into the Bay of Pigs.[56]

Chapter Eighteen

FIASCO

*"What did we buy with
all that hocus-pocus?"*

AT 6:30 A.M. on D-Day, April 17, one of the Brigade's landing ships, the *Houston*, was hit at the waterline by a rocket fired by one of Castro's British-built Sea Furies. The ship quickly began to sink stern-first as the terrified members of the Brigade clung to the decks. From a rubber raft floating near the foundering ship, William "Rip" Robertson of the CIA shouted, "Get off, you bastards! It's your fucking war!"

At 9:30 A.M. a second ship of the invasion force, the *Río Escondo*, went up in a giant fireball. Castro's planes had hit two hundred barrels of aviation fuel, ensuring that the B-26s would never be able to refuel in Cuba. Worse, a communications van sank with the ship, cutting off any air-land radio contact.

The beach at the Bay of Pigs was supposed to be deserted. The invaders found it lit by floodlights; some of the men had to swim ashore after their landing craft hit coral reefs that the CIA charts had marked as seaweed. Castro knew the Bay of Pigs well; it was one of his favorite fishing grounds. Alerted within an hour of the first shots (fired, against standing orders, by a CIA adviser), the Cuban leader had deployed columns of soldiers and tanks to resist the invasion. By Monday afternoon, the battle had clearly turned against the Brigade.[1]

On Monday afternoon Kennedy relented and authorized air strikes from Nicaragua. But many of the Cuban pilots, exhausted and afraid, refused to fly. Bissell allowed American crews to go up in the B-26s (an insubordination that Kennedy did not learn about for nearly two years). Four of the Americans were killed. One of the raids succeeded in shooting up a column of tanks, but attacks against Castro's airfields failed, in part because of low clouds. Providing air cover from Nicaragua was a difficult task: the thousand-mile round-trip flight took six hours and left only enough fuel for forty minutes over the beaches. American warplanes from the carrier *Essex*, circling offshore, watched helplessly as Castro's T-33 jet trainers shot down the slower B-26s. The T-33s would have been no match for the American F-4 Falcons of the "Blue Blaster" squadron aboard the *Essex*. When the American airmen returned to the carrier, they swore and angrily banged their helmets against the ship's bulkheads. In the combat information center the ship's officers listened glumly through weak static, as the Cubans on the beach begged for help over their walkie-talkies.[2]

At a Tuesday 7 A.M. White House briefing, Bissell told the President that the Brigade was trapped on the beaches and encircled by Castro's forces. He asked for air support from the *Essex*. Kennedy was torn. He told his brother Bob, "I'd rather be an aggressor than a bum," but to Bissell he said he still wanted "minimum visibility." While the Chief of Naval Operations, Admiral Arleigh "Thirty Knot" Burke, watched in horror, the president got up, went to the map, and moved the small magnetic model of a destroyer a few inches—out over the horizon. He wanted the Navy out of sight of the Cubans on the beach—which meant the Navy's destroyers could not provide covering fire. Burke thought to himself that Kennedy's experience in command had been as a lieutenant junior grade on a PT boat.[3]

The White House tried to keep up a facade of business as usual. Because of poor communications with the beachhead, the White House was usually several hours behind the news, but the news was never good. At 1:45 on Tuesday afternoon, the Brigade commander, José Pérez "Pepe" San Román, broadcast, "We are under attack by two Sea Fury aircraft and heavy artillery. Do not see any friendly air cover as you promised. Need jet support immediately. Pepe." His CIA handlers told him to hang on.

At a reception to honor members of Congress at 10:15 that night, President Kennedy, dressed in white tie and tails, appeared with the first lady at the top of the stairway into the front entrance hall of the White House. The Marine Band struck up a Broadway show tune, "Mr. Wonderful." The president's brother Bob grabbed Senator George Smathers by the elbow on the dance floor. "The shit has hit the fan," he told Smathers. "This thing has turned sour like you wouldn't believe."[4]

In Quarters Eye, Walt Rostow, Bissell's former Yale protégé who was now a White House aide for national security, found Bissell, looking unshaven and haggard, standing surrounded by his staff. They were shouting at each other. Bissell himself was calm. Rostow offered to drive Bissell over to the White House, where a late-night meeting had been scheduled. As the two men sped across the darkened Mall in Rostow's Volkswagen, Rostow marveled at Bissell's self-discipline.

It was an extraordinary scene that greeted them in the Cabinet Room a few minutes after midnight: The president, the vice president, the secretaries of state and defense, all in white tie; Admiral Burke and General Lyman Lemnitzer, chairman of the Joint Chiefs, in dress uniform, draped with medals. Others, about a dozen aides from the White House, Defense, and State who had been hurriedly awakened by the White House switchboard, were in corduroys and sweatshirts. Bissell, now struggling visibly to hold back emotion, made his case. The operation could still be saved, he said, but only if American warplanes were allowed to fly cover. Burke seconded him, offering to destroy Castro's air force with a couple of his carrier-based planes. Kennedy responded that he didn't want to get involved. "Hell, Mr. President, we are involved," argued the admiral. General Lemnitzer announced that the time had come "for this outfit to go guerrilla." Bissell had to inform the room that this was not an option. The mountains were eighty miles away, and there were 20,000 Cuban troops in the way. The choice for the Brigade was to take to the swamps or surrender.

Finally, sometime after 2 A.M., President Kennedy authorized six Navy fighters, with their markings painted out, to fly cover for one hour in the morning—long enough to allow the Brigade's remaining ships to unload ammunition and the B-26s to fly a bombing run against Castro's troops. Rusk protested: "That's a deeper commitment, Mr. President." Kennedy cut him off, holding his hand up to his nose. "We're already in it up to here," he said. Bissell and Burke rushed off to give the word to their troops. "Keep your chin up," Kennedy told Bissell as he left.

At 4 A.M., Kennedy wandered the south grounds of the White House, his hands thrust in his pockets, brooding. When he awoke in his bed at dawn, he was weeping.[5]

The air cover failed to materialize. Strung out, the CIA operations staff forgot to calculate the one-hour difference in time zones between Cuba and Nicaragua. The Navy jets were still on the deck when the B-26s flew over the beaches. Two more were shot down. At 2:32 on Wednesday afternoon Pepe San Román, the Brigade's commander, reported that Castro's tanks were breaking through. His men had fought bravely, but 114 were dead and many more wounded. His last message was: "Am destroying all equipment and communications. I have nothing left to fight with. Am taking to the swamps. I can't wait for you." To his CIA handler, safely aboard ship, he had a last farewell. "And you, sir," he said, "are a son of a bitch." Before they fled into the jungle, some of Román's men fired at the wakes of the departing American destroyers.

The Navy rescued twenty-six members of the Brigade over the next two days. The rest were captured or killed. A few years after the Bay of Pigs, a newsman shouted at Fidel Castro, "Why did the Americans fail?" Castro replied, "They had no air support." In Castro's prisons, the 1,189 members of the Brigade who were held there made a bitter joke of it. Every time they heard a plane fly overhead, a cry would go up in the cell blocks: "Don't shoot! Don't shoot! It's one of ours!"*[6]

IN THE war room at Quarters Eye that afternoon, Colonel Hawkins held one hand across his face, "as if hiding," writes Dave Phillips. Esterline was ashen. His deputy, Dick Drain, vomited into a wastebasket. A junior officer who had a habit of scratching his wrists under stress had bloodied his shirt cuffs. "Everyone was crying," said Alice McIlvaine, Tracy Barnes's secretary, "except Tracy, who was stoic." Barnes "attempted to cheer us up; his smiles were thin," writes Phillips.[7]

Bissell, looking somber but calm, went home at six. His assistant, Jim Flannery, was left in charge. At about ten, Flannery anxiously called his boss at home. He was worried about Esterline and Hawkins, who seemed so distraught that he was afraid they would do something drastic. "What do I do?" Flannery whispered over the phone. Bissell told him to send the two men over to his

---

* After negotiations with the Kennedy administration, Castro released the members of the Brigade in December 1962.

house. There, to Flannery's amazement, they spent a quiet evening, listening to Annie Bissell play the piano.[8]

Bissell was gracious in defeat. He turned to Arthur Lundahl, the CIA's chief photointerpreter, and said, "Now, many heads are going to roll as a result of this, but I want you to know that the hard information that you provided to us before the Bay of Pigs was absolutely right. No share of this fault should in any way attach itself to any of you. You did your job and did it well." Lundahl was not surprised. "That was Bissell and that's how he treated people."[9]

To General Maxwell Taylor, the president's military adviser, the White House seemed like a command post "that had been over-run." He had seen the same glazed eyes during the Battle of the Bulge. Dean Rusk, normally phlegmatic, angrily banged his hand down on the president's empty chair in the Cabinet Room. There was fitful talk of striking at Castro. "You've got to act or be judged paper tigers by Moscow," insisted Robert F. Kennedy. Walt Rostow calmed him down with an avuncular chat about the dangers of swinging wildly, but RFK was not far wrong about Moscow. The Russians learned of Stevenson's objections and the canceled second air strike. At the Kremlin, the hardliners began to wonder if Kennedy was weak and indecisive, easily swayed by soft liberal intellectuals. At the same time Khrushchev was wary of Kennedy, expecting that he would lash out. The Kremlin leader had been burned by the U-2 incident, fooled by Eisenhower's peaceful protestations, and forced to take a stiffer stance against Washington.

Kennedy, too, responded to the Bay of Pigs by recognizing that the Kremlin would interpret the defeat as a sign of American weakness. On Thursday, April 20, he gave a defiant speech to the American Association of Newspaper Editors and after the speech established a secret Vietnam Task Force. Kennedy told Richard Nixon that the Cuban disaster did not mean he was abandoning Southeast Asia to the communists. On the contrary, he was thinking about sending more American trainers to South Vietnam, to help build up President Ngo Dinh Diem's army.[10]

Kennedy was furious at the CIA; he threatened to break the agency "into a thousand pieces." To Ted Sorensen, Kennedy berated himself for being taken in. "How could I have been so stupid to let them go ahead?" he asked. Arthur Schlesinger had watched Kennedy and his top advisers "transfixed" by Bissell's briefings.

"They were fascinated by the working of this superbly clear, organized and articulate intelligence," he reflected. Kennedy had said of Bissell, "You can't beat brains." Now he felt he had been seduced by the aura of Bissell's secrecy. "You always assume that the military and intelligence people have some secret skill not available to ordinary mortals," the president said. Kennedy "felt sorry for Allen Dulles," he told Cord Meyer. "But he blamed Bissell." The president was not amused by Clayton Fritchey, Adlai Stevenson's aide, who remarked that the Bay of Pigs "could have been worse." How? Kennedy asked. "It might have succeeded," said Fritchey.[11]

James Reston of the *New York Times* paid a visit to Bissell that Sunday, April 23. "You know, don't you, that you've got to go," said the newsman. Bissell answered, "No, but I do now." Bissell decided to "seek an interview" with the president. He found him "affable, but firm." Kennedy told Bissell, "In a parliamentary government, I'd have to resign. But in this government I can't, so you and Allen have to go."

Bissell did not quite say it to anyone at the time, but he felt let down by Kennedy, if not betrayed. "I thought Kennedy was tough, that he wouldn't cancel air strikes and lose his first major effort. I thought Bundy was with us, too," he remarked thirty years later. He was angry with everyone, including himself, for insisting on so much secrecy. He wondered, in retrospect, why it was so important to use beat-up old B-26s instead of more modern jet warplanes. The cover wasn't going to last anyway. "What did we buy with all the hocus pocus?" he asked.[12]

In fact, Bissell had been caught in his own web. "Plausible deniability" was intended to protect the president, but as he had used it, it was a tool to gain and maintain control over an operation. "Need to know" was a useful way of keeping out meddlesome colonels and bureaucrats, including those working at the CIA. Without plausible deniability, the Cuba project would been turned over to the Pentagon, and Bissell would have have become a supporting actor.

The Bay of Pigs was more than a blow to Bissell. It marked a deep loss in the confidence, in the certainty and optimism, that had infused the Georgetown crowd. Learning the news in Paris, an ashen Joe Alsop turned to Susan Mary. "How could they have?" he asked.[13] Bissell tried to explain to his friends what had happened, but they were unpersuaded. Bissell "was devastated," said Tish

Alsop, Stewart's wife. "That Sunday, he sat in his garden with the opera blasting out the doors. It seemed to me that he had been totally taken in by the Cuban exiles, the way he talked to me that afternoon." Tracy Barnes was also worked over by his friends for his credulousness.[14]

He was "sick at heart," his wife said. "The phone rang, day and night, the families of the people killed. Tracy's only way to deal with it was to keep working. He was very bitter about how it happened—about the Kennedys." The Bay of Pigs "destroyed Tracy," said his brother, Courty. "He thought he had been betrayed. He felt let down very seriously." He did not show his resentment in public, however. Barnes and Cleve Cram of the British desk were summoned by Arthur Schlesinger to talk about another matter, and Schlesinger "took a strip off Tracy," said Cram. "It was antipathy to the agency in its rawest form. Tracy was humiliated, but he tried to be a gent. He was reserved, quiet, dignified. Afterwards, he just said, 'Well, we got away from that little shit. Let's go home and have a martini.' "[15]

Barnes was very upset with the charge that he had lied to Adlai Stevenson. "Janet told us that it almost finished Tracy off. Adlai had been a hero of his. Tracy said he didn't lie and I'm convinced Tracy told the truth," said his Rhode Island friend Ben Sturges. Schlesinger and Mac Bundy accused Barnes of at least shading the truth. "It was the CIA's proprietary attitude," said Schlesinger. "They thought what they knew was no business of anyone else." Bundy called Tracy's briefing "a dropped stitch. These guys would tell you things in an ambiguous way. They'd tell you what they wanted you to know."[16]

Barnes said that he couldn't understand why Stevenson was so angry. "My God, he knew me! He could have asked me questions," he exclaimed to his daughter Jane. "What he meant was they were all part of the same club," she said. "He was mad at Stevenson for talking about this."

Barnes was caught, as he had been all his career, between his decency and sense of honor and the dictates of his trade. He could no longer finesse the contradictions with amiable charm and a penchant for action. "I promise you I did not betray your friend Adlai," he insisted in a letter to a close friend, Marie Ridder.[17] But he was more troubled and uncertain in a second letter a few days later: "Am I guilty of bringing down the popularity of your president? Or am I not?" he asked guiltily. He compared the morning after the Bay of Pigs to a hangover. "The world needs more aspirin every day," he wrote. Then he admitted, "I am increasingly confused about the rights and wrongs of the world." [18]

AFTER THE Bay of Pigs "everyone was depressed," said Thomas Parrott, the CIA officer who acted as liaison to the Special Group, "except for those who were elated." Bissell's downfall, which Kennedy decreed be stayed for a time, meant opportunity for others, most notably Richard Helms, whose caution had been vindicated. It was clear that, after a decent interval, Helms would succeed Bissell as DD/P. At first, Barnes and Bissell tried to go about their business as if nothing had happened, but even their best friend, John Bross, shook his head in disbelief. Eating lunch with them, he said, was like eating lunch with Louis XVI after his head had been cut off. They couldn't see that their heads were in the wastebasket. [19]

President Kennedy asked Maxwell Taylor to investigate what had gone wrong with Operation ZAPATA, and Bissell and Barnes found themselves testifying before a commission that summer of 1961, like defendants in a trial. The roughest treatment came from within the agency. Lyman Kirkpatrick, the CIA's inspector general, wrote a scathing report in the fall of 1961, accusing Bissell and Barnes of "playing it by ear" by setting up a command structure that was "anarchic and disorganized." The report picks over each failure: Maritime operations, for instance, were distinguished by "a lack of qualified personnel, the confusion of responsibility, the skyrocketing costs. . . ." Overall, the operation had been "frenzied." Bissell had misled the president, failing to tell Kennedy that "success had become dubious." "Plausible deniability," the report concludes, was a "pathetic illusion." Badly stung, Bissell and Barnes demanded to write a response. In essence, they argued that the plan would have worked if Kennedy had not decided to cut off the air strikes. The IG's report, Barnes wrote Bissell in a covering letter, "is an incompetent job . . . it is biased . . . it is malicious." They privately accused Kirkpatrick of a hatchet job born of jealousy. Kirkpatrick's once promising career had been derailed by an attack of polio in 1953, and he was widely said to be bitter. [20]

Inside the CIA there was backlash against the "Grotties." The old tension between the pure spies and the covert action enthusiasts surfaced again. This is what happens when intelligence work gets corrupted by politics, scolded "the Prudent Professionals." Covert action always produces "flaps," and it was hard to think of a worse flap than this one. Allen Dulles had fallen for Barnes's charm and Bissell's arrogance, and the CIA had been disgraced. A few months after the Bay of Pigs, Barnes tried to give a pep talk to case officers in the DD/P about how well things were going, Cuba notwithstanding. In the back of the room, Justin O'Donnell, the Staff D deputy who had refused Bissell's order to assassinate Lumumba, stood up. "Tracy, there is one thing that would make things better around here, and that is if the 'Three Bs' went over the side," he said, referring to Bissell, Barnes, and Bross. The room was silent. Barnes smiled. "Justin!" he called out. "How the hell are you? Long time no see!" But Bissell was furious when he heard about the incident. He had O'Donnell shuffled off to a job in the Defense Department.[21]

Barnes put in to go to India as station chief, to atone for his sins and rehabilitate in an exotic new clime. "It was no soap," said Janet. He was told that some other post would be found for him.

Barnes could not conceal his unhappiness at home. His fiftieth birthday was on August 2, 1961. Janet tried to cheer him up with a costume party. His friends came in various guises, including as "Madame," a governess he had hated. One friend gave him a black Labrador puppy. Instead of blooming, Barnes withdrew, hugging the puppy. Barnes was so stressed, said his son Tracy Jr., that he became physically ill for weeks that summer and refused to go out.[22]

Bissell seemed more philosophical and stoic. Gordon Stewart, the chief of the Foreign Intelligence Staff, thought Bissell looked "crumpled," but Charlie Whitehurst was struck by how calm he seemed at a station chiefs' meeting that summer. He was still very busy. Bob King was surprised when his boss began planning operations that were two or three years away. "Never on God's green earth would you know he'd been fired," said King. "I said to Doris Mirage, 'I can't believe this! No farewell parties, no little lunches.' He was planning the crap out of things."[23]

He set himself to the task of harvesting the fruits of earlier labors. There was still Trujillo to be disposed of. That winter of 1961 the CIA had provided a cache of weapons—pistols and carbines—to a dissident group in the Dominican Republic intent on assassinating the local despot. In March the dissidents had begun asking for machine guns. Bissell had approved the request on May 2; "having made a considerable investment in this dissident group and its plans," he later explained, he naturally reasoned, "we might as well make the additional investment." But the Kennedy administration had vetoed the request. The CIA station chief had been instructed to tell the dissidents to "turn off" the assassination attempt because the United States was not prepared to "cope with the aftermath." According to the Church Committee, the dissidents "replied that the assassination was their affair and that it could not be turned off to suit the convenience of the United States government." Trujillo was ambushed and gunned down on May 30 by dissidents using their own weapons.[24]

John F. Kennedy was disgusted with the CIA and the disaster at the Bay of Pigs, but he was more than ever determined to get Castro. "It was almost as simple as, goddammit, we lost the first round, let's win the second," said National Security Adviser McGeorge Bundy. In the fall of 1961 the Kennedy administration set up Operation MONGOOSE (the code name was arbitrarily picked, but appropriate—a ferret trying to kill a snake) to try to overthrow Castro.

The aim of MONGOOSE was to stir up a guerrilla insurrection within Cuba. The Kennedys were enamored with "counterinsurgency" and guerrilla warfare. The president had taken to quoting Sun Tzu on the art of war, while Bobby Kennedy brought the Army's Special Forces unit, the Green Berets, up to Hyannisport, Massachusetts, on the weekend to show how they swing from trees.

MONGOOSE was a joint operation, part-Pentagon, part-CIA, run out of the White House. In place of Bissell's loose organization for the Bay of Pigs, MONGOOSE was to be "staffed up" with teams of colonels and Army guerrilla experts. The CIA component ("Task Force W") would continue to infiltrate and spy on the island, but control and order would come from higher authority. As operation director, the White House picked General Edward Lansdale, the mind behind the counterinsurgency against the communists in the Philippines and, more recently, the top American adviser to President Diem in Vietnam. Assigned to the CIA by the Air Force in the 1950s, Lansdale was essentially an independent operator. In Cuba, Lansdale planned to draw on his experience winning "hearts and minds" in the Far East. The Kennedys were impressed by Lansdale, notwithstanding the fictionalized portraits of him in Graham Greene's *The Quiet American* and as Colonel Edwin Hillandale in Lederer and Burdick's best-seller, *The Ugly American*. The Kennedys naively figured that if Lansdale had been so successful at stopping a communist insurgency in the Philippines, he could start an anticommunist insurgency in the Caribbean.[25]

Lansdale was the titular head, but the moving force behind the operation was the president's brother Robert F. Kennedy. After the Bay of Pigs the president wanted Bobby to salvage the CIA. "It's a hell of a hard way to learn things, but I have learned one thing from this business—that is, that we will have to deal with the CIA," said Kennedy. "I made a mistake in putting Bobby in the Justice Department. Bobby should be in CIA." RFK pointed out that if he was named head of the agency, the president would completely lose his ability to plausibly deny agency operations. JFK thought better of it, and his brother stayed at Justice. The younger Kennedy did, however, take a strong informal role overseeing the agency, particularly the move to get Castro.[26]

Robert Kennedy was a shrill goad. In November 1961, Bissell got "chewed out" by RFK in the Cabinet Room for "sitting on his ass and not doing anything about getting rid of Castro and the Castro regime." Bissell responded by reactivating the assassination machinery. A few days after his tongue-lashing, Bissell went to William Harvey and told him to take over the Mafia contacts from Sheff Edwards. Since Harvey was already the head of ZRRIFLE, Bissell's "stand-by executive action capability," it made sense to consolidate.

Once again Bissell had no explicit authority. He had "assumed" that Dulles had received authorization from President Kennedy, perhaps when Dulles first met with Kennedy on the Cuba operation in November 1960. But Dulles never told him so. A parade of former Kennedy administration officials testified before the Church Committee in 1975 that Kennedy had never authorized any assassination attempts and would never have condoned such a terrible act.[27] There is some evidence, however, that the Kennedys were aware of the plots.* And there is no question that RFK relentlessly prodded the CIA to "get rid of" Castro.[28]

The official who received most of this pressure was Richard Helms, who succeeded Bissell as DD/P in the winter of 1962. Helms

---

* The evidence is discussed in note 28.

had ascended to the head of the clandestine service in part by being very careful, by not taking foolish risks, by avoiding confrontation. Now he was in an impossible position. He had triumphed over Richard Bissell, but Bissell left him the assassination plot against Castro. He felt that he could not simply shut it down, or he would not be carrying out RFK's insistent demands. Yet he could not discuss assassination directly with the president or his brother without violating the code of plausible deniability. Helms personally disapproved of assassination as a tool. But as head of the clandestine service, he did nothing. He didn't really expect it to work; indeed, he hoped, in a way, that the whole business would quietly disappear.

In the fall of 1961 the Kennedys had reconsidered Bissell's value and asked him to stay on at the agency, although in a new role, as head of a new directorate of science and technology. The Corona spy satellite had finally overcome its gremlins and now orbited the Soviet Union, sending back invaluable intelligence about Soviet missile capability. The SR-71, the new spy plane that would make the U-2 obsolete, was about to come on-line. Perhaps he could develop some new technological marvel.

But Bissell turned the job down. He felt it was a demotion, that it would be too awkward to be suddenly cut off from covert actions that he had planned. "I have a horror," he wrote his daughter, "of hanging on here to a job that is not at the center of things, as so many people do." He had taken a risk in the Bay of Pigs, and now it was time to accept the consequences. In February 1962 he left the agency. At his farewell dinner at the Alibi Club, Bissell recalled, Dick Helms gave a "particularly gracious toast."[29]

Chapter Nineteen

SECRET ARMIES

"We gave them this! We gave them that! How can they not win?"

CUBA WAS ONLY one front in the Kennedys' "twilight struggle" against global communism. There was a tense standoff in Berlin, where the Wall went up in the summer of 1961, and in Asia a war was beginning that would consume the country for the rest of the decade.

With his aversion to conventional war, especially in Asia, President Eisenhower had preferred to use the CIA to hold the line. As chief of the CIA's Far East Division, Desmond FitzGerald had been in the middle of that confrontation, a "low-intensity" conflict that had become a full-blown crisis by the time the Kennedys came to power in 1961.

FitzGerald did not share the prejudice, common among Washington policymakers at that time, that Asians were an inferior race that could be intimidated or overwhelmed by American military power and presence. He had nothing but contempt for Pentagon majors who used epithets like "gook" and "slant." Based on his own experience, he knew that Asians could be effective—and more to the point, endlessly patient—fighters. He also knew, again from sometimes painful experience, that Americans were easily fooled by the clever, if corrupt, court societies of the East. All these instincts made FitzGerald wary of American involvement in an Asian land war. At the same time his romantic pride and zeal tempted him to sally forth on a more secret, individualized scale. He was attracted to the idea of supporting small resistance forces, particularly mountain fighters, against the massed power of Beijing. At "FE," these movements became his cause and his specialty.[1]

FITZGERALD'S FIRST crisis upon assuming command of FE in the summer of 1958 had come over Quemoy and Matsu, a pair of obscure rocky islands off the coast of China, now largely forgotten, but familiar symbols of the Cold War during the 1950s. In 1949, as the Chinese Nationalists fled the mainland for the island refuge of Taiwan, some 115 miles away, Chiang Kai-shek had left a large garrison of troops on Quemoy and Matsu, less than two miles from the Chinese coast. The islands were supposed to be the staging area for Chiang's fantasy of invading the mainland, but mostly they were an excuse for demagoguery and, during periodic flareups, a threat to world peace. The "China Lobby," which supported Chiang in Congress, made sure that the "G'mo" and his possessions would not be forgotten. In 1955, when Chinese Foreign Minister Zhou Enlai announced that a Chinese communist invasion of Taiwan was "imminent," President Eisenhower threatened to use tactical nuclear weapons in defense.

In the summer of 1958 the Red Chinese began heavily shelling Quemoy and Matsu. The Seventh Fleet steamed toward the embattled islands and Washington pondered whether and how to protect them. On his annual summer vacation to Maine, FitzGerald was full of determination to draw the line against the "ChiComs." "We must do something, even if it means war," he told Susan Mary Alsop as they hiked, at a brisk pace, up Sergeant Mountain near Northeast Harbor. "Des thought John Foster Dulles was being weak," she recalled. Dulles, who was dying of cancer that summer, had lost some of his resolve.[2]

Yet when FitzGerald returned to Washington from his vacation, he became more pragmatic. He had a very low opinion of the Chinese Nationalists, based on personal exposure in World War II. "He thought they were a sorry spectacle," said one of his operatives, James Lilley. "They were hated, brutal, predatory, and corrupt, and they had diddled the Americans, especially [General Joseph] Stilwell," FitzGerald's commanding officer in the China-Burma-India theater. Charles Whitehurst, who had been stationed in Taipei in 1955, was asked to brief FitzGerald. "He had cooled on the Chinese Nationalists as a weapon. He had no confidence they would ever do anything, except maybe make a deal with the com-

munists," said Whitehurst. "Des knew that seven out of ten soldiers in the Nationalist army were native Taiwanese who hated
the ChiNats. Plus, he knew we had other fish to fry." When Whitehurst began his presentation, FitzGerald coolly interrupted him.
"Let's not worry too much about Nationalist China," he said. "I
started briefing him, but he just said, 'Don't worry about it.' " On
Taiwan, the Generalissimo's son Chiang Ching-kuo was training—
with help from CIA operatives like Tony Poe—a 5,000-man special
forces team to invade the mainland. FitzGerald decided against a
recommendation to "unleash" this force against the ChiComs,
though raiding parties of a dozen men were often sent in by boat.
(The boats broke down so often that FitzGerald began calling them
"shmoats," as in "boats, shmoats!")[3]

WHILE FITZGERALD regarded Asian court society as predictably
corrupt and thin-blooded, he had a more romantic view of "mountain people." "Des believed they were history's losers, pushed out
of the fertile valleys into the hills. They were a warrior caste, with
a chip on their shoulder," said Donald Gregg, a CIA Asia hand.
"Such people were ideal for guerrilla insurgencies."

FitzGerald was fascinated with the Khamba warriors of Tibet.
"Des was flat out in his enthusiasm," said William Colby. "They
were great mountain fighters, much braver than city dwellers."
Taller than most Asians, with long faces and prominent noses, the
Khambas vaguely resembled Native Americans. They described
themselves as *ten dzong ma mi* (soldiers of the fortress of the
faith). The propaganda organs of Beijing referred to the Khambas
as "cavaliers, wild, undisciplined, and accustomed to living by
loot." When a People's Liberation Army force tried to quell a
Khamba revolt in 1953, two hundred PLA soldiers captured by the
Khambas were returned to their commanders with their noses cut
off.

FitzGerald believed that the Khambas would make an appropriate force for harassing the Red Chinese, possibly even for liberating Tibet. Since 1950, Beijing has been trying to subdue the
remote Chinese province, "the roof of the world," a theocracy with
three thousand monasteries under the divine guidance of the Dalai
Lama. But the Khambas, as well as the nominally pacifist but
restive Tibetan monks, kept resisting. By the time FitzGerald
became the head of FE, Beijing had been compelled to commit

100,000 troops just to keep the roads open in Tibet. The Khambas, a force of several thousand horsemen, had claimed, probably with some exaggeration, an estimated 40,000 Red Chinese casualties. Since 1956 the CIA had been helping them in an operation somewhat wistfully described in a classified in-house history as "one of the most romantic programs of covert action undertaken by the agency." The CIA's secret air force, Civil Air Transport (CAT), airlifted in arms by planes that the Khambas referred to as "sky-boats." The status shirt for a Khamba tribesman was made out of "sky cloth" cut from camouflaged CIA parachutes.

Based on his experience in Burma in World War II, FitzGerald had great faith in the capacity of airlifts to sustain an army even in a remote region. According to Colby, FitzGerald was enthusiastic about a new cargo plane built by Lockheed, the C-130, which could transport a twenty-one-ton payload the 2,400 miles from Bangkok to Tibet. Between October 1958 and February 1959 the CIA dropped close to ten tons of weapons and supplies to the newly constituted National Volunteer Defense Army of Tibet, which had raised its flag in front of a portrait of the Dalai Lama in June 1958.

As a Buddhist, the young Dalai Lama was supposed to be a pacifist; he was, in any event, afraid of incurring the wrath of the Red Chinese. But the Khambas, aided by the CIA, made him a romantic prince-in-exile in the spring of 1959 by helping him, disguised as a peasant, flee his palace in Lhasa over the Himalayas into India. Tony Poe, FitzGerald's favorite "knuckledragger," was the CIA's man on the ground. He later presented a crayon portrait of the Dalai Lama's flight out of Tibet to Richard Bissell, while FitzGerald told his family about Poe and the Dalai Lama racing down the runway of a remote mountain strip, a step ahead of the blazing guns of the PLA.

In Washington during the spring of 1959, the Special Group discussed Tibet on a half dozen occasions, with FitzGerald making the case for intervention. The president did not want to overtly support a revolution by the Tibetan monks, and he refused to meet with the Dalai Lama. But as often happened in the Eisenhower administration, the CIA was given license to act covertly. At Camp Hale in Colorado, a mountain base was set up in 1959 to train the Khamba tribesmen in demolition, sabotage, and radio communications. Some 250 recruits, who were never told they were in the United States, were flown in aboard C-124 Globemasters and driven from the Petersen, Colorado, airport in buses with blacked-out windows. The base guards were given shoot-to-kill orders to keep out intruders.

In the face of the Khambas' revolt, as well as the chronic restiveness of Tibet's nominally pacifist but stubborn monks, Beijing cracked down. The People's Liberation Army arrived in force and claimed to have killed 89,000 Tibetans by the end of 1959. Whole monasteries were razed, sometimes with the monks inside. When Francis Gary Powers's U-2 was shot down in May 1960, Eisenhower ordered a pause in overflights of communist territory. FitzGerald cobbled up an intricate and difficult overland supply route through old smuggling trails, however, and the operation to aid the Khambas stayed alive into the Kennedy administration.[4]

Kennedy's ambassador to India, John Kenneth Galbraith, was appalled when he learned of the Tibet operation, which was being run out of the CIA station in New Dehli. In his memoirs he describes the Khambas as "deeply unhygienic tribesmen who had once roamed over the neighboring Tibetan countryside and now relieved boredom with raids back into the territory from which they had been extruded." Galbraith understandably worried about the impact on subcontinent politics if word got out that India was a CIA staging base for cross-border raids into China. At a briefing on the Tibet operation conducted by FitzGerald and Dick Bissell in February 1961, Galbraith interrupted. "Dick," he said to Bissell, "I've had enough. This sounds like the Rover Boys at loose ends." Galbraith walked out, leaving Bissell "flabbergasted," according to Jim Critchfield, the Near East Division chief. Galbraith tried to get the Tibetan operation shut down, and he did succeed in pushing it out of India—but FitzGerald set up a new base of operations in neighboring Nepal.[5]

Camp Hale kept on training tribesmen recruited in the Himalayas, smuggled out through mountain passes, and flown thousands of miles to Colorado to learn how to use explosives and operate field radios. An embarrassing security breach had to be covered up in December 1961 when forty-seven American travelers and airport employees stumbled across a gang of Khamba tribesmen boarding a plane in Colorado Springs. The Americans were held at gunpoint and sworn to secrecy; inevitably the story leaked out, and Defense Secretary Robert McNamara had to persuade the *New York Times* not to run with it.

At about the same time, in the spring of 1961, the Tibetan operation scored a genuine success when the Khambas ambushed a

PLA convoy and captured 1,600 pages of valuable documents. From them, CIA analysts were able to find confirming evidence that the Sino-Soviet split was for real, as well as to learn useful information about the size and preparedness of the Chinese military. FitzGerald was exultant about this intelligence coup; "those blood-spattered documents seemed like the best thing that ever happened to Des," said Jim Lilley.[6]

FitzGerald was "very interested in Tibet," said Whitehurst. "He knew it was too far away, that it was difficult to support ops there. But he felt it was worth giving our best shot, and he felt that eventually the Tibetans would shake the communists out. This," Whitehurst added, "was an optimistic view." The Tibetan operation was not as far-fetched as it seems today. It was not clear in the late 1950s whether Mao would be able to control the outer provinces, or whether the revolution might not collapse of its own weight. Just getting the Dalai Lama out of Tibet kept up Tibetan Buddhism, as well as the hope of an independent Tibet that lives on thirty years later. Still, FitzGerald was overly optimistic in the opinion of some FE hands, who believed that supporting a revolt in Tibet would just get a lot of Tibetans killed without having much impact on Beijing. "It was a flea biting an elephant," said Sam Halpern. "Basically Tibet was just a nuisance to the ChiComs. It was fun and games. It didn't have any real effect." Halpern compared Tibet to the botched effort to open a "second front" with Li Mi and the ChiNats out of Burma in 1951. "I fought with Des about this. I thought we were just wasting people's lives," said Halpern.[7]

The Tibetan tribesmen couldn't help hoping for deliverance when they heard the sound of a C-130's engines overhead. After the C-130s were grounded, however, the resupply effort dwindled to a trickle during the 1960s. Meanwhile, the Chinese communist repression continued, and hundreds of thousands of Tibetans were killed. The CIA did not cause the slaughter, but the agency could not stop it, either.

PRESIDENT KENNEDY's foreign policy advisers would later use mocking terms to describe the mess they inherited in Laos. "A Kung Fu movie," George Ball, Kennedy's undersecretary of state, called it. The Eisenhower administration had somehow managed to transform a dreamy, unwarlike country, "the Land of a Million Elephants and a White Parasol," into a cockpit of superpower confrontation.

Laos seems like an obscure crisis three decades later, but in many ways it was the true beginning of the Vietnam War. On a map, Laos looked like a geostrategic linchpin to policymakers in the late 1950s and early 1960s—North Vietnam and Communist China to the north, South Vietnam and Thailand, still in the U.S. camp, but threatened, to the East and West. In 1960, Laos seemed in danger of falling to the communists. The day before Kennedy took office, Eisenhower informed him that the United States might have to go to war there. This unlikely "bastion of freedom" was "the cork in the bottle of the Far East," Eisenhower instructed Kennedy. "If Laos is lost to the free world, in the long run we will lose all of Southeast Asia." The Joint Chiefs of Staff were recommending the insertion of 250,000 troops, together with the use of nuclear weapons if China or Russia jumped in.[8]

The Laotian crisis was a classic example of heavy-handed meddling by the United States, of good intentions mixed with ignorance and arrogance. Between 1956 and 1960 the CIA had bought several elections for rightist candidates and, along with the Pentagon, financed the Royal Laotian Army at a cost of $300 million, or roughly $150 for every Laotian, two times the per capita income. The army, despite the help of American advisers, had a tendency to break ranks to go swimming or pick flowers. "Well, we made good soldiers out of the Koreans," puzzled the chairman of the Joint Chiefs, General Lyman Lemnitzer. "Why can't we make good soldiers out of the Laotians?" The CIA, State Department, and Pentagon bickered incessantly over what to do about Laos; the CIA chief of station, Henry Heckscher, refused to tell the ambassador what he was doing, and once, when he didn't like the guidance he was getting from Washington, cabled FitzGerald: "Is headquarters still in friendly hands?"[9]

The trouble began with the search for the elusive strongman, the pro-Western leader who would face down the communists and heed Washington. The Lao king, Savang Vatthana, was regarded as a hopeless lightweight who drove a '59 Edsel, quoted Proust, and cried in public. He would remain a figurehead, but nothing more. The prime minister, Prince Souvanna Phouma, was too Frenchified (he was an expert on Parisian restaurants) and had made the fatal mistake of visiting Beijing and Hanoi in 1956. A neutralist, he had to go. Washington's man was Phoui Sananikone, but he proved a disappointment and was dropped in favor of Phoumi Nosavan, an amiable colonel who had never seen combat while growing rich in the opium trade. (The switch from Phoui to Phoumi, George Ball later joked, "could have been significant or a typographical error.")[10]

In Laos in 1960, FitzGerald wanted to believe that Phoumi would show more vigor than his predecessors, and he backed his choice as CIA favorite son, assigning the Laotian colonel a permanent CIA handler, Jack Hasey. "Phoui was bad. We had not yet found that Phoumi was no damn good either," said Charles Whitehurst, who ran the CIA Laos desk. "As it turned out, neither was worth a damn." FitzGerald got an inkling that the CIA had guessed wrong again when Phoumi refused to attend his swearing-in ceremony in the capital in 1960 because a soothsayer had predicted his demise.

In August 1960 a coup by a paratrooper captain, Kong Le, caught the CIA completely by surprise. Kong Le was a disgruntled soldier, angry because his troops were always being sent out to chase the communist Pathet Lao while their commanders lolled in the capital, Vientiane. But Washington chose to treat him, like all neutralists, as a communist sympathizer. A three-way war broke out among Kong Le, Phoumi's army, and the Pathet Lao. Sensing an opportunity to make trouble, the Russians jumped in with a massive airlift that December. This was what Kennedy found awaiting him in January 1961.[11]

Sent out by his American advisers to challenge the Pathet Lao on the Plaine des Jarres in February, Phoumi's better-equipped, American-trained army broke and ran all the way back to Vientiane. "Phoumi's men set a track record," said Whitehurst. "No one got hurt unless they fell down." At the CIA there was a "lot of hand-wringing about how 'We gave them this! We gave them that! How can they not win?' What the hell! We were told the other guys didn't have a chance!" recalled Dick Bissell's special assistant, Lloyd Emerson. Kennedy went on national television in March 1961, looking grave about the crisis in Laos, which he pronounced LAY-os (the correct pronunciation, Louse, didn't seem to Kennedy like something worth defending). The president warned the Russians that "no one should doubt our resolve," but he was a little vague about what Washington was resolved to do.[12]

What Kennedy badly wanted to do was get out of Laos. He had met Phoumi on a trip to Washington. "If this is our strongman,"

Kennedy told his aides, "we're in trouble." The president asked General Lemnitzer if the United States could get troops quickly into Laos. "We can get them in all right," replied the chairman of the Joint Chiefs. "It's getting them out that worries me." Kennedy turned instead to Averell Harriman, the aging diplomat who had been shunted to the side by the younger bloods of the New Frontier, and asked him to help negotiate a solution.[13]

Harriman's aides jokingly suggested that the only solution would be for their boss, who was heir to a great railroad fortune, to buy Laos. "What would I do with it?" he growled back. Educated at Groton and Yale, Harriman was a senior statesman of the Georgetown set. FitzGerald regarded him with a "certain amusement," said Chester Cooper, but he also admired him for his toughness.[14]

Harriman looked to Souvanna Phouma, an avowed neutralist, as the answer. Persuading Souvanna to so much as lift his finger for the United States was going to be difficult, however, given that Washington had effectively driven him from power.

It is standard CIA practice to hedge bets by playing the outs as well as the ins, and in Laos the practice paid off. In Campbell "Zup" James, FitzGerald had an operative who was close to Souvanna. While other CIA men were trying to create Laotian warriors, James had worked his way into Vientiane court society. "Laos was like a big family, or a club," James later explained. "There were little feuds, but you just had to listen. They were charmed to come to my house for dinner, or go shooting with me." James's mother, a New York grande dame, had visited her son in Vientiane. "My mother charmed them," he recalled. "She was a lively, witty woman who spoke impeccable French."

Over brandy and cigars ("I sent him a steady stream of Havanas"), James had befriended Souvanna, even as Washington undermined his attempts to build a neutralist coalition. When Souvanna was driven from Vientiane in a coup in December 1960, "I passed him and his entourage leaving the capital. He said to me, 'La politique est la politique, mais l'amité est l'amité'—'politics is politics, but friendship is friendship,' " recalled James. "I said, 'We'll raise a glass to that.' "

James got his chance to renew old acquaintances when FitzGerald summoned him to his house in Georgetown in April 1961. "He told me that the president and Harriman wanted me to go and see Souvanna, who was refusing to talk to any American," said James. At CIA headquarters "the case officer asked me, 'How are you going to do this?' I said, 'I don't know.' The case officer said, 'That's not good enough.' But Des interrupted and said, 'If he had answered any differently, I would have been worried.' " FitzGerald's preference for the "nonbook" solution was justified in this case. Traveling to Paris, James was able to assuage Souvanna, who formed a coalition goverment. After long and arduous nego- tiations in Geneva in 1961–62, Harriman would work out what he called a "good bad deal" to create a neutral Laos, exactly what Souvanna had wanted before the Americans intervened.[15]

FitzGerald was frustrated by the political intrigues of Vientiane and the sloth of the lowlanders. It is hard to understand why someone as sophisticated as FitzGerald was so wrongheaded about finding a strongman in an indolent country, "but you have to re- member it was a romantic and moralistic time," said William Sul- livan, an aide to Harriman who later became ambassador to Laos. The blame for Laos can be spread throughout the State Depart- ment and Pentagon as well as the CIA. FitzGerald was not one to look back, at any rate. By the spring of 1961, he had already discovered a new champion to fight against the communists in the mountains of Laos.[16]

Vang Pao was a figure to satisfy FitzGerald's gallant vision of a wily and tough mountain fighter. At war continuously since he was thirteen—against the French, the Japanese, and now the commu- nists—Vang Pao, who was thirty-two in 1960, was a "great leader," said Vint Lawrence, a young Princeton man sent by the CIA into the mountains above the Plaine des Jarres in 1962 to help organize the hill people for guerrilla fighting. Vang Pao was a Hmong tribes- man, one of an ancient Mongol race that believed in animal spirits (*phi*) and lived by crude slash-and-burn agriculture. The Hmong— called Meo by CIA men, who in their ignorance used a Chinese term that was derisive and implied servitude—were fierce about defending their homeland. They particularly hated the Vietnam- ese, a valuable characteristic to the CIA in the early 1960s.

The enemy of the Hmong included not only the local commu- nists, the Pathet Lao, but also the North Vietnamese, who were pushing across the border and beginning to use trails down through the Laotian mountains to supply communist insurgents in South Vietnam. The Hmong were a way of keeping pressure on the North Vietnamese; as time went on they would be increasingly drawn into the fight to try to interdict the Ho Chi Minh Trail.[17]

FitzGerald got a chance to practice his faith in air supply on a grand scale in the mountains of Laos. The CIA built a web of fields—crude strips gouged out of the mountains, sometimes dog-legged and in one case running across a narrow bridge—to accommodate its short-takeoff-and-landing planes. The pilots of the CIA-owned airline, Air America, were a scruffy and wild lot, with names like "Shower Shoes" Wilson (after the rubber thong shoes he always wore) and "Weird Neil" Houston, who wore a cowboy hat and boots when he flew. Their planes carried rice and weapons ("hard rice") and sometimes drugs (the Hmong grew opium), though FitzGerald strictly forbade his men to have anything to do with the drug trade. The CIA base chief, who lived in a house decorated with a string of ears that had been chopped off the heads of dead communists, was Tony Poe.[18]

FitzGerald liked to go out to the exotic, almost primeval surroundings of the Laotian mountains to inspect this strange crew. "He arrived in a very carefully tailored safari jacket with a vast number of pockets," recalled Vint Lawrence, Poe's deputy. "We took him up to Vang Pao's house, where he entertained village chiefs and drank Scotch." William Sullivan accompanied FitzGerald on a trip in 1962. "He loved flying in those kite airplanes, landing in fields three hundred feet long," said Sullivan.[19]

FitzGerald had been specifically prohibited from going to visit Vang Pao's headquarters by Richard Bissell, who thought the trip too dangerous and cringed at what might happen if a communist raid captured so senior a CIA official. "He just wanted to see what was going on," Bissell said. The director of the clandestine service disapproved and compared FitzGerald's flouting of the rules to the time Rip Robertson, a cowboy in the Tony Poe mold, had bombed a British freighter in Guatemala, costing the CIA a million dollars. But for the most part Bissell believed that FitzGerald had "good judgment. I had a lot of confidence in him." Bissell and FitzGerald "would get into tussles," said Jim Flannery, Bissell's assistant. "Bissell loved having Des come in and fight. He was a man worthy of his mettle. Des rescued a U-2 out of a rice paddy. He had wanted a project that Bissell had resisted giving him, but when Des got his U-2 out, Bissell said, 'I guess I've got to give the damn project to him.' "[20]

Bissell and FitzGerald were in agreement about the strategic purpose of Vang Pao's secret army—L'Armée Clandestine, as it was called. Vang Pao's army had grown to 9,000 by 1961; it would swell to 30,000 by 1963. Vang Pao was grateful for the assistance, although he kept asking his CIA handlers for some kind of assurance that his people would not be abandoned someday by the Americans.[21]

Chapter Twenty

HARD TARGET

"Bobby wanted boom and bang. . . ."

LAOS WAS A PRELUDE for the Kennedys. The real fight in Asia was in Vietnam, and in 1961 and 1962 it began to draw in Desmond FitzGerald. President Kennedy had approved a commitment of troops to America's Southeast Asian ally in the fall of 1961. They were merely "advisers" at first, but by the end of 1963 almost 10,000 American soldiers would be fighting with the army of President Ngo Dinh Diem.

FitzGerald was wary of stepping up American involvement with such a weak and corrupt ally. "He thought Diem was another Chiang Kai-shek," said his daughter Frances. At the end of 1961 his trusted aide Sam Halpern gave him a very pessimistic readout after four months in the field as an operations officer in Saigon. Just riding down the highway outside Saigon, Halpern had needed to have his driver "drive like a bat out of hell to avoid sniper fire," he reported. "It was clear we didn't own the countryside." FitzGerald asked Halpern to give his "cold douche" briefing to State, Defense, and the White House. Halpern later remarked, "I was laughed at everywhere."[1]

FitzGerald was doubtful that more troops were the answer. "Des could see, you can't talk about huge battalions on parade," said Halpern. "He didn't think it could be done grandly. The army didn't know a damn thing about guerrilla warfare. They wouldn't read Che Guevara or Mao."

Robert McNamara was taking aggressive charge of the administration's effort on Vietnam. Surrounded by his Pentagon "whiz kids," his brainy systems analysts, the former auto executive wanted to quantify the military requirements for Vietnam, as if he were building Fords back in Michigan. After spending forty-eight hours in Vietnam in May 1962, McNamara declared to reporters that "every quantitative measurement . . . shows that we are winning the war." As head of FE, FitzGerald was routinely called on to brief McNamara on the CIA's current intelligence and covert action plans in Southeast Asia. As one briefing was ending in the fall of 1962, McNamara shook his head and remarked unhappily, "You know, it's hard to make sense of this war."

FitzGerald was an intuitive thinker who had no use for charts and graphs. The Far East, he believed, was particularly resistant to planners' models. As FitzGerald later recounted the story to Stewart Alsop, he paused to give a little lecture to the new Pentagon chief:

"Mr. Secretary," he volunteered, "facts and figures are useful, but you can't judge a war by them. You have to have an instinct, a feel. My instinct is that we're in for a much rougher time than your facts and figures indicate."

"You really think that?" asked McNamara.

"Yes I do," said FitzGerald.

"But why?" asked McNamara.

"It's just an instinct, a feeling," said FitzGerald. According to Alsop, "McNamara gave him a long incredulous stare, as though FitzGerald had taken leave of his senses."

FitzGerald was never again asked to brief McNamara on Vietnam. The rebuff reduced his usefulness as the CIA's man on the Vietnam team, and thus lessened his clout as the head of the Far East Division. By speaking honestly (and wisely), FitzGerald had diminished his power and created something of a quandary for his boss, Richard Helms. At just about the time he was being exiled by McNamara, a new opportunity arose that tested FitzGerald's resourcefulness and his ability to get along with the president's brother Robert F. Kennedy.[2]

THOUGH VIETNAM would over time increasingly absorb the manpower of the CIA, the agency's prime target for covert action in 1962 continued to be Cuba. As the agency's leading exponent of covert action, FitzGerald was perhaps bound to be asked to try where Bissell and Barnes had failed.* In December 1962, Helms approached FitzGerald about taking over the CIA's operations against Fidel Castro, which over the past year had devolved into a state of chaos.[3]

The job FitzGerald inherited was easily the most fraught in the agency. Even Bob McNamara, no shirker of challenges, would later describe the Kennedy administration's attitude toward Cuba as "hysterical." Robert Kennedy had become consumed with avenging his brother's embarrassment at the Bay of Pigs. Although the attorney general was deeply involved in the civil rights struggle and tackling organized crime, he was also his brother's chief adviser on the CIA. In January 1962, shortly after he had told Bissell to "get off his ass" on Cuba, RFK had declared that Castro was the administration's "top priority. . . . No time, money, effort—or manpower is to be spared." Kennedy told the "Special Group (Augmented)," the secret cell created to push for Castro's overthrow, that "the President had indicated to him that the final chapter had not been written—it's got to be done and will be done."

The Miami station, code-named JMWAVE, soon became the CIA's largest in the world: 400 CIA officers running more than 2,000 contract agents spent at least $50 million a year in an effort to avenge the Bay of Pigs. This time around, however, the roles were reversed: the administration pushed dreamy schemes, while the CIA was more realistic about the prospects for success. The political action enthusiasts, Dulles and Bissell, had been purged. Dick Helms was an old OSO man, an espionage operator who understood that intelligence networks have to be patiently built up, that policymakers cannot just snap their fingers and expect instant results. Helms was prudent about taking orders he received from Bob Kennedy. Caught in the middle, Helms pushed his men to at least give the appearance of doing something that was, in the phrase of the day, "forward leaning."[4]

---

* Before the Bay of Pigs, FitzGerald had been generally supportive, at least in corridor chatter, of "taking on Castro." But as he learned about Bissell's plan for an invasion, he had become skeptical. When Barnes had come looking for recruits for the operation in 1960, FitzGerald and other division chiefs had protected their best men. FitzGerald was uncomfortable when the CIA's inspector general blamed the fiasco partly on the low quality of personnel. FitzGerald never mentioned the Bay of Pigs thereafter, said his aide, Sam Halpern. "It was the aunt in the attic. Des's style was not to second-guess."

"Bobby wanted boom and bang all over the island," said Sam Halpern, who served as the top assistant on the Cuba operation. "It was stupid, for a simple reason. We didn't have a cotton pickin' asset on the island! I told this to Helms. We can't do it with mirrors. But the pressure from the White House was very great. I said we've got to get an intelligence base. But they wanted to set Cuba ablaze—like Churchill and Europe. Helms said to me, 'What's the matter, can't you understand the English language?'" There were ways, Helms insisted, to write reports that demonstrated determination and activity, even if they didn't show immediate results. "I said you can write all you want to, Dick, but sooner or later we've got to produce, blow up a sugar mill, you can't just do it with mirrors," Halpern recalled. "To the White House it was just pressing buttons. They didn't understand how long it took. Spies don't grow on trees."

Although General Lansdale, the operational chief of MONGOOSE, had worked for the CIA in the Philippines and Vietnam in the 1950s, he had always held himself aloof from agency headquarters and did pretty much whatever he pleased. Now he was essentially working for the Kennedys and attempting to enable their delusions.[5]

Lansdale's model was North Vietnam. He would play Ho Chi Minh by creating a cadre of guerrillas to take over the countryside and gradually squeeze the regime. The communists had been infiltrating Vietnam since the 1920s and still hadn't taken Saigon. Disregarding the experience of his own model, Lansdale hoped to march triumphantly into Havana by Election Day of 1962. He called it the "touchdown play."[6]

The "Ugly American," as the Kennedys proudly called Lansdale after the novel, was an idea man. Many of his ideas were farfetched. Among the thirty-three "tasks" he outlined for the overthrow of Castro was a plan to "incapacitate" Cuban sugar workers with biological warfare agents during the upcoming harvest. It was not clear how he planned to spray the sugar workers, as David Martin writes, "like so many insects," but there was no way that wouldn't be immediately traceable to the United States. Lansdale, whose psywar tricks in the Philippines had included leaving corpses drained of blood to look like the victims of vampires, was willing to be ruthless. Operation BOUNTY called for "a system of financial rewards, commensurate with position and stature, for killing or delivering alive known communists." The rewards, to be posted by airdropped leaflets, ranged from $5,000 for an informer to $10,000 for a high government official. (Castro would be worth only "2 cents.") The most extravagant of Lansdale's whacky ideas was to re-create, on a grander scale, a trick he had used against the Huks. In the Philippines, Lansdale had played on primitive suspicions by using helicopters at night, equipped with searchlights and loudspeakers, to pose as "the eye of God." Now he proposed to flood the Cubans with rumors of a Second Coming, in the hopes that Castro would be seen by the Catholic population as the Anti-Christ. To signify that The Hour was at hand, Lansdale wanted a submarine to surface off the coast at night and fill the sky with starbursts. CIA wags called this idea "elimination by illumination."

Laughing loudest was William Harvey, the CIA man chosen to run Task Force W, the agency group set up to implement MONGOOSE. Enamored with Ian Fleming's novels, the Kennedys had wanted the CIA's version of James Bond on Castro's case. Richard Helms gave them Harvey. "So you're our James Bond?" the president asked, taken aback, perhaps, by the sight of this squat, pear-shaped man. The secret serviceman outside Kennedy's door was equally startled when Harvey reached into his pants and handed him a .38 revolver before stepping across the presidential threshold.

Harvey was extremely suspicious of Lansdale, the boy scout guerrilla fighter who preached the Golden Rule (with certain exceptions for assassination and sabotage). His staff mocked Lansdale behind his back, calling him the "FM," for Field Marshal. Burned by Bissell's freewheeling ways, the White House wanted a strong watchdog over both Harvey and Lansdale. General Maxwell Taylor, installed by the Kennedys as the head of the Special Group (Augmented), had been shocked by the sloppy planning for the Bay of Pigs, and he was determined that "Cuba II" would be run more like a real military operation. Harvey resisted the colonels. The CIA man griped that the demand for detail was "excruciating. It went down to such things as the gradients of the beach and the composition of the sand." Kennedy's lieutenants, in turn, found Harvey to be an appalling spectacle, especially after lunch. "They thought he was crazy," explained Thomas Parrott, the CIA secretary to the Special Group. "They didn't realize he was just drunk." Mac Bundy told Parrott, "Your Mr. Harvey does not inspire great confidence." Harvey did not improve his standing by offhandedly referring to the Kennedy brothers as "fags" and "those fuckers."[7]

The result was paralysis: the Kennedys demanded instant and unrealistic results as Lansdale cooked up impossible schemes, Harvey drank his lunch, and the colonels fussed. MONGOOSE did produce a little "boom and bang" on the island: a few mortar shells were lobbed, some villagers were killed, a sugar shipment was contaminated with chemicals. But the biggest target, the Matahambre copper mines, went unscathed after the failure of two raiding parties, one aborted by a broken-down boat, another surprised by a Cuban patrol on the beach.

Castro grew stronger and better armed by his Moscow sponsors. "After Castro's crushing victory over the counterrevolutionaries, we intensified our military aid to Cuba. We gave them as many arms as Castro could absorb," writes Khrushchev in his memoirs. By early October 1962, the Kremlin had supplied over 40,000 Soviet soldiers, 1,300 field pieces, 700 antiaircraft guns, 350 tanks, and 150 jets to deter America from staging another invasion. Khrushchev had also provided his socialist comrade with nuclear-tipped ballistic missiles that could reach over half the United States.

The CIA may have helped create the Cuban Missile Crisis by its plots against Castro, but it also spotted the missiles before they were operational. In September a Cuban agent reporting to the CIA noticed suspicious construction activity in the west of Cuba, near San Cristóbal. A refugee reported seeing a long missile towed past him down a Cuban street. In mid-October the agency's U-2 spy planes photographed the missiles at their launching sites. The agency's best spy in Moscow, Oleg Penkovsky, provided manuals that showed the United States still had a little time before the missiles were made operational.

For the CIA, the discovery of the missiles was a tremendous morale booster. Even Richard Bissell was able to take some comfort from the agency's success. It was his spy plane, after all, that spotted the missiles. The Bissells were at John Bross's house in Virginia the night Kennedy went on national television to warn about the Cuban threat. The danger of the moment did not prevent old agency hands from gloating. Cord Meyer poked Annie Bissell in the ribs and said, "Isn't it neat to have the birds really come home to roost for a change?"[8]

For the next two weeks the world waited anxiously. At the

White House the "Ex Comm" of senior statesmen and soldiers groped for a solution that would force Khrushchev to back down without pushing the superpowers over the brink. The senior hawk was former Secretary of State Dean Acheson, who wanted an air strike to take out the missiles. But the balance swung toward a more measured response. Kennedy's men finally found the key in public defiance—a naval blockade of Cuba—and private horse trading—promising to withdraw America's medium-range missiles based in Turkey. After a tense wait Khrushchev backed down. Soviet ships turned back rather than defy the blockade. At the CIA the heroes were the photointerpreters who had developed the highly refined art of "reading" aerial photographs taken by the U-2. The covert action specialists were for the most part relegated to the sidelines. Anticipating that the United States might want to invade Cuba, the Pentagon instructed Harvey to infiltrate advance intelligence teams onto the island at the peak of the crisis. Robert Kennedy was furious when he learned that the men could not be recalled. At a White House meeting at the end of October, Harvey aggravated the wound by suggesting that the missile crisis was the Kennedys' fault. Kennedy stormed from the room. "Harvey has destroyed himself today," CIA Director John McCone remarked to an aide. "His usefulness has ended."[9]

Operation MONGOOSE was shelved. Lansdale was shuffled back to the Pentagon, and Harvey was sent to Rome, where he could be inebriated in a less sensitive posting. But the Kennedys were no less determined to get Castro. Desmond FitzGerald now officially became head of the successor to Task Force W, the newly designated Special Affairs Staff, on January 25, 1963.[10]

AT A party for William Colby, who took over from FitzGerald as the head of the Far East Division that January, John Horton, an old FE hand, asked FitzGerald whether his new job on the Cuba task force was "any fun." FitzGerald replied, "All I know is that I have to hate Castro."

FitzGerald understood from the outset that, after Bissell's intellectual arrogance and Bill Harvey's slovenliness, his chores were partly diplomatic. "My first job was to convince the Administration that anyone from my firm dealing with the Cuban situation is not necessarily a Yahoo bent on disaster," he wrote his daughter Frances. He tried to be at once upbeat and philosophical. "Cuba continues to be an affair in which the U.S. is every bit as emotionally hair-triggered as the Cubans themselves. As a consequence," he wrote Frances in April,

> . . . one spends one's day walking in a mine-field laid by both friend and foe and one's reactions tend to become quite sharp. Any number can play—Cubans (Castro-style), Russians, Cuban émigrés, the Senate, the press (which goes mad whenever there is blood in the water), the great rancid People and the Kennedy boys, to say nothing of the rest of the U.S. government. My first real effort has been to make the Agency's operations acceptable as respectable, which they obviously haven't been since the Bay of Pigs and this has come out very well so far. Stage two is to get everyone hitched to a consistent policy and on this I could get handsome odds. But the whole process is quite bracing and I have enjoyed it so far.[11]

FitzGerald made clear to his troops that he wanted results. Halpern tried to show him an organizational chart of the Special Affairs Staff, but he said he didn't want to see it, that he didn't want to be bothered with bureaucratic detail. "But Des. . .," Halpern protested. "You do it," said FitzGerald. He refused to sign the chart or even look at it.

The immediate results that FitzGerald wanted were pretty much the same ones Harvey and Lansdale had tried to produce: guerrilla raids and sabotage against Castro's economic infrastructure, in the hopes of "destabilizing" the regime. FitzGerald didn't really expect the Cubans to rise up and overthrow Castro in spontaneous, or nearly spontaneous, revolt. His real aim was to find a military cabal to stage a coup. As usual, FitzGerald put his faith not in the masses, but in the capacity of a few brave individuals—perhaps just one man—willing to take extraordinary risks. On March 19, 1963, FitzGerald wrote a memo acknowledging the need for a program of sabotage and economic warfare, but arguing that the CIA's "main effort" should be devoted to finding "officers disenchanted with Castro." "The real pay-off," he wrote, "will come when we are able to get actions and negotiations with key military personalities who are ready, willing and able to dispose of Castro and his immediate entourage."[12]

FitzGerald's staff felt his constant goading. "Des never had qualms about overdoing. We were never doing enough, not enough boom and bang," said Halpern. But they were relieved, after Harvey's crude squabbles with the Kennedys, to have a boss who got along with "Higher Authority," as the CIA referred to the chief executive.

"Harvey and Bobby had clashed, but FitzGerald was a more polished operator," said Ted Shackley, the Miami station chief who ran JMWAVE. "He went to the right cocktail parties and dinner parties. Our actions did not come from policy papers, they came from FitzGerald's ability to move in these circles. Harvey had been abrasive; FitzGerald was smooth as silk. . . ."

In the early summer of 1963, FitzGerald traveled to JMWAVE headquarters, a onetime Navy blimp base in Miami that operated under the cover name Zenith Technological Enterprises. He found a hardened group of paramilitary experts, including Rip Robertson, as well as other veterans of Guatemala and the Bay of Pigs.* FitzGerald brought them a target list: electric power installations, petroleum refineries and storage facilities, railroad tracks, highways, and factories. He told the senior officers of JMWAVE that he wanted a major act of sabotage every month, starting in mid-July. Station chief Shackley, "the Blond Ghost," was a coldly efficient "intelcrat," a protégé of Bill Harvey's (thus his other nickname, "Son of Pear"). He liked to be, in his favorite phrase, "forward leaning," but he was dubious about the mission FitzGerald laid out.[14]

It was costly: twenty-five CIA agents, Cuban exiles recruited as commandos, were killed or captured in five raids on the island in 1963. FitzGerald conceded that the impact of the raids was "certainly debatable." Though it was doubtful that the commandos would bring down Castro by knocking down some telephone poles or by petty acts of sabotage (the negligible Cuban underground was instructed to leave faucets running and light bulbs burning to waste energy), FitzGerald was determined to keep trying. "Des felt that if you could create an embargo or cause physical pain by blowing things up, you could have a cumulative impact. Castro would fall, either by assassination or revolt," Shackley recalled. "We were saying, 'Please don't expect that any one of these things is going to be a catalyst.' But FitzGerald felt under pressure to make these things work, and the pressure came from Robert

---

* The more flamboyant CIA paramilitary men seemed to have a thing about ears. In Laos, Tony Poe collected the severed ears of his enemies in a formaldehyde jar. Rip Robertson offered $50 to a Cuban commando, Ramon Orozco, if he brought back an ear from a raid on the island. Orozco brought back two, and Robertson paid him $100.[13]

Kennedy. He'd say, 'I saw Bobby, or I ran into Bobby, I saw him in Middleburg, here's what we've got to crank up for next month.' We would say, tactfully, we can make it work. But the question is, will these events bring Castro down?"

Back at headquarters in Langley, Halpern valued his relationship with FitzGerald as "almost father and son," but it became strained in the winter and spring of 1963. "Des's approach was a little scary," Halpern said. "We had a good base of intelligence in Cuba by '63. It had been our agent who targeted the U-2 to the missiles—we knew what was going on. Des came in, and unfortunately, because of pressure from Bobby, tried to do too much. Des did not want to be thwarted. When he wanted it done, you got it done, or he'd do it himself. With Castro he got frustrated. 'Why can't we do this?' he'd demand. He'd glare at people and make you feel uncomfortable and quote *Alice's Adventures in Wonderland*. He had contagious enthusiasms, but it was difficult to get him to stop and think, once he got the bit in his teeth." Halpern, like Ted Shackley, was inhibited. "I was just a junior officer, and I didn't have connections in Georgetown," said Halpern. "I didn't know what dinner parties he was going to."[15]

Halpern thought the relationship between Kennedy and Fitz-Gerald was unfortunate. "I think Bobby Kennedy was a bad influence on Des," he said. "He reinforced his worst instincts." Halpern said he began to "dread coming in to work in the morning," especially Monday mornings after FitzGerald had had all weekend to "run into" Kennedy and think up his own schemes—"all these hare-brained ideas," as Halpern described a series of plots that would seem like black comedy when they surfaced a decade later during the Church Committee hearings.[16]

By the time FitzGerald took over the Cuba operation, the CIA had pretty well given up on the mob as a weapon of assassination. Bill Harvey's plots with the Mafia had gone nowhere. In the spring of 1962, Harvey had given Johnny Rosselli four poison capsules and assured him "they would work anywhere and at any time with anything." Harvey and station chief Shackley also rented a U-Haul truck, filled it with $5,000 worth of explosives and weapons, left the van in a parking lot, and handed the keys to Rosselli.

But Rosselli's Cuban agents were unable—or never really tried—to kill Castro. In February 1963, just as FitzGerald was taking over Cuba operations, Harvey had a drunken farewell dinner with Rosselli, with whom he had become pals (they shared a hatred of Bobby Kennedy). FBI gumshoes, who had Rosselli under routine surveillance, looked on in disbelief.[17]

The amicable divorce from the mob did not mean an end to trying to kill Castro. FitzGerald was forced to come up with more schemes. His inclination in these matters was to exploit the hobbies of his targets. With Sukarno, it had been airline stewardesses. With Castro, it was underwater swimming.

Before FitzGerald arrived to take over the Cuban operation, a CIA officer had suggested killing Castro by poisoning his diving suit. The Technical Services Division purchased a suit, which it contaminated with fungus spores that would cause a chronic skin disease. The mouthpiece on the breathing apparatus was treated with tuberculosis bacilli. To deliver the suit, the CIA wanted to recruit James B. Donovan, the American lawyer negotiating the return of the Bay of Pigs prisoners from Cuba. Donovan had already given Castro a (noncontaminated) wet suit, however, and the scheme was discarded. It is a mystery how anyone imagined that the plot would not be easily traced—the suit was to be a gift, after all, of the United States.[18]

FitzGerald continued to look beneath the waves for a method of eliminating his target. His own idea was an exploding seashell, to be placed on the ocean floor where Castro liked to go skin diving. "He came in with this bright idea," Halpern recalled. FitzGerald's staff asked how he planned to make sure that Castro picked up the right shell. "Put a neon sign on it?" asked Halpern. Technical Services had boasted they could make a bomb out of anything, but this request stumped even Dr. Gottlieb's men. "Des thought this was a put-up job by me and TSD," said Halpern. "He was really mad. 'The President wants this,' he said."[19]

Assassination of a dictator was not a moral issue with FitzGerald. "The question always was, 'Will it work?' His attitude was, let's keep trying. Remember, he was brought up in World War II. If it's okay to shoot the guy in the trench opposite you, why not go after the guy's commander? We shot down [Japanese Navy commander Admiral] Yamamoto's plane in April 1943. We were at war in 1963. It was an undeclared war, but we were shooting at them, they were shooting at us."[20]

FitzGerald's friend from St. Mark's and Harvard, Charles Francis Adams, argued that FitzGerald "was a very disciplined man. I could sense what was going on beneath the surface, but he never talked about it," said Adams, who put FitzGerald "at a high level of honor and ethics." He speculated that, in FitzGerald's mind, playing hard against the communists was the honorable thing to do. "If you're dealing with another country that is using dirty tricks against you, you must have felt that you had to sacrifice something of your own feelings, to serve the nation. There has to be a counterforce."[21]

What would make a man as shrewd as FitzGerald indulge in plots that seem almost laughable? It wasn't animus against Castro. He could ironically joke that he was required to hate Castro, but he clearly did not share the Kennedys' obsession. His daughter Frances suggested his motives had something to do with his dread of nuclear war. FitzGerald knew how close the world had come during the Cuban Missile Crisis. At the end of World War II, FitzGerald had worried in his letter home about being a mere "stone axe" in the nuclear age. But the CIA afforded FitzGerald a chance to strike back: by eliminating Castro, he could remove the nuclear threat ninety miles offshore. It fulfilled his notion that individuals could still make a difference in a world threatened by mass destruction.

Indeed, FitzGerald saw tyrannicide as an expression of romantic individualism. "Fitz talked about how one man could change the course of history by giving up his life to kill a tyrant," said Paul Nitze, his old friend from college days. The tyrant he had in mind when he first broached the subject with Nitze was Joseph Stalin. In the early 1950s the Nitzes had loaned the FitzGeralds a small house overlooking the Potomac out at Nitze's Maryland farm. As they roamed the fields on Sunday afternoons, FitzGerald and Nitze, who was running the Policy Planning Staff at State at the time, had informally plotted the downfall of the Kremlin dictator. The talk never turned to action—there was no way to get at Stalin—but FitzGerald was completely serious, as was Nitze.

FitzGerald recalled to Nitze that as a college boy on a tour of Germany in the early 1930s, he had once passed Adolf Hitler's motorcade flashing by on the autobahn. "If only I had swerved my car," said FitzGerald, "I could have prevented World War II." FitzGerald told Nitze that he had once been nearly killed in a motor crash in college; the experience had shaken him and stirred him to contemplate the narrow margins of fate. FitzGerald was in love with the idea of seizing fate—of the bold gesture that would save millions at the cost of only one life, his own if necessary.[22]

UNDERSTANDING THE relationship between FitzGerald and Robert Kennedy is necessary to making sense of FitzGerald's actions as chief of covert action for Cuba. RFK was confounding to Fitz-Gerald. At first, he found the president's younger brother to be bumptious. But as FitzGerald watched the younger Kennedy go to work on the CIA, he was encouraged by Kennedy's boldness, his willingness to cut through the bureaucracy and demand results. But he also found Kennedy imperious and a little reckless. In their father, FitzGerald's children observed wariness and ambivalence toward Kennedy—contempt mixed with deference and even uncharacteristic subservience. At first, FitzGerald thought the president's brother was "a young punk," said Frances. But "he was scared of Bobby's power," said Barbara Lawrence. "He felt threatened by him. He felt Bobby was just there because he was the president's brother. He thought he was an amateur, and he didn't really like him." But Kennedy was a force of nature, willing to bully anyone. "He could sack a town and enjoy it," Maxwell Taylor remarked after watching the attorney general chew out the Special Group, all senior government officials. "Bob Kennedy was very difficult to deal with," said Thomas Parrott, the Special Group's secretary. "He was arrogant, he knew it all, he knew the answer to everything. He sat there, tie down, chewing gum, his feet up on the desk. His threats were transparent. It was, 'If you don't do it, I'll tell my big brother on you.' "[23]

FitzGerald, who was accustomed to outfoxing slower bureaucrats in State, Defense, and the White House, now had to contend with a raw young prince who tolerated no dissent. There is more than a little irony to the picture of FitzGerald manipulated by an amateur gamesman. That is precisely the way the "professionals" in the agency had felt about FitzGerald when he arrived from Wall Street in 1950. The difference is that FitzGerald, though cold at times, was a gentleman, while Kennedy, though capable of warmth, was not. FitzGerald had become a professional over time and he had reason to bridle at the cavalier quality of Bobby Kennedy's leadership. Although FitzGerald was too responsive to

Kennedy for Halpern's taste, he was also no pushover. FitzGerald was a formidable figure, and he resisted some of Kennedy's more unreasonable demands. At a meeting on April 3, 1963, RFK proposed sending commando raids of a hundred to five hundred men to blow up factories and attack military bases. FitzGerald calmly noted that "if such groups could be landed, it would probably be impossible for them to survive any length of time."[24]

But FitzGerald could not escape Kennedy's incessant demands. While he was out at FitzGerald's country house, his nephew Albert Francke recalled overhearing his uncle say, firmly and loudly into the telephone one Sunday afternoon in 1963, "No, Bobby, we can't do that. We cannot do that." When FitzGerald emerged from his study, his color still high, Francke asked, "What was that?" FitzGerald replied, "Oh, nothing." FitzGerald's daughter Joan Denny remembered her father entering into a towering rage upon learning that Kennedy had been meeting privately with Cuban exiles. RFK was entertaining Cuban exiles at his house at Hickory Hill and calling them at their apartments at the Ebbitt Hotel downtown, where they were housed by the agency. "Anything we told the Cubans they told Bobby," said Halpern. "It made for a strange relationship. You can't have two commanders." FitzGerald was very wary of the Cuban exiles. "I have dealt with a fairly rich assortment of exiles in the past," he wrote his daughter Frances in June 1963, "but none can compare with the Cuban group for genuine stupidity and militant childishness. At times I feel sorry for Castro—a sculptor in silly putty." Having the attorney general freelance with the Cuban exile community was, FitzGerald felt, an invitation to disaster.[25]

The exiles were even granted an audience with the president, who promised to avenge the Bay of Pigs. FitzGerald may have noted with apprehension that one of the exiles escorted into the Oval Office, Tony Varona, had earlier been hired by the CIA's mob contact, Johnny Rosselli, to make an unsuccessful attempt to kill Castro. To bring an assassin into the Oval Office, FitzGerald knew, was hardly the way to preserve plausible deniability.[26]

IN THE many attempts to "get rid of" Fidel Castro, the CIA had been always confounded by the lack of a good "delivery system"—an assassin who was at once close to Castro and willing to kill him. In the fall of 1963, FitzGerald's attention turned to a Cuban major, Rolando Cubela Secades, code name AMLASH.

First recruited as an agent by the CIA in 1961, Cubela had access to Castro and, equally important, experience as an assassin. In 1959, as a student revolutionary, he had shot and killed Batista's chief of military intelligence. Cubela had grown disenchanted with Castro and wanted to lead a coup against him. He was willing to kill Castro, though the word "assassinate" offended him; he preferred "eliminate." In October 1963 he told his CIA handlers that he wanted a show of support from the United States government. He asked to meet personally with Robert F. Kennedy.[28]

This demand was impossible, but FitzGerald agreed to meet with Cubela as RFK's "personal representative." FitzGerald sent word to AMLASH that he would see him at a CIA safe house in Paris on October 29. He came to regret the decision.

For a senior CIA official with close ties to the White House to meet with a foreign asset to discuss an assassination plot was highly unorthodox, even in that freewheeling era. It broke the rules of tradecraft, which seek to build in deniability and secrecy through the use of cut-outs and to restrict access to information on a need-to-know basis. FitzGerald was a careful professional, but in this case his activist instinct, abetted by RFK's prodding, got the better of his judgment.

The Special Affairs Staff (SAS) objected to the idea of a meeting between their chief and AMLASH. The SAS counterintelligence officer, Joseph Langosch, warned FitzGerald that Cubela might be a "dangle"—a double agent recruited by Castro to penetrate the American plots against him.* Certainly Cubela was "insecure," in the jargon of counterintelligence. He was regarded by the CIA as unstable, haunted by the memory of pulling the trigger while Batista's intelligence chief was smiling at him. With the CIA, he had

---

*In 1978, Cubela, while serving a thirteen-year sentence for his role in the assassination plot against Castro, told author Anthony Summers that CIA statements that he initiated the request for assassination weapons were "utterly false." It was the CIA that brought up the idea of assassination, he said. He also denied that he was a double agent secretly working for Castro. Cubela said that FitzGerald posed not only as Robert Kennedy's representative but also as a "senior U.S. Senator." Summers noted that Cubela was in captivity while he made these statements, but nonetheless found him to be "consistent and credible."

indignantly refused to take a lie-detector test. The Cubans were notoriously leaky, while Castro's security service, the DGI, had been well trained by the East Germans, who had a knack for working double agents.[29]

Shortly before FitzGerald was due to leave for Paris to meet AMLASH, Sam Halpern walked in on a shouting match between his boss and the SAS counterintelligence (CI) officer. "The CI man was telling Des not to go to Paris. He felt Cubela was a dangle, or that he'd talk to his friends. It was a real collision. The CI man wouldn't give and Des wouldn't give." FitzGerald decided to go anyway.

In Miami, Ted Shackley was equally frustrated. "I told Des that it was something he shouldn't do. 'If AMLASH does do something,' I told him, 'it's quite likely they'll track you down. You have a high profile. What are you going to get out of this? The only thing you'll get is the satisfaction of saying you saw the guy!' " said Shackley. "Des shrugged and went on his merry way."

FitzGerald's boss, Richard Helms, "shared the qualms [of the SAS staff]." As the head of the clandestine service, he could have vetoed the trip. "But," Helms later explained, "I was also getting my ass beaten. You should have enjoyed the experience of Bobby Kennedy rampant on your back." Helms signed off on FitzGerald's meeting with Cubela. Although FitzGerald was going in Robert Kennedy's name, Richard Helms decided it was "unnecessary" to tell the attorney general, whom he regarded as an even greater risk-taker than FitzGerald. "Bobby wouldn't have backed away," said Helms. "He probably would have gone himself." It shows the level of pressure felt by the CIA that Helms, normally careful to cover his back, didn't even bother to get Kennedy's authorization.[30]

Even so, FitzGerald was suffering from hubris, the belief (shared by Bissell, Barnes, and Wisner) that the normal rules of gravity somehow didn't apply. "He believed in his intuition," said his daughter Frances. "If he met Cubela, maybe he'd be able to tell if Cubela was trustworthy. The fact that Cubela was deemed unreliable argued for going to see himself."

"My guess is that he wanted to be a player," said Shackley. "By 1963, Des had been off the playing field for a long time. He thought it was exciting and adventurous to go back out." Halpern blamed the pressure from the Kennedys. "It was the president and the attorney general. Des was going to go all out for them. When I argued with him, he said, 'We've been through all this before. Cubela is the only guy inside who has access and is willing to try—these guys don't come often.' "[31]

FitzGerald was under an unexpected source of strain that fall that may also have affected his judgment. Well-off, though not hugely wealthy, he paid little attention to money. FitzGerald had entrusted most of his funds, about $2 million, to a college clubmate, Robert Timpson. An old Etonian, Timpson was an Englishman who had gone to Harvard and migrated to Wall Street. Though charming, he was a poor investor, and he churned and wasted FitzGerald's assets down to almost nothing. Distraught, Timpson contemplated suicide—the steward of the Brook Club caught him going out a top-floor window. For a time FitzGerald was oblivious. He left unopened on the front hall table several letters from his lawyer, Charles McVeigh (another clubmate), warning him of his dwindling assets. Finally Timpson himself arrived on FitzGerald's doorstep "looking ashen," said Barbara Lawrence. "Everyone looked tense. There were a lot of closed doors."[32]

FitzGerald was not broke—there were other family trusts that Timpson could not touch, and FitzGerald still had his CIA salary—but he could no longer afford his rather grand lifestyle. His domestic staff had grown to include a butler, a cook, various gardeners, maids and laundresses. Some had to be shed, although there was still a "couple" to handle the cooking and cleaning. That October, a few days before meeting with AMLASH, FitzGerald put his gracious redbrick house on 30th Street in Georgetown on the market and began to look for a smaller place. He sold his beloved Jaguar and bought a "mud-colored Corvair, a real ego wound," said Barbara Lawrence (according to Halpern, he took out his frustrations by driving the car as fast as physically possible between his country house in The Plains, Virginia, and the CIA's new headquarters in Langley). Game as always, Barbara FitzGerald bore up under financial strain. She began shopping at a supermarket and saved $20,000 a year in household expenses "while keeping the surface the same," said her daughter Barbara Lawrence.

"I don't have time to brood over financial problems," FitzGerald wrote his daughter Frances, who was studying in Paris. "Bills—hopefully smaller ones—will get paid and we shall be clothed and fed." FitzGerald maintained his sense of humor and whimsy under stress. On October 21 he cabled Frances: "Arriving Paris October

29 10:15 A.M. KLM 403 frabjous Tuesday 29th beamish birthday." "Frabjous" and "beamish" are expressions of delight from *Alice's Adventures in Wonderland*. At noon the twenty-ninth, FitzGerald had a cheery birthday lunch with his beloved daughter. At 5:30 P.M. that afternoon he met at a CIA safe house with the man he hoped would finally eliminate Fidel Castro.[33]

FitzGerald was a little late to the appointment, and his CIA car had to race through the Paris traffic. FitzGerald complimented his driver, CIA case officer David Laux, by telling him that he could get a job driving a taxi if espionage didn't work out. "He was very self-controlled," said Laux.[34]

FitzGerald used a false name (James Clark) but no disguise when he met Cubela. AMLASH "spoke repeatedly of the need for an assassination weapon. In particular, he wanted a high-powered rifle with telescopic sights or some other weapon that could be used to kill Castro from a distance," FitzGerald later recounted. FitzGerald responded that he "wanted no part of such a scheme." Cubela was told that "the United States does not do such things."

Or so FitzGerald told the CIA's inspector general, who was preparing a report in the spring of 1967 on the agency's assassination attempts. "The written record," the inspector general notes, "tells a somewhat different story." A memo prepared at the time by Nestor Sanchez, the case officer who was also at the meeting, stated that "nothing of an operational nature" was discussed. Cubela was "satisfied with the policy discussion." After the meeting he asked the case officer what "technical support" the United States would provide to carry out the "policy," by which he presumably meant the violent overthrow of Castro. Testifying before the Church Committee in 1975, the case officer stated that Cubela made it clear that for a coup to work, Castro would have to be assassinated first. There is no indication that FitzGerald disagreed or refused to provide "technical support."

Whatever FitzGerald did or did not say to Cubela in Paris, three weeks later—on November 19—he approved, "telling Cubela he would be given a cache inside Cuba. Cache could, if he requested it, include . . . high power rifles w/scopes." The memorandum for the record also noted that "C/SAS [FitzGerald] requested written reports on AMLASH operation be kept to a minimum." A second meeting between Cubela and his CIA case officer was set up at the Paris safe house to convey this message. At the last minute Fitz-

Gerald decided to throw in another offering to Cubela: a poison pen.

Cubela was looking for some small "exotic" weapon—a dart gun, perhaps—he could use with deadly effect in close quarters. As a medical doctor, Cubela told the CIA he was sure they could come up with some clever "technical means." The elves in the Operations Division of the Office of Medical Services worked through the night and produced a ballpoint pen—a Paper Mate—rigged with a hypodermic syringe. The needle was "so fine," Dr. Edward Gunn of Medical Services boasted to the inspector general, "that the victim would hardly feel it when it was inserted—he compared it with the scratch from a shirt with too much starch." Cubela was to be told that he could load the pen with Blackleaf 40, a nicotine-based insecticide fatal to humans that was available at the time on the shelves of hardware stores.

When Richard Helms was confronted with the story of the poison pen during the Church Committee hearings in 1975, he insisted that the CIA was just "temporizing," keeping Cubela on "the team" by giving him a few playthings. Helms, who did not really believe in assassination, considered Cubela to be a spy, not an assassin. But Halpern, FitzGerald's assistant, regarded him as an assassin and claims that FitzGerald did as well. "Des was really more interested in starting a coup, and he hoped that Cubela could organize other army officers. But in coups, he understood, people die. The way to start a coup is to knock off the top man. Des felt it was a long shot, but it might work. We were desperate. Des was willing to try anything."[35]

FitzGerald did not think it was such a long shot that he was unwilling to make a small bet, given reasonable odds. Just six days before he formally signed off on a high-powered rifle for AMLASH, he accepted a little wager from Michael Forrestal, an official on the National Security Council staff who was a member of the Georgetown crowd (his father, James V. Forrestal, had been the first secretary of defense). A memo in FitzGerald's personal files records a $50 bet with Forrestal on "the fate of Fidel Castro during the period 1 August 1964 and 1 October 1964." (Apparently, FitzGerald saw a window of vulnerability for the Cuban leader that was roughly coincident with the 1964 U.S. presidential election campaign.) "Mr. Forrestal offers two-to-one odds ($100 to $50) against Fidel's falling (or being pushed) between the dates of

1 August and 1 October 1964. In the event that such a thing should occur prior to 1 August 1964 the wager herein is cancelled. Mr. FitzGerald accepts the wager on the above terms."

The memo was dated November 13, 1963. Nine days later the assassination of John F. Kennedy dramatically increased the odds that FitzGerald would lose his bet.[36]

Chapter Twenty-One

BLOWBACK

"Now we'll never know."

ON NOVEMBER 22, 1963, Des FitzGerald had just finished hosting a lunch for an old friend of the CIA, a foreign diplomat, at the City Tavern Club in Georgetown, when he was summoned from the private dining room by the maître d'. FitzGerald returned "as white as a ghost," recalled Sam Halpern. Normally erect and purposeful, FitzGerald was walking slowly, with his head down. "The president has been shot," he said.

The lunch immediately broke up. On the way out the door Halpern anxiously said, "I hope this has nothing to do with the Cubans." FitzGerald mumbled, "Yeah, well, we'll see." In the fifteen-minute car ride back to Langley, FitzGerald just stared straight ahead. He was well aware that in Paris, at almost the moment Kennedy was shot in Dallas, one of his case officers had been handing a poison pen to a Cuban agent to kill Castro. It was at the very least a grim coincidence. FitzGerald knew that, in September, Castro had threatened to retaliate against attempts to kill him. "United States leaders should think that if they are aiding in terrorist plans to eliminate Cuban leaders, they themselves will not be safe," the Cuban leader had publicly declared. The warning that Cubela might be a "dangle," that he might be secretly working for Castro, took on an ominous new meaning. Now FitzGerald had to wonder: Had Castro killed Kennedy before Kennedy could kill him?[1]

In Paris, Cubela had just finished asking for twenty hand grenades, two high-powered rifles with telescopic sights, and twenty pounds of C-4 explosive, to be dropped on a friend's *finca* (farm), when he was told that President Kennedy had been assassinated. He was "visibly moved," according to the case officer's report. "Why do such things happen to good people?" he asked. Within a few hours the case officer received a cable from FitzGerald in Washington telling him, he later recalled, that "everything was off." The case officer was told to break off contact with AMLASH and return immediately to Washington.[2]

CIA headquarters at Langley was in a state of chaos when FitzGerald and Halpern arrived back from the City Tavern Club on Friday afternoon. "We all went to battle stations," recalled Richard Helms. "Was this a plot? Who was pulling the strings? And who was next?" In the basement vault occupied by the Special Affairs Staff, "all kinds of theories popped up," said Halpern. "Was it Castro? We had no intelligence. We didn't think Castro was that crazy. We thought maybe it had to do with KGB 'wet affairs'— sabotage and assassination."[3]

When Lee Harvey Oswald was arrested early that afternoon, the CIA began to piece his background, which was worrisome. He had defected to the Soviet Union in 1959 and then redefected back to the United States in 1962. More recently, in September, he had been spotted by CIA cameras entering the Soviet embassy in Mexico City, ostensibly to get a visa. While there, Oswald had been interviewed by a KGB agent, Valery Kostikov. This was a startling discovery. Kostikov was a member of the KGB's 13th Department, which handled "wet affairs." The deputy chief of the CIA's Soviet Division, T. H. Bagley, immediately saw the sinister implications. "Putting it baldly," he wrote to his superiors on Saturday, November 23, "was Oswald, wittingly or unwittingly, part of a plot to murder President Kennedy in Dallas?" The CIA's counterintelligence staff began working around the clock to see whom else Kostikov had been talking to in his Mexico City lair.

In due course, one of the names that turned up was Rolando Cubela. This was potentially a vital link in trying to solve the mystery of Kennedy's death. The counterintelligence staff put out a routine "trace" to see if anyone in the agency knew Cubela.

FitzGerald remained silent. Technically, he did not have to answer. Tucked away in its basement vault, compartmented from the rest of the agency, the Special Affairs Staff had received a special exemption from queries by the counterintelligence staff. Still, under the circumstances, it would seem proper to cooperate in the CIA's own investigation of the president's murder.

But FitzGerald was wary of the CIA's chief of counterintelligence, James Jesus Angleton. The legendary mole hunter was growing increasingly drunken and conspiratorial in the early 1960s. As he downed serial martinis over four-hour lunches at La Niçoise in Georgetown, he would puzzle over counterintelligence cases that had been sitting on his desk for months, even years. To him, the Sino-Soviet split was just a trick designed to lull the West, and any CIA official, up to and including the director, was a potential mole.

What would he have made of Cubela and his link to Kostikov? FitzGerald thought Angleton was mentally unstable. If Angleton was allowed into the SAS vault, Castro was safe; all action against him would stop. Angleton never did catch any moles, for all his machinations. "There is not a goddamned thing Angleton or his henchmen could have come up with," insisted Halpern in 1993. "Des thought, what the hell is Jim going to tell me?"[4]

FitzGerald had never told the director of Central Intelligence, John McCone, about Cubela. McCone was a wealthy Texas businessman who had been brought in to replace Allen Dulles after the Bay of Pigs. An outsider and a bit of a moralist, he had been kept ignorant of all the CIA's assassination plots. In the "need-to-know" world of the CIA, Richard Helms had decided that McCone did not need to know. Authority for the assassination plots was apparently something that could "spring forward" after a change of CIA directors—or even presidents. To Helms, the unrelenting pressure from Bobby Kennedy had sufficed as authorization. Besides, McCone did not want to know. When the subject of assassination was briefly raised (and quickly suppressed) at a meeting of the Special Group in August 1962, McCone, a good Catholic, had worried that if he got "involved in something like this" he might get excommunicated.[5]

On the weekend of the Kennedy assassination, FitzGerald did tell Walt Elder, the executive assistant to McCone, that he had met with Cubela in October and that one of his agents had been meeting with the Cuban turncoat the very moment Kennedy had been shot. But he did not tell Elder that AMLASH had been offered a poison pen or promised a rifle. There was no mention of an assassination plot. FitzGerald also ordered the case officer in Paris to make no mention of the poison pen in his official report.

Elder was struck by FitzGerald's clear discomfort. "Des was normally imperturbable, but he was very disturbed about his involvement." The normally smooth operator was "shaking his head and wringing his hands. It was very uncharacteristic. That's why I remember it so clearly," Elder said in 1993. He thought Fitz-Gerald was "distraught and overreacting." Elder conjectured that FitzGerald had tried to "play case officer" and found "he wasn't very good at it."[6]

It took a great deal to shake FitzGerald's stoicism. His family had never seen him weep, though his son, Des, had once seen tears in his father's eyes as they watched a late-night war movie together. FitzGerald had welled up over a scene in which an American GI flips over the body of a dead German soldier to discover a sixteen-year-old boy. FitzGerald had become an admirer of John F. Kennedy (if not his brother), and that weekend he was silent and mournful over the president's death. But he did not break down until Lee Harvey Oswald was shot.

He was sitting in front of the television with his wife on Sunday morning, November 24, when Jack Ruby stepped from a crowd and shot Oswald. FitzGerald began to cry, for the first and last time in his wife's experience. "Now we'll never know," he said.[7]

FitzGerald never said anything more about it, and he kept his secrets even from the investigators of the Warren Commission, which was never informed about AMLASH or any of the CIA's Mafia plots. ("They didn't ask," said Richard Helms.) Still, it would be a mistake to make too much of the mystery. Angleton never got over suspecting that the Russians or Cubans plotted to kill Kennedy. He thought the Russian defector Yuri Nosenko, who claimed that the Kremlin was innocent, was a KGB plant to throw the CIA off the trail. But most reputable students of the Kennedy assassination have concluded that Khrushchev and Castro did not kill Kennedy, if only because neither man wanted to start World War III.

Somewhat more plausible suspects are renegade Cuban exiles, conceivably abetted by rogue CIA agents. With his distrust and contempt for exiles, FitzGerald must have worried at least a little on this score. The FBI had been cracking down on extremist groups like Alpha 66 that wanted to overthrow Castro (the agency worried they would trip over their own plots). There had been considerable grumbling in the exile community in Miami that Kennedy had betrayed the Brigade at the Bay of Pigs. Had some hotheads tried to get even? Curiously, FitzGerald did not try very hard to investigate. "I was just told to watch the island," said Ted

Shackley. "The mainland was the FBI's territory." The officers of JMWAVE talked to some of their informants, but mostly they left the job to the FBI—which did very little, according to a report by a congressional committee set up in 1979 to re-investigate the Kennedy assassination.[8]

THE ASSASSINATION of John F. Kennedy should have marked the end of the crusade to kill Fidel Castro. Bobby Kennedy spent the winter of 1964 worrying that perhaps he had precipitated his brother's death by trying to crack down on the mob, even as top mobsters continued to work for the CIA. Lyndon Johnson had no interest in Cuba; his attention turned quickly to Vietnam.

Desmond FitzGerald, however, pushed ahead. "After the assassination, the pressure for boom and bang stopped," recalled Halpern. "We asked Des, 'Can we stop these crazy operations?' Des said we had to keep on trying." The Special Affairs Staff officers needled FitzGerald about his confidence, but FitzGerald continued to insist, "We'll get him by the end of the year." "This wasn't Bobby Kennedy anymore," said Halpern. "This was Des on his own."

On April 7, 1964, the Special Group decided to put an end to sabotage operations against Cuba. A memorandum written by CIA Director McCone stated that President Johnson had abandoned the goal of overthrowing or "eliminating" Castro. Yet on June 9, two months later, the CIA delivered two FAL automatic rifles with five magazines per weapon to Cubela in a secret drop on the north coast of Cuba.[9]

"Des wouldn't take no for an answer," said Halpern. The CIA did discontinue the boat operations—"no more shmoats," he ordered. But FitzGerald continued to try to help Cubela kill Castro. According to Halpern, FitzGerald came back from the Special Group meeting in April and announced that all sabotage ops had been stopped, but not the effort to get rid of Castro. "We told Des, 'This is the beginning of the end. You might as well face it,' " said Halpern.[10]

FitzGerald backed down slowly. The June delivery of arms was the last. Yet, on June 3, FitzGerald was still arguing with Mac Bundy for drastic measures. "While the cost would be high, it might well be worth the sacrifice if the U.S. is prepared for armed intervention in Cuba," FitzGerald wrote the national security adviser. Informally, he drily joked with Bundy's aides that while his proposal was "one-sided," the "more we worked on it the more one-sided it became." (Bundy's aide, Gordon Chase, was unamused. "Much of his logic and conclusions, frankly, leave me stone cold," he wrote Bundy.)

FitzGerald could not quite give up on Cubela. The CIA tried to put the Cuban major in touch with exile groups that might supply him with weapons on their own. Finally, in 1965, AMLASH was cut loose. The counterintelligence men at last convinced FitzGerald that Cubela was a poor security risk. Indeed, Castro was on to him: in March 1966, Cubela was arrested and tried for treason. Castro commuted his death sentence, possibly for cooperating with his secret police. For the CIA, a strange era was over.[11]

AT ABOUT the time FitzGerald was winding down AMLASH, Tracy Barnes had lunch with an old CIA friend and regaled him with tales about the agency's connections to the Mafia. Barnes spoke "with a sense of wonderment," recalled the friend. "He was saying, 'This is a crazy world we live in. Look at where we've come to.' "[12]

Barnes had a difficult time trying to rationalize his role. His family did not know about the assassination plots until after he died in 1972, but they sensed that he was groping, not very successfully, to make peace with a career that was fast waning. "I think he ended up being tormented by the kind of stuff he did," said his son Tracy Jr., who noted that "Castro was actually the kind of guy my father would have admired"—for his boldness and macho élan.

After dinner one evening Barnes said that JFK had been a good president because he was "tough. He knew the difference between who you have to kill and who you don't have to kill." As he said this, he looked "sick to his stomach," said his daughter Jane, "as if he was experimenting, trying it out, to justify it." After reading *The Spy Who Came in from the Cold*, he said, "That's what it's really like," recalled Jane. "It was like it hit him, that this really was a dirty business, no more James Bond. It was dawning on him that the CIA was not 'a second cherishing mother,' as E. Howard Hunt called it, but rather a creature that eats its own."[13]

Barnes could not bring himself to quit, however. "It would be an admission of defeat," he told Larry Houston, the CIA general counsel, after the Bay of Pigs. Stripped of his patrons when Dulles and Bissell were pushed out, he floundered about, looking for a new role. He suggested using the Peace Corps as cover for the CIA and was quickly rebuffed. For a long time he had wanted to get the CIA involved in spying in the United States, just as MI-6 ran a London field station. But under the agreement struck between Frank Wisner and J. Edgar Hoover in 1949, the United States was FBI turf; the CIA was specifically barred from spying at home.[14]

In part to give Barnes something to do, a Domestic Operations Division was established, but it was not quite what he had imagined. "Tracy got his concept, but greatly watered down," said E. Howard Hunt, who, when other division chiefs wouldn't touch him after the Bay of Pigs, was assigned to Barnes. "He wanted a real station doing ops in the United States, but he became instead the trash heap for ops no one else wanted." Barnes was put in charge of selling off proprietaries—the various airlines he had bought, at great expense and with mixed results, for the DD/P, as well as newspapers and publishing companies that were a hang-over from the Wisner era. It fell to Barnes to pay off the widows of the "sheep-dipped" Alabama National Guard pilots who had been killed in the Bay of Pigs. Barnes was also put in charge of "a couple of agents in India and Switzerland who had been forgotten about and were just sitting there, drawing expenses." His old friend Tom Braden found him in New York in the summer of 1963 selling off CIA assets through a front. Braden, who had left the CIA in 1954 to be a newspaper publisher, said, "It was sort of pathetic. He offered to sell me a newspaper. 'C'mon, Braden, you want a paper? I'll get you one, a damn good one!' He was getting rid of embarrassing assets. Yet he was cheerful and ebullient." In October 1962 he wrote his exiled mentor, Allen Dulles, "On my side, I have been trying as manfully as possible to get my own element under way, and I am frankly encouraged at the progress."[15]

Barnes was supposed to recruit foreign businessmen and students traveling in the United States to send them back abroad as agents under "deep cover." But espionage still didn't interest him much. He wanted to run political action ops, recruiting agents who could influence the local economy or political scene. He told his number two, Stanley Gaines, that he wanted to purchase a cigarette factory in Mali. "What for?" asked Gaines. "To make money," said Barnes. "We don't want to make money," said Gaines. "Well, we can put agents there," said Barnes. Gaines asked what the CIA would do with Mali cigarette makers.

Shortly after Barnes had briefed Dick Helms on his plans, including the Mali cigarette factory, Gaines was summoned to lunch with the new DD/P at his favorite restaurant, the Occidental. "Look, Stan," said Helms, "Tracy briefed me about his ops and I didn't quite understand. Maybe you can tell me what they're about." Gaines tried, explaining that he had told Barnes that the agency really wasn't in the business of making money. Helms nodded and sighed. "You keep pushing him that way," he said.[16]

Barnes also dabbled in American politics, which was strictly off-limits under the CIA's charter. He ran what he called "morale ops" to "influence people's thinking," said Elizabeth McDonald, one of his operatives. "We would try to plant editorials about candidates we regarded as pro-CIA. We knew we were not supposed to." The head of these operations was E. Howard Hunt. "This was before Watergate," said McDonald. "There were no break-ins or buggings, yet."[17]

During the 1964 presidential elections Hunt offered to spy for the Johnson administration on Senator Barry Goldwater, the Republican candidate, in order to ingratiate the CIA with the White House. The target was fairly innocuous: Hunt proposed to obtain copies of Goldwater's speeches before they were delivered. As Barnes later explained it to Chet Cooper, a former CIA analyst who had joined the White House staff, Hunt had come to Barnes and said, "Hey, I've got a great idea! We'll do a favor for the White House, get Goldwater's speeches in advance. A little 'intell'." Barnes sent Hunt over to see Cooper at the White House to offer his services. Cooper politely declined, saying that he could just send his secretary down to the Republican National Committee and she would be given advance copies without having to steal them. Hunt, said Cooper, was, as usual, "thinking black," looking for devious ways to do the routine.[18]

Barnes had often enjoyed a cocktail in his office at the end of the day. "You'd go to his office for a drink at five-thirty and you'd go home drunk at eight," said George Holmes, a clandestine service officer whom Barnes had tried to lure over to the Domestic Operations Division. "The next morning you'd realize you hadn't accomplished anything." Barnes realized he wasn't accomplishing anything, either. His friends were gently prodding Barnes, who was in his mid-fifties, to retire. Stewart Alsop and Mike Forrestal even asked his children to help persuade him to get out. "Tracy knew it wasn't his time," said Larry Houston. "He should have resigned, but he always had one more thought."[19]

His last ill-conceived idea was to try to protect Hans Tofte, who had been dumped in the Domestic Ops Division in 1962 after a failed tour of duty in South America. Barnes and Tofte had trained together in the OSS, where Tofte had been a brave commando with the Danish resistance, and Tofte had worked with Barnes to plan the coup in Guatemala. But he was a blowhard who exaggerated his exploits in Korea and a pariah. Barnes defended Tofte after he was questioned on his expense accounts, but he could not help when some CIA security officers went into Tofte's house in the spring of 1966 and found secret documents that were not supposed to leave Langley. Tofte sued the CIA for breaking into his house and allegedly stealing his wife's jewelry, and the flap spilled into the newspapers.[20]

Barnes took the blame for Tofte. Richard Helms, whom Barnes had once tried to force out during the Bissell regime, decided to squeeze Barnes. Helms had risen to become director of the CIA, and he had a long memory. He summoned his old antagonist to the director's office and recited a long list of complaints. Barnes was not tidy. He was too pro-British. He was a poor administrator. "Tracy tried to laugh it off at first, but he was stunned and hurt," said Robert Crowley, an officer in Domestic Ops. In a twist that marked the final ascendancy of the "Prudent Professionals" over the group Stewart Alsop had dubbed the "Bold Easterners," Helms ordered Desmond FitzGerald to fire Barnes. FitzGerald had become DD/P in 1965, but he was still working for Helms. In July 1966, FitzGerald had to tell his friend that his CIA career was over. "It was the hardest thing I ever did," FitzGerald told Thomas Parrott.[21]

Barnes became a "nonentity" in his final weeks, said Crowley. In a final indignity, he learned that his OSS years would not be counted toward his CIA pension. But a small farewell dinner at the Alibi Club was jolly, and Barnes resolved not to show his hurt. "He just said to hell with it," said Crowley.

A few months after he left the agency Barnes ran into Richard Bissell at an "old spooks dinner" in New York. "We didn't reminisce," said Bissell. "There was no lamenting a lost time. Tracy was his ebullient self." Still, continued Bissell, "we all realized that our period in the agency had been a kind of climax. We realized it wasn't likely to be re-created."[22]

WASHINGTON INSIDERS had regarded the brain of Richard Bissell as a great natural resource, a kind of secret weapon that favored the West in the twilight struggle. The Bay of Pigs had made those insiders ask how someone so brilliant could do something so stupid; still, there had to be a way to make use of such a valuable tool. In 1962, Bissell was made head of the Institute for Defense Analysis (IDA), a kind of in-house Pentagon think tank to evaluate weapons systems and other government high tech.

Bissell could still dazzle. Officials at the National Security Agency (NSA) marveled at how quickly he grasped the arcane science of code breaking. It was, Thomas Powers writes, as if he could empty his mind to make room for new information. But Bissell was independent-minded as well as brilliant, and there was the catch: IDA was independent in name only.[23]

IDA's offices were in the Pentagon area occupied by the Joint Chiefs of Staff. "We were just soldiers without uniforms," said Norman Christeller, IDA's general manager. "When Bissell came in, he immediately got into a fight with the generals in weapons systems analysis who wanted IDA to do the Pentagon's bidding. Bissell wanted IDA to be independent. He told the generals, 'You work for me.' They answered, 'But the Joint Chiefs are paying the bill.' "

Bissell refused to bend. He kept two secretaries busy, one just to keep track of his arguments with the generals ("I never knew if the generals knew that Bissell was recording their phone calls," said Christeller). Bissell enjoyed tearing holes in the research of the armed services and exposing weapons that were overcost and underperforming. But the military, still brooding over the fact that Bissell had "stolen" the U-2 project from the Air Force in the mid-1950s, was lying in wait. Because of the Bay of Pigs, the generals knew he was "damaged goods," said Christeller. "They fought over everything, even parking places." (Bissell refused to set aside five spaces for general officers.)[24]

Bissell finally won a philosophical battle. IDA was moved out of the Pentagon and became more independent. Even then, he wasn't satisfied. Driving to work in the morning with Christeller, he seemed discouraged. "He knew he had a lot more to offer than the job gave him," said Christeller. In the winter of 1964, Bissell was fired.[25]

Bissell left government and began consulting for the Ford Foundation. In the files of the Johnson White House is a "candidate card" under Bissell's name. It lists his prior jobs and his references (Kenneth Galbraith, Arthur Schlesinger Jr., William Bundy, Adlai Stevenson, Jerome Weisner). A marginal notation states that he "has expressed a strong desire to come back into federal service." The call never came.[26]

Looking for a new project in 1964, he contacted Frank Wisner, who was back in Washington trying to figure out what to do with his own life after the CIA. "I looked for manic prolixity," said Bissell. "I didn't see it. Wiz suggested that we start a small company in the nuclear power business. It all fell through. I still remember, though, Frank saying, 'I am really happier than I have been before.' "[27]

WISNER ARRIVED in London in September 1959, over a year after he had left the office of the DD/P. The psychiatric analysis, the painful shock therapy, had left him diminished and "diffident," said Carleton Swift, who was his number two in London. "The breakdown shook his confidence," said Cleve Cram, a senior CIA officer in London, "but it also made him less arrogant."[28]

Slowly, Wisner's spirit returned. At first, Swift essentially did the station chief's job for him, but Wisner soon became curious and demanded to see all the cable traffic. "He had an inexhaustible demand for knowledge," said Cram. A veteran gamesman, Wisner was fascinated by the rivalry between the two main branches of British intelligence, MI-5 and MI-6. He prodded the counterespionage diggers of MI-5 to produce more evidence against Kim Philby, who, remarkably, had never been arrested for treason after he was banished from the United States in 1951. Wisner felt that the old boys in MI-6, the foreign intelligence service, were somehow protecting Philby, the British mole who eventually fled to Moscow in January 1963. Wisner was never much interested in the espionage side—he was indifferent to the intelligence produced by the SIS's and CIA's one great asset in Moscow, Oleg Penkovsky—but he was as keen as ever on psychological warfare and political action.

Wisner had little role in actual operations. He did get a whiff of the old days, helping to plan a coup in Guyana, a piece of empire in South America that was leaning perilously to the left. But his real job was to get along with the British. A devout Anglophile, he did this naturally. His wife, Polly, effectively transferred her Georgetown salon to a large and elegant house at Milton Crescent. A variety of intellectuals, statesmen, politicians, and aristocrats engaged in conversation, high and low, around Wisner's dinner table. Before long Polly Wisner had renewed her friendly social rivalry with Evangeline Bruce, who as wife of the U.S. ambassador to England, the Wisners' old friend David Bruce, ran her own salon.[29]

Wisner's playfulness and gentle side returned. When his nephew Charles Reeder, a Princeton boy in London on holiday, began talking through his thick Mississippi drawl about the "Eutruscans," Wisner teased him, "I guess that's an Etruscan with a U-turn." He sensed that his little boy, Graham, was frightened and lonely about the move to England (and, perhaps, about his father's mental illness), so when he came home in the evening Wisner would sometimes crawl under the dining room table, where Graham liked to hide, and have a chat. "Then he'd go have cocktails with Isaiah Berlin," said Reeder. Wisner was bemused watching some old Romanian friends work themselves into a romantic frenzy while watching *The Prisoner of Zenda* and drinking jeroboams of champagne. His own emotions remained controlled. "You felt he could contain whatever intense feelings he had. We played golf in a sleet storm on Boxing Day. It didn't faze him at all. It was like he didn't notice it," said Reeder.[30]

Wisner began to feel useful again. "The British rather opened up their vests to him," said Swift. "He was trustworthy and his reporting was read in Washington. No one in London could touch his access. Within a year, he was fully in charge. At embassy meetings, he knew all the hot poop from the Alsops. His diffidence was gone, his confidence regained. He was going great guns, he was inside the establishment. Ambassador Bruce was a little jealous." Al Ulmer, a European station chief, listened to Wisner spin out long-range plans. "He thought he was going to make a comeback," said Ulmer.

In June 1961 the Wisners went back to Washington for a week for Frank Jr.'s graduation from Princeton. Wisner was beguiled by the court life whirling around the Kennedys. A younger, lively crowd had moved into Georgetown; hostesses were competing to have the best dinner parties. Wisner plunged in, staying up late each night and drinking an extra cocktail or two. His old friends, though glad to see him so vigorous again, wondered whether perhaps he wasn't a little manic. Richard Bissell saw Wisner at a dinner party. Afterward, Polly took him aside. "How do you think Frank is?" she asked. Bissell hesitated and answered, "I think it's starting again."

In Washington that June, Dean Rusk asked Wisner to accompany him on a diplomatic mission to Geneva, and Wisner gladly went along. Polly and Carlcton Swift went to Heathrow to meet Wisner's plane when he returned at the end of the month. Swift watched Wisner, then Polly's expression, as Wisner came down the gangway. "Oh my God," she said. "He's floating."[31]

In London, Polly tried to keep the show going. When Wisner became too loquacious at dinner, she would tease, "Down boy." Some of their friends thought she pushed him to keep up a relentless social schedule. Wisner had his spats with Polly, but she remained fiercely loyal to him. ("I don't care how bad it gets, you always stay with him," she once told a friend. "And it always gets bad.") Wisner teased his children, "Do you know who I'd marry if I had to do it all over again?" Wendy would guess her "nanny or Mrs. [Katharine] Graham." Wisner would laugh and say, "No, I'd marry your mother."

Polly Wisner knew the gossip behind her back. "People say I'm driving him crazy, for social purposes. That's not true. This is what Frank wants," she told Carleton Swift. "It's not my idea." And it was true that, despite some grumbling, Wisner was drawn to the particular mix of social life and power that distinguishes the British and American establishments. It was no less a part of his life than hers; their shared fascination was a sustaining bond.[32]

Wisner began to rave, and neither Polly nor his friends at the CIA could cover for him any longer. The end came when he called a British cabinet minister after 2 A.M. and dictated the press release that, in Wisner's opinion, the minister should have delivered earlier that day. In the spring of 1962 the DD/P, Richard Helms, had to recall his old friend to Washington. Wisner's successor was Archie Roosevelt. The new station chief carefully went through Wisner's files and then destroyed them. They were, he told his colleagues, "the ramblings of a madman."[33]

CASUALTIES OF WAR

"He was full of rue."

WISNER RETIRED FROM the CIA in August 1962. On a hunting trip to Mexico with his Mississippi cousins that summer, he was "fun to be around," said Fred Reeder. "He joked and told stories. But then he said, 'See that fellow? He's following me.' " Wisner was "haunted," said Reeder. He refused to eat in the same restaurant twice because, he explained, he was afraid of being staked out by the communists.[1]

He was also bored. The man who had run a covert empire now puttered around on his farm, managed his investments, collected small Greek artifacts, and wrote wordy book reviews praising the friends of the CIA and bashing its critics. He thought highly of *The Venetian Affair* by Helen MacInnes because it exposed Soviet disinformation techniques. But he attacked *The Ambassador* by Morris West as a "lamentably literate, albeit a bit lithuric, swelling of the litany of 'HATE-THAT-CIA!,' " in the sorry tradition of *The Quiet American*, by that "dupe" Graham Greene.[2]

Like many old CIA hands, Wisner was beginning to feel that the CIA was coming under harsh and unfair scrutiny. Because of the Bay of Pigs and the U-2 incident, the press was no longer complacently looking the other way or printing uncritical handouts. The first serious bad publicity came with the publication of the book called *The Invisible Government* by Thomas Ross and David Wise in 1964. Ross and Wise accurately revealed secret operations, and, as the title implies, questioned the assumption that a secret intelligence service is healthy in a democratic society. This was a very different view from the breathless tales of derring-do that had appeared from time to time in the Lucepress or the *Saturday Evening Post*. It marked the beginning of a steady downward slide in the CIA's media image.[3]

At first, the CIA believed it could control the bad press. The agency considered buying up the entire printing of *The Invisible Government*, but Random House said it would just print some more.[4] Wisner had always been proud of his ability to manipulate his friends in the Fourth Estate. From retirement, he did his part to stop the stain from spreading to television. On March 14, 1965, he wrote John McCone that his wife, Polly, had sat next to a young NBC producer, Edward Yates, who was doing a documentary on the CIA for David Brinkley and John Chancellor. "Polly felt that Mr. Yates made highly intemperate statements about the agency's past and present aims and accomplishments. . . ." It was clear, Wisner wrote the DCI, that "Yates had been profoundly impressed by *The Invisible Government* since he made many of the charges against the agency that are in that book." Wisner suggested that McCone "point out to their superiors in NBC the sort of damage that could result to the national interest from a nationwide, hour-long, feature television broadcast containing inaccuracies, distortions, and the perpetuation of the ugly myths, many of which are of demonstrably communist origin." But the days were over when Allen Dulles could buy off CBS with a New Year's Day champagne lunch at the Alibi Club. NBC went ahead and aired a critical documentary.[5]

Old ghosts flitted through Wisner's addled mind. During 1965 he developed a strange obsession with Martin Bormann, Hitler's chief aide. Bormann, whom Wisner liked to refer to as "the mysterious and sinister figure of Martin Bormann," was the only one of Hitler's top henchmen to give the Allies the slip in the closing days of World War II. Wisner was fascinated with stories that he had been sighted, in various disguises and aliases, around Europe and South America. Wisner's daughter, Wendy, wondered if her father's interest in Bormann represented some kind of delayed guilt about the Nazis protected by the CIA after the war.[6]

In the fall of 1965, Wisner's mania, his logorrhea, collapsed into profound depression. Janet Barnes and Jane Thompson stopped by to take Polly to lunch in Georgetown and found Wisner "so tense and anxious he could barely speak," said Thompson. "We said, 'Oh

Frank, what's the matter, bless you, dearie,' " she recalled. He tried to smile and answered, "Thank you for that." In October, Wisner was scheduled to go hunting with some old chums in Spain; his daughter, Wendy, trying to cheer him, said, "You must be excited, Dad." He replied, "I don't get excited about anything anymore." On the phone with Jim McCargar, an old CIA veteran, he reminisced gloomily about the lost revolution in Hungary and announced that he was going hunting in Spain. "The guns are in the Spanish embassy," he said, seemingly out of the blue.[7]

Wisner was obviously too sick to go to Spain. He was so depressed that his wife, Polly, worried that he would try to commit suicide. On October 28, before he drove out to his farm on the Eastern Shore of Maryland, she called the caretaker and asked him to remove the guns from the house. Wisner found one of his boys' shotguns and killed himself on October 29, 1965.

Wisner's death saddened but did not shock his colleagues. "I got a cable in Kuala Lumpur, where I was stationed," said Arthur Jacobs, the "Ozzard of Wiz" who had been Wisner's aide in the early 1950s. "The cable was from Des FitzGerald. It said that Frank had died and gave no reason, but I knew." Wisner's suicide was "entirely rational, if you can say such a thing," said his niece Jean Lindsey. "He realized that his life would be circumscribed by increasing cycles of depression. I saw Frank three days before he died and he seemed in good spirits. He talked about his children. Perhaps he had made up his mind to kill himself."[8]

At his funeral the Bethlehem Chapel in the National Cathedral was overflowing with old friends who sang "Fling Out the Banner" as Wisner's family marched down the aisle at the end of the service. "Instead of a dirge, it was exuberant, powerful, exultant," recalled Tom Braden. At Arlington Cemetery, Frank Wisner was buried as a naval commander, his wartime rank. All the top officials of the agency, from director on down, were in attendance. (The CIA posted guards to keep the KGB from seeing who was there.)

Henry Breck, a junior CIA officer out of Groton and Harvard, watched his grim-faced elders as they mourned. They were defiant and proud, but besieged. The CIA was feeling particularly embattled that October. A month earlier word had spread through the agency that the *New York Times* was embarking on a first-ever investigation of the CIA. The CIA's media liaison had sent a memo to Director McCone entitled "Subject: NEW YORK TIMES'

Threat to Safety of the Nation." The death of Wisner deepened
feelings of loneliness and betrayal among many of the Cold Warriors alongside his grave.[9]

"They felt alone," said Breck. "It was them against the Soviet
Union and the *New York Times*. They were alone on the front
lines. No one knew how bad the threat was. It was a language they
could speak only to themselves. They understood that Frank
Wisner had been driven to this terrible act by his concern for the
country's indifference."[10]

Three weeks later Desmond FitzGerald wrote Wisner's youngest son, Graham:

Why did this illness strike your father? I don't pretend a scientific
insight into these most hidden matters, but it seems to me that every
man must have his breaking point and perhaps the stronger the man
and the more remote the point, the more serious the break when it
comes. I do know that the pressures that your father bore for ten years
were enormous—certainly beyond my own full understanding of them.
Someone said of your father that he was a watchmaker in Detroit.
There is some truth in that; in fact he had to be. Our country's real-
ization that we were in a deadly cold war with Russia came late and we
were wholly unprepared to deal with it. It fell on your father's shoulders, far more than any other man, to build our defenses from the
ground up and with all speed. . . . For the whole of ten years he had to
protect us in our work from all of the traps and deadfalls of bureaucratic Washington. For all this, the watchmaker always kept ahead of
the production line and still had time and energy to give pleasure in his
company to his friends. Very great pleasure, for in the last analysis it
is as a friend that I remember him best.

Your father was a great man and nothing mars his memory.

I hope you will forgive these somewhat emotional recollections; they
would not reflect my feelings if they were not emotional and I hope to
convey to you some flavor of what others felt about your father.[11]

On January 28, 1971, six years after he died, the agency decided
to mark Wisner's passing with a private convocation of his friends
and colleagues. A plaque in his memory was dedicated and hung
permanently outside the office of the chief of the clandestine service. Richard Helms gave a short and moving speech. "Frank
Wisner was a man driven by many forces," Helms said, "an intense
man and yet, suddenly, the forces seemed to converge, surround-
ing him with a darkness like that of a great storm. Or perhaps, it
looked to him—

As if a night of dark intent
Was coming, and not a night, an age.
Someone had better be prepared for rage.
There would be more than ocean-water broken
Before God's last Put out the Light
   was spoken.[12]

AT A DINNER PARTY in Georgetown that fall of 1965, Joe Alsop began to hold forth on the nobility of America's commitment to Vietnam. The evening was a mix of generations—Des FitzGerald was there, along with his daughter Frances, and some of her friends, including Henry Breck, the young Grotonian who had signed up for the CIA partly out of admiration for men like Wisner and FitzGerald. Alsop, who was becoming an increasingly strident hawk, warmed to the romance of what he called "the Young Lords of the Delta." These were the Ivy Leaguers like Wisner's son Frank Jr., a foreign service officer, who had gone to Vietnam with the State Department or CIA to "nation build." After a few martinis Alsop began waxing about "the new Lawrences of Arabia."

"Suddenly, the younger people blew up," recalled Breck. The junior set, which had also consumed a fair amount of gin, began yelling at Alsop. Evenings with Joe Alsop were often contentious; he intentionally provoked argument. But this quarrel was more raw than most. "We yelled, 'Are you out of your mind? The war's a disaster!' " recalled Breck. The evening rapidly slid down the generational divide.

FitzGerald, for the most part, listened impassively until Frances and others began questioning the morality of American interventionism. FitzGerald turned to his daughter and her friends, and used a British put-down. "You're all so wet," he said.[13]

FitzGerald was bothered to see his daughter and Breck side with the rabble. It was one thing to have scraggly antiwar protesters waving placards on college campuses; it was quite another to be rudely accosted by his own kind in Joe Alsop's dining room. "You don't know what you're talking about," he said to Breck.

Yet FitzGerald had his own deep doubts about the Vietnam War. He had been an early and outspoken dissenter. Defense Secretary Bob McNamara had refused to be briefed by him in 1962 after FitzGerald questioned whether progress could be measured by statistics. As opposition to the Vietnam War grew in the mid-

1960s, FitzGerald would defend administration policy and do his best to carry it out. But his heart was not in the struggle. Increasingly, the same could be said about his career at the CIA.

Except to his family and closest friends, FitzGerald did not betray any low feelings. Indeed, to most he seemed upbeat and as bold as ever. His staff meetings were still "always exciting and romantic," said Edgar Applewhite. "He was confident and ebullient. He wanted the best recruits, which to him meant Harvard, Princeton, and Yale." (He was careful to add, however, that he wanted men from these institutions because they were "more competitive." He "stressed the latter point," said Applewhite, "to rule out the note of snobbery.") He did not exactly invite chumminess. "No one ever threw their arm around Des," said Bill Hood, a subordinate. But he was usually willing to listen. Except for laggards and dullards, "his troops loved him," said William Colby.[14]

The Cuba operation had been a bust, but he had gone on to clean up "WH"—the CIA's Western Hemisphere Division, which had grown by almost half in the early 1960s in response to Cuban (and Russian and Chinese) adventurism all through Central and South America. "WH had been a backwater," said Hood, who was WH's chief of operations under FitzGerald. "It was an old Hoover fiefdom [the FBI had handled Latin America during World War II], and no one in the CIA had paid any attention to it." Most of the station chiefs were former FBI agents who stayed close to the local dictators and their secret police. FitzGerald eased some out and condescended to others. "Sheriff," he'd ask mockingly when he visited an old G-man on the Latin beat. "Do we eat now or do we go directly to the whorehouse?" FitzGerald wanted more sophisticated operatives who could run political action programs, creating democratic opposition groups rather than just paying off the oligarchs.

Tim Hogan, of Andover and Yale, was FitzGerald's beau ideal. Hogan went to Brazil under deep cover and began organizing farmers and labor groups against the communists. "It was my cadres versus their cadres," he recalled. "The Chinese, Russians, and Cubans all had agents. We were all tripping over each other. Our political action was run through the Catholic Church. I felt I was really on the frontier, defending our perimeter against subversive forces." Hogan never carried a gun or felt the need for one. FitzGerald had not suddenly gone soft; rebels with weapons supplied by the CIA overthrew Brazil's leftist president, João Goulart, in

April 1964. But FitzGerald generally pushed political action over paramilitary—sometimes with a generous boost. The CIA spent $3 million to influence the 1964 elections in Chile, a dollar a vote, twice as much per voter as Goldwater and Johnson spent in the 1964 presidential campaign.[15]

By 1965, FitzGerald was widely acknowledged to be the CIA's natural chief for covert operations. In April, when Dick Helms was promoted to deputy director of the agency, most assumed that FitzGerald would become the DD/P. But Helms kept FitzGerald hanging. Nearly two months passed with no word from the seventh floor at Langley; finally, FitzGerald felt compelled to go to Helms and demand the job. This was a humiliating exercise for someone so proud, and it may have been Helms's intention to knock FitzGerald down a peg or two before giving him what he deserved.[16]

FitzGerald was not easily humbled. On the morning of June 17, Sam Halpern saw him sauntering out of the director's office. "Normally he walked briskly. I said, 'Des, did you get some good news?' and he gave me a big smile." FitzGerald's appointment as DD/P heartened the activists, including those in exile. Dick Bissell later recalled telling Tracy Barnes how "gratified" he was by the news. "I always felt that his energy and activism, backed by his considerable personal prestige, would help offset a growing conservatism and caution which I feared [in the clandestine service]," Bissell wrote John Bross.[17]

In his new role FitzGerald tried to keep his independence from Helms. The old tension, between the "Prudent Professionals" and the activists, resurfaced. When Helms pondered whether to make FitzGerald DD/P, he had asked the advice of Bill Colby, who had succeeded him as head of the Far East Division. Colby recommended FitzGerald, but cautioned Helms that "he would have to maintain tight control over him to keep him from charging off into some new Bay of Pigs." Helms had to instruct FitzGerald's deputy, Tom Karamessines, to keep an eye on the new DD/P. Karamessines took Halpern to lunch and awkwardly asked him to prod FitzGerald into being a little more forthcoming with Helms. "You're kidding," said Halpern, who wondered if he was being recruited to spy on his boss.[18]

Helms worried that FitzGerald had his own power base outside the agency, and, indeed, FitzGerald was "outgoing, cocky, and confident" at meetings with the White House, said Howard

"Rocky" Stone, FitzGerald's operations chief in Saigon. He treated Mac Bundy and Walt Rostow, the national security advisers, as his equals, and he bluffed the rest. Stone watched one afternoon in 1966 as FitzGerald casually flipped his straw hat on a hook in Bundy's office and cheekily declared, "McNamara's just given us the Pentagon. What are you going to do for us?" But the fact is that ever since the Bay of Pigs, the White House was willing to do less for the CIA.[19]

Executive branch approval was no longer pro forma. "Des had an infectious personality, he was very persuasive and gung ho, and if you weren't a skeptic, you'd be carried away," said Roswell Gilpatric, the deputy secretary of defense and a member of the Special Group. "He had a flair for covert operations. But after the Bay of Pigs we didn't approve 90 percent of them, and the ones we did approve, the agents would blow themselves up."[20]

Allen Dulles had seemed untouchable; his successors were not. Lyndon Johnson distrusted the CIA. A conspiracy theorist, the president believed that somehow (he wasn't sure how) the CIA had plotted with the Kennedys to deny him the Democratic nomination in 1960. John McCone had begun to feel increasingly squeezed out by Johnson, and in 1965 he resigned. His successor, Admiral William Raborn, an old Navy man uneducated in the intricacies of intelligence, was regarded as a simpleton. "Who's this fellow Oligarchy, anyway?" he once asked. "Red" Raborn was quickly run off by backbiting within the agency, and in June 1966 he had been replaced by Helms.* Helms was a trusted insider, but he was also a careful bureaucrat. The CIA's stature would never regain the mythic quality of the pre–Bay of Pigs era.[21]

The DD/P still presided over a large clandestine empire, particularly in the developing world. As covert action chief, Wisner had nurtured close relationships with a number of potentates, some of them quite exotic. FitzGerald looked on Third World strongmen with a mixture of bemusement and empathy. As always, just when

---

* Admiral Raborn's innocence was exasperating to FitzGerald. David Phillips, who had become the CIA's station chief in the Dominican Republic after the Bay of Pigs, recalled telling Raborn that one of the CIA's agents on the island was in the communist underground. Raborn jumped from his chair. "Have him arrested!" he ordered. Phillips noted that a muscle in FitzGerald's neck was beginning to twitch. "Is he a commie?" Raborn demanded. FitzGerald was speechless. The concept of a penetration agent was apparently new to the director of Central Intelligence.

FitzGerald seemed to verge on playing the Pasha, he was capable of redeeming himself. The haughtiness of his early years more often gave way to reflection and even empathy.

A trip FitzGerald took to the Congo in the mid-1960s is illustrative of his peculiar combination of archness and wonder. On this occasion he was the guest of Joseph Mobutu, the Congo leader backed by the CIA. He found the Congo "by turns wildly hopeful and totally hopeless," he wrote his daughter Frances. Mobutu's government "is a joke, almost." FitzGerald described dinner with Mobutu and his claque: "We were *en famille*—completely relaxed." FitzGerald was "the sportswriter at the Champ's training camp—the new Champ, full of energy, charm, and animal egocentricity." Wayne Jackson, a CIA official who accompanied FitzGerald on the trip, later recounted to his wife, Doris, that the garden outside Mobutu's house had been allowed to run to weed, but the plates on the dining room table were fancy china, inscribed with the initials "JD & MA." Jackson asked his host whom the initials stood for. "C'est moi!" answered Mobutu. "Joseph Desirée et ma femme Marie Antoinette!"

One of Mobutu's other guests had just been released from jail, to which he had been sent for disloyalty to Mobutu. "He got quietly drunk and fell disgracefully asleep during a showing of Congo News Pathé," wrote FitzGerald. "The minister of economics arrived quite tight and wholly uninvited in the middle of dinner and maintained stoutly that tomorrow was not the day to consider the budget." (He wanted to go to Paris instead.) Mobutu scolded him for his laziness—but appointed him comptroller of the currency in the morning.

It was all very entertaining, reported FitzGerald, "one of the most amusing evenings of my life. . . . And yet—what complex problems these men in their thirties deal with and how easy for us to laugh at their efforts. How would we do without our barnacled elders, established political leaders . . . and literate and patriotic citizenry? . . . Beckoning is my word for the Congo."[22]

FitzGerald did not have as much time as he wanted to visit such beckoning outposts, however. Increasingly, he was drawn into America's involvement in Vietnam. The agency was given a demanding but subordinate role to play in the war. It was counted on to collect intelligence (on the allies as well as the enemy) and to run covert action against the Viet Cong. But the leadership came from the Pentagon, White House, and State. From the beginning, the

CIA's analysts were more skeptical about the chances for success than the Pentagon or the White House staff. Instead of listening, Johnson and his lieutenants disdained the agency's men for failing to get with the program. FitzGerald had told Bob McNamara that Vietnam was a "political war" and urged him to pay more attention to winning "hearts and minds" than building up body counts. McNamara couldn't seem to grasp what he was talking about. "The communists were fighting a people's war and here we were putting in divisions. After the Bay of Pigs we turned the war over to the military and they just screwed it up," said William Colby, the chief of FE who had been a Saigon station chief.[23]

The agency's subservience was revealed in the overthrow of President Ngo Dinh Diem in 1963. Ambassador Henry Cabot Lodge was determined not to play the all-too-familiar role of patsy to the CIA's station chief; indeed, Lodge moved into the Saigon station chief's house, which he liked better than the ambassador's residence, and ordered the station chief to get rid of his large black limousine. The coup against Diem was orchestrated not by the CIA but rather by Lodge and a cabal of Kennedy advisers in the State Department and the White House. The CIA at the time opposed getting rid of Diem because it could envision the political chaos in Vietnam that was to follow.[24]

FitzGerald had been off chasing Castro during the 1963 Diem coup. When he returned to the Vietnam scene as DD/P in 1965, he tried to use some of the tricks he had learned from successful counterinsurgency programs in the Philippines and Malaya. He created "People's Action Teams"—chosen from South Vietnamese who had suffered at the hands of the Viet Cong—to roam the countryside, rooting out the enemy. The program showed early signs of success, but it was immediately swallowed up by MACV, the military command in Vietnam. "FitzGerald lamented . . . that whenever CIA developed a promising, hand-tailored operation involving perhaps 100 Vietnamese, the U.S. military command wanted to take it over, increase the size ten-fold, and change a sensitive covert man-to-man effort into a battalion-size, mechanized, impersonal campaign," wrote Ray Cline, the agency's chief analyst. By the late 1960s, the effort at "pacification"—the so-called Phoenix program—would metastasize, claiming as many as 20,000 Vietnamese deaths by "counterterror" and assassination.[25]

In the mid-1960s, the Pentagon also muscled into the CIA's secret war in Laos. The agency had largely given up on its corrupt allies in the capital, but Vang Pao, the effective leader of the Hmong (or Meo) tribesmen, continued to be a useful American client. The conflict in the mountains had become basically a stalemate—the Pathet Lao and North Vietnamese advancing in the dry season, Vang Pao and his guerrillas retaking the territory during the rainy season. MACV was not satisfied. The Ho Chi Minh Trail, the North's vital supply line to the South, snaked through the Laotian jungle. The Pentagon wanted more pressure on the North Vietnamese and on the Ho Chi Minh Trail from Vang Pao's men. After dinner one night at Joe Alsop's in 1965, Paul Nitze, who was an assistant defense secretary, asked FitzGerald and his old Laos hand, Campbell "Zup" James, if the time had not come to turn over the Hmong tribesmen to the military. Absolutely not, they answered. The program would just swell with "advisers" until it ground to a halt. FitzGerald successfully resisted giving control to the military for a time, but the coldly efficient Ted Shackley, whom FitzGerald had brought over to Laos after running JMWAVE against Castro, gradually beefed up the secret army with Pentagon help. The Hmong were increasingly dragged into the larger war against the North Vietnamese. The ultimate result was tragedy: after the United States pulled out in 1973, the North Vietnamese created a Laotian gulag to "reeducate" the mountain people. Out of a population of about 350,000, as many as 100,000 died.[26]

FitzGerald was under considerable pressure to "penetrate" the North Vietnamese, to learn Hanoi's capabilities and intentions. The CIA did about as well with Hanoi as it had with the East Bloc or North Korea in Wisner's time. Agents were dropped into North Vietnam, where they vanished. At a meeting of the president's advisers on foreign intelligence in 1967, Clark Clifford spluttered, "I can't for the life of me see why this great country can't get a few spies into this pipsqueak little country." The CIA had better luck spying on its own ally. In 1966 the CIA put a bug inside the office of the prime minister, Nguyen Cao Ky. LBJ would read the transcripts and complain about his perfidious clients.[27]

The South Vietnamese government was also riddled with communist spies. (After the war it would turn out that the North had as many as 20,000 agents throughout the South.) Counterintelligence chief James Angleton wanted to set up a special counterintelligence unit in Saigon, but secretive as ever, he failed to inform the Saigon station chief, who loudly squawked. The flap ended up in FitzGerald's office. Angleton, as was his wont, refused to attend the meeting. Looking at Angleton's empty chair, FitzGerald acidly stated, "Ah, I see Mr. Angleton is here. Now we can begin."[28]

Angleton had always gone his own way. "Angleton used to recruit DCIs," said George Holmes. He titillated Dulles with Georgetown gossip; his accounts seemed so exact that he was suspected of planting bugs in his friends' dining rooms. His power derived in part from implicit blackmail. He claimed to know everything, and few were willing to find out whether he really did. Alice McIlvaine, Tracy Barnes's secretary, observed that everyone in the clandestine service came to the DD/P's office—except Angleton. "When Angleton called, Tracy ran to his office."[29]

FitzGerald found Angleton's eccentricities exotic. An amateur poet who bred orchids, Angleton once wrote FitzGerald a poem comparing him to a potter sculpting in raw clay.[30] FitzGerald wasn't much interested in counterintelligence. He described it as "nothing but a couple of guys in the backroom examining the entrails of chickens." At first, FitzGerald left Angleton alone to root about the agency for moles. Paul Garbler, one of Angleton's victims, said that he "holds FitzGerald accountable" for not stepping in to stop Angleton's witch-hunts. (A former Moscow station chief, Garbler was unjustly suspected by Angleton of working for the KGB and banished to a posting in Trinidad.) By the mid 1960s, Angleton had become hopelessly obsessed by a "Monster Plot" to plant a high-level mole in the CIA. The Soviet Division had great difficulty trying to recruit agents; Angleton rejected them as potential "dangles" sent by the KGB.

In the spring of 1967, FitzGerald realized that Angleton was out of control, that he would have to be reined in somehow. It exasperated FitzGerald that every time he tried to get his division chiefs together for a "squawk box" conversation in the late afternoon, Angleton was nowhere to be found. He wasn't sure whether Angleton was intentionally tweaking him or still out drinking lunch. More seriously, he understood that Angleton's paranoia was corrosive to the agency. He knew that he was going to have to go to Dick Helms to discuss Angleton, although he was doubtful that the director would back him up.[31]

FitzGerald was feeling intense pressure that winter and spring, from the outside as well as within the agency. A new wave of press stories threatened to expose the agency's long reach and further undermine its image. In February 1967, *Ramparts* magazine, a left-wing publication, revealed that the CIA had secretly funded the National Student Association as a front group in the battle to win the allegiance of young student leaders from Marxist- and KGB-controlled fronts. The American press picked up the trail and ran a large number of stories exposing the agency's various ties to foundations, think tanks, labor unions, and universities. The CIA's whole system of anticommunist fronts in Europe, Asia, and South America was essentially blown.[32]

When, in January 1967, FitzGerald first heard that *Ramparts* was about to break the story, his initial response was to run a covert operation against the left-wing magazine. That winter he ordered Edgar Applewhite to try to discredit the *Ramparts* editors any way he could. "I had all sorts of dirty tricks to hurt their circulation and financing," said Applewhite. "The people running *Ramparts* were vulnerable to blackmail. We had awful things in mind, some of which we carried off, though *Ramparts* fell of its own accord. We were not the least inhibited by the fact that the CIA had no internal security role in the United States." When Applewhite returned to brief FitzGerald on his dirty tricks (which he declined to describe twenty-five years later), the clandestine chief was bemused. "Eddie," he said, "you have a spot of blood on your pinafore."[33]

The most worrisome story surfaced in March 1967, when the CIA's plot to kill Castro leaked into a widely read newspaper column. Investigative reporters Drew Pearson and Jack Anderson reported on March 3 that "President Johnson is sitting on a political H-Bomb—an unconfirmed report that Sen. Robert Kennedy may have approved an assassination plot which then possibly backfired against his late brother." The source for the article was a lawyer, Edmund Morgan, who represented mobster Johnny Rosselli—one of the mafioso hired by the CIA in the bungled plot to murder Castro. Rosselli was trying to use his former employers in the CIA as a shield to fend off deportation by the Justice Department. Rosselli told Morgan that Santos Trafficante, who had run the mob's gambling operations in Havana, had sent a team to kill Castro. But the team had been "turned" by Castro—and dispatched back to the United States to kill Kennedy. Lyndon Johnson was appalled by this report. Ever conspiratorial, he had long believed that Kennedy's death had been caused by plotters, not a lone gunman. The president confided to his adviser Joseph Califano, "I will tell you something that will rock you. Kennedy was trying to kill Castro, but Castro got him first." Angrily, the president summoned CIA Director Helms. Johnson wanted to know the details—not just about Castro, but about the CIA's involvement, if any, in the deaths of Trujillo and Diem.

Helms ordered the CIA inspector general to prepare a report. When one of the IG's men approached Sam Halpern, FitzGerald's aide asked his boss what he should say. "Tell the truth," FitzGerald said. But, as earlier noted, FitzGerald fudged on his own account of his meeting with Rolando Cubela in Paris. The line of inquiry was uncomfortable for FitzGerald; it threatened to dredge up some unsettling questions. This was not the first time that FitzGerald had heard of a link between Cubela and Santos Trafficante. In 1965, FitzGerald had ordered his men to cut off contact with Cubela after his counterintelligence officer, Joseph Langosch, gave him some disturbing news. A Cuban exile, Eladio del Valle, had tipped the CIA that Cubela was secretly in league with Trafficante. The mobster was suspect; the CIA thought he was feeding information back to Castro in hopes of recovering his gambling dynasty. Langosch concluded that the Cubela plot "had been an insecure operation prior to the assassination [of Kennedy]." Shortly after del Valle tipped the CIA, his head was split open with an axe; no murderer was ever found.

FitzGerald was not the sort to open up about his fears, but he must have been anxious when the inspector general came calling. The many conspiracy theories notwithstanding, there is no evidence that the CIA itself somehow became sucked into a plot to kill JFK. Still, as he warily answered the questions of the CIA's internal investigators in the spring of 1967, FitzGerald may have wondered again whether the attempt to kill Castro had blown back on the Kennedys. Certainly, it had blown back on the CIA.[34]

The office of the DD/P was not much fun that spring of 1967: Angleton spinning his dark webs, the "Prudent Professionals" in ascendancy, the muckraking press exposing agency secrets, the president angrily demanding explanations. FitzGerald tried to do his duty. He felt "stuck" in Vietnam. "He was a good soldier, but he wasn't crazy about it," said Sam Halpern. "He knew by now it was too late for political action, for winning hearts and minds. This was a war. We had a huge station in Saigon, but he saw that what we had started had gotten out of control. He didn't really show his misgivings, but there was a notable lack of enthusiasm. He'd just shrug."[35]

Eventually, the strain became apparent. FitzGerald's family began to realize that he was losing some of his passion for work. Barbara Lawrence was saddened that her stepfather no longer read poetry or talked about his Asian adventures in the evening. Instead, he silently watched TV. *I Spy* was his favorite; "he thought it was a riot," said Lawrence. But "something was missing. Definitely, there was a heaviness in those years. The enthusiasm was gone."[36]

"I noticed his weariness," said his best friend from boyhood days, C. F. Adams. "I had a sense that he was not in a happy state of mind." Jim Critchfield, the Near East Division chief, felt that FitzGerald had lost some of the ebullience of his early years. He seemed less confident as DD/P than he had been as a division chief. "The pressure of the job got to him," said Critchfield. "He was frustrated."[37]

In June 1967 the CIA enjoyed a success when it predicted the quick victory of Israel over the Arabs in the Six-Day War. The Pentagon and State Department had been uncertain about Arab and Israeli intentions, but FitzGerald, in his elliptical, whimsical way, had told them, "You're watching the wrong hand of the magician." Roughly translated, he meant that the United States should watch the Soviets, who were encouraging the Arabs to attack in hopes of dragging the United States into another quagmire. FitzGerald had been prescient, yet he had to look for a role as the war broke out. The director, Dick Helms, met with the president in the White House, while the division chiefs like Critchfield had their own working group. FitzGerald was odd man out.[38]

To Critchfield, FitzGerald seemed physically ill; his face was "flushed and puffy." FitzGerald was, in fact, suffering from a circulatory problem, but he refused to cut back. "He was worried about his physical softness," said Adams. "He'd be stuck in his job all day, then want to play fierce tennis."

At moments FitzGerald acknowledged that he was coming to the end of his career. On the night of July 3, he talked into the evening with Charles Child, a painter and friend from Maine (brother-in-law of the chef Julia Child) about the prospect of retirement. He was fifty-six. He was "rather calmly facing" it, Child wrote Fitz-Gerald's wife, Barbara, though he understood that, for him, leaving the CIA would be "a little death—a diminishment."[39]

The next night the FitzGeralds hooked up with Tracy and Janet Barnes for a sweet evening of reminiscence. FitzGerald had been forced by Helms to fire his old friend the year before, though in the usual fashion not even their wives knew the true circumstances of Barnes's departure from the agency. The foursome recalled happier times, when families were young and careers still on the rise. In a letter to Barbara, Janet Barnes wrote of "slinging the Gallo wine back and forth between us as we talked of ambitions and serenity and life and love and the pursuit of happiness. Desie was wonderfully warm and gentle and responsive and gave us a wonderful time. When you've known people for a very long time—dating back to St. Mark's School in my case—you quite often fall into routines and reactions—with Desie this was never possible. He grew and changed and developed along the way."[40]

Shortly before noon on a burning hot July weekend three weeks later, FitzGerald stepped onto his tennis court in The Plains, Virginia, to play mixed doubles with his wife and the British ambassador, Sir Patrick Dean, and his wife. He was lathered in ointment to protect his skin from the sun, and he was wearing a hat; still, the temperature was 97 degrees. In midservice, FitzGerald collapsed with a massive heart attack. His wife tried to revive him with mouth-to-mouth resuscitation, but he was dead before he reached the hospital.[41]

In a posthumous service, President Johnson awarded FitzGerald the National Security Medal.[42] Bobby Kennedy came to the funeral, as did Vice President Hubert Humphrey and Averell Harriman, Kay Graham, Paul and Bunny Mellon, and a "cathedral-full of grieving men from the CIA," said Campbell James, all sweating through their dark suits. They sang "Once to Every Man and Nation Comes a Moment." Frances broke down on the steps outside the church; her father was laid to rest in a small cemetery in Georgetown, beneath a dogwood tree and a birdbath hewn from Maine granite. Desmond Jr., a fifteen-year old schoolboy, could not believe that his father was really dead. "It was a mystery caused by the CIA," he said. "It all seemed too remote."[43]

The condolences poured in to Barbara. "I have just received the breaking of hearts message. To me Des was a man of rare spiritual harmonies," wrote Angleton. No one better "exemplified the best Anglo-Saxon tradition of articulate and enlightened patriotism and disciplined public service," wrote John Bross. "I am quite overwhelmed," wrote Dick Bissell.[44]

There were letters from FitzGerald's friends abroad, including the president of Mexico, the chief of the South Korean intelligence service, and one from a Mr. A. K. Deku, the commissioner of police in Ghana, thanking FitzGerald for "two Mercedes-Benz and five Peugeot cars for police surveillance work." Sidney Gottlieb, the CIA scientist who mixed the poisons, wrote Barbara, "I have just returned from the funeral, which was impressive, yet which somehow was too standard for anybody as unique and individual as Des was." Frank Wisner Jr. wrote, "More than anyone I remember, Mr. Fitz was always the first to come forward and offer me his friendship and support and sage advice during the more difficult periods of Daddy's later years."[45]

Archie Roosevelt recalled best what FitzGerald had brought to his colleagues in the CIA. Roosevelt had been in a funk about his career and the future of the CIA in the mid-1960s until he had gone to work as head of the African Division. He immediately felt the lift from FitzGerald's elevation to chief of the clandestine service. "I noticed a change in the atmosphere of that sterile, institution-like building where we spent our working day. The whole place was charged with dynamism. Formerly boring meetings became alive under the goad of his inquiring mind, and conflicting ideas flew back and forth. Now," Roosevelt concluded, "the fun is gone."[46]

AT HIS thirtieth Yale reunion in June 1963, Tracy Barnes had stayed up all night with some of his classmates from Scroll and Key, talking about the Bay of Pigs. "We had too much to drink, and Tracy opened up," recalled Andrew Rogers. "He was very cross about the Kennedys. He felt that he had unfairly taken the blame, that Kennedy had let him down." Dawn was breaking over Harkness Quadrangle by the time Barnes had finished holding forth to his fellow Keysmen.[47]

Yale had been the top of the world for Tracy Barnes as an undergraduate; it was perhaps natural for him to return to Yale for solace and reaffirmation after the CIA. Yale's president, Kingman Brewster, hired Barnes in the fall of 1966 as a personal assistant. He hoped that Barnes, with his old school charm, would pacify the alumni, who were restless about Brewster's liberal activism. Barnes was hugely relieved to move from Washington to New Haven. "Crept from darkness into light," he wrote in a note to himself that fall, "darkness of Washington into brilliant light of New Haven." Not surprisingly, Barnes quickly grew bored with chatting up Old Blues. Ever since his days starting up the Urban League in Providence after the war, Barnes had been interested in improving race relations and was more easygoing than many whites in his personal dealings with blacks. Yale's fraught relations with the local community gave Barnes a chance to pursue this interest.[48]

New Haven was one of the American cities struck by urban rioting in the summer of 1967, and militant black groups eyed the university as both a target and a source of patronage. After Martin Luther King's assassination threatened more turmoil in April 1968, Brewster made Barnes his ambassador to the inner city. Barnes was a superb envoy. "He looked like Yale," said Jonathan Fanton, a Yale administrator at the time. "Blacks didn't want to talk to another black. Tracy was the real Yale. He had that patrician's ability to relate to all people without giving the feel of talking down to them." Barnes routinely walked the streets in areas where most whites wouldn't go. "He wanted to be in touch with the toughest, most radical blacks," said Peter Almond, a graduate student who ran the Yale community relations program.[49]

Acting as peacemaker to the local militants appealed to Barnes's sense of romance and idealism. Rebe Garafalo, another graduate student who worked with him, recalled that Barnes "would call meetings to negotiate at midnight at the Dixwell Community Center in the ghetto. There'd be not a soul there. A door would be left slightly ajar, you'd go up a back stairs, and there'd be a card table and four chairs, underneath a bare light bulb. You had the sense you were being interrogated by a professional." Garafalo was taken with Barnes's spooky daring, although he observed, "There was no real reason for it. We could have met in the Yale dining room for supper. He just liked clandestine operations."

The more militant blacks tried to intimidate Barnes, once bursting into his office, knocking over chairs and papers. Someone threw an ashtray past his head. Barnes was completely unruffled. His cool bemused and gave heart to other Yale administrators, who were less insouciant about the almost daily disruptions. While Kingman Brewster was having his portrait painted in his office in Woodbridge Hall, a tremendous clatter upstairs startled the artist. "Oh, that's just Tracy having his morning meeting with the blacks," said Brewster.[50]

Barnes's most demanding adversary in the black community was Freddie Harris, a fierce militant who on one occasion, as Harris

himself put it, "tried to choke the dean of the medical school."
Unable to mau-mau Barnes, Harris came to admire him. "I was a
kidder, a joker, I'd say 'nigger' around white people. He just looked
at me and saw there was nothing there," said Harris, who later
became a minister in Detroit. "We went to his house, a fine house.
I told him I was going to sell a few brothers to get the money to
buy his house. He didn't want to buy any brothers, but he wasn't
laughing at us, he was laughing with us. He drank with us. We'd
try to shake him, but he didn't seem afraid."[51]

Barnes had long been a liberal, in his own fashion. Yale was
debating whether to admit women in 1968. Barnes's secretary,
Diana Gabriel, listened in disgust as two other administrators said
they wanted to admit only attractive women. Barnes piped up,
"Oh no, we have to have all kinds. Who are we going to get for the
unattractive men?" At first Gabriel was wary of her tweedy boss
with his society accent, but she decided that he was "a man of
honor and integrity. He had principles and ethics. He cared about
his family." She was especially struck by his affection for Janet.
"He called Mrs. Barnes 'my bride'; he was beautiful to her," said
Gabriel.[52]

Barnes generally did not discuss his career in the agency, but he
unwound a little as time went on. Gabriel asked him why men join
the CIA, and he answered, with a straight face, "Because they
crave constant danger and for the sex." After his old mentor Allen
Dulles died in 1969, he told Jonathan Fanton that the CIA needed
to "go back to where it started, when it was a very idealistic
enterprise." He lamented the new order, criticizing Richard Helms
as a poor substitute for Dulles. Yet he was conflicted about what
the agency had tried to do under the old order. In long if somewhat
guarded conversations with Peter Almond, he "talked of having
grown weary of the direction of the agency. By the time he got to
Yale, I think he was fed up with the CIA, in a profound way. I
think it killed him in the end," said Almond. "He was sick about it.
He did not speak directly, he was elliptical, but clearly he was
talking about assassinations. He was spiritually worn."[53]

He was also physically worn. His athletic prowess and ferocious
pleasure at games masked a history of angina and other minor
heart ailments. In 1969, when Barnes was still only fifty-eight, he
had a series of small strokes that made his arms go numb. Typically, he did not tell his family; he did not want to worry Janet. In
June 1970, Diana Gabriel recalled, he summoned her to his office

"and started asking me to do things he had never asked me to do before—to close things out, to finish things off. I knew something was wrong. I was scared and upset. He was calm and gentlemanly like he always was. After a while he just got up and walked out of the office." She never saw him again. Barnes had a serious stroke that night that left him bedridden for months, and for a short time, speechless.

He recovered slowly. At his house in Saunderstown, Rhode Island, he learned to speak English again in the fall of 1970 by watching *Sesame Street* with his granddaughter, Maud. He began reading Kurt Vonnegut novels, captivated by their "hard-edge sentimentality," said his former son-in-law, John Casey. In *Slaughterhouse Five*, he particularly liked the fantasy of the planet Thermidor. "Maud and I are going there," he announced. He confused cards at bridge, and his sense of direction was shaken by the stroke, but not his headlong enthusiasm. On the Fourth of July 1971 he took some friends and grandchildren out to an island in Narragansett Bay for a picnic. The fog rolled in, and Janet became anxious about getting the children home. The weather thickened; "we were all nervous," said John Fanton, the Yale administrator, who was a houseguest. "Tracy slammed down the throttle and turned back to Janet, who was sitting in the stern. He gave a big A-OK sign. She beamed, reassured. I asked him, 'Do you know where we're going?' He shrugged. 'No. Keep a watch out.' " The boat roared off in the wrong direction and almost ran into a warship at Quonset Point Naval Base.[54]

Driving back from a golf game (he still shot in the high 70s), he was pulled over for speeding in his beat-up old Dodge Dart. "You were going seventy," said the policeman. "I was not going a mile over sixty thousand," said Barnes, grinning amiably. The policeman narrowed his eyes. "Are you a wise guy?" No, Barnes cheerfully protested, he was only going sixty thousand miles an hour. The policeman asked if he'd been drinking, but finally Barnes's stroke-addled charm put the policeman at ease; he let him go with a warning.

There was, in the last years of his life, a "season of reconciliation," said his daughter Jane. "He was full of rue. It was clear he had been really thinking. He would say things like, 'History isn't moral, is it?' " His social conscience grew. He became indignant about "rich nations eating up poor nations," and urged Groton to take blacks and Scroll and Key to take women. "He became strangely mellow," said John Casey. "He'd contemplate the woods and be very sweet." He grew closer to his wife, Janet.

On February 18, 1972, he awoke in New York, where he was visiting his brother, Courty, with bad chest pains. He got on a train to New London and drove to Saunderstown, Rhode Island. He picked up his beloved dogs at the vet's and headed home. As he opened the front door, he dropped dead of a massive stroke.

At the small Episcopalian church in Saunderstown, the pews were packed with Newport society folk, former spooks, Old Blues (including almost all of Barnes's surviving classmates from Scroll and Key), and a large number of black people—civil rights activists from New Haven and Providence and ordinary townspeople who remembered Barnes's easy and open manner. They sang the "Battle Hymn of the Republic" and adjourned to Janet's for lunch. "You can't tell the difference between a funeral and a wedding," said Janet's sister. WASP rituals, like the people who attend them, can blur together in a comforting sameness, but this one was a little different, thought Marshall Dodge, Tracy's cousin and old friend for a half century, because everyone there could feel Barnes's fierce joy, even after he was gone.

Following Episcopalian tradition, there were no eulogies. Two decades after he died, Barnes's companion from the British SIS, John Bruce Lockhart, remembered him this way: "Tracy," he said, "was born out of his time. I sometimes used to see him as an Elizabethan. He was an optimist, a gallant, a romantic. His role in the Bay of Pigs should have been cutlass in hand, leading a thousand tough U.S. Marines at dead of night, with the clear objective of hanging Castro from the nearest tree."[55]

RICHARD BISSELL hung on, long after his comrades had passed away. He had been "badly spoiled" by his career in government, and he "missed the agency," he said in 1993, a year before he died. He got a job at United Technologies in Hartford in 1964, but he was "ineffective," he said. "I wrote papers about acquisitions, but we didn't make any." In 1974, when he was sixty-four, he was "forced into retirement. They wanted the office space," he recalled. "I wasn't worth what they were paying me."[56]

At home, his youngest son, Thomas, who had been born in 1959, the year Bissell became head of the clandestine service, prodded his father to tell him about his career at the CIA. "He was hesitant," said Tom Bissell. His daughter, Ann, recalled her father speaking "with modesty and pain. He didn't want to glorify what he had done, and he could live with the consequences. That's the way you played the game. He was resigned, but not really bitter." She saw no sign that he brooded or felt any moral regrets. She thought her father "had just turned the switch. He simply decided not to deal with it."[57]

Bissell had managed to remain out of the public eye for almost his entire career, except for a brief flurry of publicity right after the Bay of Pigs. But after the Watergate scandal emboldened the press and Congress to question executive authority, the agency's secrets began to leak out. In the summer of 1975, Bissell was summoned to Washington to testify before the newly created Senate Select Committee on Intelligence. Under Frank Church of Idaho, a senator with presidential ambitions, the committee was investigating the CIA's assassination plots, among other abuses contained in what CIA officials referred to as "the family jewels," a 693-page recitation of the agency's dirty tricks over the years. Testifying behind closed doors, Bissell had trouble recalling the details of the assassination plots and was caught in a number of contradictions by the committee's lawyers. Most of the senators were hostile. "How many murders did you contemplate?" demanded Senator Howard Baker of Tennessee. Bissell protested, "Well, Senator . . ." "Assassinations, I'm sorry," Baker corrected. Bissell tried, in his courtly way, to explain the concept of plausible deniability, but he was frustrated by his inquisitors' inability to grasp the concept. ("We understood it all right," said one committee member, Senator Gary Hart of Colorado, many years later. "We just didn't agree with it.") "It was a very unpleasant experience," said Bissell.[58]

At the family dinner table, he let down a little and allowed himself to complain about his interrogation. "He wasn't emotional about it, but he thought the questions were just plain stupid," said Tom. "He figured, what's the point?"

Bissell read ancient history and mystery novels; he went to the opera and traveled abroad; he did a considerable amount of charitable work. He missed his yawl, the *Sea Witch*, which he had sold in the late 1960s after he grew too old to handle her. ("Mom finally said 'enough,' " said his daughter, Ann. "She hated it.") Restlessly, Bissell walked up and down trails and mountains in Maine. "He was always way out ahead of everyone else," said Mrs. Bissell. In the evenings he would pull out his old charts and retrace his cruises—the storms, the close scrapes, the dead-reckoning land-falls in the fog.

In 1991, when he was past his eightieth birthday, he began to write his memoirs. He wanted neither to boast nor to apologize, but to leave a record for historians and for his family. The writing went slowly. The manuscript, which he finished a few months before his death, is sober and honest, as far as it goes, but not personally re-vealing. Jonathan Lewis, a young historian who had signed on to help Bissell, pressed him to deal with the moral issues involved with his work. After some thought Bissell wrote, "My philosophy during the last two or three years in the Agency very definitely was that the end justified the means and I wasn't going to be held back. Be-ginning shortly after I left, however, I came to believe with hind-sight that it had been a great mistake to have involved the Mafia in any kind of assassination attempt. I must admit this is partly a moral judgment, but it is also a pragmatic judgment."

Bissell simply did not want to deal with the moral question, said Lewis. "He equivocated. He felt he should feel that way, but I'm not convinced he did. His greatest regret, I think, was that hiring the Mafia was ineffective."

Bissell also had difficulty writing about Tracy Barnes. He felt he had to say something about his old friend, but he did not know what. What he wrote was painful to him, and it may reveal more about Bissell than Barnes—a hidden resentment from school days, perhaps, or a final, though unacknowledged, reluctance to accept full responsibility for his fate. He saved the chore for last, when he had essentially finished his manuscript and knew he was dying. "My deputy Tracy Barnes was a close friend and colleague, and our interaction was always friendly and agreeable," his passage on Barnes begins. But he goes on to say that Barnes led him astray. "I think I overestimated in those years the degree to which Tracy really embodied the philosophy of the clandestine service. I knew some fair and neutral colleagues felt that Tracy knew little more about tradecraft than I did. Some might argue that to have me rely on Tracy's judgment to support my own views was relying on ignorance to support ignorance. This," he added, "is a rather un-kind judgment on my part and perhaps very unfair."

On February 7, 1994, Bissell died in his sleep beside his wife. He did not want an elaborate burial. The only purpose of a funeral, he said, was "to get together with old friends and go off and have a few." On a sunny early spring day, his friends and children gathered by his grave to praise his sense of adventure and public service. His ashes were buried next to his mother, on the banks of a river running through the Connecticut countryside down to the sea.[59]

RICHARD BISSELL is an obscure figure today. His death was hardly front-page news; he is remembered, if at all, as the bureaucrat who took the fall for the Bay of Pigs. But he was much more. It is not a stretch to say that he personified American hubris in the postwar era. He may have been a discreet civil servant, but he accrued more real power to affect events around the world than any elected or appointed official save the president. Old CIA hands liked to refer to the DD/P as "the second most powerful man in government," and in Bissell's case, they weren't exaggerating. He believed, unselfconsciously, in America as empire, and he saw it as his job to advance American interests, preferably unencumbered by elected politicians or other bureaucrats. He did this brilliantly and sometimes recklessly. The Marshall Plan and the U-2 spy plane were in no small measure his doing. So were the assassination plots against Castro and the Bay of Pigs. The former did much to guarantee the security of the West; the latter helped create the Cuban Missile Crisis, which brought the world to the brink. It is a measure of Bissell's power as well as his self-confidence that he was able to do much of this in secret.

ACKNOWLEDGMENTS

WHEN I FIRST approached the CIA in the winter of 1992 looking for access to documents, I did not know what to expect. CIA operations are essentially exempt from the Freedom of Information Act. Still, the Cold War was over, and there was some talk of opening up archives of the early days. I was pleasantly surprised at an initial meeting with agency officials to learn that I could get access to some files under certain conditions. The conditions, however, were onerous: I would have to sign a secrecy oath allowing the agency to review my manuscript before publication. This I could not agree to do.

For nearly two years we negotiated. Finally, through my extremely able lawyer, Sven Holmes, a former staff director and general counsel of the Senate Intelligence Committee who was a partner at Williams & Connolly and has since become a federal judge in Oklahoma, an arrangement was worked out to protect my manuscript from censorship while still giving me access to certain files, mostly the CIA's own secret histories of its different divisions and their activities. The secrecy agreement I signed applies only to those materials I saw in the agency files. It does not apply to my reporting from other sources, including former agency officials. In the end, the agency was reasonable about letting me use the information from its own files. It objected only to the use of classified cryptonyms and information that would reveal "sources and methods" in a way that could genuinely harm national security. No attempt was made to block the publication of information just because it was unflattering or embarrassing to the agency.

I want to thank several agency officials for their help through a protracted and difficult process. David Gries, the former head of the Study for the Center of Intelligence, was a consistent supporter of providing access, as was his successor, Brian Latell, and Joe DeTrani, the former CIA spokesman. Ken McDonald, the head of the CIA's History Staff, graciously made available his resources, and Michael Warner of his staff was an enormous help locating material and serving as a guide. Bill McNair, Information Review Officer of the Directorate of Operations, and George Jameson of the General Counsel's Office were patient and fair-minded throughout.

Many former CIA officials helped me with their recollections. I am grateful, in particular, to Sam Halpern, Thomas Parrott, Tom Braden, James McCargar, Franklin Lindsay, Edgar Applewhite, and John Bruce Lockhart (of the British Secret Intelligence Service) for reading my manuscript and catching errors large and small. The families of my subjects were also helpful and patient with my queries, although they by no means agree with all my conclusions. My thanks especially go to Frances FitzGerald, Barbara Lawrence, Ann Bissell, Jane Barnes, Tracy Barnes Jr., Janet Barnes Lawrence, Wendy Hazard, Ellis Wisner, Frank Wisner, and Jean Lindsey. Three authors of CIA books who generously helped me are Burton Hersh, Peter Grose, and Anthony Cave Brown. I was fortunate to spend several days talking to the late Richard Bissell about his extraordinary life and career; my thanks to his wife, Annie, for her hospitality. I am grateful as well to Jonathan Lewis and Fran Pudlo for showing me Bissell's memoirs, unpublished at the time, expected out in the spring of 1996 from Yale University Press.

For the first year of my research, I had an able assistant in Adam Wolfberg, with more assists down the road from Gail Tacconelli, Steve Tuttle, and Josh Lawrence. At *Newsweek*, my colleagues Ann McDaniel and Dorothy Wickenden read the manuscript with a discerning eye. They are great editors; I have been lucky to work with them every day. Thanks, too, to my bosses Maynard Parker and Rich Smith, who give me the time to write books and don't make me feel too guilty about it. My old friend and editor Stephen Smith gave me wise counsel as always. My wife, Oscie, is, and has always been, patient, good-humored, and honest about my writing. My daughters, Louisa and Mary, helped me more than they know.

This is my third book with the one and only Alice Mayhew of Simon & Schuster; it is an honor to work with her. Thanks, too, to Eric Steel and Elizabeth Stein at S&S for their careful editing suggestions, and, once again, to my agent, Amanda Urban, who makes my writing possible.

AUTHOR'S NOTE

In connection with my research for this book, I received access to the following files of the Central Intelligence Agency:

Personnel Files (Office of Personnel)

C. Tracy Barnes
Richard Bissell Jr.
Desmond FitzGerald
Frank Wisner

Clandestine Services Histories (History Staff)

CSHP 1: [CLASSIFIED], 1961–1964
CSHP 2: CIA-Meo Activities, 1960–1964
CSHP 5: Impressions of Operations [CLASSIFIED] Laos, May 1962–March 1964
CSHP 6: The Hungarian Revolution [CLASSIFIED], 23 October–4 November 1956
CSHP 15: Funding Covert Operations, 1960–1964
CSHP 24: Report on Berlin Operations Base, January 1946–March 1948
CSHP 31: The Establishment and Early Development of the Office of Policy Coordination, 1948–October 1949
CSHP 36: Operational Program Against North Vietnam, 1960–1964
CSHP 44: The Inspection and Review Staff, DD/P, October 1952–April 1959
CSHP 52: [CLASSIFIED]
CSHP 53: Covert Support to Indonesian Revolutionary Government, 1957–1958
CSHP 56: [CLASSIFIED], 1950–1956
CSHP 98: The Illegal Border Crossing Program, 1946–1959

CSHP 105: **[CLASSIFIED]**
CSHP 121: **[CLASSIFIED]**
CSHP 150: The Berlin Tunnel Operation, 1952–1956
CSHP 163: The Evolution of Ground Paramilitary Activities at the Staff Level, October 1949–September 1955
CSHP 183: Paramilitary Ground Activities at the Staff Level, 15 September 1955–31 December 1961
CSHP 194: Major Policy Authorization for the Conduct of Covert Paramilitary Activities by CIA, 1948–1966
CSHP 195: The Origins of CIA's Clandestine Organization in the Far East, 1945–1952
CSHP 196: The 1967 Crisis in Covert Action Operations: The *Ramparts* Exposure
CSHP 208: Overthrow of Premier Mossadeq of Iran, November 1952–August 1953
CSHP 210: The Chinese Third Force Project, 1950–1953
CSHP 213: FI Staff Relations with Department of State and with Ambassadors, 1957–1967
CSHP 225: **[CLASSIFIED]**
CSHP 228: Office of Policy Coordination, 1948–1952
CSHP 267: **[CLASSIFIED]**
CSHP 279: The Third Force Effort, 1949–1953
CSHP 324: Western Hemisphere Division, 1946–1965
CSHP 335: Covert Action Operations: Soviet Russia Division, 1950–1968
CSHP 336: Development of Paramilitary Contingency Cadres, 1948–1971

DCI History Staff Publications

DCI 5: Internal Audit of the CIA, 1947–1967
DCI 8: Jack Pfeiffer's Bay of Pigs history
Roberta Knapp: *The First Thirty Years*
Nick Cullather: *Operation* **[CLASSIFIED]** (Guatemala)
Tom Ahearn: *CIA and Military Government in Vietnam*, Vol. 2
Mary McAuliffe: *A Secret World* (classified; Official Use Only)
———— "The *Ramparts* Revelations of 1967"
Hathaway and Smith: *Richard Helms as DCI*
Michael Warner: *Hearts & Minds* (draft)
———— "Picking Up the Pieces" (Bay of Pigs investigation, draft)
———— " 'A Fairly Sophisticated Point of View' " (Official Use Only)

Kevin Ruffner: Untitled first volume of his work on CIA
                    involvement with and searches for former
                    Nazis

Rhinehart, James: "Covert Action in High Altitudes,"
                    Studies in Intelligence, Spring 1976 (Tibet)

Miscellaneous Documents (various offices)

Kirkpatrick to McCone, "Evaluation of Components of the Agency," 13 November 1961, in Executive Registry Job 80B01676R, box 18, folder 10.

Bay of Pigs IG investigation and DD/P rejoinder, with related correspondence, all bound as HS/CSG-2640.

Wisner to Breckinridge, "Berlin Congress for Cultural Freedom: Activities of Melvin Lasky," 8 August 1950, in opi-42, 78-01614R, box 1, folder 4.

Robinette to Wisner, "Recommendations for Recording Equipment in Office of DD/P," 25 May 1956, in opi-40, 79-01228A, box 53, folder 8.

Sherman Kent's joke memo to Wisner on brainwashing, 1953 (mistakenly classified TS), in opi-64, Project Artichoke records.

Barnes to King, 20 January 1960, in HS/CSG-2632Z.

Bissell to King, "Goon Squads," 10 November 1960, in HS/CSG-2632AA.

DD/P Watch Office cable action log for DD/P trips, 1956, in 79-01228A, box 45.

Frank Wisner's President's Board of Consultants for Intelligence file, 1956, in 79-01228A, box 45.

Frank Wisner's relations with the press file, 1956, in 79-01228A, box 45.

Dulles to Haney, "Program [CLASSIFIED] General Plan of Action," 9 December 1953, HS/CSG-2200.

King to Dulles, "Guatemala—General Plan of Action," 11 September 1953; also Haney, "2d Interim Report," 15 March 1954, in opi-57, 79-01025A, box 1.

Arthur Jacobs's recollections of Frank Wisner, HS/HC-544.

Desmond FitzGerald, "Memorandum for the Record: American Participation in Support of General Li Mi's Guerrilla Activities in Yunnan," 10 August 1951.

History Staff "Oral History Archives" (interviews)

Richard Bissell
Douglas Blaufarb
William Colby
James Critchfield

Andrew Goodpaster
Richard Helms
Frank Lindsay
David Murphy

To the extent any material in this book reflects information from these files, that material is specifically identified in the text or the footnotes. The use of such material is covered by a secrecy agreement with the CIA and as a result was subject to prepublication review. The standard for this review was whether such material, if published, could result in the unauthorized disclosure of intelligence sources and methods that reasonably could be expected to damage the national security. All other material in the book is based on my reporting from other than CIA files, including former CIA officials, books, and documents in public archives. It is not covered by any secrecy agreement.

NOTES

I HAVE USED my chapter notes to flesh out the text in a number of places where I felt the material would slow the story down, but could still be of interest to students of intelligence or to the curious reader. Although much of the written record of the agency remains classified, almost all of the agency veterans I contacted spoke on the record. Oral history can be unreliable, but I was able to check at least the basic facts against the CIA's own official histories, which I was allowed to examine under the conditions described in the Author's Note. There are no unattributed quotes in this book. I have cited all of my sources by name, with a single exception at Chapter Twenty-One, note 12.

Key to Frequently Cited Sources

Alleged Assassination Plots	U.S. Senate, *Alleged Assassination Plots Involving Foreign Leaders: An Interim Report of the Select Committee to Study Government Operations with Respect to Intelligence Activities* (Washington, D.C.: U.S. Government Printing Office, 1975)
Bissell, *Memoirs*	Richard Bissell with Jonathan Lewis and Frances Pudlo, *Memoirs* (unpublished ms., courtesy Bissell family; scheduled for publication by Yale University Press, spring 1996)
Book IV	Book IV, *Final Report of the Select Committee to Study Government Operations with Respect to Intelligence Activities* (Washington, D.C.: U.S. Government Printing Office, 1976)
Book V	Senate Select Committee on Intelligence, Book V, *The Investigation of the Assassination of President John F. Kennedy: Performance of the Intel-*

ligence Agencies (Washington, D.C.: U.S. Government Printing Office, 1976)

CIA *Bay of Pigs*	DCI History 8: Unfinished history of the Bay of Pigs by Jack Pfeiffer
CIA *Bay of Pigs IG Report*	Bay of Pigs Inspector General investigation and DD/P rejoinder, all bound as HS/CSG-2640
CIA *Guatemala*	Nick Cullather, *Operation* [CLASSIFIED] (Washington, D.C.: CIA History Staff, 1994)
CIA *OPC History I*	Clandestine Services History 31: *The Establishment and Early Development of the Office of Policy Coordination, 1948–October 1949*
CIA *OPC History II*	Clandestine Services History 228: *Office of Policy Coordination, 1948–1952*
CIA *Paramilitary History*	Clandestine Services History 163: *The Evolution of Ground Paramilitary Activities at the Staff Level, October 1949–September 1955*
CIA *Soviet Operations*	Clandestine Services History 335: *Covert Action Operations: Soviet Russia Division, 1950–1968*
Committee on Assassinations, *Report*	Select Committee on Assassinations, U.S. House of Representatives, *Report* (Washington, D.C.: U.S. Government Printing Office, 1979)
Dulles	Wayne Jackson, *Allen Welsh Dulles as Director of Central Intelligence, 26 February 1953–29 November 1961* (Washington, D.C.: CIA History Staff, 1994)
Kennedy Records	Church Committee records declassified at the National Archives
"Report on Plots"	Inspector General of the CIA, "Report on Plots to Assassinate Fidel Castro, May 23, 1967, declassified in July 1994, National Archives

Introduction

1. Campbell James, former OSS and CIA official.
2. Although Wisner became deputy director/plans in 1951, the merger of OPC and another branch of the Directorate of Plans, the Office of Special Operations (OSO), was not accomplished until 1952.
3. Susan Mary Alsop. The romantic idealism was expressed by a number of sources. Cord Meyer, who worked for the CIA for more than two decades in senior jobs, told me, "We really thought of ourselves as waging a struggle that would decide the fate of the world for a long, long time."
4. William Colby and Peter Forbath, *Honorable Men: My Life in the CIA* (New York: Simon & Schuster, 1978). Intelligence work was "something different," outside the ordinary realm of the law. As author Mark Riebling notes in *Wedge: The Secret War Between the FBI and CIA* (New York: Knopf, 1994), p. 86, the men who ran the CIA thought they were good, and "good men can work in the moral twilight without becoming evil." See also David Atlee Phillips, *Secret Wars Diary: My Adventures in Combat, Espionage Operations, and Covert Action* (Bethesda, Md.: Stone Trail Press, 1989), p. 66.
5. Bissell and Barnes were especially liberal. Before the Bay of Pigs, Bissell remarked to E. Howard Hunt, "They don't know it, but we're the real revolutionaries." E. Howard Hunt, *Give Us This Day* (New York: Arlington House, 1973), p. 83.
6. Edgar Applewhite, McGeorge Bundy.
7. John Bruce Lockhart.
8. Thomas Powers, *The Man Who Kept the Secrets: Richard Helms and the CIA* (New York: Pocket Books, 1979), p. 5. Powers's book, written after the Church Committee investigations, was the first to really get inside the personalities and institutional culture of the CIA in the 1950s and 1960s.
9. Janet Barnes Lawrence.
10. Carleton Swift.

Chapter One: Crusader

1. Robin Winks, *Cloak and Gown: Scholars in the Secret War, 1939–1961* (New York: William Morrow, 1987), p. 54; Frank Lindsay, James McCarger, Lawrence Houston. Winks's book focuses on the ties between the agency and academe (especially Yale, which sent more than forty members of the class of '43 into intelligence work), but it is also a very readable general history of the agency.
2. Winks, pp. 52–55; Vint Lawrence.
3. Winks, pp. 20–21.

4. William Colby and Peter Forbath, *Honorable Men: My Life in the CIA* (New York: Simon & Schuster, 1978), p. 73.

5. John Ranelagh, *The Agency: The Rise and Decline of the CIA* (New York: Simon & Schuster, 1986), p. 27 (the line about gentlemen opening mail, often attributed to Stimson, actually was stated by his coauthor, McGeorge Bundy); "fair play": G.J.A. O'Toole, *Honorable Treachery: A History of U.S. Intelligence, Espionage, and Covert Action from the American Revolution to the CIA* (New York: Atlantic Monthly Press, 1991), p. 422. Ranelagh's book is a quite exhaustive overview of the agency, the most comprehensive I saw.

6. Jean Lindsey, Charles Reeder, Fred Reeder, Gardiner Green, Wendy Hazard.

7. David Wilburn Higgs, "Eastman, Gardiner and Company and the Cohay Camps: A Mississippi Lumber Empire, 1890–1937," M.A. thesis, Mississippi College, 1991, courtesy Jean Lindsey.

8. School prayer on plaque in chapel at Woodberry Forest; Merritt Cootes, Robert Winston; Woodberry School Catalogue, 1927–28; "The Fir Tree" (1928 yearbook). Courtesy Richard F. Barnhardt, assistant headmaster.

9. U.Va. described: Raymond Bice, Joseph Vaughan, Arthur Jacobs. Wisner's early days: Burton Hersh, *The Old Boys: The American Elite and the Origins of the CIA* (New York: Scribner's, 1992), pp. 188–95; London station chief: p. 423. Hersh's book is deeply reported and was an important source to me, especially on Frank Wisner. He made good use of his many interviews with former agency officials.

10. At Carter Ledyard, "Frank was an earnest man, a worrier who fussed over papers. He was not courtly. He was harassed, anxious to get on with it," said Henry Hyde, whose family was a Carter Ledyard client. Elizabeth Graham. See Francis Ellis and Edward F. Clark Jr., *A Brief History of Carter, Ledyard & Milburn* (New York: Peter Randall, 1988). For a good description of the freewheeling and sometimes amateurish ways of the OSS, see Ranelagh, pp. 38, 51, 57, 65, 68; MacFarland: Hersh, pp. 195–96 and Arthur Cox (who was with Wisner).

11. Rica Georgescu; Wisner's cables are in the OSS files in the National Archives and in the papers of Anthony Cave Brown at Georgetown University (Brown used them for his biography of William Donovan, *The Last Hero* [New York: Times Books, 1982], pp. 670–80). Wisner's cryptonym is Typhoid. See RG 226, Entry 154, Box 26, "Original Wisner Reports"; Entry 108, Box 85, "Russian Plots to Communize Romania"; see Hersh, pp. 482–85.

12. Tanda Caradja, Wendy Hazard.

13. Beverly Bowie, *Operation Bughouse* (New York: Dodd, Mead, 1947);

Robert Bishop, and E. S. Crayfield, *Russia Astride the Balkans* (New York: Robert McBride, 1948), p. 101.

14. Tanda Caradja. On January 12, 1945, Wisner personally witnessed the loading of twenty-seven boxcars of Romanians by the Russians. National Archives, RG 226, Entry 108, Box 85. In the OSS files there is no written record of Wisner's interventions.

15. Frank Wisner Jr. In March 1965, seven months before he committed suicide, Wisner wrote his own account of Romania in a sixteen-page "personal and confidential" file given to me by a friend of his, Burke Wilkinson. Wisner writes that his Balkan experience "had a profound and lasting influence upon my views of Soviet policy and contributed substantially to the shaping of my low evaluation of the prospects for a peaceful settlement of the post-war problem." The memo is formal and not very revealing, except when he discusses what happened to the Romanians who worked for him—who were all imprisoned "and in some cases" executed, except for a few who managed to hide or escape to the West. He records how he was later told that his secretary "had committed suicide by defenestration, rather than choose between the betrayal of her American friends or [sic] deportation to a Soviet POW camp."

16. Bishop and Crayfield, p. 108.

17. Robert Lee Wolff, *The Balkans in Our Time* (Cambridge, Mass.: Harvard University. Press, 1956), pp. 278–83.

18. Tanda Caradja.

19. R. Harris Smith, *OSS: the Secret History of America's First Central Intelligence Agency* (Berkeley, Calif.: University of California Press, 1972), p. 241. An excellent history.

20. Hersh, p. 159.

21. Ranelagh, pp. 80, 98; General William Quinn.

22. Peter Sichel. On his first night home, Wisner and his wife, Polly, went out to dinner to the home of old friends, John and Elizabeth Graham. "Polly wanted to go home," but Wisner was wound up and wanted to stay and drink and talk, said Elizabeth Graham. He was unable to really relax on a trip with the Grahams to Jamaica to get some sun that winter. He wrote Tanda Caradja that he was being pressed to rejoin his firm, but that he did not like New York and was considering a job in government.

23. William Corson, *The Armies of Ignorance: The Rise of the American Intelligence Empire* (New York: Dial, 1977), p. 485. An inside account, but not always reliable. SSU approach to Wisner: Colonel David Holloway to S.B.L. Penrose, August 21, 1946. Wisner said he was willing, "provided he could be sufficiently persuaded of the permanence and freedom of operation of the CIG." Frank Wisner Personnel File, CIA.

24. Walter Isaacson and Evan Thomas, *The Wise Men: Six Friends and the World They Made* (New York: Simon & Schuster, 1986), pp. 387–418.

25. Peter Grose says Wisner was advised by Allen Dulles to "find an inconspicuous slot in the government and start building up a network for political warfare from within." Grose ms., *Gentleman Spy: The Life of Allen Dulles*, p. 424. Grose's manuscript, a first-rate biography that he graciously shared with me in manuscript in the summer of 1994, was published in November 1994 by Houghton Mifflin. My citations are from the manuscript.

26. Arthur Darling, *The Central Intelligence Agency: An Instrument of Government to 1950* (College Station, Pa.: Penn State University Press 1990), pp. 250–53. The State-War-Navy Coordinating Committee (SWNCC) became the State–Army–Navy–Air Force Coordinating Committee (SANACC) on November 4, 1947.

27. Hersh, p. 224.

28. Christopher Simpson, *Blowback* (New York: Simon & Schuster, 1988), pp. 96–106. Simpson made thorough use of SANACC documents he found in the National Archives.

29. Susan Mary Alsop, *To Marietta from Paris, 1945–60* (New York: Doubleday, 1975), p. 139.

30. Townsend Hoopes.

31. Tish Alsop, Elizabeth Graham, Ella Burling.

32. For a discussion of plausible deniability, see *Alleged Assassination Plots*, pp. 11–12. This dense, intricately constructed volume is invaluable to scholars of the CIA and may be the most bizarre congressional committee report ever written.

33. Italian operation described: Trevor Barnes, "The Secret Cold War: The CIA and American Foreign Policy in Europe, 1946–1956," *The Historical Journal*, XXIV (ii/1981), pp. 399–415, and XXV (iii/1982), 649–70; James E. Miller, "Taking Off the Gloves: The United States and the Italian Elections of 1948," *Diplomatic History*, VII (Winter 1983), pp. 33–55; Winks, pp. 383–86; Simpson, pp. 90–91; Hersh, pp. 223–32.

34. For the setup of OPC, see Ranelagh, pp. 80, 93, 112–13, 115–23, 130, 133–4; Winks, pp. 383–88; Book IV. Book IV is an institutional history written by Anne Karalekas. See also a new book of documents released by the CIA History Staff, Michael Warner, ed.; *The CIA Under Harry Truman* (Washington, D.C.: Center for the Study of Intelligence, 1994). Wisner's role is described by Paul Nitze, Lawrence Houston, and Frank Lindsay. A biographical sketch authored by Wisner's friend and aide Arthur Jacobs states that Wisner met with Marshall and Forrestal sometime before June 1948, at which

time they asked him to be chief of OPC. Frank Wisner Personnel File (CIA).

35. Thomas Powers, *The Man Who Kept the Secrets: Richard Helms and the CIA* (New York: Pocket Books, 1979), pp. 34–37, 39.
36. George Kennan to author, April 9, 1992.
37. Paul Nitze.
38. Edward F. Clark Jr.

Chapter Two: Rollback

1. Thomas Parrott, Frank Lindsay, Joseph Bryan, Tom Braden.
2. Eisenhower quoted: Blanche Wiesen Cook, *The Declassified Eisenhower: A Divided Legacy of Peace and Political Warfare* (New York: Doubleday, 1981), p. 121. Psywar training: Joseph B. Smith, *Portrait of a Cold Warrior* (New York: Ballantine, 1976), pp. 85–95.
3. Psywar Workshop: "Frustrated by lack of success in amusing audiences abroad, some of the staff members took refuge in amusing themselves and their colleagues. . . Their selections of 'gamesmanship' which had an appeal to an American audience were often only bizarre or incomprehensible to the 'peasant in the piazza.' In connection with other functional staffs, the Psychological Warfare Workshop appears to have gone pretty much its own merry way." *CIA OPC History II*, p. 172. See J. Bryan III, *Merry Gentlemen (and One Lady)* (New York: Atheneum, 1985). KGB: David Atlee Phillips, *Secret Wars Diary: My Adventures in Combat, Espionage Operations, and Covert Action* (Bethesda, Md: Stone Trail Press, 1989), pp. 77–78; Christopher Andrew and Oleg Gordievsky, *KGB: The Inside Story* (New York: HarperCollins, 1990); Harry Rositzke, *The KGB: The Eyes of Russia* (New York: Doubleday, 1981). Burke: Michael Burke, *Outrageous Good Fortune* (Boston: Little, Brown, 1984); G.J.A. O'Toole, *Honorable Treachery: A History of U.S. Intelligence, Espionage, and Covert Action from the American Revolution to the CIA* (New York: Atlantic Monthly Press, 1991), p. 422. Offie: Burton Hersh, *The Old Boys: The American Elite and the Origins of the CIA* (New York: Scribner's, 1992), pp. 245–55.
4. Christopher Simpson, *Blowback* (New York: Simon & Schuster, 1988), pp. 84–89, 112–15.
5. John Loftus, *The Belarus Secret* (New York: Knopf, 1982).
6. Simpson, pp. 201–202; Michael Warner, ed., *The CIA Under Harry Truman* (Washington, D.C: Center for the Study of Intelligence, 1994), p. 292. According to an internal study by the CIA's Directorate of Operations, fewer than ten of the approximately one hundred persons brought in by the CIA act had some Nazi affiliation. Accord-

ing to the draft of a history by the CIA's History Staff, Wisner was interested in creating the "psychological fission" of the Soviet Union. "The German experience in the Soviet Union during World War II greatly intrigued the OPC. Frank Wisner, in particular, sought to learn the lessons of the German defeat in the East—a defeat he felt was due in large measure because the Nazis failed to capitalize on the anticommunist sentiment of the Russian people. Reviewing the Nazi experience on the Eastern Front, Wisner felt the U.S. 'should stop thinking of the Soviet Union as a monolithic nation and investigate the internal strains.' " Wisner recommended using émigrés as "consultants." One (recruited by Carmel Offie) was Nicholas Poppe. He had worked for the Ost-Assen Institute in Czechoslovakia during the war, doing research on the "Jewish Problem . . . in order to perfect the Nazi killing machines." The CIA hired him as a $500-a-month consultant. Kevin Ruffner, untitled first volume of his work on CIA involvement with and searches for former Nazis (CIA History Staff), pp. 69, 78, 138, 140–41, 183.

7. Simpson, p. 159; James Critchfield, Arthur Jacobs.
8. The CIA's in-house history concludes: "The almost total inaccessibility of the Soviet target outside of Berlin produced a determination to reach the target 'no matter what' that sometimes led us to operations which had very little likelihood of ever influencing Soviet policy or even individual Soviet citizens, but perhaps provided a catharsis for those who felt particularly frustrated by the situation." CIA *Soviet Operations*, p. 2. The history cites the helplessness of two case officers who could do nothing more on the day of Stalin's death than distribute some leaflets in Berlin. They composed a song to an old tsarist army tune: "It happened in Berlin/ A great event, oh friends!/ We printed leaflets/ On the day of Stalin's death. . . ." Ibid., p. 7. The report describes the difficulty of recruiting refugees: "As a member of one of those groups said in the early 1950s, 'By now, all the heroes are dead.' Fortunately, his comment was not entirely accurate, but winnowing out the heroes, or even the able, from the disillusioned and cynical mass of refugees that gathered around the DP camps of the 1940s and 1950s was a task that required much more time and experience than the agency had." Ibid., p. 5. Camps described: O'Toole, p. 451; Simpson p. 142; parachute drops: Simpson, pp. 173–74; Thomas Powers, *The Man Who Kept the Secrets: Richard Helms and the CIA* (New York: Pocket Books, 1979), p. 45; Thomas Parrott, Peter Jessup. It is sometimes said that OPC was nostalgic for the success of the OSS in World War II. But parachuting agents behind enemy lines did not work very well in that war, either. Of twenty-one teams of American agents successfully parachuted into Germany carrying radio transmitters, only one ever established com-

munication. Peter Grose, *Gentleman Spy: The Life of Allen Dulles*, msp. 305.

9. Simpson, p. 133. ZRELOPE was intended to recruit a thousand Soviet bloc émigrés as CIA assets. The project found only seventeen. CIA *Paramilitary History*, p. 48. They were trained at a cost of $30,000 apiece at Fort Meade, Maryland. Ruffner, p. 95. TsOPE is the Russian acronym for the Central Union of Postwar Emigrés. It was created because OPC wanted a group "less tainted by a history of collaboration with the Germans than NTS." The group, it was hoped, would also be more responsive to U.S. direction. "TsOPE attracted some genuinely motivated and able people, many of whom were offended by the militant and authoritative style of NTS and other émigré groups. At the same time, they were inherently synthetic and dependent." The nature of TsOPE "encouraged an unending series of intrigues and made it a haven for some who sought easy jobs and good salaries in exchange for a willingness to do whatever America requested." CIA *Soviet Operations*, p. 11.

10. Their targets were usually defectors who were preaching anticommunism to Europe. To silence émigré editors and broadcasters after World War II, the KGB used exotic weapons—various poisons, lethal cigarette packs, gas guns that left no trace to fix the cause of death. Phillips, p. 81.

11. Simpson, pp. 152–55; Arthur Jacobs, James McCargar.

12. Grose, msp. 473.

13. Eastern European operations: Ruffner, p. 68.

14. BGFIEND and British role: James McCargar. Albanian operation described: Nicholas Bethell, *Betrayed* (New York: Times Books, 1984), pp. 35–39, 55–56, 87; Tom Bower, *The Red Web* (London: Aurum Press, 1989), p. 85; Robin Winks, *Cloak and Gown: Scholars in the Secret War, 1939–1961* (New York: Morrow, 1987), pp. 393–98.

15. Tom Braden, James McCargar, Arthur Cox, Arthur Jacobs, Joe Bryan, Gratian Yatsavich. Some men were a little overwhelmed. "He was a bull," said Cox, a psywar officer. "I felt a mixture of admiration and fear when he called me to his office. He could make you feel terrified." Wisner worked very long hours. "He would be in at eight and still working at eight, with Polly on the phone, telling him he was late to dinner," said Arthur Jacobs. Wisner could be an enthusiastic schemer. He tried to hire away Najeeb Halaby from the Pentagon because he assumed that Halaby had an "in" with Louis Johnson, the defense secretary who was wary of OPC. "This was poor intelligence," recalled Halaby in an interview with the author. Halaby had been dubbed a security risk for spurious reasons. He turned down the OPC job because "Wisner had this kind of coony look and atti-

tude. He was calculating, no holds barred." Wisner had a secret recording system in his office. Three microphones were placed under his conference table, desk, and phone. Robinette to Wisner, "Recommendations for Recording Equipment in Office of DDP," May 25, 1956, in opi–40, 79–01228A, box 53, folder 8 (CIA).

16. Tom Braden, Gilbert Greenway, James McCargar, Najeeb Halaby, Charles Whitehurst; Wisner was described by Edward Green, chief of support for OPC, as "almost messianic in his attitudes" and as a good operator but not very good at management. CIA *OPC History I*, p. 15. "startled": Arthur Jacobs, Wisner bio sketch, pp. 26–27, Frank Wisner Personnel File (CIA). Jacobs vividly describes Wisner in this sketch: "His likes and dislikes were intense. He was as demanding of others as he was of himself. There was a tone of impatience and urgency about everything he undertook. . . Frequently the mood was dour and even irascible. The words he used were sometimes acidulous. The tone of his contacts was always serious. . . . His departure into humor, sometimes sophisticated and droll, and at other times, earthy, was almost startling in the somberness of his normal mien." Outside work, Wisner had "a rare charm and magnetism." Ibid. OPC was pleased to have Wisner's social contacts. An in-house history notes that he had "particularly close rapport with individuals in positions of responsibility" and listed thirty-three names, including Chip Bohlen, Bob Joyce, Paul Nitze, George Kennan, and Bob Lovett. CIA *OPC History II*, p. 525.

17. Kennan quoted, Book IV, p. 31. Sallie Pisani, *The CIA and the Marshall Plan* (Lawrence, Kan.: University Press of Kansas, 1991), p. 72; E. Howard Hunt, *Undercover* (New York: G.P. Putnam's, 1974); Gilbert Greenway. It is not clear how much of the 5 percent was used for covert operations. Bissell's recollection is that only a small portion of the money was set aside, but it was enough to make the operators feel flush. Ruddock as OPC representative in London: Lawrence Houston.

18. Ed Welles, Peter Sichel, Lawrence Houston, George Holmes; Powers, pp. 26, 42–43, 58–59. OPC paid better: CIA *OPC History I*, p. 37. Ineffectual though he was, Admiral Hillenkoetter accurately predicted that émigré groups would make poor operational allies, according to a CIA in-house history. In a memo to the National Security Council on April 15, 1948, he opposed the use of these groups because they were "highly unstable and undependable . . . completely unable to provide intelligence of real value. . ." and easily penetrated. Wisner was able to override Hillenkoetter's objections. Ruffner, p. 44

19. Grose, msp. 411.

20. Ludwell Lee Montague, *General Walter Bedell Smith as Director of*

Central Intelligence (College Station, Pa.: Penn State University Press, 1992), pp. 4–9; Bower, p. 157.
21. Lawrence Houston, Walter Pforzheimer.

Chapter Three: The Cavalier

1. FitzGerald's "Personal History Statement" for the CIA, December 1950, listed eleven clubs that he belonged to. Courtesy Frances FitzGerald.
2. "Letters from Desmond FitzGerald, March 1942–November 1943; Jan. 1944–Nov. 1945" (hereinafter "Letters"), pp. 49, 71–72. Fitz-Gerald's letters to his wife, Marietta, and his parents-in-law, the Bishop and Mrs. Peabody, were collected by the family and preserved, slightly excerpted. Courtesy Frances FitzGerald.
3. Russell Jack Smith, *The Unknown CIA: My Three Decades with the Agency* (Washington, D.C.: Pergamen-Brassey's, 1989), p. 181; "In Memoriam: Desmond FitzGerald, 1910–1967," privately printed by the CIA. Courtesy Barbara Lawrence.
4. "Letters," p. 1.
5. Ibid., pp. 8, 57.
6. Ibid., pp. 13, 21, 24, 27, 28, 34; DF to Albert and Eleanor Francke (brother-in-law and sister), September 27, 1942, courtesy Nora Cammann.
7. "Letters," pp. 34–35.
8. Ibid., pp. 25, 28–29; DF to Albert and Eleanor Francke, March 7, 1943.
9. DF to Albert and Eleanor Francke, November 17, 1942, August 26, 1943.
10. "Letters," pp. 52, 90–91, 88.
11. Barbara Tuchman, *Stilwell and the American Experience in China, 1911–45* (New York: Macmillan, 1970), pp. 414–27. Galahad casualties: Charles Romanus and Riley Sunderland, *Stilwell's Command Problems* (Washington, D.C.: Department of the Army, Historical Division, 1956), p. 240.
12. Frances FitzGerald; "Letters," pp. 60–61, 70, 80–81, 84.
13. Conclusions about air support undated, handwritten in DF Papers, courtesy Frances FitzGerald. "We preached movement and attack and often despaired. But the Chinese became accustomed to the miracle of ammmunition and food reliably supplied when needed (usually by air drops). . . ."
14. DF to Bishop and Mrs. Peabody, August 1945.
15. Frances FitzGerald, Caroline Seebohm (who is writing a biography of Marietta Tree); Marie Brenner, "The Democratic Aristocrat," *Vanity Fair*, December 1991; Malcolm Peabody, Louis Auchincloss,

Susan Mary Alsop; John Huston, *An Open Book* (New York: Knopf, 1980), pp. 120–21.

16. Paul Windels Jr.; *New York Times*, February 19, March 11, April 5 and 13, 1949.

17. Richard Stilwell to DF, November 26, 1950; DF to Stilwell, November 30, 1950, courtesy Frances FitzGerald. DF was also a friend and neighbor of Allen Dulles's. Peter Grose, *Gentleman Spy: The Life of Allen Dulles*, msp. 468.

18. Ralph McGehee, *Deadly Deceits: My 25 Years in the CIA* (New York: Sheridan Square Publications, 1983), pp. 8, 10; Donald Gregg, James Lilley, Charles Whitehurst, Tom Polgar, Frank Lindsay.

19. William Leary, *Perilous Missions: Civil Air Transport and CIA Covert Operations in Asia* (Birmingham, Ala.: University of Alabama Press, 1984), pp. 67–72. Leary's is the best public account of the CIA in Korea. Hainan: Frank Lindsay Oral History, CIA Oral History Archives.

20. Taiwan operations: CIA *OPC History II*, p. 160; Leary, pp. 126–28; "Western Enterprises": John Ranelagh, *The Agency: The Rise and Decline of the CIA* (New York: Simon & Schuster, 1986), p. 223. Third Force described: Leary, pp. 137–41; Carleton Swift, Charles Whitehurst, David Laux, John Horton, Sam Halpern. The Third Force project used 700 personnel and provided enough arms and ammunition for 200,000 guerrillas. OPC spent $25 million on the project in 1951 and $75 million in 1952. The project was authorized by NSC 48/3 on April 26, 1951. CIA *OPC History II*, p. 553. The project encountered "the same difficulties as those besetting" the Taiwan effort. CIA *Paramilitary History*, p. 37; "Our American staff knew virtually nothing of China and the Chinese and had no area training." Clandestine Services History 210: *The Chinese Third Force Project (1950–1953)*, p. 86.

21. Carleton Swift.

22. Saipan and Downey capture: Leary, pp. 137–41. Enemy uniforms: Clandestine Services History: [CLASSIFIED], p. 9. This history of OPC operations in the Korean War states that "eventually most of the guerrillas were killed, captured, or neutralized by North Korean or Red Chinese action," p. 12. Overall, 225 enemy were killed, 600 captured, five bridges and eleven buildings were destroyed. CIA *Paramilitary History*, p. 29. Tofte described: Arthur Jacobs, Thomas Parrott; Richard Helms; Ranelagh, pp. 217–18. Tofte was a Dane who escaped Nazi-held Europe in 1940, enlisted in the British Army, and fought in Asia. He worked for the OSS at the end of the war running missions in Yugoslavia. For Tofte's version of his Korean exploits, see Joseph Goulden, *Korea: The Untold Story of the War* (New York: McGraw-Hill, 1982), pp. 262–475. In 1952 the CIA's new

station chief in Seoul, John Hart, became suspicious and started putting his agents on lie detectors. Most of them had been turned and fed disinformation by the North. Hart suggested scrapping the whole operation, but Washington said no. Bedell Smith sent word to Hart the CIA "simply could not admit" its intelligence failure, especially to military intelligence. Christopher Andrew, *For the President's Eyes Only: Secret Intelligence and the American Presidency from Washington to Bush* (New York: HarperCollins, 1995), pp. 193–94. A thorough and readable study of the relationship between the chief executive and the intelligence community.

23. Frances FitzGerald. Cummings: Andrew, p. 38
24. Li Mi and "Sea Supply": Leary, pp. 129–32, Burton Hersh, *The Old Boys: The American Elite and the Origins of the CIA* (New York: Scribner's, 1992), p. 300; Charles Whitehurst, Carleton Swift, John Horton, Sam Halpern, Frances FitzGerald. FitzGerald memo: "Memorandum for the Record: American Participation in Support of General Li Mi's Guerrilla Activities in Yunnan," August 10, 1951 (CIA). Li Mi continued to receive air support when he invaded Yunnan in 1952. "Unfortunately, the ChiNat government, disregarding the advice of American officials, chose to adopt conventional warfare tactics rather than pursue the hit-and-run type of operation common to unconventional warfare." CIA *Paramilitary History*, p. 32.
25. Lansdale in Philippines: best description is Cecil B. Currey, *Edward Lansdale: The Unquiet American* (Boston: Houghton Mifflin, 1988), pp. 71, 81, 85, 87, 95, 106–107 (NAMFREL), 198–99. Technically on Air Force active duty, Lansdale was loaned first to OPC, then CIA.
26. Barbara Train. See Currey, pp. 116–17.
27. John Horton; Currey, pp. 105–106, 131.
28. "This is the way": Ranelagh, p. 226; Lawrence Houston. "Lloyd George could come into a room and not be noticed. Des FitzGerald's presence could be felt before he entered. . . . Aurell hesitated to make the smallest decision. Des suggested three ways to do the same thing—all at the same time." Joseph B. Smith, *Portrait of a Cold Warrior* (New York: Ballantine, 1976), pp. 107–11.

Chapter Four: Empire Building

1. William Sloane Coffin, Thomas Braden, Carleton Swift. "It is understandable that CIA progress in covert operations was necessarily slower than it otherwise might have been. This was true to an even greater extent in paramilitary operations, where specialized training, which is sometimes necessary, was sometimes inadequate and resulted in several instances of poor professional technique, poor judgment, and poor execution in the field and in headquarters, nota-

bly China, Korea and Albania, despite some accomplishments against the enemy in the Far East." CIA *Paramilitary History*, p. 25.

2. Thomas Powers, *The Man Who Kept the Secrets: Richard Helms and the CIA* (New York: Pocket Books, 1979), p. 101.

3. For setup of NCFE, see Blanche Wiesen Cook, *The Declassified Eisenhower: A Divided Legacy of Peace and Political Warfare* (New York: Doubleday, 1981), pp. 126–34. "Document on Terror": Christopher Simpson, *Blowback* (New York: Simon & Schuster, 1988), pp. 125–27, 135.

4. "The most important agency asset involved was the Yale Russian Chorus, a group of students from Yale University, most of whom had some facility in the Russian language and several of whom had outstanding competence. . . . Copies of the United Nations report on Hungary, for example, were brought in by Western participants and read to large crowds at the festival. One member of the Yale Russian Chorus read parts of the report from the steps of Lenin's mausoleum in Red Square. These portions of the report were translated into Russian by other members of the chorus who were scattered through the crowd . . . numerous contacts were made with the nascent Soviet dissident groups by members of the Yale Chorus. These later provided the first links to the movement which in later years was to achieve recognition throughout the world for its criticism of the Soviet system. . . . The debriefings of witting members of the Yale Chorus and other assets upon their return from Moscow stimulated great enthusiasm for this kind of approach. . . ." CIA *Soviet Operations*, p. 30.

   Students were regarded as the "future leaders." The first Soviet vice president of the International Union of Students, Aleksandr Shelepin, went on to become chief of the KGB. Among the eager young Americans recruited by the CIA to attend (as "observers") a KGB-sponsored youth rally in Vienna in 1959 was Gloria Steinem. See John Ranelagh, *The Agency: The Rise and Decline of the CIA* (New York: Simon & Schuster, 1986), pp. 246–52 (Steinem at 252). Labor: Burton Hersh, *The Old Boys: The American Elite and the Origins of the CIA* (New York: Scribner's, 1992), pp. 238–39, 295–97 (Lovestone and Brown); Culture: Cord Meyer, Tom Braden (Boston Symphony), Arthur Cox; Thomas Braden, "I'm Glad the CIA is 'Immoral,' " *Saturday Evening Post*, May 20, 1967. Eisenhower quoted: Cook, p. 121.

5. Church Committee, Book IV, pp. 31–32.

6. DF to Graham Wisner, November 26, 1965, courtesy Frances Fitz-Gerald; Thomas Parrott, Arthur Jacobs, Peter Sichel, Elizabeth Graham, John Bruce Lockhart, William Colby. "He was Malraux's *homme engagé*, a total believer. It was good versus evil. He was

much too sensitive. It was all personal and painful," said Sichel. Braden found him "frenetic," yet at the same time "kind and thoughtful. It was astonishing how much time he took to be thoughtful when people were sick or wounded or in trouble." Lockhart contrasted his "certain sweetness" with a "streak of ruthlessness." John Bruce Lockhart to author, July 14, 1993.

Wisner's writing style reveals his sense of urgency. Criticizing the East European Division for failing to control an independent-minded official in a CIA-funded group, the Berlin Congress for Cultural Freedom, Wisner wrote, "It betrays an unfortunate tendency, apparently more deep-rooted than I expected, to succumb to the temptation of convenience (doing things the easy way) and irrespective of security and other technical considerations of the utmost importance." Wisner noted that President Truman had been "very well pleased" with a report on the Congress for Cultural Freedom, and continued, "I can only hope the very rough edges which have recently appeared are not brought too sharply to the attention of these lofty officials." FGW to Breckinridge, "Berlin Congress for Cultural Freedom: Activities of Melvin Lasky," August 8, 1950, in opi-42, 78–01614R, box 1, folder 4.

7. Ludwell Lee Montague, *General Walter Bedell Smith as Director of Central Intelligence* (College Station, Pa.: Penn State University Press, 1992), pp. 91–93, 106–107, 107–108, 213–14 (WW II psy ops).
8. Lawrence Houston.
9. Montague, pp. 106–107.
10. Tom Bower, *The Red Web* (London: Aurum Press, 1989), pp. 157–58; Burton Hersch, *The Old Boys: The American Elite and the Origins of the CIA* (New York: Scribner's, 1992), pp. 363–64.
11. James Critchfield; staples: Bower, p. 154.
12. Peter Jessup; Simpson, p. 146.
13. Tom Polgar, Peter Jessup, James Critchfield.
14. John Bruce Lockhart.
15. Bower, pp. 134–35; David Murphy
16. Peter Jessup; Nicholas Bethell, *Betrayed* (New York: Times Books, 1984), p. 182; Bower, p. 164; Powers, p. 53.
17. Best source on Albania is Bethell, pp. 138–91. For Philby and Harvey see Verne Newton, *The Cambridge Spies: The Untold Story of Maclean, Philby, and Burgess in America* (New York: Madison Books, 1991), pp. 249–50, 306–41. Leonard Moseley (*Dulles* [New York: Dial, 1978], pp. 281, 285, 491), has useful interviews with Philby about Wisner. See also Kim Philby, *My Silent War* (New York: Grove Press, 1968), pp. 193–95. In the fall of 1994 three important new books appeared on Philby. Two were from the Russian side, by Philby's KGB handler, Yuri Modin, *My Five Cambridge Friends* (New York: Farrar, Straus & Giroux, 1994), pp. 186–90; and

Genrikh Borovik, *The Philby Files: The Secret Life of Masterspy Kim Philby* (New York: Little, Brown, 1994), pp. 262–93. The most comprehensive is Anthony Cave Brown, *Treason in the Blood: H. St. John Philby, Kim Philby, and the Spy Case of the Century* (Boston: Houghton Mifflin, 1994), pp. 421–24. Brown cites an unpublished memoir by Bob Joyce for Wisner's suspicions about Philby. I asked Cleve Cram, a CIA officer who read all of Wisner's 1950–51 reports on his meetings with Philby, if Wisner had shown any suspicions. Cram said no, but added that if Wisner had such suspicions he probably would not have put them on paper, but rather have talked to Bill Harvey, chief of counterintelligence.

18. Philby, p. 202. The operation to supply Yugoslavia with weapons is described in Franklin Lindsay, *Beacons in the Night:With the OSS and Tito's Partisans in Wartime Yugoslavia* (Palo Alto, Calif.: Stanford University Press, 1994), p. 334.
19. Montague, p. 213.
20. Frank Lindsay, Peter Grose, *Gentleman Spy: The Life of Allen Dulles*, msp. 511. The CIA told Grose that the document has been lost.
21. Dulles described: Louis Auchincloss, Ella Burling, Tish Alsop, Mosley, pp. 288–90; Hersh, pp. 94–95. The best sources are Grose's biography and the five-volume CIA history of the Dulles years, declassified in 1994, *Dulles*.
22. Harry Rositzke, *The CIA's Secret Operations* (New York: Reader's Digest, 1977), p. 37.
23. Grose, mspp. 354, 598.
24. Jackson, *Dulles*, I, p. 22.
25. "There was something of the little boy in Allen," said Sherman Kent, a senior agency official. "He was much attracted to the monkey business side of the agency." Grose, mspp. 508, 617. "Allen loved being the spymaster. It was candy." Tish Alsop.
26. Simpson, p. 260.

Chapter Five: The War Lover

1. Janet Barnes Lawrence, Marshall Dodge.
2. Ben Sturges, Henry Hyde.
3. Hitchcock described: Nelson W. Aldrich Jr., *Old Money: The Mythology of America's Upper Class* (New York: Knopf, 1988), pp. 48, 180–81.
4. Benno Schmidt Sr.
5. John A. Bross, *Secret Operations: Some Reminiscences* (privately printed, 1980), pp. 51–52, 56; J. A. Bross, "The Days of OSS," *Central Intelligence Retirees Association Newsletter*, Fall 1983.

6. William Colby and Peter Forbath, *Honorable Men: My Life in the CIA* (New York: Simon & Schuster, 1978), p. 36.
7. Tish Alsop, Evangeline Bruce.
8. Citation: May 7, 1945, National Archives, RG 226, Entry 92, Box 30.
9. John Casey, Evangeline Bruce.
10. Marshall Dodge, Paul Nitze.
11. Douglas Auchincloss, Janet Barnes Lawrence.
12. Joan Braden, Janet Barnes Lawrence.
13. Allen Dulles to David Bruce, December 3, 1944, National Archives, RG 226, Entry 190, Box 283.
14. William Hood; Dulles wanted Barnes to seduce Ciano, according to Allen Dulles's biographer, Peter Grose, who cites his interviews with Dulles's staff in Bern. Edda already had a lover, Emilio Pucci. The great clothing designer smuggled Count Ciano's diaries into Switzerland by designing an ample but clinging shift to make her appear pregnant. The "baby was the diaries, strapped to her waist." Peter Grose, *Gentleman Spy: The Life of Allen Dulles*, msp. 314.
15. Tracy Barnes to William Donovan, December 15, 1944, National Archives, RG 226, Entry 134, Box 215.
16. Howard McGaw Smyth, "The Ciano Papers: Rose Garden," from *Studies in Intelligence*, Allen Dulles Papers, Princeton University, Princeton, N.J.; Paul Ghali, "Dulles Got Secrets from Duce's Daughter," *Cincinnati Enquirer*, February 23, 1969.
17. Cordelia Dodson Hood, David Crockett.
18. Ambassador Vieri Traxler, David Crockett, Tracy Barnes Jr., Marie Ridder.
19. William Hood; Allen Dulles, *The Secret Surrender* (New York: Harper & Row, 1966), p. 213.
20. Henry Hyde.
21. Janet Barnes Lawrence, Jane Barnes, Tracy Barnes Jr. Barnes was taught not to reveal his emotions. In his mother's family, the Dixons, "anything in excess (except perhaps homesickness) was disapproved," wrote his cousin Priscilla Auchincloss. "Church going was regular, but perfunctory, and any close religious ties discouraged as too emotional." Mrs. Auchincloss (mother of novelist Louis) recalled hearing that one of her cousins "was going to be severely punished unless she stopped reading the Bible so hard." Louis Auchincloss; Carol Gelderman, *Louis Auchincloss: A Writer's Life* (New York: Crown, 1993), pp. 12–13; Priscilla Stanton Auchincloss, "Forward to the Members of the Dixon Association" (privately printed, 1960: courtesy Jane Barnes), p. vi.
22. Courtlandt Barnes to Jane Barnes, March 10, 1991, May 27, 1992, courtesy Jane Barnes; Louis Auchincloss.
23. Groton described: Aldrich, pp. 149–59; Gelderman, p. 38; Louis Auch-

incloss, *A Writer's Capital* (Minneapolis: University of Minnesota Press, 1974), pp. 35–41; Louis Auchincloss; Frank Ashburn, *Fifty Years On* (New York: privately printed for Groton School, 1934). The Groton School Oral History Program, Groton, Massachusetts, has a wealth of detail about the school; Endicott Peabody to Courtlandt Barnes, December 18, 1925, Groton School archives; Janet Barnes Lawrence, Clarence Pell, Charles Devens, John Casey.

24. Andrew Rogers, Charles Devens, Ezekiel Stoddard, Thomas Blagden, Marshall Dodge, Louis Auchincloss. When Barnes died, his cousin and classmate in Scroll and Key wrote a reminiscence to their clubmates, "Marshall Dodge to CSP '33, March 31, 1972, Subject: Charles Tracy Barnes (1911–1972)," courtesy Jane Barnes. See F. Scott FitzGerald, *The Great Gatsby* (New York: Scribner's, 1925), p. 6; Maynard Mack, *A History of Scroll and Key, 1842–1942* (New Haven: privately printed, 1978). Excerpts of Barnes's essay courtesy Steve Umin (a member of Scroll and Key).

25. Janet Barnes Lawrence; Allen Dulles to U.S. Civil Service Commission, September 27, 1950, Allen Dulles Papers, Princeton.

26. Barnes worked for about a year for his cousin Archie Alexander at the Department of the Army. He came to the CIA on November 12, 1951. Tracy Barnes Personnel File (CIA). PSB: Townsend Hoopes; Ludwell Lee Montague, *General Walter Bedell Smith as Director of Central Intelligence* (College Station, Pa.: Penn State University Press, 1992), pp. 203–15. For examples of its lurid Cold War rhetoric, see Psychological Strategy Board Staff Meeting minutes, August 29, 1952, PSB "Preliminary Evaluation of Our National Psychological Strategy," May 7, 1952; "Report to the President," February 22, 1952, Truman Library, Independence, Missouri; see also Walter Isaacson and Evan Thomas, *The Wise Men: Six Friends and the World They Made* (New York: Simon & Schuster, 1986), p. 497.

27. Janet Barnes Lawrence, Tom Braden.

28. Arthur Cox, Carleton Swift; H. W. Brands, *Cold Warriors* (New York; Columbia University Press, 1991), p. 61.

29. E. Howard Hunt testimony, Church Committee, JFK Records, National Archives, box 25, folder 5; Christopher Simpson, *Blowback* (New York: Simon & Schuster, 1988), pp. 152–55; Church Committee, Book IV, pp. 128–29, quotes a memo from Wisner that the CIA needed an assassination capability, but it was only a question of "keeping up with the Joneses."

Chapter Six: A Mind of His Own

1. Richard Bissell.
2. Richard Bissell, with Jonathan Lewis and Frances Pudlo, *Memoirs*,

Chapter I, "Education"; Richard Bissell; John Bross Oral History, Groton School, Groton, Massachusetts; Clarence Pell. Averell Harriman, the Cold War statesman, once told Arthur Schlesinger that "the only recipe for success is to be unhappy at Groton."

3. Groton Year Book, 1927–28 "Class History," Groton School, Groton, Massachusetts; Oliver LaFarge, *Raw Material* (Boston: Houghton Mifflin, 1945), pp. 43–44; Louis Auchincloss, *A Writer's Capital* (Minneapolis: University of Minnesota Press, 1974), p. 44.

4. Richard Bissell, Beth Kent.

5. Bissell, *Memoirs*, I, pp. 16, 19.

6. Richard Bissell, Beth Kent.

7. Joseph Alsop, with Adam Platt, *"I've Seen the Best of It"* (New York: Norton, 1992), p. 59; Groton Year Book, 1927–28 "Class History."

8. Henry Breck, Paul Wright, Paul Nitze, Richard Bissell; Bissell, *Memoirs*, I, pp. 2–9. The New England boarding schools had a strong martial ethic and suffered disproportionate casualties in wartime. At St. Paul's the boys pass a swooning angel and a list of the school's fallen on the way to morning chapel. One cannot eat at St. Mark's or pray at Groton without observing scrolls of war dead. Nelson W. Aldrich Jr., *Old Money: The Mythology of America's Upper Class* (New York: Knopf, 1988), p. 173; See Claude M. Fuess, *Phillips Academy, Andover in the Great War* (New Haven: Yale University Press, 1919); Henry Howe Richards, *Groton School in the War* (Groton, Mass.: privately printed, 1925). As a CIA official, Bissell would not feel strictly governed by the code of Christian ethics preached by the Rector. He was more affected by the lessons of power taught in the ancient history courses he loved and, more important, implicitly conveyed by the school's place in American society. Feeling obliged, while writing his memoirs, to reconcile the ethical standards taught by "established schools like Groton with the covert activities of the CIA," he stated, a little stiffly perhaps, "Many of us who joined the Agency did not feel bound in the actions we took as staff members to observe all the ethical rules that we would have observed and regarded as valid before we were members of [the CIA]. But in a larger sense, the patriotism . . . the belief in the need for the United States to play an important role in the world. . . I think these had some of their roots in our upbringing and education, and they certainly did color the atmosphere of the Agency."

9. History of the Class of 1932; 1932 Yale Banner and Pot Pourri, Yale University, New Haven, Connecticut.

10. Eugene Rostow, Walt Rostow, Fritz Liebert, McGeorge Bundy, Richard Bissell.

11. Bissell, *Memoirs*, I, pp. 3–17.

12. Aldrich, pp. 141–91.

13. Robin Winks, *Cloak and Gown: Scholars in the Secret War, 1939–1961* (New York: Morrow, 1987), p. 41; David Halberstam, *The Best and the Brightest* (New York: Random House, 1972), p. 53; Bissell, *Memoirs*, I, pp. 1–17.
14. Richard Bissell; Amory quoted in Michael Beschloss, *Mayday: Eisenhower, Khrushchev, and the U-2 Affair* (New York: Harper & Row, 1986), p. 86.
15. Bissell, *Memoirs*, III, p. 6.
16. Harlan Cleveland, Paul Nitze, Najeeb Halaby.
17. Bissell, *Memoirs*, III, p. 56.

Chapter Seven: Running the World

1. Joan Braden, Richard Bissell; Cord Meyer, *Facing Reality: From World Federalism to the CIA* (New York: Harper & Row, 1980), pp. 67–81.
2. Richard Bissell. One of Bissell's ancestors, a Sgt. Daniel Bisel (one "l"), was a spy for George Washington. Bissell, *Memoirs*, I, p. 3. Bissell took a temporary assignment until August 1954. The success of the CIA-backed coup in Guatemala that June persuaded him to sign up permanently. Ibid., II, p. 12.
3. Walter Isaacson and Evan Thomas, *The Wise Men: Six Friends and the World They Made* (New York: Simon & Schuster, 1986), pp. 490–95, 545–46; Joseph Alsop, with Adam Platt, *"I've Seen the Best of It"* (New York: Norton, 1992), p. 350.
4. Thomas Powers, *The Man Who Kept the Secrets: Richard Helms and the CIA* (New York: Pocket Books, 1979), pp. 78–80; William Bundy. Dulles did have to make a few sacrifices. Sylvia Peress, a counterintelligence specialist, was no more pink than Cord Meyer, but she lacked his war record and social connections. Dulles fired her. Homosexuals were routinely ousted as security risks. Wisner had to move his useful fixer, Carmel Offie, off the books because he had been arrested on a morals charge and couldn't get a security clearance. (He became a bagman for the CIA's labor fronts in Europe.) There were persistent suspicions at FBI and State, never proved, that Offie was working for the Soviets. Bill Harvey, the CIA's counterintelligence chief, thought Offie was a mole. James McCargar; Burton Hersh, *The Old Boys: The American Elite and the Origins of the CIA* (New York: Scribner's, 1992), pp. 442–44; Mark Riebling, *Wedge: The Secret War Between the FBI and CIA* (New York: Knopf, 1994), p. 117.
5. Avis Bohlen (daughter).
6. Susan Mary Alsop, *To Marietta from Paris, 1945–60* (New York: Doubleday, 1975), p. 266.

7. For the Georgetown scene generally: Jean Friendly, Oatsie Charles, Evangeline Bruce, Tish Alsop, Janet Barnes Lawrence, Joan Braden, Katharine Graham, Avis Bohlen, Ella Burling, Susan Mary Alsop, Tom Braden, Paul Nitze, Richard Bissell.
8. Joseph Alsop, p. 388. See his description of the "bore factor," an important consideration he used in seating dinner parties. A table of twelve could afford only one bore. Very dull but powerful men or very stupid but beautiful women were counted as "half bores."
9. Louis Auchincloss, Susan Mary Alsop.
10. Paul Nitze.
11. Richard Bissell. Joseph Alsop, p. 191; Stewart Alsop, *The Center: People and Power in Political Washington* (New York: Harper & Row, 1968), p. 194; James Reston, *Deadline: A Memoir* (New York: Random House, 1991), p. 209. Alsop's method is described by Wayne Jackson in his CIA history of Allen Dulles. Alsop "would make outlandish statements about Soviet capabilities, trying to provoke CIA officials to confirm, contradict, or at least comment on." Jackson was at a dinner party one night at Susan Mary Patten's (she later married Alsop) when he saw the method at work with a senior CIA official who "did comment and contradict and in the course of doing so, disclosed information which he should not have mentioned." Jackson, *Dulles*, IV, pp. 43–44.
12. Courtesy Bob Merry, who is writing a biography of the Alsop brothers, and Michael Beschloss, who gave me his copy of Alsop's FBI file obtained under the Freedom of Information Act.
13. Jean Friendly; Reston, p. 186; Joan Braden.

Chapter Eight: Coup

1. Thomas Powers, *The Man Who Kept the Secrets: Richard Helms and the CIA* (New York: Pocket Books, 1979), pp. 55–56.
2. John Bruce Lockhart. The original British code name was Operation Boot.
3. Selwa Roosevelt, Kermit Roosevelt.
4. Kermit Roosevelt, John Bruce Lockhart, John Waller. Operation AJAX is described by John Ranelagh, *The Agency: The Rise and Decline of the CIA* (New York: Simon & Schuster, 1986), pp. 261–64; Roosevelt gives his own telling in *Countercoup: The Struggle for the Control of Iran* (New York: McGraw-Hill, 1981), pp. 261–64. For a lively account, see Stephen Ambrose, *Ike's Spies: Eisenhower and the Espionage Establishment* (New York: Doubleday, 1981), pp. 188–234. CIA headquarters mood described: Clandestine Services History 208: Overthrow of Premier Mossadeq of Iran, November 1952–August 1953 (CIA), pp. 59, 64.

5. Arthur Schlesinger Jr.
6. They had all traveled to Europe with steamer trunks and nannies as boys, and they remained essentially Eurocentric. Their horizons were limited by their cultural biases as well as their limited experience. FitzGerald, with his interest in Asia, was probably the most sophisticated of the lot. But, like Wisner, he was heavily influenced by the British colonial model. Tracy Barnes had liberal views toward developing democracies, but he had never actually been to one. When Bissell was administering the Marshall Plan, "he was quite uninterested in rich versus poor issues or the developing countries," said his deputy, Harlan Cleveland. "He left those to me." Bissell was a student of empire, and his favorite poem, "Take Up the White Man's Burden," gives a clue to his visceral attitude.
7. The best account of this theory, and the most readable account of the Guatemala coup, is Stephen Schlesinger and Stephen Kinzer, *Bitter Fruit: The Untold Story of the American Coup in Guatemala* (New York: Doubleday, 1982), pp. 106–107. For the CIA sections, Schlesinger and Kinzer drew on the interviews conducted by R. Harris Smith for a biography of Allen Dulles that was never completed. Peter Grose bought the research for his biography of Dulles, *Gentleman Spy: The Life of Allen Dulles* (Boston: Houghton Mifflin, 1994).
8. Bissell doubted that United Fruit had much to do with the coup, according to Jonathan Lewis, who helped him with his memoirs. He said he never heard Dulles talk about the fruit company. For the most recent (and best) scholarship on PBSUCCESS, see Piero Gleijeses, *Shattered Hope: The Guatemalan Revolution and the United States, 1944–1954* (Princeton, N.J.: Princeton University Press, 1991), pp. 7, 135, 363. Another notable and well-researched work on the Guatemala coup is Richard H. Immerman, *The CIA in Guatemala* (Austin, Texas: University of Texas Press, 1982).
9. David Atlee Phillips, *The Night Watch* (New York: Atheneum, 1977), pp. 34–35.
10. Richard Bissell, Janet Barnes Lawrence.
11. Roosevelt, p. 209; Kermit Roosevelt.
12. Grose, mspp. 536, 540.
13. Richard Bissell, Jake Esterline (ran the war room in Washington), Gilbert Greenway (handled air operations), Enno Hobbing (Haney's number two in Opa-Locka), E. Howard Hunt (political action for Haney). See Schlesinger, pp. 110–17, Gleijeses, pp. 288–93. Tracy Barnes and the head of the Western Hemisphere Division, J. C. King (later moved aside by Dulles to give Wisner a "free hand"), presented the "Guatemala General Plan of Action" to the Department of State on September 9, 1953. The plan calls for psywar and paramilitary operations but is sketchy. CIA *Guatemala*, pp. 27–28. Wisner

wrote Dulles, "The plan is stated in such broad terms it is not possible to know exactly what it contemplates, particularly in the latter phases. . . ." Wisner did "not regard this as a particular drawback," since adjustments could be made. Wisner to DCI, November 11, 1953. Barnes and Dulles added the psywar capacity to the plan, according to a still-classified CIA history, Roberta Knapp, *The First Thirty Years* (Washington, D.C.: CIA History Staff, 1994), p. 134.

14. E. Howard Hunt; Phillips, p. 34.
15. E. Howard Hunt, *Undercover: Memoirs of an American Secret Agent* (New York: Putnam, 1974), pp. 96–97; Tad Szulc, *Compulsive Spy: The Strange Career of E. Howard Hunt* (New York: Viking, 1974), pp. 66–67; Joseph B. Smith, *Portrait of a Cold Warrior* (New York: Ballantine, 1976), pp. 94–95; Schlesinger, p. 166.
16. Phillips, pp. 34–43.
17. Carleton Swift, Jake Esterline, Enno Hobbing.
18. Enno Hobbing.
19. Gleijeses, pp. 292–93, 373.
20. Barnes on Armas: CIA *Guatemala*, p. 52; Schlesinger, pp. 147–53. The CIA lost track of the freighter: "The deception . . . was excellent, a flustered Wisner told Allen Dulles." Grose, msp. 543.
21. Schlesinger, pp. 131–46; Gleijeses, p. 255.
22. Even though Arbenz disclosed the plot, including CIA involvement, the press looked the other way. CIA *Guatemala*, p. 39. Gleijeses, pp. 368–69; Harrison Salisbury, *Without Fear or Favor* (New York: Times Books, 1980), p. 479.
23. E. H. Hunt, Jake Esterline, Enno Hobbing, Albert Haney.
24. Wisner's doubts: Richard Bissell. John Bruce Lockhart observed Wisner's cautious streak on big covert actions, noting that Wisner was initially wary of Iran, too. Considers aborting operation: CIA *Guatemala*, p. 38; security breaches: ibid., p. 41; "rather naked" memo, black flights suspended: ibid., p. 42.
25. Phillips, pp. 40–49; Schlesinger, pp. 170–95; Gleijeses, pp. 319–42; Enno Hobbing, Richard Bissell, Jake Esterline. See also Gregory Treverton, *Covert Action: The Limits of Intervention in the Postwar World* (New York: Basic Books, 1987), pp. 68–75. Air attack "pathetic": CIA *Guatemala*, p. 69. After three days of action, two of the invasion's four prongs had been turned back (one by the Salvadoran police) and one had been halted by "minor resistance." Ibid., p. 69.
26. Arbenz crackdown: CIA *Guatemala*, pp. 63–64. Bissell, *Memoirs*, II, p. 30.
27. Richard Bissell.
28. Richard Bissell. Gleijeses (pp. 341–42) debunks the notion that the planes and radio psywar frightened Arbenz. His officer corps turned on him because they feared an invasion by the Marines. The agency's

classified history by a member of the CIA History Staff, Nick Cullather, supports this view. "Agency legend developed, promoted by Bissell and other officials close to the operation, that Arbenz 'lost his nerve' as a result of psychological pressure of air attacks and radio propaganda. In fact, Arbenz was deposed in a military coup, and neither the radio nor the air attacks had much to do with it. It was natural, however, for [the operation's] officers to feel these elements had been decisive. In the operation's last days, they were all that was left." CIA *Guatemala*, p. 75. The CIA's bombing may have had an effect on Colonel Diaz. According to State Department reporting, it helped soften him up to accept Ambassador Peurifoy's insistence that he lead a coup. See Christopher Andrew, *For the President's Eyes Only: Secret Intelligence and the American Presidency from Washington to Bush* (New York: HarperCollins, 1995) pp. 209–10. Only one Guatemalan in fifty owned a radio, but city dwellers were more likely to. The psywar radio campaign was helped when a freak accident knocked the government radio station off the air for three weeks in late May. CIA *Guatemala*, pp. 27, 57. British freighter: The CIA's official history of the Dulles era, declassified in 1994, states that the compensation was never paid and claims that the "investigation showed that the ship was sunk by a pilot and plane furnished by President Somoza of Nicaragua." Jackson, *Dulles*, III, p. 44.

29. Enno Hobbing; Gleijeses, pp. 352–53; Schlesinger, pp. 206–15.
30. Press reaction: Gleijeses, pp. 368–69.
31. Wisner cable: CIA *Guatemala*, p. 79. Jake Esterline, Tom Braden; Phillips, pp. 49–50; Schlesinger, pp. 218–19. "Only one" was not true: at least forty rebels died in combat, plus seventy-five in the jails. CIA *Guatemala*, p. 84.
32. Janet Barnes Lawrence, Richard Bissell; *Saturday Evening Post*, October 30, 1954.
33. Carleton Swift, John Fanton.
34. David Ignatius, "In from the Cold: A Former Masterspy Spins Intriguing Yarns of His Past Intrigues," *Wall Street Journal*, October 10, 1979; Howard Stone; Gleijeses, pp. 368–72; Richard Bissell.
35. Enno Hobbing; Schlesinger, pp. 184, 189, 221; Grose, mspp. 548, 550; Richard Bissell, Janet Barnes Lawrence. Medal: Tracy Barnes Personnel File (CIA).

Chapter Nine: The Spy War

1. Thomas Polgar, Peter Jessup, Jim Critchfield.
2. Gordon Stewart; John Ranelagh, *The Agency: The Rise and Decline of the CIA* (New York: Simon & Schuster, 1986), pp. 138, 288–96; David Martin, *Wilderness of Mirrors* (New York: Harper & Row,

1980), pp. 76–89. Operation Gold was the British code name for the tunnel. John Bruce Lockhart of the SIS says the Americans were not brought in for their money and technical know-how, as is commonly assumed, but because the site was in the American sector, and the British needed the United States to build a radar station as cover.

3. Jim Critchfield, Janet Barnes Lawrence.

4. Ranelagh, pp. 295–96.

5. Gordon Stewart. The Soviets may not have wanted to blow Blake, a prime asset, by shutting down the operation quickly. Also, the Soviets did not know about American code-breaking technology—Blake had been kept in the dark about that. The Russians may have figured that the West could intercept their messages, but not read them. Finally, Peter Grose speculates that the post-Stalin leadership in the Kremlin wanted the West to be reassured that a surprise attack was not imminent. Grose, *Gentleman Spy: The Life of Allen Dulles*, msp. 574.

6. Janet Barnes Lawrence, John Bruce Lockhart. Barnes described in Germany: Thomas Parrott, Peter Jessup, Jim Critchfield, Alice McIlvaine, Bill Hood, Henry Pleasants. In his annual fitness report by the CIA, Barnes was marked down in the categories, "is security conscious" and "tough minded." The report cites his "charming personality." Tracy Barnes Personnel File (CIA).

7. Thomas Parrott; Martin, p. 66–67. Between 1945 and 1961 the police in Berlin counted 229 actual kidnappings and 328 attempts by communist security forces. There is no figure for kidnappings by the West. Peter Wyden, *The Wall: the Inside Story of Divided Berlin* (New York: Simon & Schuster, 1989), p. 94.

8. Peter Jessup, Thomas Parrott. The story is probably based on an old tale variously said to involve a university campus in Boston or a federal agency in Oklahoma City. The voice from heaven in one of these versions belongs to a different Harvey—Paul, the radio commentator. David Atlee Phillips, *Secret Wars Diary: My Adventures in Combat, Espionage Operations, and Covert Action* (Bethesda, Md.: Stone Trail Press, 1989), p. 302.

9. Martin, p. 22; Carleton Swift, Thomas Parrott.

10. "Finger the terns": Martin, pp. 67–68.

11. Mary Cutler Buehl, Thomas Parrott, Jim Critchfield.

12. Church Committee, Book IV, pp. 52–53.

13. Janet Barnes Lawrence, Jane Barnes.

14. James McCargar.

15. Peter Jessup, Jim Critchfield, Bill Hood.

16. Ranelagh, pp. 285–88.

17. John Prados, *The Presidents' Secret Wars* (New York: Morrow, 1986), p. 123. Of all the CIA books, Prados made the best use of

available documents, especially from the National Security Council.

18. Ray Cline, *Secrets, Spies and Scholars: Blueprint of the Essential CIA* (Washington, D.C.: Acropolis Books, 1976), pp. 186–87.

19. Janet Barnes Lawrence, Oatsie Charles, Jane Thompson, Fisher Howe, Edgar Applewhite. His sensitivity to criticism was cited in two fitness reports, November 5, 1954 and April 13, 1957. Frank Wisner Personnel File (CIA).

20. Frank Wisner Jr.

21. Tanda Caradja; Wisner correspondence courtesy Burton Hersh from his Freedom of Information Act request from CIA: W. B. Smith to J. Edgar Hoover, December 22, 1952; Allen Dulles to J. Edgar Hoover, April 19, 1954; Sheffield Edwards to Sam Papich, May 24, 1955. Hoover quoted in Mark Riebling, *Wedge: The Secret War Between the FBI and the CIA* (New York: Knopf, 1994), p. 100. Hoover also liked to spy on Allen Dulles. Hoover's files on the CIA director include a report from a "confidential source" who saw Dulles at a Georgetown restaurant "with an attractive middle-aged woman not his wife . . . drinking considerably . . . talking in a loud voice." Dulles was carrying on about the British, whom he disliked, and making fun of a senator. J. P. Mohr to Tolson, "Re: Allen Dulles," August 7, 1953. Courtesy CIA History Staff.

22. Burton Hersh, *The Old Boys: The American Elite and the Origins of the CIA* (New York: Scribner's, 1992), pp. 324, 376.

23. Ellis Wisner, Graham Wisner, Frank Wisner Jr., Wendy Hazard, Barbara Lawrence.

24. Hersh, pp. 384–85; Charles Saltzman.

25. Lawrence Houston, Gilbert Greenway.

Chapter Ten: Collapse

1. Burton Hersh, *The Old Boys: The American Elite and the Origins of the CIA* (New York: Scribner's, 1992), p. 391; for discussion of Radio Free Europe, see note 10.

2. Al Ulmer, Richard Bissell.

3. John Bruce Lockhart to author, July 14, 1993. The dinner is also briefly described in Hugh Thomas, *Suez* (New York: Harper & Row, 1966), p. 114.

4. On October 8, Kim Roosevelt, the CIA's top Middle East hand, flatly predicted that the British would send an expeditionary force to reclaim the Suez Canal, which had been nationalized by Nasser in July 1956. Communications intercepts gave further warning. But James Angleton's Israeli sources deceived him, saying that no action was imminent. Peter Grose, *Gentleman Spy: The Life of Allen Dulles*, mspp. 621–28. The intelligence community's "watch" report on Octo-

ber 24 spoke of a "receding danger of hostilities." It only predicted an Israeli attack "in the near future" on October 28. The attack was launched the next day. Allen Dulles described the Sinai invasion as a "mere probing action." Jackson, *Dulles*, V, pp. 11–15.

5. James McCargar, Janet Barnes Lawrence.
6. Christopher Simpson, *Blowback* (New York: Simon & Schuster, 1988), p. 265.
7. Jane Thompson, William Hood, John Mapother.
8. No weapons or Hungarian speakers: Clandestine Services History 6: *The Hungarian Revolution* [CLASSIFIED], *23 October–4 November 1956* (CIA), pp. 76, 95. Wisner cables: DD/P Watch Office cable action log for DD/P trips, 1956, in 79–01228A, box 45 (hereinafter "Cable Log"). Full copies of Wisner's cables could not be located by the CIA. Interestingly, the covering letter on the Cable Log, dated November 26, 1956, is a request from Richard Helms, who was the chief operations officer of the DD/P, to James J. Angleton, chief of the counterintelligence staff, to pull together Wisner's cable traffic. Since Angleton was not in the normal chain of command and was sometimes used for special projects requiring discretion, it is a reasonable guess that Wisner's cables were disturbing to their recipients in Washington, and that Helms quietly asked Angleton to pull them together for review.

A myth has grown up over the years that the CIA had links to cells of dissidents in Hungary that could be "activated" as a paramilitary force. See William Corson, *The Armies of Ignorance: The Rise of the American Intelligence Empire* (New York: Dial, 1977), pp. 419–21, for an improbable conversation between Wisner and Allen Dulles; Hersh, p. 392; and Grose, msp. 626. These accounts sometimes use the code name Red Sox/Red Cap. In fact, according to John Mapother, a case officer in the Vienna station, the CIA had no such assets. "Red Sox" and "Red Cap" are code names for different operations.

9. Richard Bissell; William Colby and Peter Forbath, *Honorable Men: My Life in the CIA* (New York: Simon & Schuster, 1978), p. 134.
10. Tom Polgar. The CIA was very sensitive to the charge of having inspired the revolution. Almost immediately, Radio Free Europe was largely cleared of complicity by internal studies and by a German study. Cord Meyer, *Facing Reality: From World Federalism to the CIA* (New York: Harper & Row, 1980), pp. 121–30. But the CIA's declassified study of the Dulles era notes that RFE picked up signals from low-powered radio stations in Hungary and broadcast their calls for revolution throughout the country. Jackson, *Dulles*, III, p. 101. See also Simpson, pp. 266–67, for an account of how "Radio Free Moscow" pledged American relief to the Hungarians. The station was

run by the Russian nationalist group NTS, which was financed by the CIA. Wisner heard complaints on his trip to the border on November 11.

11. "Criticism of RFE broadcasts into Hungary": "Cable Log." In 1954, Wisner had approved Operation Veto, followed by Operation Focus, to encourage dissent in Hungary and Czechoslovakia with radio broadcasts and balloon drops. John Prados, *The Presidents' Secret Wars* (New York: Morrow, 1986), pp. 123–27. However, when Wisner briefed the President's Board of Consultants on Foreign Intelligence Activities in 1956, he insisted that "in both operations the people were encouraged to undertake only such action as would not bring about reprisals by the regime." Frank Wisner PBCFIA file, 1956, in 79–01228A, box 45 (CIA).

12. Marie Ridder. In a memo to Cord Meyer, chief of the International Organizations Division, on December 12, Wisner said he had seen Walter and Marie Ridder in Vienna on November 11. The Ridders, he reported, were blaming RFE for inciting revolution. Wisner said he tried to "straighten them out." Frank Wisner's relations with the press file, 1956, in 79–01228A, box 45 (CIA).

13. William Colby.

14. Thomas Powers, *The Man Who Kept the Secrets: Richard Helms and the CIA* (New York: Pocket Books, 1979), pp. 94–96.

15. Arthur Schlesinger, Jr., *Robert Kennedy and His Times* (Boston: Houghton Mifflin, 1978), pp. 455–56.

16. Wisner and PBCFIA: memorandum of meeting with General Cassidy, executive officer of PBCFIA, October 16, 1956. "Mr. Lovett and Ambassador Bruce had been somewhat astonished by the informal disposition of PP [psywar and paramilitary] affairs at the OCB [Operations Coordinating Board, executive branch oversight of covert action] conversations at lunch without records, etc." Frank Wisner PBCFIA file. For PBCFIA report, see Hersh, pp. 412–13.

17. Wisner's illness was diagnosed as "oriental fulminating hepatitis." His family believes that it contributed to his mental problems by affecting his central nervous system. They suspected (though there is no proof) that the clam had been poisoned by the KGB. Wendy Hazard, Jean Lindsey.

18. Manic depression symptoms and treatment described to author by Frederick Goodwin, M.D., former director of the National Institute of Mental Health.

19. Stewart Alsop, *The Center: People and Power in Political Washington* (New York: Harper & Row, 1968), pp, 225–29. For Helms, see Powers, pp. 96–97, 103, 108, 117, 122, 126, 135.

20. Selwa Roosevelt.

21. Gordon Stewart, James Critchfield.

Chapter Eleven: Brother's Keeper

1. James Lilley, Charles Whitehurst.
2. Ralph McGehee, *Deadly Deceits: My 25 Years in the CIA* (New York: Sheridan Square Publications, 1983), pp. 39–40, 50.
3. James Lilley, Charles Whitehurst; Jackson, *Dulles*, I, p. 72.
4. Barbara Lawrence.
5. Barbara FitzGerald to Eleanor Francke, October 4, 1956; DF to Eleanor Francke, January 4, 1957, courtesy Nora Cammann.
6. E. Howard Hunt.
7. Al Ulmer.
8. James Lilley.
9. McGehee, pp. 32–33. The Inspection and Review Staff's "summary assessment" of the Far East Division in October 1955 concluded that "a. the FE operation effort of the Agency was unsatisfactory; b. Results obtained by the FE Division did not warrant this large expenditure of money or the large number of employees." The report recommended abolishing the China Base. "The China Base performed no function that could not be delegated to Station Chiefs or to the FE Division HQS (which in many cases duplicated the work of related subordinate divisions)." Clandestine Services History 44: *The Inspection and Review Staff, DDP, October 1952–April 1959* (CIA).
10. Townsend Hoopes, *The Devil and John Foster Dulles* (Boston: Little, Brown, 1973), p. 350; John Prados, *The Presidents' Secret Wars* (New York: Morrow, 1986), pp. 130–32; Joseph B. Smith, *Portrait of a Cold Warrior* (New York: Ballantine, 1976), pp. 217–18.
11. Smith, pp. 205, 230.
12. Prados, pp. 134–35. The $10 million figure may be an exaggeration. According to the Dulles history, the Special Group approved withdrawing $843,000 from the CIA reserve on November 23, 1957, though it notes additional withdrawals were also made. The Dulles history stresses that the Defense and State Departments were heavily involved in the Indonesia operation. Jackson, *Dulles*, III, p. 109. Wisner cautions NSC: Clandestine Services History 53: *Covert Support to Indonesian Revolutionary Government, 1957–1958* (CIA), p. 49. Cuts out Allison: ibid., p. 37.
13. Smith, pp. 238–40; Robert Maheu, and Richard Hack, *Next to Hughes: Behind the Power and Tragic Downfall of Howard Hughes by his Closest Adviser* (New York: HarperCollins 1992), pp. 71–75.
14. Smith, pp. 240–48; Prados, pp. 135–45.
15. Avis Bohlen.
16. Sam Halpern.
17. William Crowley.

18. Janet Barnes Lawrence, Richard Bissell, Barbara Train, Paul Nitze.
19. Sam Halpern; Powers writes that Wisner was "subdued by hospital attendants and carried out of the building by force, while DDP officials watched in shocked silence." Thomas Powers, *The Man Who Kept Secrets: Richard Helms and the CIA* (New York: Pocket Books, 1979), pp. 96–97. The Wisner family says this story is untrue. The Jacobs biographical sketch in Wisner's personnel file says he went on leave in June 1958 and was hospitalized on September 12, 1958. Frank Wisner Personnel File (CIA).
20. Paul Nitze.
21. Frederick Goodwin, M.D.
22. Powers, p. 96.
23. Janet Barnes Lawrence.

Chapter Twelve: High Flier

1. Gilbert Greenway; Wisner becomes chief of station, Burton Hersh, *The Old Boys: The American Elite and the Origins of the CIA* (New York: Scribner's, 1992), p. 423.
2. Dulles: Leonard Mosley, *Dulles* (New York: Dial, 1978), p. 294; Bissell: Lloyd Emerson, Walter Pforzheimer, Jim Flannery, Eleanor Dulles, Gordon Stewart, Richard Bissell. Bissell's fitness reports marked him down slightly in the categories of "able to see another's point of view," "calm," "unemotional," "even disposition," and "gets along well with people at all social levels." Richard Bissell Personnel File (CIA).
3. Michael Beschloss, *Mayday: Eisenhower, Khrushchev, and the U-2 Affair* (New York: Harper & Row, 1986), pp. 84–93, 106. An authoritative account of the U-2 development and shoot-down in May 1960. See also Clarence L. "Kelly" Johnson, with Maggie Smith, *Kelly: More Than My Share of It All* (Washington, D.C.: Smithsonian Institution Press, 1985). Johnson, perhaps the greatest airplane designer ever, made a formidable team with Bissell, the great facilitator. Years after the U-2, when Johnson had to work again with Pentagon bureaucrats, he lamented, "Whatever happened to the days of Richard Bissell?" Complaining to Arthur Lundahl, the CIA's chief photointerpreter, about all the red tape, Johnson grumbled, "I'm not coming back to Washington anymore." Bissell, *Memoirs*, V, p. 18. While Ed Land worked for Polaroid, he refused to allow his company to do any work for the government (to keep government auditors away from internal company data). The actual film was developed and manufactured by Kodak. Frank Lindsay.
4. Beschloss, p. 110. Bissell estimated that five pilots died developing the plane. Bissell, *Memoirs*, V, p. 38.

5. Beschloss, pp. 8, 121; Richard Bissell.
6. Dino Brugiani.
7. Jackson, *Dulles*, I, p. 56.
8. John Ranelagh, *The Agency: The Rise and Decline of the CIA* (New York: Simon & Schuster, 1986), pp. 316–18.
9. Bissell, Memoirs, V, p. 50.
10. Richard Bissell.
11. The CIA itself was slow to recognize that the missile gap was a fiction. Its intelligence estimates were based on "worst case" scenarios that allowed the possibility that the Russians would have a three-to-one edge in ICBMs in the early 1960s—notwithstanding the fact that the U-2 did not see a single ICBM site. In his congressional testimony Allen Dulles, ever the conciliator, was too cautious to take on both the Air Force, which hyped the threat partly for budgetary reasons, and Senator Stuart Symington, who hyped it for political reasons. For an understated but thorough account, see Jackson, *Dulles*, V, pp. 39–139. See also Dwight D. Eisenhower, *The White House Years*, Vol. II: *Waging Peace, 1956–1961* (New York: Doubleday, 1965), p. 389. See note 10 of Chapter 16 there for a discussion of the CIA's position on the missile gap.
12. Richard Helms.
13. Deborah Shapley, *Promise and Power: The Life and Times of Robert McNamara* (Boston: Houghton Mifflin, 1993), pp. 66–74.
14. Richard Bissell, Eleanor Dulles.
15. Richard Bissell.
16. *Ibid.*
17. Janet Barnes Lawrence. See Richard Deacon, *"C"—A Biography of Sir Maurice Oldfield* (London: Macdonald, 1985).
18. Richard Bissell.
19. Jane Barnes, Tracy Barnes Jr., Janet Barnes Lawrence, Ben Sturges, John Casey, Ella Burling, Oatsie Charles.
20. Ann Harriet Bissell, Beth Kent, Mrs. Richard (Ann) Bissell, Tom Bissell, Winthrop Bissell, Fritz Liebert.

Chapter Thirteen: A Clandestine World

1. Richard Bissell; Bissell, *Memoirs*, V, p. 79.
2. Sam Halpern, Donald Gregg; Jackson, *Dulles*, III, pp. 94–107.
3. Ed Welles. For examples of KGB intrigue in the Third World, see Vladislav Zybok, "Spy vs. Spy: The KGB vs. the CIA, 1960–1962," *Cold War International History Project Bulletin* (Washington, D.C.: Woodrow Wilson Center, Fall 1994), pp. 28–29.
4. Lyman Kirkpatrick, Richard Bissell; Jackson, *Dulles*, I, p. 52.
5. Robin Winks, *Cloak and Gown: Scholars in the Secret War, 1939–*

1961 (New York: Morrow, 1987), p. 389. Campbell James, who became involved in Italian ops in the 1960s, says the $25 million figure is high; he estimated $15 to $20 million.

6. Ted Atkins.

7. Sam Halpern.

8. Charles Peters.

9. Sam Halpern.

10. David Ignatius, "In from the Cold: A Former Masterspy Spins Intriguing Yarns of His Past Intrigues," *Wall Street Journal*, October 10, 1979.

11. Carleton Swift; Thomas Powers, *The Man Who Kept Secrets: Richard Helms and the CIA* (New York: Pocket Books, 1979), pp. 123–24; Ralph McGehee, Deadly Deceits: My 25 Years in the CIA (New York: Sheridan Square Publications, 1983), pp. 72–73 (calls Jantzen "Rod Johnson"). CIA operatives sometimes showed a kind of earnest naiveté toward the natives. The most famous example was Edward G. Lansdale, who was first close to Ramón Magsaysay in the Philippines and then tried to cultivate Ngo Dinh Diem in South Vietnam. Lansdale was acidly portrayed by Graham Greene in *The Quiet American* as Alden Pyle, the CIA man who tried to teach the peasants town hall democracy. Lansdale made it all sound simple; in his counterinsurgency lectures on Vietnam in the early 1960s, he said, "Just remember this: Communist guerrillas hide among the people. If you win the people over to your side, the guerrilas have no place to hide. With no place to hide, you can find them. Then, as military men, fix them . . . finish them!" Stanley Karnow, *Vietnam: A History* (New York: Viking, 1983), p. 221. Some of the agency's operatives were basically con artists. Miles Copeland, the most colorful of the Middle East hands, wrote "good cables to Allen [Dulles]," said Carleton Swift. "He'd make a lot out of nothing" by boasting that he was the last to see the prime minister and suggesting that he could arrange a coup. Copeland claimed he practiced something called "cryptodiplomacy," described in a couple of unreliable books written after his retirement. Working with Allen Dulles on a special political action staff that the DCI created, Copeland dreamed up what he called "W&W (Weird and Wonderful)" projects like the search for a "Muslim Billy Graham," a "great mystagogue" who could be manipulated by the CIA (the appropriate holy man was never found). Carleton Swift; McGehee, p. 72; Miles Copeland, *Without Cloak or Dagger* (New York: Simon & Schuster, 1974), *The Game Player: Confessions of the CIA's Original Political Operative* (London: Arum Press 1989), pp. 121, 134–35.

12. Carleton Swift, George Holmes.

13. Some ambassadors refused to be left in the dark. David Bruce, the

author of the scathing PBCFIA report in 1956, was ambassador to West Germany in the late 1950s. When he heard that the CIA was considering building another Berlin Tunnel, he ordered the station chief not to "put a shovel in the ground without telling me first." Peter Grose, *Gentleman Spy: The Life of Allen Dulles*, msp. 713.

14. Church Committee, Book IV, pp. 51–52. For the CIA's official history of presidential authorization in this period, see volume III (Covert Action) of Jackson, *Dulles*. CIA men always insist that they acted with presidential authority, but the grant could be extraordinarily broad. According to Peter Grose, Bedell Smith once worried that he might be breaking the law with a particularly audacious covert action. He told Truman about his concerns, and the president "reached into his desk drawer, pulled out a single sheet of White House stationery, scrawled a few words on it, folded and handed it to the general without saying a word. As Smith unfolded the paper, he saw his own name granted a blanket presidential pardon, signed by Harry S. Truman. The absolution before the law was unlimited and undated." Grose, msp. 420. There was, even in the early days, an oversight committee to approve OPC operations. It consisted of the deputy secretaries of defense and state and the president's national security adviser. They met on Tuesdays for lunch. Frank Lindsay.

15. Jackson, *Dulles*, IV, pp. 101–12; Michael Beschloss, *Mayday: Eisenhower, Khrushchev, and the U-2 Affair* (New York: Harper & Row, 1986), p. 129.

16. Leonard Mosley, *Dulles* (New York: Dial, 1978), p. 457.

17. Beschloss, p. 126

18. William Colby and Peter Forbath, *Honorable Men: My Life in the CIA* (New York: Simon & Schuster, 1978), p. 180.

19. Richard Bissell.

20. Powers, pp. 124–25; Jim Flannery.

21. Peter Sichel, Edgar Applewhite.

22. Powers, p. 125.

23. Bissell described: Jim Flannery, Bob King, Lloyd Emerson.

24. Bob King.

25. Although Bissell owned some fine things, he was, like many New England Brahmins, almost ludicrously frugal. He bought slacks at a discount warehouse in Pennsylvania and drove a Ford with a hole in the roof (he used an umbrella as a patch). Mrs. Richard Bissell.

26. Jim Flannery, Bob King, Charles Whitehurst; Colby and Forbath, pp. 149–50.

27. Donald Gregg, Jim Flannery.

28. Powers, pp. 124–26.

29. The CIA had limited success recruiting deep penetration agents. There were none worth mentioning before Lieutenant Colonel Pyotr

Popov of Soviet Military Intelligence walked into the Vienna station in the winter of 1952–53 and offered his services. Popov spied for five years before he was caught and executed. Some of his reports helped reassure Washington that the Kremlin was not close to starting a war. Grose, msp. 513–14; Christopher Andrew, *For the President's Eyes Only: Secret Intelligence and the American Presidency from Washington to Bush* (New York: HarperCollins, 1995), p. 214. The first station chief in Moscow was seduced by a Russian maid, a "swallow" in the KGB, in 1956. Andrew, pp. 212–13.

30. Paul Garbler, Lloyd Emerson. Bissell may have been listening to James J. Angleton, who was suspicious of all defectors and agents-in-place.

31. FitzGerald described: Charles Whitehurst, Donald Gregg, Sam Halpern, Campbell James, Chester Cooper, David Laux, John Horton, William Colby.

32. Colby and Forbath, p. 147.

33. Campbell James described: David Laux, Chester Cooper, Campbell James.

34. Tony Poe described: Vint Lawrence; Christopher Robbins, *The Ravens: the Men Who Flew in America's Secret War in Laos* (New York: Crown, 1987), pp. 124–27. See also John Prados, *The Presidents' Secret Wars* (New York: Morrow, 1986), p. 162. Ears: David Corn: *Blond Ambition: Ted Shackley and the CIA's Crusades* (New York: Simon & Schuster, 1994), p. 134. Poshepny told Roger Warner, "FitzGerald saved my ass many times. Lotta guys wanted to nail me. They thought I was some kind of nut. But he got me a lot of these good jobs." Roger Warner, *Back Fire: The CIA's Secret War in Laos and Its Link to the Vietnam War* (New York: Simon & Schuster, 1995), p. 75.

35. DF to Frances FitzGerald, March 25, 1955, courtesy Frances Fitz-Gerald; Frances FitzGerald. It turns out that the intelligence reports, discounted at the time, were, if anything, underestimates of the brutality of Mao's regime. Mao may have been responsible for some 40 to 80 million deaths in his attempts to "purify class ranks" in the 1950s and 1960s. *Washington Post*, July 17, 1994.

36. Barbara Lawrence, Desmond FitzGerald Jr., Frances FitzGerald, Joan Denny, Doris Jackson.

Chapter Fourteen: Plots

1. "There will be no communist government": Joseph Smith, *Portrait of a Cold Warrior* (New York: Ballantine, 1976), p. 324. Setup of Cuba operation: Peter Wyden, *Bay of Pigs: The Untold Story* (New York: Simon & Schuster, 1979), p. 27. Wyden's book is the best account of

the Bay of Pigs, very deeply reported from the participants. See Thomas G. Patterson, *Contesting Castro: the United States and the Cuban Revolution* (New York: Oxford University Press, 1994), for background on how the United States mishandled Castro.

2. Wyden, pp. 24–25; David Atlee Phillips, *The Night Watch* (New York: Atheneum, 1977), p. 86. For an excellent analysis of how PB-SUCCESS paved the way, see Richard H. Immerman, *The CIA in Guatemala* (Austin, Texas: University of Texas Press, 1982), pp. 187–196.

3. Lyman Kirkpatrick, Howard Stone, Bill Hood, Jake Esterline, Richard Bissell.

4. Hunt in Uruguay: Tad Szulc, *Compulsive Spy: The Strange Career of E. Howard Hunt* (New York: Viking, 1974), p. 77; Hunt's "flight of truth:" CIA *Bay of Pigs*, p. 230. Helms described: Phillips, p. 87. Phillips calls Flannery "Abe."

5. Jim Critchfield, Al Ulmer. The inspector general's report on the Bay of Pigs in 1961 was scathing about the staffing of the operation: "None of the most experienced senior operating officers of the project participated fulltime. Of the 42 officers in top operating jobs (GS 12–15), 17 rated in the lower one-third, nine in the lowest tenth." CIA *Bay of Pigs IG Report*, p. 42.

6. David Corn, *Blond Ambition: Ted Shackley and the CIA's Crusades* (New York: Simon & Schuster, 1994), p. 81.

7. Phillips, p. 92; Wyden, pp. 32–33.

8. Phillips, p. 89; Janet Barnes Lawrence, Richard Bissell.

9. Many of the old-time covert action operators were skeptical that Barnes and Bissell could pull off the operation. Bill Harvey, in particular, was dubious. He had come back to Washington from Germany to run Staff D, a supersecret group of code breakers, and he would often go out for drinks in the evening with Doris Mirage, Bissell's secretary. "He thought Bissell was naive," said Mirage. "You need to be a bastard to work in the bowels of the CIA, and Bissell wasn't." Larry Houston, the CIA general counsel, became increasingly critical of Barnes as an administrator. "He was slipshod in the way he ran things," said Houston. "It was just his way. It took me a long time to catch on because he seemed so plausible." Doris Mirage, Lawrence Houston.

10. Jane Barnes, Janet Barnes Lawrence.

11. Oatsie Charles, Michael Beschloss, *The Crisis Years: Kennedy & Khrushchev, 1960–1963* (New York: HarperCollins, 1991), p. 135; Henry Brandon, *Special Relationship: A Foreign Correspondent's Memoirs, from Roosevelt to Reagan* (New York: Atheneum, 1988), p. 111. Allen Dulles and the Kennedys swapped copies of the James Bond novels. Dulles knew that Bond was an improbable spy, al-

though he was romantic about the reason: "I feel that James Bond in real life would have had a thick dossier in the Kremlin after his first exploit and would not have survived the second." Peter Grose, *Gentleman Spy: The Life of Allen Dulles,* msp. 704. As John Bross later related the story to R. Harris Smith, the morning after the dinner party Bross told Dulles about Fleming's suggestions and made light of the whole thing. Bross "was puzzled that Allen's amusement was not as hearty as he had anticipated." Compartmented from the Cuban operation, Bross did not know that Bissell and Barnes at that moment were working up a similar program of psywar against Castro. Grose, msp. 709.

12. Inspector General of the CIA, "Report on Plots to Assassinate Fidel Castro," "Report on Plots", p. 13.
13. Nixon role: CIA *Bay of Pigs,* pp. 246, 274. Barnes cautioned Bissell against becoming involved with Nixon's friend William Pawley, former U.S. ambassador to Peru and Brazil and a businessman with extensive investments in Cuba, because he was too right-wing. Ibid., p. 253.
14. "Report on Plots," pp. 11–12.
15. Jake Esterline, Richard Bissell.
16. *Alleged Assassination Plots,* pp. 72–73.
17. Miles Copeland, *The Game of Nations* (New York: Simon & Schuster, 1969), p. 202 ("break him in half"); Paul Nitze and James McCargar (Stalin); Jake Esterline (Arbenz).
18. Jake Esterline, Richard Bissell; *Alleged Assassination Plots,* pp. 93–94. The plot is described in the testimony of Edward Hinkle, JFK Records, Church Committee, National Archives, box 35, folder 5, and Bissell phone conversation with Joe DeGenova, June 5, 1975, box 31, folder 1.
19. Sidney Gottlieb. For the best account of Gottlieb and MKULTRA, see John Marks, *The Search for the Manchurian Candidate* (New York: Dell, 1979), pp. 59–112. Olson's family charged in 1994 that he was pushed. Sam Halpern.
20. Richard Bissell, Sidney Gottlieb. Grose writes that Wisner may have understood the seriousness of the LSD experiments. He required that he approve any use of LSD by Gottlieb and his department. Grose, msp. 564.
21. Richard Bissell testimony, JFK Records, Church Committee, National Archives, box 35, folder 1; *Alleged Assassination Plots,* p. 4; Richard Bissell and Bob King.
22. Ted Atkins, Sidney Gottlieb; *Alleged Assassination Plots,* p. 181; Thomas Powers, *The Man Who Kept the Secrets: Richard Helms and the CIA* (New York: Pocket Books, 1979), pp. 161, 163. Many accounts wrongly state the target was General Abdul Karim Kassem.

Chapter Fifteen: Shoot-Down

1. Richard Bissell, Frank Lindsay, John Ranelagh, *The Agency: The Rise and Decline of the CIA* (New York: Simon & Schuster, 1986), pp. 324–25; Walter A. McDougall, . . . *the Heavens and the Earth: A Political History of the Space Age* (New York: Basic Books, 1985), p. 224; William E. Burrows, *Deep Black: Space Espionage and National Security* (New York: Random House, 1986), pp. 109–10. The Corona later proved to be highly reliable.
2. Bissell, *Memoirs*, V, p. 59.
3. Richard Bissell; Michael Beschloss, *Mayday: Eisenhower, Khrushchev, and the U-2 Affair* (New York: Harper & Row, 1986), pp. 5–9, 233–38, 241–42, 368.
4. In his memoirs Bissell says that the pilot's decision to commit suicide was "left entirely to his own judgment. He was under no orders to do away with himself." Bissell, *Memoirs*, V, p. 76.
5. Jackson, *Dulles*, V, pp. 39–139.
6. Bissell, *Memoirs*, V, p. 67.
7. Ibid., p. 74; Bob King, Richard Bissell.
8. Beschloss, p. 60.
9. Ibid., pp. 250–51, 258.
10. Ibid., p. 254, 258. It is interesting that Alsop continued to rail about the "missile gap" despite the fact that the U-2 couldn't find any ICBM deployments. He was being fed hyped intelligence reports by Senator Stuart Symington, a chauvinist who behaved irresponsibly throughout the whole controversy. Why didn't Bissell, who could be indiscreet with Alsop, tell his friend that the missile gap was fiction? The answer may be that Bissell, a hardliner ever suspicious of the Russians, thought the gap was theoretically possible in the future. See Bissell, *Memoirs*, V, pp. 80–81. He was reflecting the institutional bias of that Cold War time. Under pressure from the Air Force, and because it used "worst case" scenarios, the CIA's own National Intelligence Estimates misstated the progress of the Soviet ICBM program. NIE 11–5-57 in March 1957 predicted that the Soviets would "probably" have up to 10 ICBMs by mid-1959, with 100 ICBMs a year later, and 500 two or three years after that. The CIA failed to recognize that the early Soviet ICBM, the SS-6, was too crude for wide-scale deployment. NIE 11–8-59, approved February 1960, predicted that "the probable Soviet ICBM program would provide on the order of 140–200 ICBMs in launchers by mid-1961." In fact, as the Corona spy satellite discovered in 1961, the Soviets had perhaps a dozen. The United States, by contrast, already had an invulnerable "Triad": 32 Polaris missiles in submarines, 16 Atlas

ICBMs, 60 medium-range missiles in Britain, and was installing 45 medium-range missiles in Turkey. Jackson, *Dulles*, V, pp. 39–139; Richard Reeves, *President Kennedy*, (New York: Simon & Schuster, 1993), p. 59.

11. Ibid., pp. 239, 379.

12. David Atlee Phillips, *The Night Watch* (New York: Atheneum, 1977), p. 145; Thomas Powers, *The Man Who Kept the Secrets: Richard Helms and the CIA* (New York: Pocket Books, 1979), pp. 185–186; *Alleged Assassination Plots*, pp. 191–96.

13. Ranelagh, pp. 339–40; Bissell, *Memoirs*, VI, p. 8.

14. Richard Bissell, *Alleged Assassination Plots*, pp. 53–54.

15. Cable cited at ibid., p. 15. See also pp. 52–70. Gottlieb is identified as Joseph Schneider, Lawrence Devlin as Victor Hedgman. Did this cable mean that Eisenhower authorized the assassination? "That is in the eye of the beholder," Bissell writes in his memoirs. "I think if you had asked Ike at that moment, he probably would have said, 'I sure as hell would rather do it without killing him, but if that's the only way, then it's got to be that way'—Eisenhower was a tough man behind that smile." Bissell, *Memoirs*, VI, p. 14. For the case that Eisenhower did know of and authorize the assassination attempt, see Peter Grose, *Gentleman Spy: The Life of Allen Dulles*, mspp. 724–25.

16. *Alleged Assassination Plots*, pp. 14–51; Richard Bissell, Robinson McIlvaine.

17. Carleton Swift, Sam Halpern; David Martin, *Wilderness of Mirrors* (New York: Harper & Row, 1980), pp. 121–23, "Report on Plots," p. 39. By the early 1960s, the NSA had twice the budget of the CIA and was overwhelmed with information from U-2 and satellite photos and electronic intercepts. Boxcars full of highly classified tapes lined up on railway tracks outside NSA headquarters in Fort Meade, Maryland. In the 1950s the CIA had success intercepting Third World communications, but less against the Kremlin. After an early success that helped ferret out Philby as a mole (the Venona traffic), the intelligence community found SIGINT far harder against the Soviets than the Germans, whose codes the Allies had cracked. Chrisopher Andrew, *For the President's Eyes Only: Secret Intelligence and the American Presidency from Washington to Bush* (New York: HarperCollins, 1995), pp. 216–19, 260, 273, 359.

18. Justin O'Donnell is identified as Michael Mulroney in *Alleged Assassination Plots*, pp. 37–41; Richard Bissell.

19. *Alleged Assassination Plots*, pp. 47–49; Martin, p. 123.

20. *Alleged Assassination Plots, pp. 49–51.*

21. Ibid., p. 73; "Report on Plots," pp. 11–12.

22. *Alleged Assassination Plots*, p. 74; Bob King. In his memoirs, Bissell

writes, "I believe that I first learned about the plan from Sheff Edwards. . . . Sheff was frank with me about what he was doing and I also authorized him to continue. I was willing to take some responsibility for decisions but really on the assumption that Sheff could handle their implementation. The genesis of the idea did not originate with me (as has been attributed by some authors and historians) and I had no desire to become personally involved in its implementation, mainly because I was not competent to handle relations with the mafia. . . ." Bissell, *Memoirs*, VI, p. 110. This explanation seems disingenuous. Before the Church Committee, Edwards testified that "Bissell asked him to locate someone who could assassinate Castro." *Alleged Assassination Plots*, p. 74. As chief of CIA security, Sheff Edwards was responsible for safeguarding agency secrets, not for carrying out covert actions. He had to be drafted by Bissell to become involved in the Cuban operation. It may be true that Edwards told Bissell he had some mob connections that could carry out the assignment, but it is almost surely true that Bissell went to Edwards in the first place because he thought Edwards might have some "assets" not available to the Directorate of Plans. The CIA's Office of Security had a number of former FBI agents who could find their way around the underworld. Bissell liked to circumvent his own bureaucracy and reach out to different divisions to handle difficult jobs. See *Alleged Assassination Plots*, p. 74, footnote 3. The Cuba Task Force was compartmented from this assassination planning. There was some talk in that group that after the invasion Castro would be assassinated by the "white hats" in the invasion force. They were supplied by the CIA with weapons with silencers. CIA *Bay of Pigs*, p. 281.

23. *Alleged Assassination Plots*, pp. 74–77; Robert Maheu and Richard Hack, *Next to Hughes: Behind the Power and Tragic Downfall of Howard Hughes by his Closest Adviser* (New York: HarperCollins, 1992), pp. 112–17.
24. *Alleged Assassination Plots*, pp. 95, 109, 111.
25. Ibid., pp. 77–79; "Report on Plots," pp. 57–61.
26. Ibid., pp. 23–32; *Alleged Assassination Plots*, pp. 79–83.
27. Richard Bissell.

Chapter Sixteen: *Plausible Deniability*

1. Gary Hart; Thomas Powers, *The Man Who Kept the Secrets: Richard Helms and the CIA* (New York: Pocket Books, 1979), pp. 181–84.
2. Richard Bissell; Alleged Assassination Plots, pp. 111–12.
3. Chester Cooper, Thomas Parrott, Lyman Kirkpatrick, F.A.O. Schwarz Jr.; Stephen Ambrose, Eisenhower's biographer, writes

that it would have been "out of character" for Eisenhower to order an assassination. Stephen Ambrose, *Eisenhower: The President* (New York: Simon & Schuster 1984), p. 557. But Grose cites the testimony of White House science adviser George Kistiakowsky, who sat in on high-level meetings, that Eisenhower kept firm control over any plots involving "use of force" against offending foreign politicians: "The president got very angry and said he won't even let his agency heads take action . . . that all plans should be brought to him for decision." Grose writes, "Defenders of presidential virtue only insult Eisenhower's intelligence in suggesting that he did not understand the intimations he was receiving from his aides, and the signals he was sending back when he let opportunities pass without a negative response." Peter Grose, *Gentleman Spy: The Life of Allen Dulles*, mspp. 723–24. Christopher Andrew points to a memo by Gordon Gray, kept secret for thirty years, that turned up when *Foreign Relations of the United States 1958–1960* (Washington, D.C.: U.S. Goverment Printing Office, 1991) was published in 1991. When Allen Dulles suggested sabotage against Cuba in February 1960, Gray noted that Eisenhower "wondered why we weren't trying to identify assets for this and other things as well across the board including even possibly things that might be drastic." Christopher Andrew, *For the President's Eyes Only: Secret Intelligence and the American Presidency from Washington to Bush* (New York: HarperCollins, 1995), pp. 252, 582 quoting *FRUS 1958–1960*, vol. 6, p. 789. See also Chapter 20, note 28 there for a discussion of presidential authorization by Eisenhower and Kennedy.

4. Ibid., pp. 718, 664; Bob King, Richard Bissell.
5. F.A.O. Schwarz Jr. "I was still naive about what secrets could be kept and what secrets leaked," said Bissell, who added that he was lulled by his relations with the Alsops and the generally good press enjoyed by the agency. "It was a different era. Frank Wisner used to talk about his 'friends in the press.' I was naive about goofs. But I was never guilty. I had chagrin that I had not foreseen where this would lead to, but not guilt." Richard Bissell.
6. "Report on Plots," pp. 67–74; *Alleged Assassination Plots*, pp. 74–85 (see footnote on p. 85); William Hundley (chief of Organized Crime Division of Justice Department in Kennedy administration).
7. Richard Bissell, Bob King, Doris Mirage; Bissell, *Memoirs*, VI, p. 111. Goon squads: The Pfeiffer history notes "extensive plans for the formation of goon squads throughout much of Latin America in an attempt to counter the pro-Castro elements of various nations. The goon squad program was of considerable interest to the DDP, Mr. Bissell." The report records "disruption in Mexico City of 400 Castro sympathizers gathered to celebrate the 26th of July movement

through the use of stink bombs set off in the meeting place; in Lima, Peru, a counter-demonstration against some 200 Castro sympathizers gathered to celebrate the 26th of July movement. . . In San José, Costa Rica, a meeting of the Amigos de Cuba was broken up . . . an agent in the station sprayed the two principal speakers, prominent Cuban leftists, with 'Who, Me?' (an obnoxious scent)." CIA *Bay of Pigs*, p. 238. In November 1960, Bissell wrote the chief of the Western Hemisphere Division, "I noted with great interest the discussion of the use of goon squads in the minutes of the November 1 meeting. . . . I would greatly appreciate receiving, in due time, a report on the progress you have realized in expanding your capacity for this type of action." Bissell to King, "Goon Squads," November 10, 1960, in HS/CSG 2632AA (CIA).

8. Robert Komer, Eleanor Dulles, Chester Cooper.
9. Alice McIlvaine, Chester Cooper, Jane Barnes.

Chapter Seventeen: Invasion

1. Richard Bissell; Robert Amory Oral History, Kennedy Library, Boston, Mass.; see Harris Wofford, *Of Kennedys and Kings* (Pittsburgh: University of Pittsburgh Press, 1980), p. 358.
2. Richard Reeves, *President Kennedy* (New York: Simon & Schuster, 1993), p. 72.
3. Richard Bissell.
4. Reeves, p. 72.
5. Richard Goodwin, *Remembering America: A Voice from the Sixties* (Boston: Little, Brown 1988), pp. 169–70.
6. Chester Cooper, George Ball.
7. Richard Bissell, Reeves, p. 72.
8. Thomas C. Reeves, *A Question of Character: A Life of John F. Kennedy* (New York: Free Press, 1991), pp. 217–18; Michael Beschloss, *The Crisis Years: Kennedy and Khrushchev, 1960–1963* (New York: HarperCollins, 1991), p. 103.
9. Peter Grose, *Gentleman Spy: The Life of Allen Dulles*, msp. 738.
10. Christopher Andrew, *For the President's Eyes Only: Secret Intelligence and the American Presidency from Washington to Bush* (New York: HarperCollins, 1995), p. 259; Bissell, *Memoirs*, VI, p. 24. According to Grose, Bissell "sent discreet messages through his old friend Adlai Stevenson" that he would be willing to take a leave from his CIA job to work on the Kennedy campaign. Grose, msp. 730.
11. Richard Bissell.
12. Powers, *The Man Who Kept the Secrets: Richard Helms and the CIA* (New York: Pocket Books, 1979), p. 126.
13. Alice McIlvaine, Lloyd Emerson, Bob King, Richard Bissell; Powers,

p. 135. In his memoirs Bissell suggests that Dulles "told me that it might have been better if Helms had moved to another position in the Agency, an idea which was never enacted." In later years Bissell regretted not consulting Helms. "One of my major mistakes as DD/P, and particularly in the Bay of Pigs, was not finding a way to make an ally of Dick Helms." Bissell, *Memoirs*, VI, pp. 64–66.

14. Richard Bissell, Beschloss, p. 103 (says in Moorish living room; Bissell recollects by pool. Bissell, *Memoirs*, VI, p. 24). JMARC: CIA *Bay of Pigs*.

15. The initial budget for JMARC in March 1960 was $4.4 million (political action $950,000, propaganda $1.7 million, paramilitary $1.5 million, intelligence $250,000). By August, the cost was up to $25 million; it became $46 million by April 1961. The Cuba operation had 40 operators in March 1960 and 588 by April 1961. CIA *Bay of Pigs*, pp. 3, 8, 66. See Peter Wyden, *Bay of Pigs: The Untold Story* (New York: Simon & Schuster, 1979), p. 55. Wyden also draws on an excellent early book on the Bay of Pigs, told from the point of view of the Cuban exiles, Haynes Johnson, *The Bay of Pigs: The Leaders' Story of Brigade 2506* (New York: Dell, 1964). See also Trumbull Higgins, *The Perfect Failure: Kennedy, Eisenhower, and the Bay of Pigs* (New York: Norton, 1987) for a sharp analysis of the operation.

16. CIA *Bay of Pigs IG Report*, p. 98.

17. Richard Bissell. The CIA's own intelligence estimate in December declared that Castro was "firmly in control" of Cuba and that "internal opposition to the Castro regime" was "still generally ineffective." Bissell, *Memoirs*, VI, p. 25. This National Intelligence Estimate is in the National Security Archives, *Cuban Missile Crisis, 1962* (Alexandria, Va.: Chadwick-Healy, 1990). Pleas for help: CIA *Bay of Pigs IG Report*, p. 109.

18. Wyden, p. 69; Jake Esterline. In his memoirs Bissell writes, "I always seemed to be advocating a larger brigade while Colonel Hawkins appeared to have a lesser sense of urgency about a further build-up at this particular time." Bissell knew that he had a manpower crisis on his hands. In asking for three hundred additional slots for the Cuba Task Force, Bissell wrote Dulles, "I am convinced that we may be simply running out of suitable people in the Agency in certain categories." Bissell, *Memoirs*, VI, p. 21. The CIA's in-house history of JMARC is very harsh on Barnes, whom it criticized for being at once uninformed, opinionated, and off-the-cuff. "A review of the written record shows one of the most voluminous correspondents was [Tracy] Barnes. A great deal of his written material is repetitious ad nauseam." Barnes "belabored issues that were common knowledge to the principals of [the Task Force]. . . . Barnes appears

to have suffered a severe case of verbal diarrhea." CIA *Bay of Pigs*, pp. 174, 189.

19. Thomas Parrott; Wyden, pp. 54, 61–63, 84; Powers, p. 139; Robert Amory Oral History, Kennedy Library, Boston.
20. Wyden, p. 52.
21. Ibid., pp. 46–47, 84–85.
22. Ibid., pp. 31, 72–73; Luis Aguilar, *Operation Zapata* (Frederick, Md.: University Publications of America, 1981), p. 59; Jackson, *Dulles*, III, p. 117.
23. Wyden, pp. 88–92. The body of the Joint Chiefs report was actually quite skeptical about the chances for success. The executive summary was more sanguine. Bissell chose to base his briefing on the latter. It is not clear whether Bissell himself really read the main report. Going over it thirty years later with Jonathan Lewis for his memoirs, he seemed surprised by all the caveats raised by General Lemnitzer's report. In his memoirs, Bissell simply states, "The inconsistency between the body of [Lemnitzer's] memoranda and the executive summary did not fix itself in my mind as an important fact at the time. It is hard to speculate why it did not receive more attention." Jonathan Lewis; Bissell, *Memoirs*, VI, pp. 30–37, 62.
24. McGeorge Bundy, Bob King; Beschloss, p. 105.
25. *Alleged Assassination Plots*, pp. 181–84; F.A.O. Schwarz Jr.
26. Richard Reeves, p. 84.
27. Beschloss, p. 105.
28. Wyden, pp. 99–100; Richard Reeves, pp. 70–71.
29. Richard Bissell; Lucien Vandenbroucke, "The Confessions of Allen Dulles," *Diplomatic History*, Fall 1984. Bissell publicly responded to the Vandenbroucke article in the same issue: "There was never any trace of a conspiratorial alternative operational plan based on the assumption that the President's hand would be forced," he wrote. But he went on, "Many of us, like Dulles himself, believed that there was a possibility that, in the event of trouble, restrictions would be relaxed, possibly even on the use of U.S. aircraft." Dulles and Bissell may have made a mistake confusing Eisenhower, who frequently commented that when "you commit the flag, you commit to win," with Kennedy, who was more worried about covering his political flank. Recent research indicates that Eisenhower may have been willing to commit U.S. military forces in Guatemala in 1954 had the CIA plot failed. It is possible that Dulles and Bissell assumed that Kennedy would be ready to do likewise in Cuba. See David Atlee Phillips, *Secret Wars Diary: My Adventures in Combat, Espionage Operations, and Covert Action* (Bethesda, Md.: Stone Trail Press, 1989), pp. 137, 178.

30. McGeorge Bundy.

31. David Atlee Phillips, *The Night Watch* (New York: Atheneum, 1977), pp. 101–102.

32. Richard Bissell.

33. "Mutiny": Haynes Johnson, Jake Esterline; Johnson, pp. 75–76, 227; Bissell's truthfulness: Edgar Applewhite. In his memoirs Bissell allows that he was not altogether forthcoming with the president. "It could very well be that the fear of cancellation became so absorbing that I managed to ignore or suppress relevant facts," he writes. He recognized that, in retrospect, he and Dulles should have canceled the operation themselves after the landing site was moved from Trinidad (thus eliminating the "guerrilla option"), the landing was shifted to nighttime, and especially when the air support was cut down. But he somewhat meekly protests, "Allen and I had been edged into the role of advocates." More stoically, he later writes, "I have never denied that we were culpable and I am more than happy to accept the blame personally." Bissell, *Memoirs*, VI, pp. 52–54. In truth, Bissell had not been "edged into the role of advocate." He had put himself in a position where he was both selling his plan and acting as the only man who really knew enough to judge it. This was a familiar trap for CIA officials in this era, and it was made worse by the Kennedys' contempt for bureaucracy, a void Bissell rushed to fill.

34. Powers, p. 145. Bissell said the decision to cut out the DD/I was Dulles's. He noted, however, that Bob Amory was well aware of what was going on in part because he had access to the CIA's reconnaissance of Cuba. Bissell, *Memoirs*, VI, p. 67. Amory was present at a briefing on the invasion plan in January 1961. CIA *Bay of Pigs*, pp. 194–95.

35. Wyden, pp. 93, 98–99, 111. An intelligence report on March 16 predicted that the invaders would be augmented by an active resistance force of 2,500 to 3,000. Once lodgment was achieved, the report predicted the invaders would be supported by 25 percent of the population and opposed by no more than 20 percent. Opposition "will largely disintegrate" and 35 to 40 percent of the army "will defect." Clandestine Services History: [CLASSIFIED], enclosure 4, p. 1.

36. Allen Dulles, "My Answer to the Bay of Pigs," unpublished article, Allen Dulles Papers, Princeton University, Princeton, N.J.

37. Beschloss, p. 139.

38. Richard Reeves, p. 76; John Ranelagh, *The Agency: The Rise and Decline of the CIA* (New York: Simon & Schuster, 1986), p. 451; Beschloss, pp. 107–108.

39. Wyden, pp. 146–51; Richard Reeves, pp. 79–83.

40. Wyden, p. 160; Richard Bissell, Jake Esterline.

41. Bissell's impatience and frustration showed through in a letter he

wrote to his old friend and partner Kelly Johnson of Lockheed that March. "I have learned of your expected additional delay of the first flight from 30 August to 1 December 1961. The news is extremely shocking on top of our previous slippage from May to August. . . . I trust this is the last of such disappointments short of a severe earthquake in Burbank." Years later Bissell wrote, "This seems to be a rude and unnecessarily harsh reaction." But it may reveal the stress he was under. Bissell, *Memoirs*, V, p. 90.

42. Ibid., VI, p. 73; Beschloss, p. 114; Wofford, pp. 347–48.
43. Pierre Salinger, *With Kennedy* (New York: Avon, 1966), p. 194.
44. Wyden, p. 170; Bissell blamed the Joint Chiefs, particularly his old Air Force foe Curtis LeMay, for persuading JFK that air cover was not absolutely essential. The Air Force had refused to help Bissell train the Brigade—sour grapes, possibly, over getting cut out of the U-2. Bissell, *Memoirs*, VI, pp. 60–61.
45. Wyden, pp. 152–58; Phillips, *The Night Watch*, pp. 105–106; Jake Esterline. A CIA historian, Jack Pfeiffer, wrote an article, "Adlai Stevenson and the Bay of Pigs," that was declassified in 1994. (It is in the *Studies in Intelligence* collection at the National Archives, box 8, folder 99.) Two years after the Bay of Pigs, in response to allegations in the first real exposé of the CIA, Thomas Ross and David Wise, *The Invisible Government* (New York: Random House, 1964), that he had misled Stevenson, Barnes wrote a memo to the DD/P defending his role. He said that at his briefing on April 8 he had told Stevenson about the operation "in detail," though he did not mention the air raid because he claimed it had not been "worked out" yet. Yet the record shows that the air raid had been planned by April 5. "There is no way that Barnes could have been ignorant of the decision to launch air strikes on D-2 or D-Day," the CIA historian writes. The article quotes Jake Esterline as saying harshly, "We didn't feel that Tracy understood it well enough himself to brief anybody." The article also quotes Dick Drain, Esterline's number two, in a similar vein: "Knowing Tracy, I've always had severe doubt that Tracy made it very clear to the Ambassador. He was sent up there to make it clear to him . . . on the whole works . . . I think Tracy, dealing with Adlai—in a way they were two of a type—dealt with him, probably the way, just intuitively, Tracy dealt with everyone—very pleasantly, kind of elliptically, lots of smiling and graciousness, interjection of completely non-connected events, shook hands, laughed, and said what a great time he'd had; and came back and announced that he had briefed the Ambassador." Richard F. Pedersen, chief of the political section of the U.S. Mission to the United Nations who was present at Barnes's briefing, wrote the CIA historian, "The briefing totally misled Ambassador Stevenson, Ambassador Plimpton, and

me as to the scope and timing of what was underway." Pedersen
stated that Barnes indicated that there would be no U.S. forces or
personnel involved and that nothing would happen during the U.N.
General Assembly.

46. The CIA article on Stevenson and the Bay of Pigs states that the CIA
signed off on Stevenson's remarks, buying into the misleading cover
story, before the U.N. General Assembly. It doesn't identify who
gave the approval, except as "the responsible person at the CIA"—
presumably Barnes, who was Bissell's designated liasion to State and
Defense, although it is also possible that Stevenson went to someone
else who was not "witting." Secretary of State Dean Rusk compounded the confusion. He knew about the air attack, but he mistakenly thought the "defector" landing in Key West was a real one, so he
failed to warn Stevenson until Saturday afternoon—too late. Pfeiffer.

47. Phillips, *The Night Watch*, p. 106.

48. Wyden, p. 189. Stevenson later said, "Tracy Barnes came up and
briefed us. . . . He assured us this was simply a question of helping
the exiles and this was not in any way a U.S. operation. In light of
what happened I suppose this can be regarded as less than candid."
Hugh Thomas, *The Cuban Revolution* (New York: Harper & Row,
1977), p. 330.

49. Phillips, *The Night Watch*, pp. 106–107; Janet Barnes Lawrence.

50. Wyden, pp. 194–96. For JFK's venereal disease, see Nigel Hamilton,
JFK: Reckless Youth (New York: Random House, 1992).

51. Wyden, p. 196.

52. Ibid., pp. 194–99. Rusk complained in his memoirs that he had never
seen a written copy of the invasion plan. "It is true that he had not
seen a tidy, complete operational plan in writing; even I hadn't,"
wrote Bissell. "In this kind of operation, because of the alleged or
fancied requirements for maintaining tight security, an absolute minimum was written down. I believe now that this sloppiness in not
reducing plans to writing (if only to have a record) can be open to
criticism. There was no big sheaf of documents tabbed on the edge
containing all the elements of the plan, as there would be in the
military. There wasn't time for it and there weren't enough people to
prepare it." Bissell, *Memoirs*, VI, p. 81.

53. Richard Bissell, Wyden, pp. 163, 202–203.

54. Wyden says the time was about 7 P.M. (p. 199); Bissell says 9:30 P.M.
Cabell and Bissell stressed Stevenson's impact on Rusk. In a May 7,
1961 memo to General Maxwell Taylor, charged by JFK with investigating the Bay of Pigs, they wrote: "The Secretary described Ambassador Stevenson's attitude in some detail. Ambassador Stevenson
had insisted that air strikes would make it impossible for the U.S.
position to be the same." Bissell, *Memoirs*, VI, pp. 75–76.

55. Richard Bissell, Jake Esterline; Wyden, pp. 198–204.
56. Wyden, pp. 206–210.

Chapter Eighteen: Fiasco

1. Peter Wyden, *Bay of Pigs: The Untold Story* (New York: Simon & Schuster, 1979), pp. 219–20, 229–30.
2. Ibid., pp. 235–36, 243–44.
3. Ibid., pp. 266–67.
4. Ibid., pp. 268–69.
5. Walt Rostow; Wyden, pp. 270–71; Richard Reeves, *President Kennedy* (New York: Simon & Schuster, 1993), pp. 93–95; Michael Beschloss, *The Crisis Years: Kennedy and Khrushchev, 1960–1963* (New York: HarperCollins, 1991), p. 123.
6. Wyden, pp. 272–88. Survivors rescued: *CIA Bay of Pigs IG Report*, p. 33.
7. David Atlee Phillips, *The Night Watch* (New York: Atheneum, 1977), p. 109; Alice McIlvaine.
8. Wyden, p. 293; Jim Flannery.
9. Bissell, *Memoirs*, V, p. 22
10. Wyden, p. 289; Harris Wofford, *Of Kennedys and Kings* (Pittsburgh: University of Pittsburgh Press, 1980), p. 353, Beschloss, pp. 148–49; Reeves, pp. 98–99.
11. Thomas Powers, *The Man Who Kept the Secrets: Richard Helms and the CIA* (New York: Pocket Books, 1979), p. 144; Wofford, pp. 357–63. Kennedy wisely took the blame in public. "There's an old saying that victory has a hundred fathers and defeat is an orphan," he quipped at a press conference. In one of the small ironies of history, that "old saying" was traced back to an entry in the Ciano diaries which Tracy Barnes had managed to secure for Allen Dulles 16 years before. Peter Grose, *Gentleman Spy: The Life of Allen Dulles*, msp. 757.
12. Richard Bissell.
13. Susan Mary Alsop.
14. Janet Barnes Lawrence, Avis Bohlen, Tish Alsop.
15. Courtlandt Barnes, Cleve Cram.
16. Ben Sturges, McGeorge Bundy.
17. Jane Barnes, Marie Ridder.
18. Marie Ridder.
19. Thomas Parrott, Marie Ridder.
20. Jackson, *Dulles*, III, p. 135. CIA *Bay of Pigs IG Report*, pp. 36–38, 56, 61, 64, 123. Bissell's and Barnes's response is titled "An Analysis of the Cuban Operation." "Malicious": Barnes to Bissell, January 19, 1992 (CIA).

21. Robert Crowley. Bissell's 1961 fitness report for Barnes, written about a month after the IG report on the Bay of Pigs, demonstrates loyalty, but it seems slightly surreal in light of the facts. "Perhaps the most important part of his duties . . . was the handling of a variety of major special assignments. This he performed in a manner which earned him my complete confidence in his judgment, energy, and effectiveness. . . . His work involved much negotiation with other departments, especially the Department of State, in which he conducted himself with great skill. I would name as his most unusual and valuable quality his imaginativeness about new approaches to the functions of the clandestine service." Tracy Barnes Personnel File (CIA).
22. John Casey, Janet Barnes Lawrence, Tracy Barnes Jr., Jane Barnes.
23. Gordon Stewart, Doris Mirage, Bob King.
24. *Alleged Assassination Plots*, pp. 207, 212–13, 262.
25. McGeorge Bundy.
26. Wofford, p. 364.
27. *Alleged Assassination Plots*, pp. 141, 314–15. Bissell told the Church Committee that he did not authorize an assassination attempt but rather reactivated the Mafia contacts through Harvey. Helms, who succeeded Bissell as DD/P, testified that he merely went along with plans already in progress. Harvey believed he had authorization from Bissell. Incredibly, Bissell did not brief the new DCI, John McCone. Ibid., pp. 151, 187, 311.
28. Did Kennedy authorize the assasination plots? Two anecdotes are often cited: In March 1960, Kennedy asked his friend George Smathers what the world would think if Castro were assassinated. Smathers answered that the United States would get the blame, and Kennedy agreed it was a poor idea. He told Smathers that he had been "given to believe" that Castro would be dead by the time the Cuban exiles hit the beaches in the upcoming invasion. "Someone was supposed to have knocked him off, and there was supposed to be absolute pandemonium," Smathers later told historian Michael Beschloss.

   Then in November, a few days after RFK berated Richard Bissell for his inaction toward Cuba, President Kennedy asked journalist Tad Szulc, "What would you think if I ordered Castro to be assassinated?" Szulc answered that the situation in Cuba would not improve, and that the United States should not engage in immoral acts. Kennedy said, "I agree with you completely," but that he was under "terrible pressure" from his advisers. Szulc thought he heard the president say that the pressure came from his "intelligence people." Beschloss, pp. 138–39.

   Robert F. Kennedy was certainly aware of the CIA/Mafia plot to kill Castro. The only question is when he learned of it. Bissell never told Kennedy directly, he later testified. But he may have let him know in a "circumlocutious" fashion. A memo from Sheff Edwards to Attorney General Kennedy in May 1961 quoted Bissell as saying that the "planning" against Castro included the "use of Giancana and the underworld." In the same memo Edwards described how Robert Maheu had been used as a "cut-out" to deal with Giancana so the CIA would not be directly involved with "dirty business." The word "assassination" was never used, but an earlier memo to J. Edgar Hoover of the FBI reported that Giancana was bragging about knocking off Castro. It is quite likely that Hoover filled in RFK on the details.

The CIA itself did a year later, in May 1962. At his request, Kennedy was briefed "all the way" on the CIA/Mafia plots against Castro. Kennedy was angry with the CIA officials who briefed him. "I trust if you ever do business with organized crime again—with gangsters—you will let the attorney general know," he said. Kennedy had been trying to prosecute Giancana, and he knew that the Chicago don would use his CIA service as a shield.

Kennedy did not, however, instruct the CIA to stop trying to kill Castro. This is a very important point to old agency hands—it is the dog-that-didn't-bark in the mystery over presidential authorization that arose during the Church Committee hearings. CIA officials insist that they were under unrelenting pressure from Bobby Kennedy to "get rid" of Castro. He never came out and used the word "assassination," but he made it clear enough—given the dictates of plausible deniability—that he wanted Castro gone, and it was the CIA's job to make this happen any way it could. *Alleged Assassination Plots*, pp. 121–123, 127, 132–33, 324, 330–31; Sam Halpern, Richard Helms. Bissell believed that both Eisenhower and Kennedy knew and approved of the plots to kill Castro—but only in general terms. "I have never believed for a moment that Allen [Dulles] went to the President and said, 'I'm trying to use the mafia to get Castro assassinated.' Indeed, I am sure that just did not happen." On the other hand, "I also don't think Bobby Kennedy would have concealed these plans from his brother. I feel he would have said that we are trying in every way we can to get rid of this guy, and that may mean using some pretty unpleasant methods. The President might have replied that it is really vital to get rid of him and you go right ahead, or he might have said I agree with you and hope you can get rid of him." Bissell, *Memoirs*, VI, p. 109. My own surmise, based on the somewhat sketchy evidence, is that in the winter of 1960, before the Bay of Pigs, Dulles gave JFK some vague hint that the CIA was trying to kill Castro, and Kennedy didn't stop him or press him on the details. Then, in the fall of 1961, when Bobby Kennedy became directly in-

volved in Cuba, he learned the specifics of the Mafia plot, partly from
the FBI and then from Harvey et al. Bobby probably filled in JFK.
(See note 26 to Chapter 20.) My guess, however, is that Eisenhower
never knew of the plots. In any case, in the early days—in 1960 when
the plotting started—Bissell was willing to authorize the plots based
on the merest nods and winks from Dulles, who himself may not have
known of the Mafia involvement until much later. The rationale was
plausible deniability, but Bissell was quite comfortable with the freedom from accountability that plausible deniability permitted.
29. Richard Bissell; RB to Ann Harriet Bissell, March 11, 1964, Bissell,
Memoirs, VII, p. 3.

Chapter Nineteen: Secret Armies

1. Frances FitzGerald.
2. Susan Mary Alsop.
3. Charles Whitehurst, James Lilley.
4. Donald Gregg, James Lilley, William Colby, Sam Halpern. The best,
   most detailed public source on the Tibet operation is John Prados,
   The President's Secret Wars (New York: Morrow, 1986), pp. 184–87.
   See also Michael Peissel, *The Secret War in Tibet* (Boston: Little,
   Brown 1973), pp. 3–15, 75–81, 107, 140–53, 163–65, for a more florid
   but firsthand account. "Romantic Program": between October 1958
   and February 1959 the CIA dropped about 20,000 pounds of arms and
   ammunition to the Khambas. The Tibetans called their training camp
   in the Rocky Mountains "Dumra" (Garden Spot). Between 1959 and
   1960, 250 Tibetans were trained there. An earlier training base on
   the East Coast had caused respiratory problems. James M. Rhinehart, "Covert Action in High Altitudes," *Studies in Intelligence*,
   Spring 1976 (hereinafter CIA *Tibet*), p. 20.
5. Jim Critchfield, Richard Bissell; John K. Galbraith, *A Life in Our
   Times* (Boston: Houghton Mifflin, 1981), pp. 394–97.
6. Prados, pp. 168–69; Victor Marchetti, and John D. Marks, *The CIA
   and the Cult of Intelligence* (New York: Knopf, 1974), pp. 115–116;
   James Lilley. The Khambas killed a ChiCom regimental commander
   and captured 1,600 pages of documents that told the CIA that the
   cadres of the People's Militia were paper only, that the Chinese economy was in poor shape; and that the Sino-Soviet rivalry was severe.
   Rhinehart, p. 22.
7. Sam Halpern.
8. George Ball, *The Past Has Another Pattern* (New York: Norton
   1982), pp. 361–62; Richard Reeves, *President Kennedy* (New York:
   Simon & Schuster, 1993), p. 31; Charles A. Stevenson, *The End of
   Nowhere* (Boston: Beacon, 1972), is a comprehensive account but

very densely written. The best on-the-ground account is Roger Warner's *Back Fire: The CIA's Secret War in Laos and Its Link to the Vietnam War* (New York: Simon & Schuster, 1995). See also J. Graham Parson, Chester Cooper, and Winthrop Brown Oral Histories, Kennedy Library, Boston.

9. Charles Whitehurst; Reeves, pp. 74, 111; David Corn, *Blond Ambition: Ted Shackley and the CIA's Crusades* (New York: Simon & Schuster, 1994), p. 124. Some CIA operatives were cynical about the brand of democracy they were importing: one CIA man told Charles Stevenson, "We thought that politics is politics the world over, so we tried to transplant Tammany." Stevenson, p. 48.

10. Christopher Robbins, *The Ravens: The Men Who Flew in America's Secret War in Laos* (New York: Crown, 1987), p. 104; Prados, pp. 262–65; Stevenson, pp. 25–170; Ball, p. 362.

11. Charles Whitehurst; see Winthrop Brown Oral History, Kennedy Library. Brown could see that Phoumi was a loser, but Washington was obdurate. According to John Horton, a case officer in FE, Fitz-Gerald pushed Heckscher's successor, Gordon Jorgensen, to stand up to Ambassador Brown, who FitzGerald thought was "soft."

12. Reeves, p. 75; Charles Whitehurst, Lloyd Emerson; Bissell himself went to Vientiane for a firsthand look in January 1961 and listened in disbelief as the military outlined its plan for defeating the Pathet Lao. "Even that much contact with reality convinced me that we were dealing with a situation a million miles from the precision, order, and purposefulness of the Department of Defense. The plan proposed by the Joint Chiefs of Staff included elegant lines of troop deployment, bold military manuevers, and predictions that the Plaine des Jarres would be seized by parachute on approximately the 10th day of the operation. I found this assessment and the briefing almost surreal." Bissell did not speak up. This was a Pentagon show. Just as he expected the JCS to defer to the CIA on Cuba, Bissell kept silent about the Pentagon's war plans in Laos. "This experience can be taken as an example of how the bureaucracy in Washington is sometimes detrimental to policymaking," he writes. Bissell, *Memoirs*, VI, pp. 43–44.

13. David Halberstam, *The Best and the Brightest* (New York: Random House, 1972), pp. 97–98. Although Bissell had little faith in a military solution, he also disapproved of sending Harriman to seek a cease-fire. He protested to his friend and fellow hawk Walt Rostow that this "was just going to throw away all the U.S. assets in Laos. Walt replied that he sympathized, but the President's view in effect was that we couldn't attempt to win in Laos." Bissell, *Memoirs*, VI, p. 44.

14. William Sullivan, Chester Cooper.

15. Campbell James.

16. William Sullivan. The code name for the agency's support of Vang Pao was Operation Momentum. FitzGerald personally authorized the operation on a trip to Laos in January 1961. Warner, pp. 24–26.
17. Vint Lawrence; Jane Hamilton-Merritt, *Tragic Mountains: The Hmong, the Americans, and the Secret Wars for Laos, 1942–1992* (Bloomington, Ind.: Indiana University Press, 1993), p. 5.
18. Air America described: Christopher Robbins, *The Invisible Air Force: The Story of the CIA's Secret Airlines* (London: Macmillan, 1979) and *The Ravens*. The French subsidized the Hmong army by selling its opium to Emperor Bao Dai of Vietnam for a high markup. Though the CIA prohibited its operatives from engaging in the opium trade, David Corn makes a convincing case that the agency turned a blind eye to opium trading by the Hmong. Corn, pp. 127, 147–51.
19. Vint Lawrence, William Sullivan.
20. Jim Flannery, Richard Bissell.
21. Hamilton-Merritt, pp. 131–40; Vint Lawrence.

Chapter Twenty: Hard Target

1. Frances FitzGerald, Sam Halpern.
2. Stewart Alsop, *The Center: People and Power in Political Washington* (New York: Harper & Row, 1986), p. 157; William Colby and Peter Forbath, *Honorable Men: My Life in the CIA* (New York: Simon & Schuster, 1978), p. 259; David Halberstam, *The Best and the Brightest* (New York: Random House, 1972), p. 348.
3. *Alleged Assassination Plots*, p. 141. Mongoose described: John Prados, *The Presidents' Secret Wars* (New York: Morrow, 1986), pp. 211–17; John Ranelagh, *The Agency: The Rise and Decline of the CIA* (New York: Simon & Schuster, 1986), pp. 383–90. The most detailed description is in David Corn's biography of Ted Shackley, the station chief of JMWAVE, *Blond Ambition: Ted Shackley and the CIA's Crusades* (New York: Simon & Schuster, 1994), pp. 74–119. Corn made good use of the Church Committee documents in the National Archives declassified as a result of a congressional act requiring disclosure about the Kennedy assassination.
4. Sam Halpern; Christopher Andrew, *For the President's Eyes Only: Secret Intelligence and the American Presidency from Washington to Bush* (New York: HarperCollins, 1995), p. 275.
5. Harris Wofford, *Of Kennedys and Kings* (Pittsburgh: University of Pittsburgh Press, 1980), p. 386.
6. Bissell felt Lansdale was simply trying to do all over again what he had failed to do in the Bay of Pigs. "Mongoose bore a remarkable resemblance to CIA's original planning for the Bay of Pigs. I am still convinced that his plan did not embody a new concept or sequence of

activities radically different from those contemplated in the Agency's Operation Zapata." Bissell, *Memoirs*, VI, p. 103.

7. Thomas Parrott, Sam Halpern; Thomas Powers, *The Man Who Kept the Secrets: Richard Helms and the CIA* (New York: Pocket Books, 1979), pp. 173–79; Corn, p. 82 ("fags").

8. Bissell, *Memoirs*, V, p. 82. The notion that Kennedy's secret war in Cuba provoked the Soviets into a disproportionate response has been hotly disputed by Kennedy aide Arthur Schlesinger Jr. Certainly, Castro was well aware of the activities of JMWAVE; the many Cuban exiles on the agency payroll in Miami were notoriously talkative and thoroughly penetrated by Castro's East German–trained security service. In 1989, Kennedy's secretary of defense, Robert McNamara, conceded, "If I had been in Moscow or Havana at that time, I would have believed the Americans were preparing an invasion." The CIA's own postmortems of the Cuban Missile Crisis concluded that Khrushchev believed that the creation of a Soviet missile base in Cuba would discourage the United States from trying to overthrow the Castro regime. Arthur Schlesinger, Jr., *Robert Kennedy and His Times* (Boston: Houghton Mifflin, 1978), p. 526; Corn, p. 94.

9. Corn, p. 93. There is some dispute over the effectiveness of the CIA. Some historians claim that the information about the missile sites came from a walk-in refugee in Miami. This is a misreading of the documents, contends Sam Halpern, the executive officer of MONGOOSE. In fact, he says, CIA assets in Cuba targeted the U-2 flights that found the missiles at San Cristóbal. See Mary S. McAuliffe, "Return to the Brink: Intelligence Perspectives in the Cuban Missile Crisis," *The SHAFR Newsletter*, June 1993; Samuel Halpern, "Revisiting the Cuban Missile Crisis," ibid., March 1994.

10. For narratives of the missile crisis, see Michael Beschloss, *The Crisis Years: Kennedy and Khrushchev, 1960–1963* (New York: HarperCollins, 1991), pp. 431–575; Richard Reeves, *President Kennedy* (New York: Simon & Schuster, 1993), pp. 370–425; an excellent book from the CIA end is Dino Brugiani, *Eyeball to Eyeball: The Inside Story of the Cuban Missile Crisis* (New York: Random House, 1991).

11. John Horton, DF to Frances FitzGerald, April 11, 1963, Frances FitzGerald Papers, Boston University.

12. DF to Director of Central Intelligence (John McCone), March 16, 1963, *Kennedy Records*, box 16, folder 4.

13. Corn, p. 74.

14. Ibid., p. 81.

15. Minutes of DF briefing of President Kennedy, November 12, 1963, Kennedy Records, box 11, folder 1. FitzGerald told the president that sabotage operations had "raised the morale" of the Cuban people and kept pressure on Castro by adding to his economic problems. He

said there were indications that some military leaders might back away from Castro, though he described the military as generally loyal. He said the CIA was trying to encourage military officers to "dare to talk and plot Castro's downfall with each other." He asked for Kennedy's permission to push ahead with sabotage and harassment. The Special Group approved on November 14. A week later Kennedy was assassinated. LBJ rescinded the order on December 20, 1963.

16. Sam Halpern.
17. *Alleged Assassination Plots*, pp. 84–85, footnote 4; David Martin, *Wilderness of Mirrors* (New York: Harper & Row, 1980), pp. 145–46; "Report on Plots," pp. 53–54; Schlesinger, p. 484.
18. *Alleged Assassination Plots*, pp. 85–86; Sam Halpern, Sidney Gottlieb. Gottlieb recalls that the wet suit idea originated with FitzGerald. The 1967 IG report states it is not clear whether Harvey or FitzGerald started the plot, though FitzGerald "seemed to say" that it was his idea. "Report on Plots," p. 75. Halpern says the plot was conceived before FitzGerald took over the Cuba operation and notes that Donovan's work with Castro was done in December—a month before FitzGerald's arrival.
19. Sam Halpern, "Report on Plots," p. 77. FitzGerald even bought two volumes on "Caribbean Mollusca."
20. Sam Halpern.
21. Charles F. Adams.
22. Paul Nitze.
23. Frances FitzGerald, Barbara Lawrence, Thomas Parrott.
24. "Meeting on Cuba," April 3, 1963, Kennedy Records, box 11, folder 1.
25. Sam Halpern, Albert Francke, Joan Denny, DF to Frances Fitz-Gerald, June 25, 1963, Frances FitzGerald Papers, Boston University.
26. Beschloss, pp. 141–43; Schlesinger, p. 494. Of course, the president at the time was foolish enough to be sleeping with Judith Exner Campbell, a girlfriend of both Rosselli and Giancana (and Frank Sinatra, who fixed her up with JFK). There is speculation—but no strong evidence—that the Mafia moll played the role of courier between the president and the mob. Exner has claimed that she carried some envelopes back and forth, but she is perhaps not the most credible witness. "I couldn't imagine her being privy to any kind of secret information," said William Campbell, her ex-husband. "She wouldn't understand it anyway. I mean . . . they weren't dealing with some kind of Phi Beta Kappa."

As noted in Chapter Eighteen, note 28, Robert F. Kennedy was aware of the Mafia plots against Castro. Briefed by the CIA in May

1962, he had warned the agency never to use the Mafia again—that is, without clearing it first with the attorney general. The agency had taken heed, within the peculiar confines of plausible deniability. Although the CIA told Kennedy at the May briefing that the Mafia operation had been shut down, in fact Harvey that spring gave Rosselli poison pills and a van containing weapons. It is not clear if Kennedy knew about this particular plot. Richard Helms is the last one alive who would know for sure, and he will not answer directly, though he says that RFK was an unrelenting goad to "get rid of" Castro. RFK may have been insulated from some of the details, but he was in a position to know a great deal about the connections between the Mafia and CIA. According to Halpern, the Special Affairs Staff had a case officer devoted full-time to talking to Mafia contacts provided by none other than Robert F. Kennedy. The case officer, who was given an Italian pseudonym, met with Mafia contacts to pick up intelligence about Castro. The information had been supposedly funneled out by the mob's "stay-behind" agents in Havana who hoped, one day, to get their gambling casinos restored. The meetings were set up through the office of the attorney general; according to Halpern, the calls were placed by Kennedy's secretary, Angie Novello (she has no recollection of this). The operation was an intelligence-gathering one (Halpern says the information was mostly useless); it was not part of an assassination plot. Robert Kennedy's biographer Arthur Schlesinger Jr. argues that Kennedy was innocent of trying to kill Castro. In 1967, when stories of the assassination plots began to emerge in the press, Kennedy angrily told his aides, "I didn't start it. I stopped it. . . . I found out that some people were going to try an attempt on Castro's life and I turned it off." Richard Helms, Angie Novello, Sam Halpern; Schlesinger, pp. 494, 498.
27. Anthony Summers, *Conspiracy* (New York: Paragon, 1989), p. 323.
28. Sam Halpern, *Alleged Assassination Plots*, pp. 86–87.
29. Church Committee, Book V, p. 17; Committee on Assassinations, *Report*, p. 112.
30. Sam Halpern, Ted Shackley, Richard Helms.
31. Frances FitzGerald, Doris Jackson, Ted Shackley, Sam Halpern.
32. Barbara Lawrence, Albert Francke.
33. DF to Frances FitzGerald, undated, probably Thanksgiving 1963, Frances FitzGerald Papers, Boston University; DF to Frances FitzGerald, October 21, 1963, courtesy Frances FitzGerald.
34. David Laux.
35. *Alleged Assassination Plots*, pp. 88–89, 174–78; "Report on Plots," pp. 88–93; Sam Halpern, Richard Helms. The case officer, Nestor Sanchez, testified before the Church Committee that AMLASH just

wanted the pen for self-defense. He rejected the pen when offered, perhaps because it did not suit his needs. Kennedy Records, box 35, folder 4.

36. The wager is in FitzGerald's personal papers, dated November 13, 1963, courtesy Frances FitzGerald. This date is one day after Fitz-Gerald briefed Kennedy on the progress of the Cuban operation and one day before the Special Group approved his plan of continued covert operations against the Castro regime. See note 15.

Chapter Twenty-One: Blowback

1. Sam Halpern.
2. "Report on Plots," pp. 93–94.
3. Richard Helms, Sam Halpern.
4. Church Committee, Book V, pp. 23–29; Sam Halpern.
5. *Alleged Assassination Plots*, p. 164; "Report on Plots," p. 114; Walt Elder.
6. Walt Elder.
7. Barbara Train, Desmond FitzGerald Jr.
8. Haynes Johnson, Richard Helms, Ted Shackley; Church Committee, Book V, pp. 57–60; Committee on Assassinations, *Report*, pp. 127–29, 239, 257. The FBI did run down a number of leads, but it failed to make use of its own Cuba section in the Domestic Intelligence Division. Allen Dulles was a member of the Warren Commission. His first allegiance was to the CIA, writes Peter Grose; Dulles "sought with the utmost subtlety to neutralize the impulses of his fellow commissioners to pursue lines of inquiry that might expose CIA operations, even though they had nothing to do with the Dallas shooting." Peter Grose, *Gentleman Spy: The Life of Allen Dulles*, msp. 780. See also, Evan Thomas, "The JFK Cover-Up," *Newsweek*, November 22, 1993. For conspiracy theories, see Anthony Summers and Robbyn Summers, "JFK: Case Reopened," *Vanity Fair*, December 1994. The article claims that FitzGerald was presiding over a meeting with Cuban exiles on a new plot to overthrow Castro on the morning of November 22, 1963. If such a meeting took place, FitzGerald was not at it, according to his executive assistant, Sam Halpern.
9. *Alleged Assassination Plots*, p. 177, "Report on Plots," p. 87. In 1963, JMWAVE had authorized eighty-eight missions to Cuba, of which fifteen were canceled. Of the rest, four directly involved sabotage, including blowing up a sawmill and oil facility. CIA teams encountered Cuban forces ten times. David Corn, *Blond Ghost: Ted Shackley and the CIA's Crusades* (New York: Simon & Schuster, 1994), pp. 103–104, 112. On March 6, 1964, FitzGerald wrote Mac

Bundy a letter reviewing the program's goals and accomplishments. The letter shows that he had not given up hope of finding his man on a white horse: "The ultimate object of the program was not mass uprisings but to encourage disaffected elements within the military establishment and other power centers to carry out a coup." Sabotage was "a sort of firing pin for internal unrest and to create the conditions for a coup, which was to be the main force leading to Castro's defeat." FitzGerald cited "five rather low key raids," the effectiveness of which was "certainly debatable." He acknowledged that "Castro is on a strong upswing," and that a covert program of sabotage to overthrow Castro is "not realistic." But, he went on, "our program to get in touch with and subvert members of the military establishment and other exile groups in Cuba continues. Its chance of success naturally rises and falls with the state of morale inside Cuba and is influenced by the success or inactivity of our other programs and the U.S. position in general." He concluded, "as part of an integrated program, we still have at least a fighting chance to get rid of Castro." DF to McGeorge Bundy, March 6, 1964, Kennedy Records, box 38, folder 1.

10. Sam Halpern.
11. "Report on Plots," pp. 106–11. DF, "A Reappraisal of Autonomous Operations," June 3, 1964; Gordon Chase to McGeorge Bundy, June 16, 1964; Department of State Intelligence and Research Division, "Meeting Notes," June 4, 1964, Kennedy Records, box 39, folder 1.
12. Confidential interview.
13. Tracy Barnes Jr., Jane Barnes.
14. Lawrence Houston.
15. E. Howard Hunt, Tom Braden, Tracy Barnes to Allen Dulles, October 4, 1962, Allen Dulles Papers, Princeton University, Princeton, N.J.
16. Stanley Gaines.
17. Elizabeth McDonald
18. Chester Cooper.
19. George Holmes, Lawrence Houston, Jane Barnes.
20. Stanley Gaines, Thomas Parrott, Marlys Chatel (Tofte's widow), Robert Crowley. Chatel described her late husband as "an authentic hero who kind of blew up. He had a drinking problem." See Morton Mintz, "Tofte Case Blows Covers High and Low," *Washington Post*, October 16, 1966.
21. Thomas Parrott, Richard Helms. Through the end Barnes received excellent fitness reports. His last, on May 12, 1966: "He has continued to perform at the same high level of competence." Tracy Barnes Personnel File (CIA).

22. Robert Crowley, Lawrence Houston, Richard Bissell.
23. Thomas Powers, *The Man Who Kept the Secrets: Richard Helms and the CIA* (New York: Pocket Books, 1979), p. 118.
24. Bissell was, in fact, trying to implement government policy. In 1962, the Bell Report, a formal policy document of the executive branch, called for a clearer separation between the Defense Department and IDA. Bissell, *Memoirs*, VII, pp. 9–10.
25. Norman Christeller, Bob King.
26. Bissell's card file is in the office files of John Macy, dated October 1964, LBJ Library, Austin, Texas.
27. Richard Bissell.
28. Carleton Swift, Cleve Cram, Henry Hyde, Al Ulmer.
29. Carleton Swift, Wendy Hazard; Burton Hersh, *The Old Boys: The American Elite and the Origins of the CIA* (New York: Scribner's, 1992), p. 424.
30. Charles Reeder.
31. Carleton Swift, Al Ulmer, Richard Bissell.
32. Wendy Hazard, Benno Schmidt Sr., Jean Lindsey.
33. Selwa Roosevelt.

Chapter Twenty-Two: Casualties of War

1. Fred Reeder.
2. Burke Wilkinson, an old foreign service hand and friend of the Wisners, gave me a file of correspondence that included the book reviews. "HATE-THAT-CIA" is from a letter to Sherman Kent, April 13, 1965. Wisner wrote, "I keep hearing from my wife, Squirrel-eye, and other friends that you are telling people that Morris West's latest and most novel novel, 'The Ambassador,' is a GOOD BOOK!"
3. Thomas Ross and David Wise, *The Invisible Government* (New York: Vintage, 1974), is a remarkable piece of reporting for its time, given how little the public really knew about the CIA. For attacks on the news media, see Frank Wisner to Allen Dulles, February 3, 1964, Allen Dulles Papers, Princeton University, Princeton, N.J.
4. David Wise.
5. Frank Wisner to Allen Dulles, May 12, 1965; FW to John McCone, March 14, 1965, Allen Dulles Papers, Princeton University.
6. Burton Hersh, *The American Elite and the Origins of the CIA* (New York: Scribner's, 1992), p. 439.
7. Jane Thompson, Wendy Hazard, James McCargar.
8. Arthur Jacobs, Jean Lindsey. A month before he killed himself, Wisner told Helms that he was giving up his consultancy with the CIA. Frank Wisner Personnel File (CIA).

9. Harrison Salisbury, *Without Fear or Favor* (New York: Times Books, 1980). p. 519.

10. Henry Breck.

11. DF to Graham Wisner, November 21, 1965, courtesy Frances Fitz-Gerald.

12. I received a copy of Helms's remarks in an unmarked envelope mailed to my home.

13. Henry Breck.

14. Edgar Applewhite, William Hood, William Colby.

15. Tim Hogan; John Ranelagh, *The Agency: The Rise and Decline of the CIA* (New York: Simon & Schuster, 1986), p. 390 (Brazil); Gregory Treverton, *Covert Action: The Limits of Intervention in the Postwar World* (New York: Basic Books, 1977), pp. 18, 20–21 (Chile).

16. Thomas Parrott.

17. Richard Bissell to John Bross, August 3, 1967, courtesy Frances FitzGerald.

18. William Colby, Sam Halpern.

19. Howard Stone. CIA veteran David Murphy credited Wisner with reviving a somewhat moribund Soviet Division when he became DD/P. He called DF a "unique type who did not hesitate to push forward his ideas with all deliberate speed and vigor." David Murphy Oral History, CIA Oral History Project.

20. Roswell Gilpatric.

21. Ranelagh, pp. 423–24; Christopher Andrew, *For the President's Eyes Only: Secret Intelligence and the American Presidency from Washington to Bush* (New York: HarperCollins, 1995), p. 309. It's not clear what conspiracy LBJ had in mind, outside a general distrust of the Kennedys. DF and Raborn: David Atlee Phillips, *The Night Watch* (New York: Atheneum, 1977), pp. 170–71.

22. DF to Frances FitzGerald, March 15, 1966, Frances FitzGerald Papers, Boston University; Doris Jackson.

23. William Colby.

24. Ranelagh, pp. 432–35; Richard Reeves, *President Kennedy* (New York: Simon & Schuster, 1993), pp. 535–52, 565–77, 588–621; Sam Halpern. Once the coup plotting was under way, the Saigon chief of station recommended that "we do not set ourselves irrevocably against the assassination plot, since the two alternatives mean either a bloodbath in Saigon or a protracted struggle which would rip the Army and the country asunder." McCone made it clear, however, that assassination should not be part of the plan. *Alleged Assassination Plots*, pp. 217–23.

25. Ray Cline, *Secrets, Spies and Scholars: Blueprint of the Essential CIA* (Washington, D.C.: Acropolis Books, 1976), p. 214; Ranelagh, pp. 436–41.

26. Campbell James; Roger Warner, *Back Fire: The CIA's Secret War in Laos and Its Link to the Vietnam War* (New York: Simon & Schuster, 1995), pp. 125–46; Jane Hamilton-Merritt, *Tragic Mountains: The Hmong, the Americans, and the Secret Wars for Laos, 1942–1992* (Bloomington, Ind.: Indiana University Press, 1993), pp. 148–540; John Prados, *The Presidents' Secret Wars* (New York: Morrow, 1986), p. 295, Christopher Robbins, *The Ravens: The Men Who Flew in America's Secret War in Laos* (New York: Crown, 1987), p. 337.

27. Sam Halpern. Clifford quoted: Douglas Blaufarb Oral History, CIA Oral History Project. North Vietnam was called "the great blank" by intelligence operatives. In his CIA Oral History, Richard Helms said, "I was willing to do almost anything to try to get it, including putting peaceniks from the United States into the peace movement to see if they could get something via Sweden or other peaceniks who travelled to Hanoi. In other words, we turned the box out on all the tricks that we could think of to do this, but as I look back on it, it was no great success . . . a hard nut to crack, and we didn't crack it. I think we might have done a slight bruise job on one side of the nut, but that was all." CIA Oral History Project.

28. Sam Halpern.

29. George Holmes, Alice McIlvaine.

30. Barbara Lawrence.

31. Paul Garbler, Sam Halpern.

32. Ranelagh, p. 251.

33. Edgar Applewhite, Robert Kiley. Kiley, who was the last CIA official in charge of the NSA, said that James Angleton was more aggressive than FitzGerald in looking for a way to stop *Ramparts* from publishing. Angleton believed the article was a "Soviet plot." When Applewhite returned from his mission to dig up dirt on the *Ramparts* editors, "I told him that the *Ramparts* hippies had reached a journalistic threshold in describing the incidence and practice of fellatio on the West Coast. He asked, what is fellatio? When I told him he cracked up. The practice was not new to him but that word was. In his weekly staff meeting a few weeks later he regaled his nonplussed division chiefs with an explanation of fellatio." The CIA heard rumors from "N.Y. publishing circles" on January 2, 1967 that *Ramparts* was doing a story. The CIA's in-house history of the affair states that "possible examination by the Agency of *Ramparts* income tax returns was discussed by IRS but was not accomplished." After the leak, two hundred clandestine service case officers worked round the clock for two weeks on damage control. Clandestine Services History 196: The 1967 Crisis in Covert Action Operations: The *Ramparts* Exposure (CIA), pp. 26, 33, 59.

34. Halpern; David Martin, *Wilderness of Mirrors* (New York: Harper &

Row, 1980), p. 219; Mark Riebling, *Wedge: The Secret War Between the FBI and CIA* (New York: Knopf, 1994), pp. 170–73, 218–41. In 1971 the CIA approached the Immigration Service to stall deportation proceedings against Rosselli in order to avoid public disclosure of his involvement with the agency. In 1976, Rosselli was hacked up, stuffed into an oil drum, and dumped into the sea near Miami. A year earlier—just before he was scheduled to testify before the Church Committee—Giancana was shot seven times in the throat and mouth as he was frying sausages in his Chicago kitchen.

35. Sam Halpern.
36. Barbara Lawrence.
37. C. F. Adams, Jim Critchfield. Helms cut out DF: "Dick could have included Des in the meetings with Angleton and me, but I think he knew Des well enough to know that Des would be out and about town doing his own thing." James Critchfield Oral History, CIA Oral History Project.
38. Jim Critchfield, Eugene Rostow.
39. Charles F. Adams, Charles Child to Barbara FitzGerald, undated, probably July 1967, courtesy Frances FitzGerald.
40. Janet Barnes to Barbara FitzGerald, undated, probably July 1967, courtesy Frances FitzGerald.
41. Barbara Lawrence.
42. Sam Halpern.
43. Campbell James, Desmond FitzGerald Jr.
44. James J. Angleton to Barbara FitzGerald, July 23, 1967; John Bross to Barbara FitzGerald, July 25, 1967; Richard Bissell to Barbara FitzGerald, August 3, 1967, courtesy Frances FitzGerald.
45. A. K. Deku to Barbara FitzGerald, September 2, 1967; Sidney Gottlieb to Barbara FitzGerald, July 25, 1967; Frank Wisner Jr. to Barbara FitzGerald, July 24, 1967, courtesy Frances FitzGerald.
46. Archie Roosevelt to Barbara FitzGerald, August 29, 1967, courtesy Frances FitzGerald.
47. Andrew Rogers.
48. Undated, probably fall 1966, courtesy Janet Barnes Lawrence.
49. Barnes at Yale: Jonathan Fanton, Peter Almond, Rebe Garafalo, Diana Gabriel, Freddie Harris, Janet Barnes Lawrence. Special thanks to Geoffrey Kabaservice.
50. Janet Barnes Lawrence.
51. Freddie Harris.
52. Diana Gabriel.
53. Peter Almond.
54. John Casey, Jonathan Fanton, Jane Barnes.
55. John Bruce Lockhart to author, August 30, 1994.
56. Richard Bissell; Bissell, *Memoirs*, VII, "Private Life."

57. Tom Bissell, Ann Bissell.
58. Gary Hart; Bissell testimony before Church Committee, Kennedy Records, National Archives, box 35, folder 1. In the mid-1970s, at the time of the Church Committee, new congressional regulations, and a purge of the covert-action case officers by Jimmy Carter's DCI, Admiral Stansfield Turner, Bissell found himself "profoundly depressed by the state of the intelligence community, because of the articles on it, and by the state of the nation because of the strength of pacifist and isolationist sentiments in Congress." Bissell, *Memoirs*, VII, p. 11.
59. Jonathan Lewis, Bissell, *Memoirs*, pp. 68–70, 108. Funeral described by Ann Bissell.

INDEX

Acheson, Dean, 24, 51, 56, 100, 148–149, 291
Adams, Charles Francis, 45, 295–96, 332
Africa, 107, 181, 188, 221
   Congo, 220, 221–25, 326
Albania, 38–39, 40, 68, 70, 71, 72, 85, 88, 119, 213, 242
   brainwashing fears and, 211
Allison, John, 158
Almond, Peter, 335, 336
Alsop, Corinne, 90
Alsop, Joseph, 26, 27, 63, 89, 104–6, 170, 200, 266
   Bissell and, 89, 90, 91, 240, 240n
   in KGB trap, 106
   sensitive information and, 105
   U-2 incident and, 219
   Vietnam War as viewed by, 322
Alsop, Stewart, 27, 63, 99, 104, 105, 106, 150, 170, 176, 286, 313
   sensitive information and, 105
Alsop, Susan Mary Patten, 11, 26, 49, 101n, 104–5, 266, 274
Alsop, Tish, 27, 102, 176, 266–67
Alsos Mission, 85
ambassadors, 184, 193
Amory, Robert, 95, 237
Anderson, Jack, 330
Angleton, James, 205, 307, 308, 328–329, 331, 333
Animal Farm (Orwell), 33
Applewhite, Edgar, 11, 187, 249, 323, 330
Arabs, 332
Arbenz, Jacobo, 111–13, 115–23, 125, 126, 159, 203, 204, 207, 209, 247, 249, 250
Armas, Carlos Castillo, 115–16, 117, 119, 120, 121, 123, 124, 126, 247

Asia, Asians, 50–51, 55, 107, 153, 180, 184, 199, 273
   American prejudice toward, 48, 273
   China, *see* China, Chinese
   court society in, 273, 275, 281
   FitzGerald and, 43, 44, 46–48, 50, 53–59, 153–57, 192, 193–200, 213, 237, 273–78, 280–83, 285, 286, 291
   Indonesia, *see* Indonesia
   Japan, 153, 155, 171
   Korea, 53, 156, 180, 279; *see also* Korean War
   Laos, 156, 195, 196, 199, 278–84, 285, 327–28
   Philippines, 50, 57–58, 60, 63, 105, 155, 156, 193, 270, 271, 288, 289, 327
   Taiwan, 51, 156, 183, 274, 275
   Thailand, 50, 56, 156, 182, 183–84, 279
   Vietnam, 50, 156, 265, 270, 282, 288; *see also* Vietnam War
assassination, 85
   of Kennedy, 304, 305–6, 307–9, 330–31
   KGB and, 36–37, 306
assassination plots, CIA, 113, 214, 230–36, 310
   authorization for, 222, 230–32, 245, 271, 307
   Barnes and, 234, 235–36, 237, 336
   Bissell and, 210, 212, 213, 220, 222–23, 225–26, 227, 228, 229, 230–35, 245, 251, 271, 272, 339, 340, 341
   against Castro, 208n, 209–10, 220, 225–29, 230–31, 232, 233, 234, 235–36, 245, 251, 271, 272, 294–295, 298–304, 305–10, 330–31, 341

assassination plots, CIA (*cont.*)
  Church Committee and, 185, 209,
    224, 226, 230, 231, 233, 234, 245,
    270, 271, 294, 302, 303, 339
  Dulles and, 231–32, 235, 271
  FitzGerald and, 295, 299–304, 305–
    310, 331
  against Lumumba, 220–25, 226,
    232–33, 269
  McCone and, 307, 309
  against Stalin, 37, 209
  against Sukarno, 213, 232–33
  against Trujillo, 220, 269–70, 331
Atkins, Ted, 182*n*, 214*n*
atomic bomb, 48, 70, 199
Auchincloss, Douglas, 78
Auchincloss, Louis, 73, 90
Aurell, George, 59

Bagley, T. H., 306
Baker, Howard, 339
Ball, George, 239, 278, 280
Bankruptcy Ball, 102, 106
Barnes, Courtlandt, 81, 267, 338
Barnes, Courtlandt, Jr., 82
Barnes, Jane, 135, 174, 175, 207, 236,
    267, 310, 337
Barnes, Janet, *see* Lawrence, Janet
    Barnes
Barnes, Katharine, 81
Barnes, Tracy, 9, 74, 75–86, 103, 107,
    137, 138, 144, 161, 162, 214, 238,
    310–14, 332–33, 334–38
  Alps trip of, 80
  assassination plots and, 234, 235–
    236, 237, 336
  background of, 10, 81–83, 173
  Bissell and, 88, 172, 173, 340
  as Brewster's assistant, 334–35
  CIA assets sold by, 311
  CIA joined by, 10, 83
  Ciano diaries and, 79
  in Cuba operations, 12, 119, 204,
    205, 206, 207, 209, 210, 215, 237,
    242–43, 244, 249, 254–57, 259,
    260, 264, 267, 268, 269, 287, 334,
    338
  danger and adventure courted by,
    75, 76, 78, 79, 81, 82, 86, 127, 243
  death of, 82, 310, 338
  in domestic operations, 311
  A. Dulles and, 74, 79, 84, 127, 130,
    139, 173, 311

firing of, 313, 332–33
  funeral for, 338
  German Mission commanded by,
    127, 129, 130, 132–34, 136, 153
  Germans captured by, 78, 133
  gloomy side of, 135, 198
  in Guatemala operation, 112, 113,
    114, 115–16, 117–18, 119, 120,
    123–24, 126
  Harvey and, 130–31, 132–33
  heart ailments of, 336–37, 338
  Helms disdained by, 240–41
  money and, 81–82
  moral sensibilities of, 11, 78, 134,
    135, 310, 336, 337
  in OSS, 76–81, 313
  as parachutist, 77, 78, 80, 84, 133
  physical appearance and character
    of, 78, 79–80, 81, 82, 83, 84, 86,
    117–18, 127, 130, 131, 133–34,
    173, 174–75, 207
  political dabbling of, 312
  race relations as interest of, 335–36
  schooling of, 82–83, 88, 91, 92, 173,
    334
  security discipline and street
    smarts lacking in, 114, 130, 131,
    132, 133
  as SIS liaison, 172–73
  social issues as concern of, 335–36,
    337
  strokes suffered by, 337, 338
  Tofte defended by, 313
  and torture of defectors, 134
  trusting nature of, 80, 114
  as viewed by his children, 173–75,
    207, 236
  in World War II, 10–11, 75–81, 83,
    113, 133, 134, 207
Barnes, Tracy, Jr., 144, 174–75, 310
Barone, Billie, 161
Bartlett, Charles, 238
Batista, Fulgencio, 203, 220, 254, 299
Bay of Pigs invasion, 12, 88, 119,
    241–69, 270, 289, 292, 311, 318,
    324, 325, 327, 334, 338
  aftermath of, 264–69
  Bissell in, 119, 192, 204–6, 241,
    244–55, 257–58, 259–60, 261–63,
    264–67, 268–69, 270, 287, 314,
    341
  Bundy and, 245, 246, 247–48, 251,
    258, 266, 267, 270

deadline for, 251, 253, 254, 257–58
escalation of, 241, 242, 244, 248
expert analysis ignored in, 249–50
FitzGerald and, 287*n*
initial idea for, 204–6, 241
investigation of, 268
Kennedy and, 241, 244–49, 250,
    251–52, 253–54, 255, 257–59, 261–
    263, 265–66, 267, 268, 270, 271,
    287, 298, 308, 334
Nixon and, 208*n*
Stevenson's briefing on, 254–55,
    256–57, 258, 259, 265, 267
task-force system and, 245
trimming of, 246–47, 248, 252, 253–
    254, 255, 257
Beerli, Stan, 258
Berle, A. A., 252
Berlin, 32, 131, 133, 135–36, 246,
    273
    kidnappings in, 131
Beschloss, Michael, 166, 186, 217
Bissell, Ann, 176, 178, 339
Bissell, Annie (Mrs. Richard Bissell),
    176–77, 178, 265, 290, 339–40
Bissell, Marie, 89–90, 341
Bissell, Richard, 9, 86, 87–97, 98–99,
    106, 107, 143, 161, 165–73, 175–
    178, 179, 186–92, 313–15, 333,
    338–41
    Alsop brothers and, 89, 90, 91, 105,
        176
    assassination plots and, 210, 212,
        213, 220, 222–23, 225–26, 227,
        228, 229, 230–35, 245, 251, 271,
        272, 339, 340, 341
    background of, 10, 88–97, 173
    in Bay of Pigs invasion, 119, 192,
        204–6, 241, 244–55, 257–58, 259–
        260, 261–63, 264–67, 268–69, 270,
        287, 314, 341
    Bay of Pigs investigation and, 268
    Barnes and, 88, 172, 173, 340
    character of, 88, 89, 92–93, 171,
        173, 176–78, 187, 188–91, 237
    children of, 173, 175–76, 178
    Church Committee testimony of,
        339
    CIA joined by, 10, 87–88, 98–99
    CIA left by, 272
    control needed by, 187, 249
    covert action as viewed by, 88, 90–
        91, 186–87, 210–11, 212, 213, 214

Cuban Missile Crisis and, 290
in Cuba operations, 119, 192, 204,
    205, 206, 208, 209, 210, 215, 220,
    225–26, 227, 228, 229, 230, 241,
    244–55, 257–69, 271, 287
death of, 338, 340–41
Dulles and, 99, 105, 118, 139, 181,
    232, 240, 241
made Dulles's successor as CIA di-
    rector, 239, 240
on FitzGerald, 324
at Ford Foundation, 87, 98, 213,
    315
Georgetown society and, 99, 103
Guatemala operation and, 112, 118–
    119, 120–21, 122, 124, 125, 126,
    171
Helms made successor to, 268,
    271–72
on Hungarian situation, 146–47
impatience of, 168, 188, 189, 190,
    247
as Institute for Defense Analysis
    head, 314–15
intellect of, 10, 87, 88, 90–91, 93,
    95, 96, 180, 188, 237, 266, 314
intelligence analysts ignored by,
    190, 249–50
isolationism and, 94
Kennedy administration and, 237–
    238, 239, 240
Laos and, 283
Lumumba and, 220, 221, 222–23
Mahdawi plans and, 214
as Marshall Plan organizer, 10, 87–
    88, 95–97, 172, 180, 187–88, 341
memoirs written by, 340
moral sensibilities of, 233, 234, 339,
    340
music loved by, 177–78
as nonconformist, 91–92, 93, 94,
    99
organizational improvements made
    by, 187
railroads and timetables as interest
    of, 90, 94, 95, 180
retirement of, 338–40
risk-taking of, 92–94, 177, 190, 220,
    252, 272
rock climbing of, 93
roof climbing of, 92–93, 171
sailing of, 89–90, 93–94, 98, 176–77,
    252, 253, 339, 340

Bissell, Richard (*cont.*)
  satellite project of, 216, 217
  schooling of, 10, 88–89, 90–93, 171,
    173, 179, 234
  as shipping planner, 90, 94–95,
    120–21, 187
  sloppiness of, 188, 191
  spies as viewed by, 191–92
  SR-17 developed by, 171–72, 253
  State Department invite to, 239
  tardiness of, 188, 189
  as teacher, 10, 93, 95
  as technocrat, 170–71, 191, 211,
    212, 272
  Tibet operation and, 276, 277
  at United Technologies, 338
  U-2 developed and run by, 165–71,
    172, 176, 191, 204, 212, 216, 217–
    218, 220, 314, 341
  Wisner and, 10, 87–88, 98, 139,
    317
  made Wisner's successor as chief of
    covert operations, 165, 172, 179–
    180, 186–87, 203
  in World War II, 10–11, 90, 94–95,
    120–21, 187
Bissell, Richard, Jr., 176
Bissell, Thomas, 338–39
Black Chamber, 17
Blake, George, 129–30
Bloodstone, Operation, 25–26, 34
Bogotá, 42
Bohlen, Avis, 101, 102–3, 104, 160,
    162, 198
Bohlen, Charles "Chip," 24, 26, 27,
    34, 35, 40, 101, 102, 104, 160,
    162, 198
  on Khrushchev, 219–20
  McCarthy's targeting of, 100, 101,
    138
Bonano, Joe, 234
Bormann, Martin, 319
Bowie, Beverly, 21
Bowles, Chester, 239, 240, 253
Braden, Thomas, 33, 39, 61, 62, 63,
    64, 78, 84, 98, 103, 311, 320
Bragadiru, Mita, 20, 21
brainwashing, 211
Brandon, Henry, 207
Braun, Eva, 79
Brazil, 323–24
Breck, Henry, 91, 320, 321, 322
Brewster, Kingman, 334, 335

Bross, John, 73, 76, 88, 107, 187, 268,
    269, 290, 333
Brown, Irving, 62
Bruce, David, 77, 79, 148–50, 316
Bruce, Evangeline, 77, 101, 101*n*,
    148, 316
Brugiani, Dino, 168
Bryan, Joe, 33, 64, 84, 131
Bullitt, William, 34
Bundy, McGeorge, 11, 93, 94, 239,
    289, 309–10, 325
  Bay of Pigs and, 245, 246, 247–48,
    251, 258, 266, 267, 270
Bundy, William, 100, 185, 252
Burgess, Guy, 69, 70
Burke, Arleigh, 262, 263
Burke, Michael, 33–34, 39, 127
Burling, Ella, 27, 103
Burma, 53–54, 55–56, 156, 193, 276,
    278

Cabell, Charles Pearre, 258
Cabot, John Moors, 111
Cabot, Thomas, 111
Cairo Tower, 182
Califano, Joseph, 330–31
Cambodia, 184, 190
Cannon, Clarence, 181
Caradja, Tanda, 20–21, 22, 138–39
Casey, John, 77, 175, 337, 338
Castro, Fidel, 203–4, 220, 232–33,
    237, 310
  Cuban loyalty for, 249–50
  Cubela in plot against, 299–303,
    305–6, 307, 309, 310
  Fleming's ideas on, 207
  Kennedy assassination and, 305,
    306, 307, 308, 330–31
  plots to assassinate, 208*n*, 209–10,
    220, 225–29, 230–31, 232, 233,
    234, 235–36, 245, 251, 271, 272,
    294–95, 298–304, 305–10, 330–31,
    341
  plots to embarrass, 207–9, 225
  plots to overthrow, 204–10, 240,
    270–71, 286–98, 302, 303; *see also*
    Bay of Pigs invasion
  psychological warfare against,
    206–9, 215, 288
  Soviet aid to, 203, 241, 290, 291
  see also Cuba
Castro, Raul, 209, 210, 236
CAT (Civil Air Transport), 51, 276

Central America:
  Guatemala, *see* Guatemala
  Nicaragua, 204, 255, 256, 259, 262, 264
Central Intelligence Agency (CIA), 28, 42, 97
  accountability of, 29, 97, 148–49, 184–85, 230–31
  ambassadors and, 184, 193
  classified records of, 10, 13, 118
  coups orchestrated by, 106, 107–10, 111–26, 151, 186, 190, 316
  culture of secrecy in, 235
  developing nations and, 110–26, 180, 181, 182, 183, 325
  domestic spying and, 311
  drug experiments by, 12, 208, 211–212, 213, 214
  Eastern European operations of, 36, 37–38, 65, 71, 73, 110, 119, 127–37, 142–48, 149–50, 152, 154, 180
  elitism in, 97, 99, 110
  émigrés imported by, 35
  excesses of, 12, 72, 211–12, 214
  failures of, 10, 11–12, 36, 42, 56, 60, 71, 73, 186, 190, 233
  Far East operations of, *see* Asia
  foreign government officials recruited by, 181–84
  friendship used as recruitment tool by, 182–84
  front groups used by, 61–62, 98, 330
  funding of, 40–41, 63, 85, 181
  Georgetown society and, 39–40, 99, 101–6, 108
  Germans recruited by, 34–35, 74
  International Organizations division of, 61, 62, 64, 98
  Ivy League schools as recruiting ground for, 15–16
  media and, *see* press
  medical aid given by, 182
  morality and, 11, 134, 146, 233
  Office of Special Operations in, 28–29, 41–42, 43, 52, 150
  parachute missions of, 36, 67, 71, 72
  PBCFIA report on, 148–49
  police forces trained by, 182
  policymaking by, 39–40, 180, 193
  reputation of, 12, 186, 210, 318, 329–30
  Security Office of, 225–26
  technical development in, 170–71, 191, 208, 211, 212–13, 295
  type of men in, 9, 68–69, 91, 108, 132, 149, 233
  unsuccessful operations shut down in, 72, 152
  Western Hemisphere division of, 323
  see also Office of Policy Coordination; Office of Special Operations; *specific people, places, and topics*
Central Intelligence Group, 28
Charles, Oatsie, 102, 103, 137, 207
Charusathien, Praphat, 183
Chase, Gordon, 310
Chennault, Claire, 51
Chiang Ching-kuo, 183, 275
Chiang Kai-shek, 51, 155–56, 183, 274, 285
Child, Charles, 332
Chile, 324
China, Chinese, 46–48, 156, 194, 195, 274–78
  China Mission and, 153–57, 199
  communist, 12, 51–56, 153, 156, 180, 190, 196, 199, 274–75, 276, 278, 279
  FitzGerald and, 44, 46–48, 53–56, 153–57, 193, 199, 274–78
  Nationalist (KMT), 51–52, 53–54, 56, 155, 187, 193, 195, 274–75, 278
  Soviet split with, 278, 307
  Third Force movement in, 52–53
  Tibet and, 275–78
Christeller, Norman, 314–15
Church, Frank, 230, 339
Church Committee (Select Committee to Study Governmental Operations with Respect to Intelligence Activities), 185, 209, 224, 226, 230, 231, 233, 234, 245, 270, 271, 294, 302, 303, 339
Churchill, Winston, 42, 109, 162
CIA, *see* Central Intelligence Agency
CIA Act (1949), 35
Ciano, Edda, 79
Ciano, Galeazzo, 79
Civil Air Transport (CAT), 51, 276

Clark, Edward, 31
Cleveland, Harlan, 96–97
Clifford, Clark, 40, 328
Cline, Ray, 183, 327
Cloak and Dagger, 17, 33–34
Cloak and Gown (Winks), 16
Coffin, William Sloane, 60
Colby, William, 11, 16–17, 63,
    147–48, 181, 186, 192, 193,
    275, 276, 291, 323, 324,
    327
Committee of Five Million, 49, 58
communism, 10, 12, 199
    efficacy of covert action against,
        66–67, 71–72, 73
    front organizations and, 25, 61–62,
        98, 330
    Marshall Plan and, 28
    phony resistance organizations
        and, 67
    Truman Doctrine and, 24
    Western culture as weapon against,
        61–62
    see also specific people and places
Conant, James Bryant, 129
Congo, 220, 221–25, 326
Cooper, Chester, 193, 195, 231, 236,
    238, 281, 312
Copeland, Miles, 187
Corcoran, Thomas, 51, 111
Corona project, 216, 217, 272
Corson, William, 24
covert action, 41–42, 149, 180, 181,
    182, 184, 210, 269
    Bissell's view of, 88, 90–91, 186–87,
        210–11, 212, 213, 214
    Bowles's view of, 239
    5412 Committee and, 184–85
    FitzGerald's philosophy of, 193
    Rusk's view of, 239
    see also psychological warfare;
        specific actions
Cox, Alfred, 53–54
Cox, Arthur, 62, 84
Cram, Cleve, 267, 315
Critchfield, James, 35–36, 65, 129,
    130, 132, 133, 136, 152, 181–82,
    277, 332
    Cuba operations and, 205–6
Crockett, David, 80
Crosby, Bing, 159
Crowley, Robert, 313
Crowley, William, 160

Cuba, 125, 273
    Barnes and, 12, 119, 204, 205, 206,
        207, 209, 210, 215, 237, 242–43,
        244, 249, 254–57, 259, 260, 264,
        267, 268, 269, 287, 334, 338
    Bissell and, 119, 192, 204, 205, 206,
        208, 209, 210, 215, 220, 225–26,
        227, 228, 229, 230, 241, 244–55,
        257–69, 271, 287
    Dulles and, 207, 210, 227, 231, 240,
        241, 247, 250, 258, 266, 269, 271,
        287
    exiles of, 298, 308, 310, 331
    FitzGerald and, 286–87, 291–98,
        299–304, 305–10, 323, 327, 331
    Fleming's ideas on, 207
    invasion of, *see* Bay of Pigs invasion
    Kennedy administration's attitude
        toward, 270, 271, 291, 296
    Kennedys and, 231, 241, 244–55,
        257–59, 261–63, 265–68, 270–72,
        287–94, 296, 297–98, 299, 300,
        307, 309, 330, 334
    missiles in, 290–91, 294, 296, 341
    see also Castro, Fidel
Cubela Secades, Rolando, 299–303,
    305–6, 307, 309, 310, 331
    Trafficante and, 330–31
Cummings, Mansfield, 55
Cutler, Mary, 134, 135, 198
Cutler, Robert, 134
Czechoslovakia, 32, 42, 152, 158

Dalai Lama, 276, 278
Dean, Patrick, 143, 333
de Gaulle, Charles, 169
DeLarm, Jerry, 113, 119, 123
del Valle, Eladio, 331
Denny, Joan, 200–201, 298
Devens, Charles, 82
Devlin, Lawrence, 222, 223, 224, 225
Díaz, Carlos Enrique, 123
Diem, Ngo Dinh, *see* Ngo Dinh Diem
Dillon, C. Douglas, 221, 244
displaced persons (DP) camps, 25, 34,
    36, 38, 68, 72, 136
"Document on Terror," 61
Dodge, Marshall, 75, 77, 82, 338
Doherty, John, 123
Dominican Republic, 204, 220–21,
    269–70, 325n
Donovan, James B., 295
Donovan, William, 9, 20, 24

Doolittle, Jimmy, 167
Doolittle Report, 134–35
Doster, George Reid, 259
Downey, John, 52
Drain, Dick, 205, 255, 264
Droller, Gerry, 205, 206, 243
drug experiments, 12, 208, 211–12,
      213, 214
Dulles, Allen, 23–24, 29, 37, 43, 61,
      64, 66, 72–74, 78–80, 85–87, 101,
      105, 110, 128, 149, 154–55, 172,
      181, 185–86, 190, 237, 241, 258,
      274, 307, 325
   administrative style of, 164–65, 185
   assassination plots and, 231–32,
      235, 271
   Barnes and, 74, 79, 84, 127, 130,
      139, 173, 311
   Bissell and, 99, 105, 118, 139, 181,
      232, 240, 241
   Bissell made chief of covert opera-
      tions by, 165, 172
   Bissell made successor to, 239, 240
   character of, 73, 74, 139
   CIA funding and, 181
   made CIA head, 73
   code used by, 235
   Cuba operations and, 207, 210, 227,
      231, 240, 241, 247, 250, 258, 266,
      269, 271, 287
   death of, 231, 274, 336
   decline of, 232, 239–40
   FitzGerald and, 192, 193
   Guatemala and, 111, 112, 113, 115,
      117, 118, 119, 120, 123–24
   Hungary and, 146, 147
   Indonesia and, 158
   Iran and, 108, 109
   Khrushchev speech and, 136–37
   Lumumba and, 221–22
   McCarthy and, 98, 100
   Nasser and, 209
   in OSS, 78–79, 80–81
   Soviet view of, 186
   spying as viewed by, 73–74, 154,
      165, 168
   U-2 and, 165–66, 167, 168, 169, 219
   Wisner and, 139, 141, 164
Dulles, Clover, 74
Dulles, Eleanor, 171, 235
Dulles, John Foster, 73, 85, 101, 110,
      149, 186
   death of, 232, 239–40

Georgetown society vs., 101
   Guatemala and, 111, 123
   Hungary and, 146
   Indonesia and, 157–58, 159–60
   Iran and, 108, 110
   McCarthy and, 99, 100, 101
   neutralism and, 157

Eden, Anthony, 143, 167
Edwards, Sheffield, 100, 225, 226,
      229, 271
Egypt, 143
Eisenhower, Dwight D., 42, 58,
      73, 85, 100, 101, 109, 110,
      111, 119, 120, 124, 134, 144, 146,
      149, 152, 180, 227, 228, 240, 250,
      273
   China and, 274, 276, 277
   CIA-monitoring measures of, 148,
      184–85
   Cuba operations and, 230, 231, 243–
      244, 247
   détente with Soviets desired by,
      217, 218, 219–20, 265
   Doolittle Report and, 134–35
   5412 Committee created by, 184–
      185
   Hunt and, 205
   Laos and, 278–79
   Lumumba and, 222
   PBCFIA created by, 148, 150
   on psychological warfare, 32, 62
   U-2 and, 165–66, 167, 168, 169,
      170, 217–18, 219–20, 265, 277
Elder, Walt, 307–8
Emerson, Lloyd, 165, 190, 192, 280
England, *see* Great Britain
espionage, *see* spying
Esterline, Jake, 124, 204, 205, 208,
      209, 210, 248, 249, 252, 254, 255,
      264
Europe, 36, 37–38, 65, 71, 73, 110,
      119, 127–37, 142–48, 149–50, 152,
      154, 180
   Soviet takeovers in, 9, 12, 19, 20,
      21–22, 25, 32, 33, 199
   see also specific countries

Fanton, Jonathan, 335, 336, 337
Far East operations, *see* Asia
Farland, Joseph, 220–21
Farouk I, King, 182
Farr, Finis, 33

Federal Bureau of Investigation
(FBI), 23, 70, 106, 138, 187, 225,
226, 239, 243, 311, 323
  Cuban extremists and, 308–9
  Meyer and, 98
5412 Committee, *see* Special Group
Fiorini, Frank, 299*n*
FitzGerald, Barbara Green Lawrence,
49, 50, 155, 200, 201–2, 301, 308,
332–33, 334
FitzGerald, Desmond, 9, 44–50, 63,
82*n*, 103, 138, 153–57, 184, 192–
202, 238, 239, 322–34
  as action-oriented, 194, 324
  "Alice in Wonderland" quotes of,
198, 294, 302
  assassination plots and, 295, 299–
304, 305–10, 331
  atomic bomb as viewed by, 48, 199,
296
  Barnes fired by, 313, 332–33
  character of, 44–45, 49, 54–55, 59,
68, 154, 160, 192, 194, 197–98,
200, 323, 324–25, 326
  China and, 44, 46–48, 53–56, 153–
157, 193, 199, 274–78
  CIA joined by, 10, 43, 50
  conflicting tendencies in, 194
  Congo trip of, 326
  in Cuba operations, 286–87, 291–98,
299–304, 305–10, 323, 327, 331
  cultural differences as viewed by,
44, 46, 47–48, 193, 197
  death of, 333–34
  elitism and romanticism of, 44–45,
54–55, 68, 192, 198, 199
  emotional distance of, 201, 202
  exotica collected by, 196
  in Far East Division, 43, 50, 53–59,
153, 192, 193–200, 213, 237, 273–
278, 280–83, 285, 286, 291
  fight against communism as viewed
by, 193, 194, 199
  financial problems of, 301
  funeral for, 333, 334
  gloomy side of, 198–99
  made Helms's successor as chief of
covert operations, 324, 334
  illness of, 332
  J. Kennedy's assassination and,
305–8, 331
  R. Kennedy and, 291, 293–94, 297–
298, 299, 300

  in Laos operations, 280, 281–82,
283
  McNamara and, 286
  and media criticism of, CIA, 330
  morality of, 11, 295–96
  recruitment style of, 194–96
  reform movement of, 49–50, 58
  skin condition of, 47, 197, 333
  in Tibet operation, 275–78
  tyrannicide as seen by, 296–97
  Vietnam War and, 285, 286, 322–
323, 326, 327, 328–29, 331
  as viewed by his children, 200–201
  weariness in, 331–32
  Wisner's mental illness and, 157,
158, 160, 161–62, 321
  Wisner's suicide and, 320, 321
  in World War II, 10–11, 44, 45–48,
153, 197, 276, 295
FitzGerald, Desmond, Jr., 201, 202,
308, 333
FitzGerald, Frances, 47, 49, 55, 198–
199, 200, 201, 285, 291, 292, 296,
297, 298, 300, 301–2, 322, 326,
333
Fitzgerald, F. Scott, 83
FitzGerald, Marietta (Marietta Tree),
26, 45, 48–49, 101
Flannery, Jim, 187, 188, 189, 191,
256, 264–65, 283
Fleming, Ian, 172–73, 186, 207, 289
Ford Foundation, 87, 98, 213, 315
Forrestal, Michael, 303–4, 313
Forrestal, James, 27, 29, 303
France, 24, 28, 62
  Barnes in, 77, 78
  Bissell's U-2 operations and, 169
  in Suez crisis, 143
Francke, Albert, 298
Friendly, Alfred, 101, 106
Friendly, Jean, 101, 103, 106
Fritchey, Clayton, 266
Fulbright, William, 251–52

Gabriel, Diana, 336–37
Gaines, Stanley, 311–12
Galbraith, John Kenneth, 277
Garafalo, Rebe, 335
Garbler, Paul, 329
Gates, Thomas, 206*n*, 244
Gehlen, Reinhard, 74
Gehlen organization, 35–36
George, Lloyd, 59

Germany, 24, 25, 32, 64, 65–66, 87,
  127–34, 136, 171
  Barnes and, 78, 127, 129, 130, 132–
  134, 136, 153
  Berlin, 32, 107, 131, 133, 135–36,
  246, 273
  intelligence agency in, 78–79
  Italy and, 80
  League of Young Germans in,
  65–66
  Soviet Union and, 79, 80
  Wisner in, 22–23, 25
Giancana, Sam, 227–28, 233–34
Gilpatric, Roswell, 325
Gleijeses, Piero, 112, 122
Goldwater, Barry, 312, 324
Gooch, Robert, 19–20
Goodwin, Richard, 238
Gottlieb, Sidney, 211–12, 214, 215, 217,
  222–23, 224, 225, 228, 295, 334
Goulart, João, 323–24
Graham, Elizabeth, 27
Gray, David, 259
Gray, Gordon, 83–84, 141, 160, 162,
  222, 231
Great Britain, 24, 55, 110, 143–44,
  156, 172, 181
  in Albanian operation, 38–39
  intelligence operations in, 55; *see
  also* Secret Intelligence Service
  Iran and, 108, 109
  Malaya and, 156, 193
  "thrusters" of, 194
  U-2 and, 167, 168–69
Green, Gardiner, 18
Greenway, Gilbert, 40–41, 114, 141,
  164
Gregg, Donald, 50, 180, 190–91, 197,
  275
Grose, Peter, 37, 73, 232
Gruson, Sydney, 117
Guatemala, 106, 111–26, 148–49, 151,
  158, 159, 171, 186, 204, 205, 207,
  209, 247, 249, 250
  Cuba operation and, 203, 204, 206,
  207, 241, 243, 247, 250, 253
Guevara, Ernesto "Che," 125–26, 203,
  206, 209
Gunn, Edward, 303
Guyana, 316

Hainan, 51
Haiti, 204

Halpern, Sam, 64, 160, 161, 182–83,
  194, 195, 197, 278, 285, 287, 288,
  292–94, 298, 300, 301, 303, 305–7,
  309, 324, 331
Haney, Al, 115, 117–18, 120, 124
Harkness Hoot, 91–92
Harriman, Averell, 27, 95, 281, 282,
  333
Harris, Freddie, 335–36
Hart, Gary, 339
Harvey, William, 69, 70, 130–33,
  134, 205, 223, 224, 245, 271, 289–
  295
Hasey, Jack, 280
Hawkins, Jack, 242, 248, 250, 252,
  253, 264
Hazard, Wendy, 140
Heckscher, Henry, 115, 279
Helms, Richard, 53, 60, 150–52, 160,
  164, 165, 170, 191, 192, 194, 240–
  241, 268, 272, 286, 312, 313, 317,
  329, 331, 332, 336
  made Bissell's successor as chief
  of covert operations, 268, 271–
  272
  made CIA deputy director, 324
  Cuba operations and, 205, 206,
  272, 287, 288, 289, 300, 303, 307,
  331
  FitzGerald promoted by, 324
  Kennedy assassination and, 306,
  308
  U-2 and, 170
  Wisner commemorated by, 321–22
Hersh, Burton, 23
Herter, Christian, 206*n*
Herwarth von Bittenfield, Hans, 34
Hilger, Gustav, 34–35
Hillenkoetter, Roscoe, 30, 42
Hiss, Alger, 100, 132
Hitchcock, Tommy, 75–76
Hitler, Adolf, 12, 17, 34, 35, 66, 68,
  79, 94, 232, 319
  FitzGerald and, 296
Hmong tribe, 282, 283, 328
Hobbing, Enno, 115, 117, 120, 123,
  125
Hoffman, Paul, 96
Hogan, Tim, 323
Holland, Henry, 120
Holmes, George, 41, 184, 312, 329
Hong Kong, 52, 194
Honorable Men (Colby), 11, 17

Honourable Schoolboy, The (le Carré), 11
Hood, Cordelia Dodson, 79–80
Hood, William, 80, 130, 145, 323
Hoopes, Townsend, 26–27, 84
Hoover, J. Edgar, 23, 69, 106, 138, 186, 225, 227, 239, 323
Horton, John, 58, 193, 194, 197–98, 291
Houston, Lawrence, 41, 64, 141, 310–311, 313
Howe, Fisher, 137–38
Hoxha, Enver, 38, 39
Hungary, 142–48, 149–50, 152, 160
Hunt, E. Howard, 85, 114, 115, 118, 155, 205, 208, 310, 311
  in Cuba operation, 20, 206, 243, 252, 260
  Goldwater speeches and, 312
Huston, John, 49
Hyde, Henry, 81

Ignatius, David, 183
India, 277
Indonesia, 157–60, 192, 196
  Sukarno in, 157–60, 213–14, 226, 232–33, 295
Institute for Defense Analysis (IDA), 314–15
intelligence work, *see* spying
Invisible Government, The (Ross and Wise), 318–19
Iran, 106, 107–10, 112, 125, 183
Iraq, 214
Isaacson, Walter, 10
Israel, 143, 332
Italy, 24, 28, 62, 88, 181
  elections in, 11, 28–29
  German forces in, 80

Jackon, Dwayne, 326
Jackson, William Harding, 30–31, 43, 64
Jacobs, Arthur, 19, 37, 53, 63, 320
James Campbell "Zup," 195, 196, 281–282, 328, 333
Jantzen, Robert, 183–84
Japan, 153, 155, 171
Jessup, Peter, 36, 65, 130, 136
JFK, 12
John, Otto, 105
Johnson, Haynes, 249
Johnson, Kelly, 166, 167, 176

Johnson, Lyndon B., 93, 309, 312, 315, 324, 327, 328, 330
  CIA distrusted by, 325
  FitzGerald's death and, 333
Jones, Lem, 260
Joyce, Bob, 30, 40, 41, 69

Kaplan, Gabriel, 58
Karamessines, Tom, 324
Kassem, Abdul Karim, 214
Kennan, George, 24, 26, 27, 29, 30, 34, 35, 71
  in creation of OPC, 29, 30, 40
  German diplomats and, 34–35
  uncharacteristic remark made by, 211
  on U-2 incident, 220
  warnings of, about Soviets, 24, 29, 30
Kennedy, John F., 12, 69, 170, 207, 228, 237–38, 239, 240, 257, 273, 297, 310, 325
  Asia and, 273, 277, 278, 279, 280–281
  assassination of, 304, 305–6, 307–9, 330–31
  Bay of Pigs and, 241, 244–49, 250, 251–52, 253–54, 255, 257–59, 261–263, 265–66, 267, 268, 270, 271, 287, 298, 308, 334
  Cuban exiles and, 298
  Cuban Missile Crisis and, 290
  Cuba operations and, 231, 241, 244–255, 257–59, 261–63, 265–68, 270–272, 287–93, 296, 300, 334
  Hoover and Dulles appointed by, 239
  Laos and, 278, 279, 280–81, 285
  MONGOOSE and, 270–71, 288, 289, 290
Kennedy, Joseph P., 239, 251
Kennedy, Robert F., 271, 287, 295, 297, 325, 333
  character of, 297
  Cuban exiles entertained by, 298
  Cuba operations and, 253, 262–63, 265, 270, 271, 272, 287, 288, 289, 290, 291, 293–94, 296, 297–98, 299, 300, 307, 309, 330, 334
  FitzGerald and, 291, 293–94, 297–298, 299, 300
Kent, Beth, 89, 178
Kent, Sherman, 250

KGB, 33, 36–37, 105, 132, 135, 320,
 329, 330
 Alsop and, 106
 assassinations and, 36–37, 306
 CIA view of, 33
 Oswald and, 306
Khamba warriors, 275, 276–78
Khrushchev, Nikita, 136–37, 170, 246
 Castro and, 290, 291
 détente with U.S. desired by, 217,
  218, 219–20, 265
 Kennedy and, 265
 U-2 incident and, 219 20, 265
 see also Soviet Union
Killian, James, 165
King, Bob, 166, 188, 189, 191, 213,
 218, 232, 234, 245, 255, 269
King, J. C., 117, 204
Kipling, Rudyard, 16
Kirkpatrick, Lyman, 181, 231, 268
Kong Le, 280
Korea, 53, 156, 180, 279
Korean War, 16, 42, 43, 50, 51, 53–
 56, 68, 83, 85, 110
 brainwashing in, 211
Kostikov, Valery, 306, 307

Land, Edwin, 167
Langosch, James, 299, 331
Lansdale, Edward G., 57–58, 105,
 156, 192, 193, 270–71, 288–89,
 290, 291, 292
Laos, 156, 195, 196, 199, 278–84, 285,
 327–28
Latin America, 107, 108, 323
 Brazil, 323–24
 Cuba, *see* Cuba
 Guatemala, *see* Guatemala
 Nicaragua, 204, 255, 256, 259, 262,
  264
Laux, David, 195, 197, 302
Lawrence, Barbara, 140, 155, 196,
 200, 202, 297, 301, 332
Lawrence, Janet Barnes, 12, 75, 76,
 78, 81, 82, 83, 102, 112, 124, 126,
 129, 132, 135, 161, 172, 173, 175,
 176, 206n, 207, 257, 267, 269,
 332–33, 336, 337, 338
 Wisner and, 144, 162–63, 319
Lawrence, Vint, 282, 283
League of Young Germans, 65–66
le Carré, John, 11
LeMay, Curtis, 71, 166

Lemnitzer, Lyman, 263, 279, 281
Lewis, Jonathan, 105, 340
Liebert, Fritz, 93, 94, 177
Lilley, James, 51, 154, 155, 156, 194,
 274, 278
Li Mi, 53, 55–56, 193, 278
Linares, José, 126
Lindsay, Frank, 51, 70–72
Lindsey, Jean, 18, 320
Linse, Walter, 131
Lippincott, William, 15, 16
Lockhart, John Bruce, 11, 66–67, 108,
 130, 143, 338
Lockheed Corporation, 166, 167, 276
Lodge, Henry Cabot, 111, 327
Loftus, John, 35
Lorenz, Marie, 299n
Lovestone, Jay, 62
Lovett, Robert, 27, 149
LSD, 12, 208, 211–12
Luce, Clare Booth, 74, 148
Luce, Henry, 74, 117
Lumumba, Patrice, 220, 221–25, 226,
 232–33, 269
Lundahl, Arthur, 265

MacArthur, Douglas, 53, 54, 56
McCargar, Jim, 37, 39, 40, 320
McCarthy, Joseph, 99–101, 138
 Hoover and, 138
McCarthyism, 98–101, 138
McCone, John, 291, 307, 309, 319,
 320–21, 325
McDonald, Elizabeth, 312
MacFarland, Lanning, 20
McGehee, Ralph, 156–57
McGuire, Phyllis, 227–28
McIlvaine, Alice, 133, 235, 236, 264,
 329
Maclean, Donald, 70
McLean, Neil, 38
McNamara, Robert, 171, 246, 277,
 287, 325
 Vietnam War and, 285–86, 322, 327
McVeigh, Charles, 301
Mafia, 12, 226–29, 233–34, 235, 251,
 271, 294–95, 298, 308, 309, 310,
 330–31, 340
Magsaysay, Ramón, 57–58, 63, 105,
 156
Mahdawi, Colonel, 214, 228
Maheu, Robert, 226, 227–28
Malaya, 156, 193, 327

Malaysia, 156
Mapother, John, 136, 145
Marshall, George C., 29, 42
Marshall Plan, 10, 28, 40–41, 62, 87,
    95–97, 172, 180, 187, 341
Martin, David, 131
Marx, Groucho, 33
Maury, Jack, 192
Mayday (Beschloss), 217
medical aid, 182
Meyer, Cord, 64, 98, 100, 101, 189–
    190, 266, 290
Middle East, 107, 109, 180, 181, 182
    Iran, 106, 107–10, 112, 125, 183
    Iraq, 214
    Suez crisis in, 143–44, 145, 172, 173
mind control, 211
Mirage, Doris, 188, 234, 269
Mitchell, Leslie, 173
Mobutu, Joseph, 326
Mohammed Reza Shah Pahlavi, 108,
    109, 183
MONGOOSE, Operation, 270–71,
    288–91
Monzón, Elfegio, 123, 124–25
Morgan, Edmund, 330
Mosley, Leonard, 185
Mossadegh, Mohammed, 108, 109,
    110, 183
Murphy, David, 67
Mussolini, Benito, 79, 80

Naguib, Bey, 182
Nasser, Gamal, 157, 182, 209
National Committee for a Free Eu-
    rope, 61
National Football League, 16
National Movement for Free Elec-
    tions (NAMFREL), 58
National Security Act (1947), 29
National Security Council, 29
National Student Association, 330
Neoal, 277
Ngo Dinh Diem, 265, 270, 285, 331
    overthrow of, 327
Nguyen Cao Ky, 328
Niarchos, Stavros, 74
Nicaragua, 204, 255, 256, 259, 262,
    264
Night Watch, The (Phillips), 112, 248
Nitze, Paul, 26, 40, 50, 77–78, 84, 91,
    100, 105, 106, 160–61, 251, 296,
    328

    on Bissell, 96
    Wisner's illness and, 161, 162
Nixon, Richard M., 27, 170, 265
    Cuba operations and, 208*n*, 265
Nosenko, Yuri, 308
Noyes, Charles P., 255

O'Connell, James P., 226–27, 229
O'Donnell, Justin, 223–24, 269
Office of Occupied Territories, 24
Office of Policy Coordination (OPC),
    32–43
    Albanian operations of, 38–39, 40,
        68, 70, 71, 72, 85, 119
    assassinations and, 36–37
    atmosphere at, 16–17
    creation of, 9, 15, 29–30, 32, 41, 50,
        70, 71
    émigrés recruited by, 34–35, 85
    excesses of, 40–41
    funding of, 40–41, 63
    growth of, 63
    Marshall Plan and, 28, 40–41, 87–88
    merged into CIA, 9, 58
    OSO merged with, 43, 54, 58, 151
    OSO vs., 41–42, 150–51
    Pentagon and, 32
    refugee army organized by, 34, 36
    Smith and, 43
    staffing of, 15, 16–17, 33–35
    see also Central Intelligence
        Agency
Office of Special Operations (OSO),
    28–29, 52, 150
    OPC merged with, 43, 54, 58, 151
    OPC vs., 41–42, 150–51
Office of Strategic Services (OSS), 9,
    15, 28, 31, 33, 64, 66, 150, 153,
    187
    Barnes in, 76–81, 313
    folding of, 9, 23
    Dulles in, 78–79, 80–81
    SSU and, 23, 24
    Wisner in, 9, 19–23
Offie, Carmel, 34–35, 36, 61, 109
Old Boys, The (Hersh), 23
Oldfield, Maurice, 172
Olson, Frank, 212
OPC, *see* Office of Policy Coordination
Operation Bughouse (Bowie), 21
Orta, Juan, 228–29
Orwell, George, 33
OSO, *see* Office of Special Operations

OSS, *see* Office of Strategic Services
Oswald, Lee Harvey, 306, 308

Panama, 204
Parrott, Thomas, 33, 36, 63, 131, 132, 133, 134, 231, 268, 289, 297, 313
Pash, Boris, 85
passports, forging of, 65
PBCFIA (President's Board of Consultants on Foreign Intelligence Activities), 148, 149–50
PBSUCCESS, *see* Guatemala
Peabody, Endicott, 48, 82, 90, 91
Peabody, Mike, 196
Pearson, Drew, 106, 330
Penkovsky, Oleg, 191–92, 290, 315
Peurifoy, John E., 116–17, 123
Philby, Harold "Kim," 38, 39, 68–70, 71, 72, 85, 108, 119, 132, 138, 156, 211, 315
Philippines, 50, 57–58, 60, 63, 105, 155, 156, 193, 270, 271, 288, 289, 327
Phillips, David, 33, 114
    in Cuba operation, 204, 205, 206, 209, 248, 255–56, 257, 260, 264
    in Guatemala operation, 112, 114–115, 121, 122, 124, 204
    Raborn and, 325*n*
Phoui Sananikone, 280
Phoumi Nosavan, 280–81
Plimpton, Francis T. P., 255
Poland, 67–68, 142
Polgar, Thomas, 67, 127, 147, 206
police forces, training of, 182
Pope, Allen Lawrence, 159
Poshepny, Tony "Tony Poe," 195, 196, 242, 275, 276, 283, 293
Powers, Francis Gary, 219, 220*n*, 228, 277
Powers, Thomas, 30, 42, 60, 148, 187, 191, 314
President Kennedy (Reeves), 238
President's Board of Consultants on Foreign Intelligence Activities (PBCFIA), 148, 149–50
press, 105–6, 117, 120, 123, 124, 125, 129, 159
    CIA criticized in, 318–19, 320–21, 329–30
    Cuba invasion and, 243, 249, 253, 256, 265
    Khrushchev's speech released to, 137

Tibet operation and, 277
U-2 incident and, 218–19
Price, Leontyne, 18
propaganda, 26, 28, 30, 33
    in Cuba operation, 204, 206, 209, 248, 260
    radio broadcasts as tool for, *see* radio stations
    Soviet, 10, 23, 24, 25, 30
    Wisner and, 60–62, 63–64
    see also psychological warfare
psychological warfare, 17, 24, 29, 32–33, 62, 64, 83–85, 87, 88
    Barnes's use of, 113, 207, 209, 215
    against Castro, 206–9, 215, 288
    Eisenhower on, 32, 62
    in Guatemala operation, 113, 121, 124, 247
    in Indonesia, 158–59
    Lansdale's use of, 57, 288–89
    workshop for, 33, 64
    see also propaganda

Quinn, William, 23

Raborn, William, 325
radio stations, 61, 152
    in Cuba operation, 206, 260
    Radio Free Europe (RFE), 61, 137, 142, 147
    Radio Liberation, 61
    Radio Warsaw, 67
    Voice of Liberation, 114–15, 121, 122, 124, 204, 247
Ranelagh, John, 168
Reeder, Charles, 17, 18, 19, 316
Reeder, Fred, 18, 318
Reeves, Richard, 238
Reston, James, 106, 120, 141, 219, 266
Ridder, Marie, 147, 267
Ridder, Walter, 147
Riebling, Mark, 138
Roa, Raul, 256
Robertson, William "Rip," 115, 116, 122, 125, 242, 261, 283, 293
Rogers, Andrew, 334
Romania, 9, 19, 20–22, 66, 199
Roosevelt, Archie, 108, 228, 317, 334
Roosevelt, Cornelius, 108, 228, 235–36
Roosevelt, Kermit "Kim," 108–10, 112, 125, 182, 228

Roosevelt, Selwa, 108
Roosevelt, Theodore, 94, 108
Rositzke, Harry, 33, 35
Ross, Thomas, 318–19
Rosselli, Johnny, 226, 229, 294–95, 298, 330
Rostow, Eugene, 92, 93, 94
Rostow, Walt, 93, 263, 265, 325
Rowan, Dan, 227–28
Ruby, Jack, 308
Ruddock, Merritt, 41
Rusk, Dean, 239, 246, 256–57, 258, 259, 263, 265, 317
Russell, Richard, 185
Russia, *see* Soviet Union

Salinger, Pierre, 253
Saltonstall, Leverett, 185
Saltzman, Charles, 24, 140–41
Sanchez, Nestor, 302
San Román, José Pérez "Pepe," 262, 264
satellites, 105, 216, 217, 272
Schlesinger, Arthur, Jr., 23, 110, 251, 253, 265–66, 267
Schmidt, Benno, 76
Schroder Banking Corporation, 111
Schwarz, F.A.O., Jr., 231, 245
Scott, Hugh, 219
Secret Intelligence Service (SIS), 11, 38, 66, 128, 130, 143, 191, 315
    Barnes as liaison to, 172–73
    brainwashing fears and, 211
    in Iranian coup, 108, 109
    Soviet moles in, 129–30; *see also* Philby, Harold "Kim"
    Soviet telephone lines tapped by, 128
    U-2 and, 168
Secret Surrender, The (Dulles), 80–81
Senate Select Commitee on Intelligence (Church Committee), 185, 209, 224, 226, 230, 231, 233, 234, 245, 270, 271, 294, 302, 303, 339
Seven Society, 19
Shackley, Ted, 293, 294, 300–301, 309, 328
show trials, 211
Sichel, Peter, 23–24, 42, 197
Sihanouk, Prince, 190
SIS, *see* Secret Intelligence Service
Six-Day War, 332
60 Minutes, 35

Smathers, George, 203, 262–63
Smith, Russell Jack, 44
Smith, Walter Bedell, 37, 42–43, 54, 55, 58, 64–65, 72–73, 84, 86, 211
    Philby and, 70
    United Fruit and, 111
Somozo, Anastasio, 113, 115, 120
Sorensen, Ted, 237, 253, 265
Souvanna Phouma, Prince, 195, 279, 281–82
Soviet Union, 10, 28, 56, 170
    agents infiltrated into, 67
    Arabs and, 332
    assassinations and, 36–37, 210
    Bay of Pigs and, 265
    bomber gap and, 168, 170
    Castro aided by, 203, 241, 290, 291
    China's split with, 278, 307
    CIA's phone tapping tunnel and, 128–30
    Congo and, 221, 222
    deportation to work camps in, 21–22
    détente between U.S. and, 217, 218, 219–20, 265
    Dulles brothers as seen by, 186
    emerging nations and, 180–81
    European expansion of, 9, 12, 19, 20, 21–22, 25, 32, 33, 199
    Germany and, 79, 80
    global ambitions of, 24–25, 134–35, 180–81
    Guatemala and, 112, 123, 126
    Hungarian revolution and, 142–47
    ICBMs in, 217, 218, 219
    Indonesia and, 158
    intelligence agency of, 33; *see also* KGB
    Iraq and, 214
    Italy and, 181
    Kennedy assassination and, 306, 308
    lack of Western knowledge about, 128, 170
    Laos and, 280
    mind control techniques and, 211
    missile gap and, 170, 217, 218
    morality in methods of fighting, 134–35
    OPC formed as response to, 29–30
    Oswald and, 306
    refugee army organized against, 25–26, 34, 36

Soviet Union (*cont.*)
　satellites and, 105, 216, 217, 272
　as U.S. ally, 20, 21–22, 23
　U-2 and, 165, 166, 167–68, 169–70,
　　171, 216, 217–20, 265
　Wisner's view of, 9, 10
　in World War II, 19, 22
　see also communism; Khrushchev,
　　Nikita
Special Group (5412 Committee),
　184–85, 206*n*, 222, 231, 244, 276,
　287, 289, 297, 307, 309
spying, 28
　American attitudes toward, 17
　Bissell's view of, 191–92
　covert action vs., 41–42
　domestic, 311
　Dulles' love of, 73–74, 154, 165
　FitzGerald's view of, 194
　planes for, 171–72, 253, 272; *see
　　also* U-2
　satellite for, 216, 217, 272
SR-71, 171–72, 253, 272
SSU (Strategic Services Unit), 23,
　24, 28
Stalin, Joseph, 12, 17, 22, 24, 71, 135,
　142, 296
　deportations ordered by, 21, 135
　planned assassination of, 37, 209
Stalinism, Khrushchev's speech on,
　136–37
State-Army-Navy-Air Force Coordi-
　nating Committee, 24, 26, 34
State Department, 51
　CIA vs., 184, 193, 237, 238–39
　ECA and, 97
　German diplomats and, 34–35
　McCarthyites and, 99
　OPC and, 34, 39, 40, 41, 55
　Wisner at, 24–29
Stevenson, Adlai, 101, 238, 254
　Bay of Pigs and, 254–55, 256–57,
　　258, 259, 265, 267
Stewart, Gordon, 128, 151–52, 165,
　269
Stilwell, Joseph, 46–47, 274
Stilwell, Richard, 50, 52, 58
Stimson, Henry, 17
Stone, Howard, 135, 183, 324–25
Strategic Services Unit (SSU), 23,
　24, 28
Sturges, Ben, 174, 267
Sturgis, Frank, 299*n*

Sturges, Sandol, 207
Success, Operation, *see* Guatemala
Suez Canal, 143, 145, 172, 173
Sukarno, 157–60, 213–14, 226, 232–33,
　295
Sullivan, William, 282, 283
Sulzberger, Arthur Hays, 117
Sulzberger, Cyrus, 63
Sumatra, 158, 159
Swift, Carleton, 12, 52, 53, 56, 84,
　132, 184, 315, 316, 317

Taiwan, 51, 156, 183, 274, 275
Tammany Hall, 49–50
Taylor, Maxwell, 265, 268, 289, 297
television, CIA documentary on,
　319
Thailand, 50, 56, 156, 182, 183–84,
　279
Thanarat, Sarit, 184
Thayer, Charles, 34, 35, 71
　McCarthy's targeting of, 100, 101,
　　138
Thompson, Jane, 137, 145, 319
Thompson, Llewellyn, 137, 145
Tibet, 275–78
Timpson, Robert, 301
Tito, Marshal, 71
Tofte, Hans, 53, 187, 313
Toscanini, Arturo, 80
Toscanini, Valli, 80
Trafficante, Santos, 227, 228, 229,
　330–31
Traxler, Adele, 80
Traxler, Vieri, 80
Tree, Marietta Peabody FitzGerald,
　26, 45, 48–49, 101
Tree, Ronald, 49
Trojan plan, 68
Trotsky, Leon, 24
Troy, Hugh, 33
Trujillo, Rafael, 220–21, 269–70, 331
Truman, Harry S., 23, 42, 56, 87,
　148–49
Truman Doctrine, 24
Truscott, Lucian, 65, 66, 67, 127, 152
TsOpe, 36
Tuchman, Barbara, 47
Turkey, 291

Ukraine, 36
Ulmer, Al, 142, 155–56, 158, 206,
　316

United Fruit Company, 111–12, 117,
  126, 260
United Technologies, 338
U-2, 165–71, 172, 176, 191, 204, 212,
  216–20, 257, 272, 314, 341
  Cuban Missile Crisis and, 290, 291,
    294
  FitzGerald and, 283
  poison pin for pilots of, 217, 219,
    228
  Soviet interception of, 216–20, 265,
    277, 318

Vang Pao, 282, 283–84, 328
Varona, Tony, 229, 298
Vatthana, Savang, 279
Vientiane, battle of, 195, 280
Vietnam, 50, 156, 265, 270, 282, 288
Vietnam War, 279, 285–86, 322–23,
  326–29, 331
  CIA role in, 326–27
  People's Action Teams in, 327
Voice of Liberation, 114–15, 121, 122,
  124, 204, 247
Volcano Plan, 67

Walz, Skip, 15–16
Washington, D.C., 26, 27
  Georgetown society in, 26–28, 39–
    40, 99, 101–6, 108, 140, 151, 160–
    161, 316–17
Welles, Ed, 42, 181
Whitehurst, Charles, 40, 54, 154, 190,
  199, 269, 274–75, 278, 280
Whitman, Anne, 111
Whitman, Edmund, 111
Whitney, Harry Payne, 82
Whitney, John Hay, 77, 172
Wilderness of Mirrors (Martin), 131
WIN, 67
Wise, David, 318–19
Wise Men, The (Thomas and Isaac-
  son), 10
"Whiffenpoof" song, 16
Whitman, Anne, 219
Winks, Robin, 16
Wisner, Ellis, 140
Wisner, Frank, 9–10, 17–43, 60–66,
  75, 106, 116, 133, 135–41, 187,
  197, 204, 209, 315–17, 318–22,
  325
  Albania operation and, 68, 70, 211
  Anglophilia of, 68–69, 316

Alsop brothers and, 104, 105, 106
Asia operations and, 157, 158, 159,
  160
background of, 10, 17–19, 37
Barnes and, 10, 83, 84, 133, 139
Berlin riots and, 107
Bissell and, 10, 87–88, 98, 139, 317
Bissell made successor to, 165, 172,
  179–80, 186–87, 203
as book reviewer, 318
children and, 140, 161
CIA as viewed by, 42
CIA failures and, 60, 66, 67–68, 72
control needed by, 63–64, 118–19,
  145–46
convocation commemorating,
  321–22
education of, 18–19
farm of, 139–40, 162, 318
funeral for, 320
gamesmanship of, 18, 19, 315
in Germany, 22–23, 25
Guatemala operation and, 113, 114,
  115, 116, 117, 118–19, 120, 122,
  124
FitzGerald recruited by, 10, 43, 50
Helms and, 150–52, 160, 164
hepatitis contracted by, 148, 150,
  151, 162
hiring practices of, 15, 35, 149
Hoover and, 23, 138–39
Hungarian revolution and, 142–48,
  149–50, 152, 160
Iran and, 108, 109
Khrushchev speech and, 137
as London station chief, 164,
  315–17
McCarthy and, 138–39
management style of, 40
and media criticism of CIA, 318–19
mental illness of, 31, 137, 138,
  140–41, 142, 143, 144, 145, 147–
  148, 150, 151–52, 160, 161–63,
  164, 198, 315, 316, 317, 318–20,
  321
Meyer and, 98
moral upbringing of, 17–18, 19, 37
OPC created by, 9, 15, 29–30, 41,
  50, 70, 71
OPC Far East Division and, 50,
  51–52
in OSS, 9, 19–23
Philby and, 68–69, 70

policymaking of, 39–40
press and, 63–64, 105–6, 139, 141
propaganda operations of, 60–62,
  63–64, 137
psychiatric treatment of, 162–63,
  164, 315
refugee army plans of, 25–26, 34,
  36, 136, 152, 242
retirement of, 318–20
in Romania, 9, 19, 20–22, 66, 199
Roosevelt on, 108–9
socializing of, 27–28, 39, 137–38,
  316–17
Soviets as viewed by, 9, 10, 19, 21,
  22, 23, 24, 28, 135
in State Department, 24–29
suicide of, 12, 320–21
technology and, 212
on tour of CIA stations, 143, 147,
  148, 149, 158, 159, 160
Truscott and, 66
U-2 and, 168
in World War II, 10–11, 19–20, 66
Wisner, Frank, Jr., 22, 143, 316, 322,
  334
Wisner, Graham, 140, 316, 321
Wisner, Polly, 39, 138, 151, 162, 316,
  317, 319, 320
Wisner, Wendy, 319, 320

Wolff, Karl, 80
World Federation of Trade Unions,
  62
World War II, 9, 32, 171, 180, 210,
  246
  Alsos Mission and, 85
  Barnes in, 10–11, 75–81, 83, 113,
    133, 134, 207
  Bissell in, 10–11, 90, 94–95, 120–21,
    187
  FitzGerald in, 10–11, 44, 45–48,
    153, 197, 276, 295
  FitzGerald on, 296
  intelligence operations compared
    with, 50–51, 66–67, 71
  leaflet drops in, 64
  Philby in, 68
  spying and, 17
  Wisner in, 10–11, 19–20, 66
Wright, Paul, 91

Yates, Edward, 319
Yugoslavia, 71

Zahedi, Fazlollah, 125, 183
ZAPATA, *see* Bay of Pigs invasion
Zemurray, Sam, 111
Zero Hour (Bundy), 94
Zhou Enlai, 274